Lewis

A BIOGRAPHY

Michael Bakewell was born in Birmingham in
1931 and educated at Bishop Vesey's Grammar
School, Sutton Coldfield and King's College,
Cambridge. Most of his life has been spent in
radio and television with occasional excursions
into the theatre. After working as Head of Plays
in BBC Television in the sixties, during some of
the most exciting years of television drama, he left
to become a freelance writer and director of
documentaries on an improbable range of subjects
from Caspar David Friedrich to Housing of the
Elderly.

Over the last few years he has also written a series
of biographical radio features on Stendhal,
Richard Hughes, John Cowper Powys, Dickens,
Chekhov, Tolstoy and Lewis Carroll. He lives
outside Colchester with his wife, Melissa.

MICHAEL BAKEWELL

Lewis Carroll

A BIOGRAPHY

Mandarin

A Mandarin Paperback
LEWIS CARROLL

First published in Great Britain 1996
by William Heinemann Ltd
This edition published 1997
by Mandarin Paperbacks
an imprint of Reed International Books Ltd
Michelin House, 81 Fulham Road, London SW3 6RB
and Auckland, Melbourne, Singapore and Toronto

Copyright © Michael Bakewell, 1996
The author has asserted his moral rights

A CIP catalogue record for this title
is available from the British Library
ISBN 0 7493 9893 0

Typeset in Sabon by
Deltatype Ltd, Birkenhead, Merseyside
Printed and bound in Great Britain
by Cox & Wyman Ltd, Reading, Berkshire

For Melissa,
who has encouraged, helped and suffered this
book at every stage, kept it afloat, driven me round
its locations and read its text with a patient and
diligent eye,
with my love,
and for Leo,
companion of my morning walks round Richmond and of my
first visit to Croft Rectory.

Acknowledgements

The first biography of Lewis Carroll, by his nephew Stuart Dodgson Collingwood, was published in the year of his death and is still unsurpassed as a portrait of its highly complex subject. A succession of biographies since then have all shed light on the personality and work of Lewis Carroll, particularly those by Derek Hudson and Anne Clark. The publication of the diaries, edited by Roger Lancelyn Green, and of the letters, edited by Morton N Cohen, with the assistance of Roger Lancelyn Green, changed the face of Lewis Carroll studies, and the constant flow of new information through the Lewis Carroll Society and from the C L Dodgson Estate under its senior trustee, Philip Dodgson Jaques, is continually adding to our understanding. To all of these I am deeply indebted.

I am grateful to A P Watt Ltd, on behalf of the Executors of the C L Dodgson Estate for permission to quote from copyright material by Lewis Carroll and from the diaries, edited by Roger Lancelyn Green, from the letters, edited by Morton Cohen and from *Lewis Carroll and the House of Macmillan*, edited by Morton Cohen and Professor Anita Gandolfo. Every effort has been made to trace copyright holders of text and photographs to clear permissions. I regret any inadvertent omissions, which can be rectified in future editions.

I would like to express particular gratitude to Rosemary Hart for asking me to write a series of programmes on the life of Lewis Carroll for BBC Radio 4 and thus setting me on the path, and to John Pearson for his encouragement and initiative.

Thanks are also due to the staff of the Guildford Muniment Room (Surrey Record Office); to the Governing Body of Christ Church and especially to Janet McMullen of Christ Church Library; to Mrs M J St Clair for permission to quote from the Hargreaves manuscripts at Christ Church; to the British Museum; to the staff of the Newspaper Library at Colindale; and to Robin Harcourt Williams, librarian and archivist to the Marquess of Salisbury.

Great thanks must also go to Mr and Mrs Peter Atkinson for taking me round the Rectory and the garden at Croft, to Beverly Davies, to Deborah Rogers, to my editors at Heinemann, Tom Weldon and Kate Goodhart. Above all I have to thank my wife and my old friends John and Helen Patrick for their unselfish sacrifice of their time and energy and for the invaluable contribution of their knowledge and expertise.

This book was scheduled for publication in July 1995, but was held up over matters of copyright. The delay has at least given me the opportunity to read several new books on Lewis Carroll, including *The Red King's Dream* by Jo Elwyn Jones and Frances Gladstone, and Morton Cohen's authoritative new biography. *The Red King's Dream* is an agreeable ramble down the highways and by-ways of Carrolleana which sets out to expose the real identities of the characters in the Alice books, but the attempt to prove that Ruskin is the Gryphon, Darwin the Puppy and Lionel and Hallam Tennyson are Tweedledum and Tweedledee, only serves to needlessly restrict the genius of Lewis Carroll.

I have not considered it necessary to revise this book in the light of Morton Cohen's invaluable biography, but readers will find occasional references to it in the notes.

Contents

List of Illustrations

Gertrude Chataway and two drawings by Dodgson (*courtesy of the Dodgson Family Collection*)

Dodgson's sitting room at Christ Church and The Chestnuts (*courtesy of the Dodgson Family Collection*); the four eldest children of the Marquess of Salisbury (*by kind permission of the Earl of Selborne*)

Isa Bowman, Charles Dodgson and Gertrude Thompson (*courtesy of the Dodgson Family Collection*)

Illustration by Gertrude Thompson; Evelyn Hatch (*courtesy of The Rosenbach Museum and Library, Philadelphia*)

A Note About Names

The initial difficulty in writing a life of the author of *Alice's Adventures in Wonderland* is to decide what to call him. The man himself was exceptionally punctilious and precise about modes of address. 'Lewis Carroll' is not really appropriate, since it only applies to part of his work and scarcely at all to his life. 'Charles' is out of the question. He would have considered it an intolerable liberty: only the most devoted of his child-friends, Isa Bowman, was permitted to call him 'Uncle Charles'. Therefore, although I have occasionally called him by his Christian name when a child and a schoolboy, for the most part he is referred to as 'Dodgson', though he would doubtless have preferred 'Mr Dodgson'.

The second difficulty is that all the eldest sons of the Dodgson family were called 'Charles', as was his mother's father. Dodgson's father, grandfather and great-grandfather all bore the name. His father I have chosen to call 'Dodgson Senior', even before the birth of his son, or the 'Reverend Dodgson'. From the time of his appointment as Archdeacon to the see of Ripon he is referred to by that title.

Introduction

'The Rev. C.L. Dodgson', wrote Virginia Woolf, 'had no life,' and, in the sense that he did not elope with a bed-ridden lady poet, or search for the source of the Nile, or declare himself the head of a fledgling Balkan republic, I suppose that this is true. He spent the first eighteen years of his life largely within his father's rectories, and passed the remainder of it within the cloistered confines of Christ Church College in Oxford. Yet the man who spent his holidays at Eastbourne for nineteen successive summers once ventured as far as Moscow, and the unremarkable mathematician who churned out twenty-five obscure volumes with titles like *The Enunciation of the Propositions and Corollaries in Euclid* wrote two books which have been translated into every language in the world and are in almost as many homes as the Bible and Shakespeare.

To a stranger he cannot have been an appealing character. He was fussy and easily offended, old-maidish and excessively prudish, storming out of theatres at the sight of a man dressed as a woman, publicly denouncing W.S. Gilbert for allowing the words 'Damn me' into the *Pirates of Penzance* and shouting at a child-actress for daring to sing and dance *Ta-ra-ra-boom-de-ay* in his rooms. He would turn away from a lady when helping her over a stile, so as not to catch even a glimpse of her ankles. He invariably wore clerical black, closely buttoned up to the neck, with gloves and a top-hat, even at the height of summer. He carried himself bolt-upright, was deaf in one ear, suffered from housemaid's knee and had a pronounced stammer. He was such a dull tutor that his pupils organised a round robin asking to be transferred to another teacher.

And yet, here was a man who was the adored companion of dozens and dozens of little girls who clearly idolised him and loved every minute spent in his company. He performed conjuring tricks for them, delighted them with clockwork musical toys, hid under tables, devised endless games and puzzles, took them to plays and pantomimes and holidays at the sea, escorted them to church and occasionally took nude photographs of them. Above all, he told them endless enchanting stories, drawing sketches to illustrate them as he talked, while his eager listeners clamoured for more.

He led an inner life of such constant vitality and variety as to suggest that he was a kind of English Leonardo (another exponent of mirror writing). In his journals, mathematical formulae jostle with observations on the dialogue of Dickens and the progress of the Crimean War. His restless mind was always devising bewildering mazes and unbreakable ciphers, regulations for lawn tennis tournaments or new braking and steering systems for his tricycle, the Velociman. He contrived a machine for writing in the dark, designed a new form of postal order and invented an early form of Scrabble. Through the long night hours he kept evil or blasphemous thoughts at bay with problems involving triangular billiard tables, or counters in bags, or cylindrical towers. He campaigned against vivisection and for vaccination, and concocted a scheme for transporting the population of Tristan da Cunha to the coast of South Africa.

The key to his multi-faceted personality lies in his childhood, which he somehow managed to preserve within himself, untouched, throughout his life. Where Dickens endured a 'childhood so unhappy and so painfully humiliating' that for years he could not speak of it and spent the rest of his life trying to write it out of himself, Dodgson's early years seem to have been a time of unclouded happiness which again and again he would strive to recapture and perpetuate in the company of innumerable child-friends. As he grew older, their company became more indispensable to him. Little girls became the air he breathed and without them he would feel himself withering away. 'Children are three-fourths of my life,' he said, and this was no exaggeration. In many ways he never really grew up, concealing the child within behind a mask of fastidious remoteness. He was permanently on the threshold of the adult world, watching his little girl friends pass into a mature life where he could not follow.

So great has seemed the disparity between the dry, pedantic, unsmiling don and the personality of Lewis Carroll that inevitably there have been attempts to present the man as a split personality. It has even been suggested that Dodgson never wrote the works on which his fame rests, but that they were ghosted by another writer not renowned for her public sense of humour, Queen Victoria. Yet Charles Lutwidge Dodgson and Lewis Carroll are essentially one and the same, and the personality of the man who created *Alice's Adventures in Wonderland* can be traced in practically everything he wrote – with the exception of some of the more abstruse mathematical treatises. Lewis Carroll was hidden from view in the lecture hall or common room, but he was always there when a child happened by.

The other popular delusion is that Dodgson/Carroll was a kind of patron saint of childhood, an unworldly dreamer far removed from the realities of everyday life. But no unworldly dreamer could have coped with the complexities of collodion wet-plate photography and no gentle saint would have driven illustrators, printers and publishers to despair by the relentless exactitude of his criticism and by the ferocious accuracy of his eye (or his magnifying glass). Charles Dodgson was, in fact, very shrewd, very practical, highly capable and extremely demanding. Virtually everything that he wrote, from a pamphlet on *The Profits of Authorship* (which sold for sixpence) to the two volumes of *Sylvie and Bruno*, found its way into print. The list of his published works comes to well over 250 items. Even his photographs went on public sale.

Dodgson sought out his own illustrators and tracked down his own translators. He mastered every aspect of typography and graphic reproduction and frequently infuriated practitioners by his expertise in their craft. He was a determined and highly imaginative promoter of his own work, constantly devising new ways of keeping his name (or rather Lewis Carroll's) before the public with a succession of new editions. He was also a pioneer of marketing – who but Dodgson could have invented the 'Wonderland Postage Stamp Case'? – but he was appalled when he discovered that he had unwittingly sanctioned a tin of biscuits decorated with illustrations from *Through the Looking Glass.*

There are many conflicting aspects of Dodgson: his simple and sincere faith, his horror of a universe without motivation and without God, his obsession with logic to the point where it almost became a religion in itself. He could distil nonsense from everything which crossed his path, he needed to reinvent and reinterpret everything in his own terms and turned the most unlikely subjects into games. He was a man of youthful, inextinguishable high spirits, yet was also a misanthrope who withdrew from society but still utterly depended upon the company and the affection of little girls. All this was united in the complex and unique genius of Lewis Carroll.

I
'The happy spot where I was born'

Lewis Carroll is so deeply associated with the landscape of Victorian Oxford, with summer afternoons on the river and quiet college gardens, 'the happy time of pinafores, treacle and innocence',[1] that it always comes as something of a surprise that his alter ego, Charles Lutwidge Dodgson, was born on a bleak January day in 1832 in the reign of William IV, in a remote corner of rural Cheshire and passed the first eleven years of his life in surroundings more like a farmyard than a country vicarage.

Dodgson's birthplace may have been relatively inglorious, but he could lay claim to a highly colourful collection of ancestors who certainly were not[2]. Among his more astonishing forbears were Matilda, an illegitimate daughter of William the Conqueror, Yvo de Talbois, a Count of Anjou, and Sir William Skeffington, Henry VIII's commissioner to Ireland. Biographers[3] have been quick to seize on Dodgson's descent from Edwin and Morcar, the Earls of Mercia and Northumbria who make a fleeting appearance in the Mouse's recital of 'the driest thing I know' in *Alice's Adventures in Wonderland*, and from Sir Richard Hoghton, who was entertaining King James I when that notably eccentric monarch is said to have conferred a knighthood on a loin of beef:

> The leg of mutton got up in the dish and made a little bow to Alice; and Alice returned the bow, not knowing whether to be frightened or amused.

No one, so far as I know, has claimed that Dodgson's ancestress, Lady Godiva, was responsible for his passion for photographing little girls in the nude.

This extraordinary pedigree derived not from the Dodgson side of the family, but from the Lutwidges. His great aunt, Elizabeth Anne, had married a Major Charles Lutwidge and his father, Dodgson Senior, had also married a Lutwidge, his first cousin Frances Jane. Further connections with the Skeffingtons, the Raikes and the Hoghtons combined to give Dodgson an exotic and highly complicated family tree which, with a certain amount of ingenuity, could be manipulated to relate him to Queen Victoria. In comparison with the Lutwidges, the Dodgsons were a more prosaic, stolid family. The name seems to have derived from one Dodge of Offerton, near Stockport. There were Dodgsons who had been merchants in the north of England in Tudor times, and one had been Mayor of York in 1517, but since the eighteenth-century the Dodgsons had produced a long line of Church of England clergymen.

Dodgson's father and mother shared a common grandfather, Charles Dodgson, Bishop of Ossory and Ferns, and subsequently, Bishop of Elphin. The Bishop's eldest son, Dodgson's grandfather, broke with family tradition and went into the army. He became a Captain in the 4th Dragoon Guards, but his career was cut short in 1803 when he was killed by a group of Irish rebels at Philipstown. The violent death of his grandfather was to colour Dodgson's whole attitude to the Irish question. He became a staunch opponent of Home Rule, detested Parnell and recorded with relish his 'disgrace as corespondent in a divorce suit'.[4] One cannot help wondering how he would have reacted had he known that Parnell had consoled himself during a period of political crisis by reading *Alice's Adventures in Wonderland*.[5] Captain Dodgson fathered two sons, Charles, the father of our Charles Dodgson, and Hassard Hume, who was born two weeks after the Captain's death. Nine years later, their mother, Lucy, married again. Her husband was George Marwood, who became a canon of Chichester Cathedral. Their only daughter, Margaret Anne, was to marry William Wilcox and to bear him thirteen children. These were the 'Whitburn Wilcoxes', the clan of cousins who were all to become close friends of Charles Dodgson and to figure frequently in his life.

Charles Dodgson Senior had been born in 1800 in Hamilton, a royal burgh some twelve miles from Glasgow. He can scarcely have known his father and by the time of his mother's second marriage, he would have been at Westminster School. He never seems to have contemplated any future other than the church. At Christ Church, Oxford, he distinguished himself by taking a double first in Classics and Mathematics and was considered one of the most outstanding men of his year. In 1825, when he proceeded to his degree, everyone was convinced that he had a brilliant future ahead of him.

By the 1820s the Church of England had become a serious business. Gone were the days of easy living, the absentee vicar and the hunting parson, days when a clergyman could devote his entire existence to ornithology or lepidopterology or the pleasures of the table. The cosy deism of the eighteenth-century had been put to flight by the very fears conjured up by the French Revolution. Religion had become a bulwark against anarchy, atheism and the spread of subversive liberal ideas, and the popularity of evangelicalism and non-conformism had spurred the Anglican Church to put its own house in order – to root out corruption, absenteeism and pluralism. An Act of 1803 compelled the clergy to reside in their own parishes. Out of 10,000 livings it was revealed that 6,311 lacked resident incumbents.

Dodgson Senior was the embodiment of the new sense of purpose which had taken over the church. For him the priesthood was a sacred calling, not an occupation like any other. Instinctively a High Churchman, and of a grave temper, he deliberately distanced himself from the fervours and simplicities of evangelicalism. At Oxford, he cultivated the friendship of like-minded souls: Charles Longley, six years his senior and a reader in Greek at Christ Church, and Edward Bouverie Pusey, who in the 1830s, with Keble, Newman and Froude, was to be in the vanguard of the Oxford Movement. Longley and Pusey went on to become two of the leading churchmen of their century, Longley as Archbishop of Canterbury, Pusey as the leader of the High Church in Oxford. Dodgson Senior, the intellectual equal of his friends, who at Christ Church had seemed to promise so much, let his talents waste away in an obscure and poverty-stricken country parish. At the age of twenty-eight, he married his first cousin, Frances Jane Lutwidge. In later years the Reverend Dodgson would advise his son to remain at Christ Church for at least ten years before venturing out into the world, getting married and finding a parish. Presumably he had reason to regret his own impulsive rush into matrimony. The problem was that Christ Church, like all Oxford colleges, was deeply rooted in its monastic origins. A College Fellowship was granted on the understanding that the holder would remain celibate and would proceed to Holy Orders. The higher orders, the heads of colleges, the Canons and professors were free to marry, but mere fellows, known as Students in the case of Christ Church, were denied the pleasures of the married state. Choosing a wife meant forfeiting their place. This was to pose no problem for Charles Dodgson, but his father had not been prepared to wait.

The parishes which Christ Church held in its gift were offered in rotation as they became vacant, and a man might have to wait for a long time before a living came up which he considered suitable to his status and income. Many a prospective marriage must have withered and died in the interim. One can only suppose that Dodgson Senior and Frances Jane were far too deeply in love even to contemplate the long wait. He accepted the first living on offer, the remote and impoverished perpetual curacy of Daresbury. Frances Jane must have been every bit as determined and as certain as he was. Whatever Dodgson Senior's academic qualifications, he had very little to offer his bride beside a far from desirable parish isolated from family and friends. They had nothing but one another.

Dodgson Senior and Frances Jane were married on 5th April, 1827, at Christ Church in Hull. Like her husband, Frances Jane was the child of a military man, Major Charles Lutwidge of the 1st Lancashire Militia, and he too had served in Ireland. More fortunate than Captain Dodgson, he had left the army to become Collector of Customs in Hull. Frances Jane must have been something of a beauty, as her only surviving portrait shows, and she and her sister Lucy were known as the 'swan-necked sisters'. She was said to have been 'one of the sweetest and gentlest women that ever lived, whom to know was to love'. In her surviving letters she comes across as affectionate, practical, highly organised and in a permanent hurry, writing always in 'dashing haste',[6] totally unconcerned about herself, interested only in her family and her large network of relations.

As a young man Dodgson Senior was romantically good-looking and renowned for the charm of his conversation, his wit and humour. However, his humour was not allowed to trespass on religious territory. He was not one to take his calling lightly and would never countenance any levity on scriptural matters. Although he was to overcome the handicap of his early marriage and rose slowly through the ecclesiastical hierarchy to become a Canon of Ripon and Archdeacon of Richmond, he never seems to have been stretched to his full capability.

'My dear father,' wrote Dodgson many years later, 'was what is called a "High Churchman".' Although Dodgson Senior had left Christ Church before the dawning of the Oxford Movement, he was deeply sympathetic towards its objectives and was linked to it through his friend Pusey, who was one of its guiding lights. The aim of the Tractarians, as the Movement's followers were called, was to bring a new sense of religious purpose to the church, to divorce it from the secularisation which had so severely compromised it and to endue it with a new purity and spiritual vigour. At the same time they endeavoured to demonstrate that the Church of England could claim its descent, not from the machinations of Henry VIII, but from the faith and teaching of the Early Fathers. The movement placed great emphasis on church ritual and brought its adherents perilously close to the Church of Rome – John Henry Newman, who had been the leader of the movement converted to Catholicism in 1843.

*

As the crow flies, Daresbury (Dodgson Senior's first living) is little more than sixteen miles from the centre of Liverpool, but in the 1820s it might have been at the end of the universe. Two-and-a-half miles away the Mersey wound slowly up to the rapidly expanding town of Warrington, but Daresbury was lost amid the open fields of a small farming community. It was a very insignificant place indeed and its population numbered only 143. Dodgson's nephew and first biographer, Stuart Collingwood, said that the parsonage was so secluded that even the passing of a cart was an event.[7] Today the site of the old parsonage in Morphany Lane is surrounded by a network of busy roads serving Warrington, Runcorn and Chester, but the place somehow manages still to give off an air of peace, as if it were miles from anywhere and had never been disturbed.

Now only the stones of the well and a commemorative plaque give any indication that the parsonage once stood there – it was destroyed by fire in 1883. The house had been built in 1819 and was a good two miles from the church, since the incumbent of that time was reputed to be more interested in farming his land than in his clerical responsibilities. In the photographs it looks to be of quite a modest size, but the house somehow contained seven bedrooms, two sitting-rooms, a study and a room that the Reverend Dodgson was to convert into a school. There were outbuildings which included a shippon, or cowshed, and a laundry. Apart from Daresbury itself, the Reverend Dodgson's curacy took in five other villages:[8] Moore, where the hall was reputed to be haunted, Keckwick, Hatton, a closely-knit community from which it was rare for people to marry outside, Preston Brook and Newton-by-Daresbury, where the parsonage stood. All told, the Reverend Dodgson's flock consisted of some 1,800 souls. There was no assistant, only Messrs Crouchley and Wright, churchwardens, and Mr Houghton, the clerk. The Dodgsons had a pony and gig, but the new perpetual curate seems to have covered much of his extensive parish of villages on foot with, according to local tradition, his lunch tied up in a red spotted handkerchief.

The living to which the Reverend Dodgson had succeeded was not even a parish in its own right, but a 'Parochial Chapel' of the mother church of Runcorn, of which he was perpetual curate, almost the lowest rung on the ecclesiastical ladder. He did not receive the church tithes, and his total annual income was £191.10s.11d. Out of this he had somehow to support his family and to pay his rates and taxes. 'The Revenues of the Perpetual Curacy of Daresbury certainly admit of improvement,' he commented grimly.[9] The Parochial Chapel had been built in 1550, during the

Reformation, and was a ramshackle structure with ugly box pews and a high pulpit. Only the tower remains now – the rest of the old church was swept away in a drastic restoration in 1870 and replaced by a conventionally Victorian building. In a side chapel, a stained-glass window of 1934 commemorates Daresbury's most famous son. Dodgson and Alice kneel, rather incongruously, behind a shepherd, adoring the Virgin and Child, while characters from *Alice's Adventures* disport themselves below. The font in which the Dodgson children were baptised now stands rather forlornly outside in the churchyard, where it serves as a bird bath.

The Reverend Dodgson was determined to make his mark on his first living and set about his new duties with commendable vigour. He established a Sunday School, gave lectures for the parishioners three times a week, visited the poor and the sick. There was a community of bargees on the Trent and Mersey Canal, a mile-and-a-half from the parsonage, who refused to attend Divine service in church because they would not venture beyond their natural element, the water. The perpetual curate was not a man to let such a difficulty stand in his way. He persuaded Mr Egerton, a wealthy local landowner, to put up the money to convert one of the barges into a floating chapel and conducted a service there every Sunday at midday. Another barge served as a school.

In the year after their arrival at Daresbury Mrs Dodgson bore her first child, Frances Jane, followed two years later by a second daughter, Elizabeth Lucy. All told, ten children were to arrive during the Dodgsons' sixteen years at Daresbury, which must have stretched their slender resources to breaking point. On 27 January, 1832, their first son, Charles Lutwidge, was born. A few days before his son's birth, the Reverend Dodgson had written to the Christ Church Treasury expressing his gratitude for their efforts to secure a 'potato tithe' which might bring him an additional £200 a year. It was a very gloomy letter:[10]

> I am very glad to hear a good account of my old friends – for myself I
> am going on as well as a man can be supposed to do, without
> prospects, living on a precarious Income and subject to a constant
> drawback on his domestic comforts. I already begin to experience the
> anxieties incidental to my situation having at this moment two
> Vacancies for Pupils unfilled.

Dodgson never said very much about his birthplace in later life, and he never returned to Daresbury once he had left it. He did think well enough of the place to consider adopting 'Dares' as a pseudonym before finally settling for 'Lewis Carroll', but only the well-known lines in 'Faces in the Fire' give any idea of what he thought about it:

An island farm, 'mid seas of corn
Swayed by the wandering breath of morn –
The happy spot where I was born.

Fragmentary recollections of the boy's childhood survive, like faded snapshots: little Charles playing in the marl pits – marl was a loam dug out and laid on the fields as manure – or climbing trees. He made friends of toads and snails and 'tried also to encourage civilised warfare among earthworms by supplying them with small pieces of pipe with which they might fight if so disposed.'[11] Seeing his elder sisters and his mother continually engaged in various acts of charity he set himself to peeling rushes with the strange notion that the pith might be given to the poor.

There were children with whom the young Dodgson would have played. At nearby Morphany Hall[12] lived the Darbyshires, a family of Quakers, and Mrs Darbyshire was known to the children as Aunt Dar. There were children at Hallam Hall and Daresbury Hall as well, but the only childhood friend whose existence we know for certain was Thomas Vere Bayne, son of the Headmaster of the grammar school at Warrington. Father and son used to come over to the service at Daresbury every Sunday. Vere Bayne was Dodgson's friend for life. He was three years older than Charles, and they were to be dons together at Christ Church, close and constant friends.

As the family steadily increased the boy would not have had to look beyond the parsonage for playmates. Caroline Hume was born in 1833, Mary Charlotte two years later, Skeffington Hume the year after that, Wilfred Longley in 1838, Louisa Fletcher in 1840, Margaret Anne in 1841 and in 1843, the year in which the Dodgson family finally left Daresbury, Henrietta Harington. Despite the presence of his two elder sisters, Charles, as the eldest son, became the children's acknowledged leader and established a firm control over them that was to last for the rest of their lives. He devised and regulated their games, and became the family entertainer and resident magician.

There was plenty to keep the children occupied. Although Mrs Dodgson employed a permanent nursemaid, Mary Cliffe, and there were other servants for the house and laundry, the girls were expected to help with the washing, dressing and caring for the younger children and in carrying out their charitable duties around the parish. Outside the parsonage, Daresbury had its share of wonders – a smithy, a cornmill, a rope and twine maker and even a small sessions house where trials were conducted. Two miles from the parsonage, at Preston Brook, there was a long tunnel on the Trent and Mersey Canal and barges were slowly propelled through it by

'Leggers', lying on their backs walking the boats along with their feet on the tunnel roof. From nearby Daresbury Firs the children would have caught their first sight of a railway train, making its way through Keckwick on the Lancashire and Cheshire Junction railway – Dodgson's childhood was the time of the great railway explosion. Seven years before he was born there were less than fifty miles of track in the country, and by the time he left Daresbury there were more than two thousand miles, with lines running from London to Bristol, Liverpool, Manchester and York. The railway ran through the children's games, their poems and their nightmares:

> Is that not an angry snake?
> Lo! he twists his writhing tail!
> Hear the hisses he doth make!
> See his yellow coat of mail.
>
> Distant howls still louder grown,
> Angry mutterings sounding near,
> All proclaim with solemn tone,
> Something dreadful coming here![13]

Only one excursion outside Daresbury has been recorded, a holiday in Beaumaris on the isle of Anglesey. The railway had not yet made its way into north Wales and the journey there by coach would have taken three days. Only Telford's bridge over the Menai straits seems to have left any lasting impression on Charles Dodgson, for it crops up many years later in the song which he gave to the White Knight in *Through the Looking Glass*:

> I heard him then, for I had just
> Completed my design
> To keep the Menai bridge from rust
> By boiling it in wine.

But there must have been other expeditions. In the Dodgson family papers at Guildford there is a brown folder of skeleton maps indicating the main stages on routes to Beaumaris, York, Richmond and Oxford; these may well be journeys that the boy made with his father. He certainly went to stay with his grandfather in Hull, and his first surviving letter, addressed to his nurse, is from somewhere he calls Marke. It was written when he was five.

> I love you very much, and tend you a kitt from little Charlie with the horn of hair. I'd like to give you a kitt, but I tan't because I'm at Marke. What a long letter I've written. I'm twite tired.[14]

Even at that early age he seems to have been obsessed with kisses. Millions of kisses were to feature in his letters to little girl friends. Kisses figure largely in one of his mother's earliest letters, written to her son while she was staying in Hull with her father. Charles and the other children may have been staying with the Darbyshires at Morphany Hall.

> I hope my sweetest Will says "Mama" sometimes, and that precious Tish has not forgotten. Give them and all my other treasures, including yourself, 1,000,000,000 kisses from me, with my most affectionate love. I am sending you a shabby note, but I cannot help it. Give my kindest love to Aunt Dar, and believe me, my own dearest Charlie, to be your sincerely affectionate
> Mama.[15]

The boy did not receive many letters from his mother, and this one evidently became something of a talisman which he guarded jealously. 'No one is to touch this note,' he wrote on the back, 'for it belongs to C.L.D.' and, to make doubly sure, 'Covered with slimy pitch, so that they will wet their fingers.'

Charles, like his younger brothers, was initially educated at home, taught first by his mother, and then by his father. There was a school in Daresbury village, but it was not the kind of place to which the Dodgsons would have sent their eldest son. Frances Dodgson kept a scrupulous account of her son's progress. There is a little book in the family papers with a pebble cover inscribed 'Charles Lutwidge Dodgson. 1839'[16] which records his own reading and the books which he read with her. The books which he read to himself included *The Pilgrim's Progress, Christ's Repository Truths* and *Stories from Scripture*. His 'Religious Reading with Mama' noted *Baker's Scripture Characters* and *The Juvenile Sunday Library*. There was also a section in her notebook headed 'Daily Reading: Useful – Private' which tells us that he had studied *The Parents' Cabinet* and had some knowledge of the 'biggest animals', travels and geography. He had also slogged his way through *Edgeworth's Early Lessons* and *The Little History of France*.

Religion was, of course, an inescapable part of his upbringing. The boy had been provided with a series of sacred texts written out on small pieces of card so that he could carry them about with him and bear them in his mind throughout the day: 'All mankind are sinners and therefore cannot save themselves', 'Repentance is necessary in order to be saved through Jesus Christ', 'Man is not able to forsake sin without the help of God', 'God sees and knows all things'.[17] The texts had a profound effect upon Dodgson, and their constant presence helped to shape his religious opinions in his later life. He was never far from a religious text. His diaries abound in them.

Inevitably there have been attempts to put Dodgson's relationship with his father and mother into a conventionally Oedipal framework, with the Reverend Dodgson cast as a gloomy Victorian tyrant who came between his son and the boy's love for his mother. In no way is this borne out by the facts. Everything we know about the Reverend Dodgson underlines his love and concern for his family and his constant desire to help and understand them. His son did not always agree with him or share his views, but there was no conflict between them and the father (the Reverend Dodgson) does not seem to have tried to inflict his opinions on his son.

Dodgson seems to have been a patient, obedient and supremely cheerful child. Rebellion or resistance to his parents' wishes would have been totally alien to his nature. To judge from one of the Reverend Dodgson's letters, at this stage in their lives, father and son seem to have shared an enthusiasm for extravagant absurdity. The boy had asked his father to bring back various items for him on a trip to Leeds and had evidently been nagging him about it. The Reverend Dodgson's reply is a bravura display of ruthless nonsense:

> As soon as I get to Leeds I shall scream out in the middle of the street, Ironmongers – Ironmongers. Six hundred men will rush out of their shops in a moment – fly, fly, fly in all directions – ring the bells, call the constables – set the town on fire. I will have a file & a screwdriver, & a ring, & if they are not brought in directly, in forty seconds I will leave nothing but one small cat alive in the whole town of Leeds & I shall only leave that, because I am afraid I shall not have time to kill it.[18]

It was through Dodgson Senior that Charles came to love mathematics, one of the profound passions of his life, and he always spoke of his father's mathematical skills with deep respect, considering him far superior to any of his teachers at Rugby. A family anecdote tells of the boy's early commitment:

> One day, when Charles was a very small boy, he came up to his father and showed him a book of logarithms, with the request, 'Please explain.' Mr Dodgson told him that he was much too young to understand anything about such a difficult subject. The child listened to what his father said and appeared to think it irrelevant, for he still insisted, 'But, please, explain!'[19]

By the early 1840s there were signs that the Reverend Dodgson's long years in the wilderness were at last coming to an end. At Ripon, in

Yorkshire, a new diocese had been created and in 1836 the ancient Minster of the town became England's newest cathedral. The first Bishop was the elder Dodgson's Christ Church friend, Charles Longley. Longley needed the support of men he knew and could trust and he asked Dodgson to become his Examining Chaplain. The post involved considerable responsibility with very little in the way of additional income, but the elder Dodgson eagerly seized the opportunity. It would mean somehow carving time out of the work he had to do at Daresbury, but this must have seemed a small price to pay for moving into a sphere where his abilities could at last be demonstrated. One of his first duties in the new diocese was to deliver the sermon at Longley's first ordination ceremony on 15th January, 1837. A series of Ordination Sermons followed over the years in which the Reverend Dodgson defined the high responsibilities of the clergy and the unique nature of their calling. They were workers together with God:

> in the advancement of his kingdom upon earth; as accredited ambassadors of his will; as appointed ministers and stewards of his mysteries; to mankind, as shepherds set over them in the Lord, to watch for their souls, to feed them with the bread of life, to lead them forth beside the waters of comfort: ...[20]

The Reverend Dodgson's sternly uncompromising view of the duty of the Ministry to 'spend all and be spent in the single work of winning souls to Christ' would be one of the factors which would prevent his eldest son proceeding to full Holy Orders.

Dodgson Senior thought well enough of his sermons to publish them, and he went on to bring out works of formidable dullness at regular intervals, instilling in his son the notion that a man is judged by his ability to bring out at least one new book every year.

The title of one of the Reverend's books, *The Providence of God manifested in the Temporal Condition of the Poorer Clergy* must have come straight from the heart. The elder Dodgson's financial situation was growing increasingly desperate. By 1840 there were eight children to be supported and another on the way. Bishop Longley set to work to try to secure a profitable living for his Examining Chaplain somewhere in his own diocese. His first attempt, at Catterick, failed, but the comfortable parish of Croft on Tees looked to be a likely possibility. Admittedly the incumbent was still living, but the Reverend James Dalton had held Croft since 1805 and was rumoured to be in poor health. Rather than wait for his demise, Longley wrote off to Sir Robert Peel, the prime minister and patron of the living, to try to reserve it for his protégé, but Peel refused to be committed in advance and the Bishop and his Chaplain had to wait for a year-and-a-half before the Reverend Dalton moved from the Rectory to the churchyard. Longley lost no time in writing again to Sir Robert, urging the elder Dodgson's outstanding qualifications and stressing his desperate financial plight. Not content with his own efforts he assembled an army of friends, supporters and local worthies, including Mr Egerton of Tatton Park, to campaign on his candidate's behalf. Peel, enmeshed by political and economic difficulties, had better things to do, and the never-ending representations of Longley and his faction must have come close to losing Dodgson the position. Peel wrote testily to Longley telling him that he wished he had been left at liberty to make up his own mind about the Reverend Dodgson's suitability for the post. A few days later, however, a gracious letter from Sir Robert arrived at Daresbury, conferring upon the elder Dodgson the vacant living of Croft, on condition that he agreed to reside there. Dodgson wrote off gratefully to Sir Robert and set out, at the earliest opportunity, to explore his new parish.

For his son, now close to his eleventh birthday, it was the end of what we can only judge to be an era of almost cloudless content. Yet Charles left Daresbury without regret. He never looked back with nostalgia to his rural idyll. Landscape and nature were never to hold any great importance for him and in later years his family and friends were often shocked by his total indifference to a fine view or a pretty flower. It was his inner landscape which absorbed him.

2

'The children of the North'

Fair stands the ancient Rectory,
The Rectory of Croft,
The sun shines bright upon it
The breezes whisper soft.[1]

Croft is in the North Riding of Yorkshire on the old road over the Tees from Northallerton to Darlington, the main route to the Border country and Scotland. It was an area rich in the supernatural. The Tees had its own malignant spirit, known as Peg Powler, who lurked about the river at Piercebridge a few miles upstream, demanding sacrifice. The Manor House at Darlington was haunted by the murdered Lucy Jarrett whose bloody fingerprints could not be washed from the wall. Nearby were the celebrated 'Hell Kettles', supposedly bottomless pits where the souls of the dead could be heard screaming in agony, and Monksend, in Croft itself, was supposed to be called after a monastery destroyed by an earthquake. 'It would have to be a very tiny earthquake!' thought Alice.

Croft had a population of around 700 souls. In the eighteenth-century it had been a flourishing spa but, with the rise of industrial Darlington, it was entering a period of steady decline. 'I am told that the place is going fast out of fashion as a watering place, for wh. I am not sorry,' wrote the new incumbent, 'as that migratory sort of population never does much good to the state of a Parish.'[2] The Reverend Dodgson saw Croft for the first time while he was attending Bishop Longley at Ripon. He went over for half-a-day to take stock of what was to be the Dodgson family home for the next twenty-five years. 'The house is a good old-fashioned Rectory', he told his brother Hassard, 'with no *beauty* outside or inside, but as far as I cd judge, in its state of disablement and disorder, possessing the elements of abundant comfort.'[3] He set to work sketching plans of the three floors of the house and its surrounding buildings. There was a drawing room and a dining room, each twenty-five feet in length and 'decidedly too narrow in proportion', a small study, a small sitting-room,

> numerous bedrooms of all sorts and sizes, Servants' Hall, Butler's
> Pantry, Housekeeper's Room, Scullery, Laundry, Brewhouse, Larder,

Dairy, Coach House, stabling for seven horses, Tithe Barn, Pig-sties, Henhouse – a large and excellent kitchen garden with a capital south wall, a small flower garden, separating the House from the road.

He calculated that he would have to increase his domestic establishment by 'a sort of half Housemaid, half Kitchen-maid' but since, by his reckoning, his income had now risen to £910 a year, he was certainly in a position to afford it.

The Reverend Dodgson had assured Sir Robert Peel that he would take up residence at Croft 'with as little delay as circumstances will admit of', but first the Rectory had to be made ready for his family, and the 'disablement and disorder' which had befallen the house during the last years of James Dalton's tenure put to rights. The putting to rights involved raising the ceiling of the bedroom on the first floor, and while this work was being carried out the children paid a visit to Croft to survey their new domain. They marked the occasion by making a deposit of a mysterious hoard of family objects in the new nursery floor. This came to light in 1950 when the Rectory was being converted into flats. The offerings seem to have been chosen to represent individual members of the family: a fragment of Mrs Dodgson's handwriting, a scrap of the Reverend's induction paper, a thimble, a fragment of clay pipe, a small penknife, a hair-slide, the lid of a child's teapot, a crab's shell, a little white glove and a left shoe belonging to one of the girls. They are all very Carrollean objects and most of them make an appearance in Alice in one form or another. The whole enterprise must have been masterminded by young Charles, as the children's leader. His particular contribution was a block of wood on which he had written:

> And we'll wander through
> the wide world
> and chase the buffalo.[4]

The only member of the Dodgson family destined to wander through the wide world was the as yet unborn Edwin Heron, although buffaloes did from time to time wander through the verse of Lewis Carroll:

> He thought he saw a Buffalo
> Upon the chimney-piece:
> He looked again, and found it was
> His sister's husband's niece.

There can be little doubt that the treasure was hidden there for posterity to discover, rather like the cache which was placed beneath Cleopatra's Needle when it was re-erected on the Victoria Embankment in 1878. As if to confirm the formality of the whole proceedings, the children had added another inscription: 'This floor was laid by Mr Martin and Mr Sutton June 19th 1843'.

While the Rectory was being refurbished, Frances Jane had given birth to her tenth child, Henrietta Harington. Nothing now stood in the way of the family taking possession of their new home. Before they left Daresbury, they gathered in the church to receive a farewell address from the churchwardens:

> It is, Sir, to your persevering energies, and truly Christian labours, that we are indebted for that first of Blessings to the poor and the uneducated, the establishment and the successful maintenance of a Sunday School, now most numerously and regularly attended ... Nor is it, Sir, to you alone, that our gratitude is due. During these sixteen years we have seen that your labours of Christian love and active benevolence have been shared by the excellent and amiable ladies of your family ...[5]

There was no shortage of Christian labours awaiting the Dodgsons at Croft:

> There will be much to do in the way of improvement [noted the new Rector] there is only one Sermon, &, as is generally the consequence, the Church attendance almost entirely confined to the Morning Service. There are also no more than 35 children under Church, or indeed any Religious Education ... the Sacrament is administered only 5 times a year.[6]

The church of St Peter stood close by the old bridge over the Tees. The Rectory was a leisurely two minutes' stroll away on the other side of the road. The church dated back to Norman times, though most of the existing fabric was of the thirteenth- and fourteenth-century. 'Very respectable' was how the Reverend Dodgson described the place, though one wonders what he made of the figure of a Romano-British fertility god built into the wall by the south porch. It has been most efficiently emasculated although this has not altogether wiped the smile off its face. In the Dodgsons' day, the church was dominated by two vast and ungainly family pews. To the south stood that of the Chaytors, a wealthy Newcastle merchant family; to the north stood, and stands still, the monstrously ostentatious two-storey pew of the Milbankes, a kind of cross between a beach hut on stilts and a box at the opera. Like the Chaytors, the Milbankes were descended from prosperous Newcastle merchants. Both families had been granted baronetcies. Twenty years before the Dodgsons' arrival, Annabella Milbanke had entered into an unfortunate marriage with Lord Byron and they had spent their 'treaclemoon', as the poet called it, at nearby Halnaby Hall. Beneath the Chaytor pew stood a fifteenth-century screen which was to be the cause of one of the first clashes between the Reverend Dodgson and his flock. Sir William Chaytor wanted it restored, Dodgson wished it to stay as it was. 'Imperfect as it is, it gives an air of unusual antiquity to that part of the church.' Sir William contended that it was his screen and he had the right to do with it whatever he wished. He told the new incumbent that he considered it 'more becoming in a rector to avoid quarrelling with his parishioners'. Eventually Chaytor took the law into his own hands, and cut down part of the screen. The Reverend Dodgson protested to Longley, and Chaytor received a stern rebuke from the Archdeacon of Ripon. There the matter seems to have ended: peace must have been restored, since the Dodgson sisters became frequent visitors at Sir William's mock-Norman Clervaux Castle.[7]

In every church associated with Dodgson, there have been attempts to link what he would have seen there with the creatures of his dream-worlds. There is a gryphon on the pulpit at Daresbury, another lurks beneath a misericord at Ripon. At Croft on the sedilia, there is a pig which has, perhaps, deserted its sty along with a riotous group of wild men of the woods, a ram's head and a man and woman fighting. What really caught the boy's imagination at Croft was the Rectory garden. Much has been made of the importance of the Deanery garden at Christ Church but if ever there was a garden to which he would spend his life trying to find the key, it was the one at Croft. The Reverend Dodgson's predecessor, James Dalton, had had a consuming passion for horticulture and filled the large garden with rare and exotic plants, including 'the night-blowing Cereus, whose flowers after an existence of but a few hours, fade into the waning sun'.[8] The children's favourite was what they called the 'umbrella tree' under which they indulged in their 'elephant hunts', and there was an acacia tree beneath which Charles used to lie at full length, reading.

Dodgson saw the potential for an elaborate railway game in the Rectory garden. One of the first railway stations in the world had been built at nearby Darlington. George Hudson, the 'railway king', was frequently to be seen with the Milbankes in their hideous pew, turning his back ostentatiously on the Reverend Dodgson during the sermon while his wife unfurled her parasol. Charles would build his own railway: 'stations' would be situated at regular intervals around the garden, while a train, made out of a wheelbarrow, a barrel and three 'trucks', would trundle from one to another, carrying his brothers and sisters. He devised a detailed set of rules, regulations and penalties which were the basis of the game. The duties of the station master, presumably Charles himself, were very clearly spelled out:

> Station Master must mind his station and supply refreshments: he can put anyone who behaves badly to prison, while a train goes round the garden. He must ring for the passengers to take their seats, then count 20 slowly, then ring again for the train to start. There shall be a place at the L station for lost luggage. If there is anyone to go, a flag is to be hoisted.[9]

If a passenger fell out of the train, which was probably very likely, he was to lie still until picked up. A passenger had to be run over three times before he was entitled to a doctor. If a passenger could not afford the fare, he was to work his passage by making tea for the Station Master 'who drinks tea at all hours' and grind sand for the company – 'what use they make of it they are not bound to explain'. Trains puff and rumble their way constantly through Dodgson's life and work. There were few weeks that did not see him on a train from Oxford to London or Guildford or Eastbourne or on long, improbable, wearisome treks to Darlington or Whitby. Trains figure in *Sylvie and Bruno, Through the Looking Glass* and *A Tangled Tale*, where the railway regulations are even more fantastic than they were in the garden at Croft.

> 'Take your places on the spring-boards!' shouted a porter.
> 'What are *they* for?' Clara asked in a terrified whisper.
> 'Merely to help us into the trains.' The elder lady spoke with the nonchalance of one quite used to the process. Very few people can get into a carriage without help in less than three seconds, and the trains only stop for one second.[10]

At first the Dodgson children seem to have camped out in the Rectory rather than taking full possession of it. The girls continued to share rooms as they had done at Daresbury, as if reluctant to relinquish the snug intimacy of their Old-Woman-who-lived-in-a-Shoe existence. Charles, as befitted his position, set himself up in a room of his own. He was shortly going away to school and needed peace and quiet for his studies, but he must have spent much of his time devising new tricks, games and surprises with which to divert his brothers and sisters. Not only did he invent all their games, he had to be the star performer in them. 'As a little boy, I was simply detestable,' he once confessed to a friend. He would dress up in a brown wig and a long white robe and would descend to perform magic tricks at which the other children would be suitably bemused and astounded. All his life he needed to astonish and bewilder people, whether he was putting obscure problems of logic to his fellow dons or devising puzzles for little girls. He fed on their exclamations of perplexity, wonder and delight. At Croft, his sisters and young brothers must have provided an ideal captive audience. The games and tricks and conundrums were nothing new. Even the railway game had probably first been played at Daresbury, but it was at Croft that, in every sense, Charles first came into his own.

While his eldest son was keeping the family entertained, the Reverend Dodgson was getting to grips with his new parish. The church roof was in a perilous state and had to be renewed. A school had to be provided for the children of Croft, where they could be trained in Christian knowledge and get a solid grounding in reading, writing and arithmetic and where the girls could be instructed in needlework. An old cow-shed near the Rectory was pulled down to provide the site. Dodgson raised the money from his parishioners and the local worthies, making a substantial contribution out of his own pocket, and Bishop Longley came over from Ripon to lay the foundation stone. The school opened in 1845. The Rector gave a great deal of his time to teaching there, as did his wife, supported, with varying degrees of enthusiasm, by the rest of the family. In one of the magazines written by the children there is a visit to *The Village School* written by an unidentified 'R.Y.' which perhaps portrays one of the elder Dodgson sisters in action:

> 'Sally Brown! don't talk or you'll catch it!'
> 'Please'm, I wasn't talking!'
> 'Don't answer! Go into the coal hole!' (pushes her in, and locks the door) 'and there you'll stay till midnight. John Dobbs! Don't wink!' (gives him a violent blow on the back).[11]

1844 saw Charles's twelfth birthday and the beginning of his own school career at Richmond. Only ten miles away from Croft, Richmond had something of a fairy-tale atmosphere about it. The town stood at the entrance to one of the most spectacular of the Yorkshire dales, Swaledale, and stood on a steep hill, dominated by the ruins of a great castle. To the north the keep of the castle looked down onto the busy market-place and the Chapel of Holy Trinity. To the south a precipitous slope led down to the turbulent waters of the Swale. King Arthur and his knights were said to sleep in a cave in the castle rock, and there were tales of buried treasure and of a drummer boy who had vanished into a labyrinth of secret passages. Richmond School, where Charles arrived on 1st August, stood on a road leading down the hill off Frenchgate in the churchyard of St Mary's, a twelfth-century foundation, unlucky enough to fall into the clutches of that passionate restorer, Sir George Gilbert Scott, later in the century. The school could trace its own history back some four hundred years, but in Dodgson's day it owed its high reputation to the energies and learning of the redoubtable Doctor Tate, reputed to be the finest classical scholar in England. Sydney Smith, who once shared a coach with Tate, described him as 'dripping in Greek', and, according to one of the school's old boys, he had 'a profoundly human reverence for port'. Tate had died the year before Charles's arrival at Richmond and had been succeeded by his son, James Tate II. He was a sensitive, mild, rather timid character, with a curious habit of looking at himself in the polished inside of his watch case before launching into one of his rare fits of discipline. Charles always remembered his 'kind old schoolmaster' with great affection and made a point of calling on him whenever he was in the neighbourhood. Tate considered his pupil a 'gentle, intelligent and well-conducted boy'.[12] They were well matched.

Everything we know of Charles's years at Richmond confirms that he was very happy there. It was not a large school, 120 boys in all. He was taken into Tate's own house as one of sixteen boarders and was immediately accepted into the headmaster's family of which there were seven. Charles was particularly taken with 'a little girl who came down to dinner the first day, but not since',[13] the first (or at least the first recorded) of several hundred little girls who were to catch his eye.

The churchyard of St Mary's served as the school playground, although the Rector was constantly complaining about the noise and the damage caused by the pupils. Since in the winter the boys would take the benches out of the classroom and use them as toboggans to go careering down between the tombstones, this is not altogether surprising. 'The chief games', Charles told his sisters, 'are foot-ball, wrestling, leap-frog and fighting.'[14] There was a 'plague stone' in the churchyard, said to mark the burial place of 1,000 victims, which new boys were warned not to go near for fear of infection. Charles was subjected to some remarkably restrained initiation rituals which he seems to have suffered cheerfully. One was 'King of the Cobblers' in which he sat, as King, in a circle of boys, and having ordered them to 'Go to work', as instructed, was assailed with kicks and blows from all sides. Having survived this and similar ordeals, he was accepted into the school confraternity and announced with satisfaction, 'the boys play me no tricks now'. There was a tradition among his sisters, recorded with some surprise by Collingwood, that 'in later school days he was famous as a champion of the weak and small, while every bully had good reason to fear him'.[15]

Charles was under a strict injunction from his father to report back to him the texts of the sermons he heard preached at St Mary's, but in his first letter home he had to confess he had been unable to hear a word of the one preached at morning service and he seems to have had only the haziest notion of the evening one. This may have been due to the restlessness of his fellow pupils or the acoustics of St Mary's, but it may be the first indication of the incipient deafness which was to strike him a few years later at Rugby. At the time, however, he seemed more concerned that he had lost his toothbrush.

'You may fairly anticipate for him a bright career,' Tate told the Reverend Dodgson, 'you must not entrust your son with a full knowledge of his superiority over other boys, but let him discover this as he proceeds.'[16] James Tate's first report on his pupil was quite remarkably perceptive in its grasp of the boy's character. It also indicated the way in which the man was to develop. He believed that Charles had 'an uncommon share of genius', possessed 'knowledge far beyond his years' and was 'so jealous of error, that he will not rest satisfied without a most exact solution of whatever seems to him obscure'.[17] In the years to come Dodgson's jealousness of error would be of great personal advantage when pursuing mathematical or logical problems, but it was to prove perfectly intolerable when applied to other people. It was to make him the scourge of his publisher and his printer and was to lead to endless disputations with the Steward of his college over such matters as the precise time at which the Christ Church letter-box was emptied. Tate also mentioned 'one or two faults', particularly the boy's wayward and highly individual treatment of the syllabic quantities of the verse of Virgil and Ovid. Charles was 'marvellously ingenious in replacing the ordinary inflexions of nouns and verbs, as detailed in our grammars, by more exact analogies, or convenient forms of his own choosing'. Tate had put his finger on another Carrollean characteristic. Everything he touched invariably involved a degree of reinvention – whether a theorem by Euclid, or 'Twinkle, twinkle little star', it had to be recreated in his own terms to make it his own. He would devise his own system for remembering important dates and calculating on what day of the week a particular date might fall. Even the Symbolic Logic to which he devoted all his time and energy in later years was not Logic as the Professor of that subject might have taught it. It was, as the White Knight would have put it, 'My own invention.'

Richmond possessed a famous theatre which has survived intact to our own time. All the great players of the day, Kean, Kemble, Macready, appeared there. Dodgson almost certainly never entered it while he was a schoolboy. Even if Tate had allowed his pupils to enter a place of public entertainment, the Reverend Dodgson refused to countenance theatre-going. But Charles would have been well aware of its existence, he would have seen the posters and playbills and recreated the performances in his own restless imagination.[17a]

In the Rectory at Croft he had a theatre of his own, built with the help of a local carpenter. Charles wrote all the plays himself, manipulated the puppets and probably played most of the parts as well. His father's ban did not extend to entertainment in the home, and the plays were performed before the entire family, other relatives and friends. Word of the Dodgson family theatricals must have spread throughout Croft since the boy's 'exploits with a collection of puppets and a miniature theatre' were still remembered in the village at the time of the Lewis Carroll centenary in 1932. The most popular of the plays was *The Tragedy of King John*, but as this has not survived we have no way of knowing whether it was a full-blown tragedy or a comic burlesque in the manner of one written when he was thirteen on Shakespeare's *Henry IV Part* 2:

PRINCE HAL: My gracious lord! my father!
This sleep is sound indeed, this is a sleep
That from this golden rigol hath divorced
So many English –
KING: What meaneth rigol, Harry?
PRINCE HAL: My liege, I know not, save that it doth enter
Most apt into the metre.
KING: True, it doth.
But wherefore use a word which hath no meaning?
PRINCE HAL: My lord, the word is said, for it hath passed
My lips, and all the powers upon this earth
Cannot unsay it.[18]

King John figures, if only obliquely, in the only one of Charles's family entertainments to survive, a surreal operetta entitled *La Guida di Bragia*:

I went in immediately after, and said 'Your majesty has lost your luggage, have you not?' 'Yes', said the king, in accents of the deepest sadness, 'I lost it all, when – when I went to the Wash' – 'Did your majesty go to the Wash?' I enquired – he answered, 'I did' – Whereupon I remarked with a smile 'and much you needed it!'[19]

La Guida di Bragia, opera-speak for *Bradshaw's Railway Guide*, was probably written while Charles was at Rugby School and performed for an audience of Dodgsons and Wilcoxes at Croft. The script includes detailed directions for lighting, scene-setting and sound effects. It is a lively, knockabout hybrid of comic patter, satire, light opera, with occasional anticipations of Lewis Carroll, as in this foretaste of 'If you'll tell me what language "fiddle de-dee" is, I'll tell you the French for it.'

> SPOONEY: I say, old feller, what language is that?
> MOONEY: What a donkey you are, Spicer, he can't understand that, you must talk to him in his own language.
> SPOONEY: How in the world am I to do that, Moggs, when I don't even know what it is?[20]

The plot, such as it is, concerns two characters called Mooney and Spooney (or Moggs and Spicer) who take a job on the railway, on the condition that they sing while they work:

> MOONEY: A *Bradshaw's Railway Guide*, on legs, stood visibly before me, and at the same moment I heard a hollow voice ... which said, 'Mooney, why singst thou not, Spooney, why singst thou not?'[21]

They fail to carry out their side of the bargain and Bradshaw takes revenge by changing the timetable. One suspects that the entertainment derived from Charles's difficulties in making his way from Rugby to Darlington via Birmingham. No one ever succeeds in catching a train:

> HUNTSMAN: Where's the station-master? I want to go to London by the 9.45.
> MOONEY: The 9.45, sir? That's gone rather more than half an hour ago.
> HUNTSMAN: Oh dear, dear, how unlucky I am! When's the next train?
> SPOONEY: The next train is 11.5.
> HUNTSMAN: Oh, that'll do! give me a ticket for that!
> MOONEY: But that train goes to Lincoln, sir.
> HUNTSMAN: Oh, never mind, I'm sure to miss it, so it don't signify! only give me a ticket.[22]

The most original and the only genuinely funny character in the play is Mrs Muddle, a compound of Mrs Malaprop and Sarah Gamp, who is so worried about the hazards of railway travel that she insists on 'ensnaring her life'.

> MRS MUDDLE: Then, young man, mark my words! If any of them collections happens, or the steam Indian blows up, or I get run over and killed in one of your funnels, which I could never see the sense of yet, & they never light 'em up, mark my words it'll be manslaughter! and if it *be*, which I'm mortally certain it will, I'll write to the nugepaper! there!

SPOONEY: But my dear madam, it can't be manslaughter, in any
              case. It will only be woman-slaughter.[23]

Charles could never resist a bad joke, but he took his marionette theatre
very seriously, as he took all things. He had learned from a very early age
that every activity that was not manifestly religious ought to be justified by
some kind of moral purpose. In the prologue to his entertainment he says:

> Why can't we have, in theatres ideal,
> The good, without the evil of the real?[24]

It was, of course, a means of justifying what he was doing to his father, but
he did come to believe very firmly that the theatre possessed a great
potentiality for good. Unfortunately, as far as he was concerned, the good
all too often became confused with the harmless. In over forty years of
theatre-going, Dodgson went out of his way to avoid any experience that
was at all demanding, with the exception of Shakespeare's plays. This was
partly due to his prudishness – even the plays of Pinero were capable of
shocking him – partly because he was invariably accompanied by little
girls, but also because there was something in him that resisted the
demands made on him by great art. This was also true of music:

> In listening to first rate music there is a sense of anxiety and labour,
> labour to enjoy it to the utmost, anxiety not to miss our opportunity:
> there is, I verily believe, a sensation of pain in the realisation of our
> highest pleasures, knowing that they must soon be over.[25]

As a result Dodgson kept carefully away from demanding experiences
likely to remind him of his own mortality and confined himself to a lifetime
of trivial, but undeniably safe, entertainment.

The Rectory, particularly when Charles came home for the holidays, must
have been a noisy, high-spirited, very active place, bubbling over with
energy and invention. By 1845 there were ten children. As a community
they were wholly self-sufficient: they had no need of the outside world. To
some degree this must have had a cocooning, smothering effect. There are
no signs of adolescent rebellion, no suspicion of conflict between the
parents and their loving children. All one happy family, all ill-equipped to
cope with life beyond Croft. They had a strong sense of their own family
identity.

> From all the house and garden,
> Its inhabitants come forth,
> And muster in the road without,
> And pace in twos and threes about,
> The children of the North.[26]

Charles always kept his sisters firmly in their place. His authority as the eldest son was not to be called into question:

> *Sister, do not raise my wrath.*
> *I'd make you into mutton broth*
> *As easily as kill a moth!*[27]

It was half humorous in tone, but there was an assumption of confident superiority behind it. His puzzle – 'Which is best, a clock that is right only once a year, or a clock that is right twice a day?' was originally devised for his sister Elizabeth, and preserves his brother–sister tone perfectly:

> 'Ah, but,' you say, 'what's the use of its being right twice a day, if I can't tell when the time comes?' Why, suppose the clock points to eight o'clock, don't you see that the clock is right at eight o'clock? Consequently when eight o'clock comes your clock is right. 'Yes, I see that,' you reply. Very good, then you've contradicted yourself twice: now get out of the difficulty as you can, and don't contradict yourself again if you can help it.[28]

The younger boys had not yet made any incursion into his territory, nor were they ever to do so, but he was keeping a watchful eye on the nine-year-old Skeffington, to judge from the Mosaic injunction at the end of one of his letters home from Richmond:

> My dear Skeff,
> Roar not lest thou be abolished.[29]

1845 saw the 'publication' (the stitching together between two pieces of cardboard) of his first collection of verse, *Useful and Instructive Poetry*. Much of it is what one might expect from a clever and rather precocious schoolboy, but there are gleams of Lewis Carroll. The witty and grotesque illustrations are full of character and the perfect complement to his verses, as startling in their way as those of Edward Lear. In a note on the various books and magazines which he wrote and compiled during childhood, Dodgson said that the first poem was suggested by one by Winthrop Praed in *The Etonian*. The poets Praed and Charles Stuart Calverley were to be the presiding influences over much of his early verse. His own poem was about a tedious fairy who was constantly telling him what he must not do:

> *'What may I do?' At length I cried,*
> *Tired of the painful task.*
> *The fairy quietly replied.*
> *And said 'You must not ask.'*
> Moral. *You mustn't.*[30]

Most of the poems, like the Duchess's conversation, carry morals. They are his comment on the didactic, 'improving' poems he read at his mother's knee, verses like:

> When up the ladder I would go,
> (How wrong it was I now well know)
> Who cried, but held it fast below?
> MY SISTER.

In Charles's darkly subversive sister poem he plans to put her in an Irish stew. There is a sustained note of subtly contained rebellion. The poems are gently anarchic, ridiculing the rules and regulations which governed the children's daily life.

> Learn well your grammar,
> And never stammer,
> Write well and neatly,
> And sing most sweetly,
> Be enterprising
> Love early rising,
> Go walk six miles,
> Have ready quick smiles,
> with lightsome laughter,
> Soft flowing after.
> Drink tea, not coffee;
> Never eat toffy.
> Eat bread with butter,
> Once more, don't stutter.[31]

Stuttering was the Dodgson family affliction. Of the seven sisters there was only one who was not to be handicapped to some degree. Two of them, Elizabeth and Caroline, stammered very badly, two moderately and two slightly. The as yet unborn Edwin would also develop the family problem. What must it have been like when they were all gathered together! How the whole family came to be afflicted in this way remains a mystery. It is unusual for women to stammer, yet here were six within one family. There has been no shortage of suggestions, but none is valid in terms of our medical knowledge. The most common theory was that it derived from the close kinship of their parents, but this would now be considered an old wives' tale. Florence Becker Lennon was certain that it was because the naturally left-handed Dodgson had been forced to write with his right hand,[32] but there is no evidence whatsoever that he was left-handed. The theory that it was the result of the tyranny imposed by the Reverend Dodgson has no factual basis either. The truth is that there is no single simple cause of stammering. It can run in families and younger children can imitate the speech difficulties of their elders. It is not a neurotic symptom, nor is it necessarily caused by stress or anxiety, although these can make it worse. Descriptions of Dodgson's stammer vary considerably. To his friend Gertrude Thomson it was a 'slight hesitation'; Mrs Stretton, on the other hand, said that as a child she found his stammering bouts 'quite terrifying'. There was a suggestion that he never stammered when he was with children, but there are many references to his handicap by his little girl friends. What is certain is that nervousness and self-consciousness only made it worse. Dodgson tried for many years to find a remedy for his affliction. The fear of sticking on certain consonants, 'p' and hard 'c', was often enough to put him off reading the lesson in church, yet he never allowed it to stand in the way of anything he really wanted to do.

Until the end of 1845, his speech impediment seems to have been the only problem in an unusually happy life. But the cloudless existence of his childhood was about to receive a severe jolt in the form of Rugby School. For the first time in his life he was to find himself persecuted, alone, and comfortless. It was an ordeal which came close to breaking him, and which he never forgot.

3
'Work more profitless than play'

The Reverend Dodgson was determined to provide his son with the best education which lay within his means. He wrote to his brother, Hassard:

> ... with respect to the sons of poor parents I am strongly of the opinion that a sum of money spent in Education, is far more profitable to a Boy who will profit by it, than the prospect of getting it at his father's death.[1]

At that time there were only seven schools in the country which could provide what the Reverend Dodgson would have considered a sufficient education – Eton, Harrow, Charterhouse, Winchester, Shrewsbury, Westminster and Rugby. The Bishop of Elphin, Captain Dodgson and the Reverend Dodgson himself had all been Westminster boys, but by the 1840s the reputation of the school was at an all-time low. Had Charles gone to Westminster, he would have been there to witness the arrival of Henry Liddell, who was appointed Headmaster in May 1846, and they would have met as master and pupil, rather than as Dean of Christ Church and Student of Mathematics. It was at Westminster that Liddell's daughter and Dodgson's future heroine, Alice, was born in 1852.

Rugby was then at the height of its reputation. Although the foundation dated back to the sixteenth-century, the fame of the school was largely the achievement of its late Headmaster, Thomas Arnold. Utterly humourless, almost totally insensitive to art and literature, he was convinced that young boys were fundamentally wicked creatures who had to be brought to a 'sense of corporate duty' and responsibility. With missionary zeal he had established a high standard of academic teaching and an unparalleled moral tone. Despite some highly controversial public floggings (Arnold was not a man to spare the rod) he had made Rugby 'a place of truly Christian education' and, in the words of Carlyle, 'a temple of industrious peace'. The school's success had been crowned by the arrival of the London to Birmingham Railway which had transformed Rugby from a sleepy backwater of 2,500 inhabitants into a busy and thriving railway junction.

It must have been the school's high academic record which had attracted

the Reverend Dodgson. He would scarcely have approved either of
Arnold's religious views or his politics. The Headmaster of Rugby had
been a controversial and frequently unpopular figure. He had died
suddenly of angina on his forty-seventh birthday in 1842. His devoted
followers closed ranks and transformed him into a teacher of almost
mythical significance, an archangel of the public schools. This did not
make the task of his successor, Dr Archibald Tait, an easy one. 'Oh, my
dear Tait,' wrote his friend Lake, 'I do not envy you if you get it. I quite
quake for the awful responsibility of putting on that Giant's armour.'[2] Tait
was a Scot and, as a child, had been nicknamed the 'little Bishop'. In
private life he was reticent and withdrawn, dominated by his purposeful
wife. His favourite expression was that 'there was a great deal to be said on
both sides'. He ended his days as Archbishop of Canterbury.

Charles Dodgson's name was entered in the register of the school on
28th January, 1846. It was his fourteenth birthday. At Richmond, he had
been a big fish in a very modest-sized pond; at Rugby, where there were five
hundred pupils, he was lost, bewildered and much set upon. 'I cannot say
that I look back upon my life at a Public School with any sensations of
pleasure,' he wrote nine years later, 'or that any earthly considerations
would induce me to go through my three years again.'[3] The corridors no
longer rang to the screams of pathetic little boys roasted in front of the fire,
nor were pupils forced to run the gauntlet through ranks of their fellows
wielding knotted handkerchiefs, and Arnold had put a stop to the bizarre
rites of passage like 'clodding' – pelting with hard balls of kneaded soil. Yet
persecution was still rife. Fagging was obligatory and was brutally
enforced. 'If you do not provide servants to clean the boys' boots or to wait
on them at meals, undoubtedly the most powerful will get things done for
them by the weaker', had been Arnold's rather bland comment. A silent
witness to Charles Dodgson's miseries is one of his school books preserved
in Harvard College Library. On the fly leaf, in an elegant script, he has
written,

> C.L. Dodgson
> School House,
> Rugby.

One of his persecutors has added, after the signature, 'Is a muff.'

School House was Tait's own house, but it was very different from
Dodgson's cosy home at Richmond. There were eighty boys living in close
and insanitary proximity but what plagued Charles most was what Sydney
Smith described as 'the tyranny and servitude of the long dormitory', an
experience which haunted him for the rest of his life. In 1857 he paid a visit

to the school at Radley and admired the 'Snug little bedroom' assigned to each boy:

> From my own experience of life at Rugby I can say that if I could have been thus secure from annoyance at night, the hardships of the daily life would have been comparative trifles to bear.[4]

The public school dormitory must have had something of the atmosphere of a Roman arena, and Charles would have had to submit to its cruelties and indignities in whichever school he had attended. All we know of Charles's ordeal is that the bigger boys stole the blankets from the younger ones, leaving them to shiver all night in the cold, but he was probably subjected to more refined cruelties. The question inevitably arises as to whether Charles was persecuted sexually: homosexuality was common at public schools, although there is no established record of it at Rugby. It is a convenient hypothesis which might help to account for his arrested sexual development but it remains another of the unanswerable questions in Charles Dodgson's life. 'Rugby almost crushed him', said Collingwood, 'his shy and sensitive nature could not stand the ways of public school.'[5]

Rugby was a school where a boy was expected to prove himself on the playing field; it was part of the code of virile Christianity on which the school prided itself. Team sport was an area in which Dodgson positively did not excel. 'His abilities', said his nephew, 'did not lie much in the field of athletics,' which is probably a considerable understatement. Even so, he would have been forced to take part in 'big-side' football, and endure the miseries of a muddy field in a cold, wet English winter. Cricket, on the other hand, seems to have had some appeal for him at least as a spectator, for two cricket prints hung on the wall of his room. In many respects it was a game that should have fascinated the author of *Through the Looking Glass*, though his only recorded reference to the game does not suggest much enthusiasm:

> I only played cricket once. I was put on to bowl. After the first ball I was taken off, the captain remarking that the ball, if it had gone far enough, would have been a wide.[6]

As a result of one of Tait's reforms, Charles did at least have a study of his own where he could shut himself away from the hostile world. Once over the initial shock of his new life, his work began to go well. His wayward individualities in Latin verse were corrected either with the cane, which was in frequent use or, more probably, by his being compelled to write out thousands of lines.

> During my stay I made I suppose some progress in learning of various

kinds, but none of it was done *con amore*, and I spent an incalculable time in writing out impositions – this last I consider one of the chief faults of Rugby School.[7]

It is interesting to note that, despite these experiences, Dodgson was one of the last dons in Christ Church to punish undergraduates who failed to turn up to his lectures by setting them impositions.

The boy was in fact doing considerably more than making 'some progress'. His mathematics master, Mr Mayor, told the Reverend Dodgson that he had not had a more promising boy of his age since he came to Rugby. Charles considered Mr Mayor his best teacher, 'Papa excepted'. At the end of his first year, in a class of fifty, he came first in mathematics and second in Classics. At the end of his second year, in June 1847, Mrs Dodgson wrote, as always in 'dashing haste', to her sister Lucy Lutwidge to tell her that 'dearest Charlie' had come home with two large prize books, Arnold's *Modern History* and Thierry's *Norman Conquest*.

> Dearest Charlie is thinner than he was but he looks well and is in the <u>highest</u> spirits: <u>delighted</u> with his success at school – he is going to write to you himself – he sends you love and <u>humblest</u> apologies and says he <u>will</u> write very soon.[8]

Although during the course of his life Dodgson wrote 'wheel-barrows-full' of letters, he was not noted for replying promptly. Correspondents sometimes had to wait five or ten years for a reply. One of his rules in *Wise Words about Letter Writing* was 'Don't fill <u>more</u> than a page and a half with apologies for not having written sooner.'

At Rugby letters were his lifeline to the Rectory paradise from which he had been exiled. Letters did not arrive as frequently as he might have wished and this is confirmed by a lively sketch he made of his sisters dragging forcibly away 'The only sister who *would* write to her brother, though the table had got "folded down"!' The other sisters are depicted 'sternly resolved' to get off to '"Halnaby and the Castle", tho. it is yet "early, early morning"'. The sketch is signed 'Rembrandt'. Very few of Charles's own letters from Rugby have survived. The tone of those that have is lively and buoyant with no hint of the miseries he was enduring; complaining about one's lot would have been against the Dodgson code. If Dodgson resented the fact that his father had committed him to one of the ante-rooms of Hell, he never let it show, nor is there the least hint that he resented the fact that his sisters remained safely ensconced in the Rectory paradise. Wisely, in his letters home, he confined himself to his achievements not his disasters, and made much mention of his prize books, of which he was accumulating quite a library. For each book he had to obtain his father's sanction, but one can scarcely see the Reverend Dodgson objecting to Whiston's *Josephus* or Wheatly's *A Rational Illustration of ... the Book of Common Prayer of the Church of England*. Charles also wanted his father's permission to purchase Liddell and Scott's longer *Greek Lexicon*. The *Lexicon* had taken Henry Liddell nine years to compile and had become a most unlikely runaway bestseller. It was to figure in Dodgson's squibs ridiculing Liddell's architectural reforms when he was Dean of Christ Church – his New Belfry was compared to 'a gigantic copy of a Greek Lexicon'.

Not all his reading was as clerically-oriented as his choice of prizes would suggest. In the course of a long letter to Elizabeth, written to prove what a long letter he could write if he put his mind to it, he told her that he had been reading the first number of 'Davy Copperfield'. He thought the plot poor, but was greatly amused by Mrs Gummidge. The letter ends on a sustained note of nostalgia. Will his room be ready for him when he comes home? Have his cricketing prints been framed? When is Papa going to the Ordination?

> Are the mats finished? Is Skeffington's ship finished? Have you left off fires yet? Have you begun the evening walks in the garden? Does Skeffington ride Henderson's pony much now? Has Fanny found any new flowers yet? Have you got any new babies to nurse? Mary any new pictures to paint? Has Mr Stamper given up the ball-room yet? Will you tell me whose and when the birthdays in next month are?[9]

The whole life of the Rectory is conjured up in those few sentences, and one can feel why it meant so much to him. It is one of the most vivid things he ever wrote, a simple, unguarded expression of longing. This is the childhood world to which he always wanted to return and which he was always trying to recreate in the company of shoals of little girls. Nothing was ever to take its place.

4
'Very local magazines'

The holidays at Croft were now more precious than ever, the time when
Charles could be most fully himself. He was now devoting all his energies
to editing and writing a series of magazines:

> indeed they might be called <u>very local</u> magazines, as their circulation
> was confined to the inmates of Croft Rectory.[1]

The first, *Useful and Instructive Poetry*, was written entirely by Charles
himself and proudly dedicated to Wilfred and Louisa. There were eight
magazines in all. Four, *The Comet, The Rosebud, The Star* and *The Will
O'The Wisp*, have vanished without trace. The second, however, entitled
The Rectory Magazine, has survived.

> This was the first started for general contribution, and at first the
> contributions poured in one continuous stream, while the issuing of
> each number was attended by the most violent excitement through the
> whole house: most of the family contributed one or more articles to
> it.[2]

Family magazines were not at all uncommon. The Rossetti children had
one to which the whole family contributed, called the *Hedge Rose*, but this
was a very sober affair compared with any which had the young Charles
Dodgson at the helm. The value of *The Rectory Magazine* rests, not so
much on its literary merits, which are extremely slight, as on the insight it
gives us into the other members of the Dodgson family and the picture it
provides of life at Croft Rectory. Eight members of the family contributed
under a series of initials which were identified in a table at the front of the
book. Charles, apart from his rather self-conscious editorial contributions –

> The beginning of a new periodical is always an anxious moment for
> the editor: the question naturally suggests itself. 'What if it should fail
> altogether?'[3] –

wrote under a series of different initials: VX, BB, FLW, JV, FX and QG.
His was naturally the lion's share. Although the book is dated 1850 the
bulk of the contributions were written much earlier, probably in 1847,

when Charles was fifteen. Elizabeth Lucy was seventeen and her principal contribution was *A Tale without a Name*, a bustling piece of social satire about a 'female person' (she could scarcely be dignified with the title of Lady) who rushes and hops about the little villages of Morton from dawn to dusk entirely covered in a large pink cloak, asking alarming questions like, 'Have you been down that street?' Much more original is a curious piece called *Battiana* which concerns a bat which is eager to prove that it is the most superior bird in existence. The bat boasts that it is a 'link in creation' and that no other creature, except perhaps the flying fish and the ladybird, possesses this distinction:

> I do not mention a cupboard because I believe it to be so entirely domestic an animal ... that it cannot be included amongst wild birds.[4]–

suggesting that Charles did not have a monopoly on surrealist humour in the Dodgson household. The kind of nonsense that we have come to associate with Lewis Carroll was obviously something of a common currency at Croft. The fourteen-year-old Caroline Hume's contribution was a poem in unsteady metre about a boy being eaten by a shark. Mary Charlotte, who would have been fifteen, showed that she shared the family appetite for grotesque disasters with a poem called 'The Whirlwind':

> *The air was filled with shrieking mice,*
> *The houses rolled along,*
> *Till they reached the edge of the precipice;*
> *One crash and they were gone.*[5]

Skeffington, eleven, began what promised to be a lively serial about Farmer Gubbins who, resplendent in a green and scarlet waistcoat, bewails the fact that he will have to give up eating hot suet and cream since he is becoming so fat that he can hardly walk. When his son appears dragging a 'young rascal', Skeffington's inspiration seems to have failed him. It is difficult to tell whether the nine-year-old Wildred Langley was intending to be funny or not in his 'Tale of the Wars' about a messenger who comes to tell the Queen that her son has been killed:

> *The Queen she fell in a swoon,*
> *The porter in a fit:*
> *The messenger looked round the room,*
> *And then went out of it.*[6]

Or did he receive some assistance from his brother? The title page does carry the information that the edition has been 'carefully revised and improved'.

The only contribution by an adult is from Lucy Lutwidge. Charles's aunt, an honorary member of the children's clan. This was an advertisement for a Maid of All Work for 'Happy Grove, Mount Pleasant', which, making allowances for a considerable ironic exaggeration of the maid's workload, sounds very much like a description of life at Croft Rectory. The family is described as 'large but quiet', and they keep cows, pigs and poultry. The maid will be expected to cure hams and bacon, and make the occasional cheese. She is to have breakfast on the table at nine, luncheon at twelve, dinner at three, tea at six and supper at nine. She is expected to lend a hand in baking and brewing.

> A cheerfulness in disposition and a willingness to oblige
> indispensable. Wages £3.3s a year, with or without sugar accordingly
> as she gives satisfaction.[7]

The 'with or without sugar' sounds rather like the Mock Turtle but tea and sugar seem frequently to have been written into conditions of employment. A maid in Albany Street, London, in 1847 was paid £10 a year 'finding her own tea and sugar.'

Charles's own contributions vary considerably in their quality, and many of them fail to rise above the schoolboy level. There is 'Musings on Milk' which, in anticipation of the Dormouse, is concerned with things beginning in 'M'. The grand total, with some repetition, is eighty-two words – 'Murky misanthropes. Much they merit manacles!' There is no mention of 'mousetraps' or 'muchness'.[8]

Two serial stories stretch his talents rather further. In the first Sydney Hamilton leaves his father's home rather than give up his friend Edmund Tracey. He is plunged into a series of wild adventures which demonstrate Charles's natural aptitude for the cliff-hanger.

> He started up: a low, black grove skirted the road, and, as he gazed
> upon it, two men sprang forth into the moonlight, one of whom seized
> the horse's bridle.[9]

There appear to be a good many private jokes, including a reference to the Rectory porridge – 'a curious and indefinite compound bearing a striking resemblance to a dirty paste, and a flavour not unlike a mixture of slate pencil dust and sand'. The other, 'Crundle Castle', was perhaps intended as a satire on life with the Chaytors at Clairvaux Castle and is chiefly memorable for the introduction of the frightful spoilt child Guggy, who was to resurface many years later as Uggug in *Sylvie and Bruno*.

As the family magazines progressed the other members of the clan lost interest:

Gradually all departed,
Leaving me to write alone.

The Rectory Umbrella was written entirely by himself and the title suggests both the tree under which the children played and the protection which the Rectory afforded them against the world outside. In the frontispiece a merry old gentleman is sheltering beneath an umbrella with panels marked: 'tales, poetry, fun, riddles, jokes', shielding himself from little demons who are hurling down rocks of spite and despair. It was a perfect expression of the way in which Dodgson would use his imagination to defend himself. The decline in interest in the magazine by the other children may have been the result of Charles's 'King of the Castle' attitude, but they may just have had other things to do. Skeffington would have been doing his best to study; he was a dogged but slow worker. The girls had occupations of their own in the Rectory and in Croft, where the elder sisters were teaching at the school during the week and taking the Sunday School at weekends. They were also beginning to enjoy a much more extensive social life than had ever been possible at Daresbury. And there was a new baby to be cared for, Edwin Heron, the last of Frances Jane's eleven children, born in 1846. The Reverend Dodgson was taking on extra responsibilities at Ripon where he had been appointed Archdeacon.

Dodgson returned to Rugby and was almost immediately struck down by mumps. He caught it very badly, and wrote home to say that the complaint had left him 'more deaf than usual'. He had in fact lost the hearing of his right ear. It did not seem to get in the way of his writing – he was producing a steady stream of poems and parodies. A children's game played with metal fishes caught with magnets prompted a zoological paper on these curious beings, 'Fishs':

> Skin hard and metallic; colour brilliant, and of many hues; body hollow (surprising as this fact may appear it is <u>perfectly true</u>); eyes large and meaningless; fins fixed and perfectly useless.[10]

Another of his zoological papers was devoted to the 'Lory', a species of parrot that was to rise again, phoenix-like, in *Alice's Adventures*.

> The time and place of the Lory's birth is uncertain: the egg from which it was hatched was probably, to judge from the colour of the bird, one of those magnificent Easter Eggs (– Of these a full description may be found in the sixth number of the 'Comet' –) which our readers have doubtless often seen; the experiment of hatching an Easter egg is at any rate worth trying.[11]

Under the heading of 'Difficulties' he posed a problem which never ceased to fascinate him and to which he would return again and again: 'Where does the day begin?'

> Supposing on Tuesday it is morning at London; in another hour it will be Tuesday morning in the west of England; if the whole world were land we might go tracing Tuesday Morning, Tuesday Morning all the way round, till in 24 hours we get back to London again ... But we <u>know</u> that at London 24 hours after Tuesday morning it is Wednesday morning. Where then, in its passage round the earth, does the day change its name? Where does it lose its identity?[12]

Ten years later Dodgson wrote a letter to the *Illustrated London News* on the subject and in 1860 it was the theme of a lecture he gave to the Ashmolean Society. He never seems to have come to any particular conclusion. A practical, if not a metaphysical solution to the problem was provided by the general acceptance of the International Date Line in 1884.

Although he considered so much of his time at Rugby wasted, he had done well academically. Admittedly, Dodgson would probably have done equally well anywhere else. Curiously enough, the enduring legacy of Rugby was not the prizes he had won there, nor his unhappy memories of being bullied, but the spiritual teaching of Thomas Arnold. Although Charles did not enter the school until four years after the great man's death, nothing had diminished the memory of his teaching. Arnold believed that man was involved in a perpetual battle with moral evil, that his every action was committed in the full presence of God, and that his body was the temple of the Holy Spirit. All these ideas were to have a profound effect upon the young Dodgson. 'Nowhere is Satan's work more manifest than in turning holy things to ridicule,'[13] Arnold had told a group of boys who had been misbehaving during chapel. Dodgson was to make this one of his own most resolutely held beliefs, causing him to close his ears against the blasphemous anecdotes of his fellow dons, or to sweep out of theatres in a towering rage.

It is possible that Arnold's influence may have undermined that of the boy's father. Arnold was fiercely opposed to anything which came between man and his creator:

> Is it anything less than a positive blasphemy to require the mediation of an earthly priest between the Christian and his true divine mediator?[14]

This was not an attitude which would have found favour with the Archdeacon – Reverend Dodgson conferred a unique importance on the role of the priesthood, particularly in the administration of the sacraments, and he had followed the Tractarians in placing great emphasis on church ritual. Under Arnold's influence, his son began to see ritual as little more than self-glorification and as an obstacle to the simple acts of observance and worship which were at the heart of his own faith. In later life he would make a point of remaining seated when the choir entered the church in procession, believing that to stand gave the choirboys too great a sense of their own importance. Dodgson's beliefs were to be marked by their simplicity and their sincere humility.

Some ninety years after Dodgson had left Rugby, the school did its best to make amends for the miseries it had inflicted upon one of its most celebrated pupils. His portrait was hung in the Speech Room, and a memorial tablet, decorated with figures from Tenniel's drawings, was unveiled in the chapel. The secretary of the Old Rugbeian Society drew some consolation from the knowledge that 'the conditions which troubled him have long since passed away' and hoped that Dodgson would have rejoiced 'at the desire of the school to do honour to his memory'.[15]

5
'It lies in a valley, almost, and fogs are chronic'

Archdeacon Dodgson never seems to have considered for a moment that his eldest son would choose any career for himself other than the church. With the unfortunate exception of his own father, the Dodgsons had done nothing else for generations. Nor would he have considered any university for his son but Oxford, the greenhouse of the Church of England, nor any college but the one he had himself attended, Christ Church. Always a man to make use of his friends, the Archdeacon wrote to Dr Pusey asking him what the possibilities were of his son being nominated for a Studentship (a Fellowship) at the College.

This was a time when the Canons held Studentships in their pockets, and could distribute them at will. But Pusey replied, rather cautiously, that while it would give him great pleasure to recommend the son of his old friend, he could not put him forward if there were other candidates of superior merit. The Archdeacon had no alternative but to enter his son as a mere undergraduate or commoner in the hope that he might eventually progress to a Studentship. Accordingly, Charles arrived at Christ Church to matriculate on 23rd May, 1850. This was not a very exacting procedure. The candidate underwent a *viva voce* examination by one of the college tutors in which he was asked to construe a few lines of Homer or Virgil and to translate a short passage from English into Latin. There was also a test in elementary mathematics which Dodgson would have passed without giving the matter a second's thought. The following day, he was taken to the Senate House to sign a document subscribing to the thirty-nine Articles of the Church of England and promising to abide by the Statutes of the University, a ragbag of ancient regulations which obliged him among many curiosities:

> to refrain from all taverns, wine-shops and houses in which they sold wine or any other drink, and the herb called nicotiana or 'tobacco;' not to hunt wild beasts with dogs or snares or nets; not to carry cross-bows or other 'bombarding' weapons, or keep hawks for fowling; not to frequent theatres or the strifes of gladiators; and only to carry a bow and arrow for the sake of honest recreation ...[1]

Dodgson was now accepted as a member of the university, but he could not take up his place at Christ Church. The reason for this was quite simple – there was no accommodation. The old Laudian statutes, enacted to govern the university in the seventeenth-century, were still in force. Every undergraduate was compelled to keep residence within the walls of his own college. And there was no prospect of Charles moving into college before the following January. The only alternative was to return home to Croft where he had been since leaving Rugby the previous December.

One can only suppose that he was overjoyed. The year at Croft is one of the few totally blank periods of his life. There are no letters; there is no diary. Collingwood writes rather speculatively about 'that painful era of self-consciousness which prefaces manhood' and goes on: 'The natural freedom of childhood is dead within us: the conventional freedom of riper years is struggling to birth.'[2] This is surely wide of the mark. If anything was flourishing in Charles Dodgson it was 'the natural freedom of childhood'. It was never to die – that was his problem and his particular genius. That year at Croft was probably spent prolonging as far as possible the precious days of his childhood, living in a world of his own creation, entertaining his brothers and sisters with tricks and games and puzzles, devising and performing plays for the marionette theatre, writing what had now become a one-man family magazine and living a life of perfect contentment beneath the Rectory umbrella. He produced a rambling tale of a Baron, a Magician and a hideous toad which he called *The Walking Stick of Destiny*. The story has at least one Carrollean moment when the Baron's servant, seriously confused by his master's eccentric discourse, is asked whether his master is at home and replies: 'The fish, sir, was the cook's affair, I had nothing whatsumdever to do with it,' which, on reflection, he immediately afterwards corrects to, 'the trains was late, so it was unpossible as the wine could come sooner'.[3]

By January 1851 there was still no accommodation available for Charles in Christ Church, and the Archdeacon decided to take action. He persuaded an old friend living in the college, Horace Jacob Ley, a Reader in Rhetoric, to allow Charles the use of one of his own rooms. Ley and his tenant subsequently became great friends, and Ley was to become one of Dodgson's early photographic 'victims'. At the beginning of the Easter Term of 1851, Dodgson moved into his own rooms in Peckwater Quad.

Charles Dodgson was to live in Oxford for the next forty-seven years and would never leave it for longer than three months at a time – yet he never felt moved to write anything about the place. He delighted in taking relatives, friends and little girls on tours of the city and he even commemorated Maggie Bowman's visit with a poem, but it tells us precious little about Oxford:

> Then hand in hand in pleasant talk
> They wandered and admired
> The Hall, Cathedral and Broad Walk,
> Till Maggie's feet were tired.[4]

Apart from his satires on Liddell's architectural reforms the only reference to Oxford in any of his major works comes at the end of *Alice's Adventures Underground* – 'She saw an ancient city, and a quiet river winding near it along the plain, and up the stream went slowly gliding a boat with a merry party of children on board …' and even that was cut when *Underground* became *Wonderland*. In his letters he only mentions the disadvantages of the climate. 'It lies in a valley, almost, and fogs are chronic.' In 'The Deserted Parks' he does give us a description of what must have been one of his daily walks, but it is closer to a parody of Goldsmith than to an evocation of Oxford:

> How often have I loitered o'er thy green,
> Where humble happiness endeared the scene!
> How often have I paused on every charm,
> The rustic couple walking arm in arm –
> The groups of trees, with seats beneath the shade
> For prattling babes and whisp'ring lovers made –
> The never-failing brawl, the busy mill
> Where tiny urchins vied in fistic skill –
> (Two phrases only have that dusky race
> Caught from the learned influence of the place;
> Phrases in their simplicity sublime,
> 'Scramble a copper!' 'Please, sir, what's the time?')[5]

Oxford in the early 1850s was slowly awakening from the long sleep of the eighteenth-century. The storm clouds of reform were gathering over the torpid colleges, but nothing had happened as yet to change the appearance of the place. The streets were, for the most part, unpaved and dusty. There was no 'north Oxford', no suburbs: the city was still largely confined to the line of its medieval walls and surrounded by fields. If Dodgson wanted to go for a walk in the open countryside, he had only to walk down St Aldate's and cross Folly Bridge. Only the presence of the railway indicated that the town was connected to the nineteenth-century, and Oxford had done everything in its power to keep that at bay. A railway had been proposed as long ago as 1837 but Christ Church, which owned most of the land through which it was to pass, had firmly opposed it. Bills for a railway between Oxford and London were laid before Parliament in 1837, 1838 and 1840, but were thrown out by the House of Lords. The university trembled for the moral welfare of its undergraduates if they were to be afforded a swift and easy passage to London. When, in 1843, the university yielded to the inevitable, many of the older dons simply refused to recognise its existence. Nor was the university going to let the railway have everything its own way. The existence of a railway did not mean that anyone could travel on it. A series of clauses, which might have been composed by young Charles Dodgson for the Croft Rectory railway, were inserted into the Bill to give the university firm control over it:

> If the said Vice Chancellor shall notify to the proper Officers, Book-keeper, or Servant of the said Company that any Person or Persons about to travel in or upon the said Railway is a member of the said University not having taken the Degree of Master of Arts or Bachelor of Civil Law ... the proper Officer shall immediately thereupon, and for the space of 24 hours, refuse to convey such Member of the said University, notwithstanding such member may have paid his Fare.[6]

In everyday affairs and in the whole process of education, the colleges were everything and the university nothing. The colleges were virtually little universities in themselves, self-governing and self-administering. There were hardly any inter-collegiate lectures. The subjects open to study were strictly limited. Science degrees were as yet unheard of. Honours could be taken in classics or mathematics or both. History consisted of the study of Herodotus, Thucydides, Livy and Tacitus; philosophy of Plato and Aristotle. Modern philosophy – Leibnitz or Spinoza, for example – would have been anathema. A man went to Oxford to receive an education fit for a gentleman. After he had taken his degree he would return to his country estates, enter Parliament or, and this was the greater number, the Church of England. If he chose to remain at Oxford and to become a fellow of his college, he held the post for the rest of his life and nothing very much was expected of him. So long as a fellow remained unmarried and proceeded to Holy Orders, it was practically impossible to unseat him.

> The whole body of Oxford men [said T.E. Kebbel] were, in many respects, like one gigantic common-room: all members of a highly exclusive society; all members of the Church, and, with some very few exceptions, which did not in the slightest degree affect the tone or manners of the place, all gentlemen.[7]

Oxford was a city of curious anomalies, but none quite so curious as the constitution of Christ Church. 'It is a theoretically impossible place,' wrote Falconer Madan:

> How can a College, with its own quadrangles and Chapel, and with
> its alternations of term and vacation, its closing time at 9 p.m. and its
> four hundred undergraduates [he was writing in 1923] be the same
> institution as the Cathedral Establishment of the Diocese, including a
> Dean and Chapter complete and a cathedral entirely within the
> College?[8]

Christ Church never managed to resolve the dilemma. It was the largest,
grandest and wealthiest college in Oxford. The Cathedral, tucked away
behind Tom Quad, was the smallest in England, and the Bishop of Oxford
was all too frequently made aware of his inferiority to the Dean and
Chapter of the college. During Dean Gaisford's long reign the Bishop was
denied the use of the Chapter House and given very little access to his
Cathedral.

   In the years since Dodgson's father had taken his degree, Christ Church
had suffered something of an academic decline. It was certainly not the
most suitable college for a student of mathematics. Indeed, an undergraduate who really proposed to take the subject seriously and to explore the
most advanced theories of the day, would have gone to Cambridge where
the torch bearers of English mathematics, Cowley, Babbage and Hamilton, held sway. At Oxford the revolution in the study of mathematics that
was taking place in Germany was viewed with profound suspicion.
Dodgson was an instinctive conservative. New developments in mathematical thinking had little interest for him, at least at that time. His only wish
was to sit at the feet of Euclid and to explore more deeply and more
thoroughly the traditional mathematics he had learned from his father and
in which he had distinguished himself at Rugby. For the time being, the
undistinguished and unadventurous teaching of the subject that prevailed
at Christ Church was entirely suited to his taste and needs. Mathematics
ran through almost every moment of his waking day, it accompanied him
in his long solitary walks, and it sustained him through tormented and
sleepless nights. His passion for the subject, acquired, like so much else,
from his father, was awakened early in childhood and remained with him
until the last days of his life. He published a succession of mathematical
text books and papers which easily outnumber his literary work, and he
made at least one important contribution to mathematical method by his
treatise on determinants.

   Although he taught the subject at Christ Church for twenty-six years to
a succession of more-or-less reluctant undergraduates, mathematics was
essentially part of his inner world. He was constantly devising problems
for himself to solve. It was a way of giving occupation to a mind which
could never be turned off, which could never stop itself thinking. It was

also a way of imposing certainty and order on a disorderly world. Puzzles, games and conundrums seemed to arrive virtually of their own accord, and with them he would entertain his child-friends or torment his fellow dons. Confronted with a pretty little girl he would give her a wire puzzle or ask her to solve a problem about ferrying sheep across a river. He seems to have derived an almost sensual satisfaction from setting a problem to which he alone knew the correct solution. The desire to perlex and to astonish never left him. Mathematical problems, puzzles, logical conundrums, were all ways he could amaze his audience, as he had amazed his sisters at Croft.

When Dodgson first came to Christ Church there were marked distinctions between the grades of undergraduates. First came the Gentlemen Commoners. Many colleges judged their status by the numbers of the nobility they were able to attract. The gilded youth wore, appropriately, golden tassels in their caps to distinguish them from the vulgar herd and gowns of silk. In Hall they dined at High Table (a privilege to which the Fellows of the college were not entitled). To be a Gentleman Commoner it was not absolutely necessary to be a member of the aristocracy – parent could pay, as did John Ruskin's father, for the privilege of seeing his son sit at table with the men of rank and blood. Next came the Scholars, wearing a full gown with deep, wide sleeves. They had won one of the scholarships conferred by the College. The Commoners, of whom Dodgson was one, wore short, plain gowns. At the base of the pyramid were the Servitors, who were educated at reduced fees in return for performing various humble tasks – waiting in Hall, lighting fires and so forth.

> The position of undergraduates [wrote Dodgson's nephew] was much more similar to that of schoolboys than is now the case; they were subject to the same penalties – corporal punishment, even, had only just gone out of vogue! and were expected to work, and to work hard.[9]

For some, however, particularly the wealthy, Oxford meant freedom from paternal authority, a chance to educate themselves in the way of the world rather than Homer or Virgil. Thomas Hughes who, like Dodgson, had come to Oxford from Rugby, described the life of the 'fast set' of Gentleman Commoners:

> London wine merchants furnished them with liqueurs at a guinea a bottle, and wine at five guineas a dozen.... They drove tandems in all directions, scattering their ample allowances, which they treated as pocket money, about roadside inns with open hand, and going tick for

anything which could possibly be booked ... they hunted, rode steeple chases by day, played billiards until the gates closed, and then they were ready for vingt-et-un, unlimited loo, and hot drink in their own rooms, as long as anybody could be got to sit up and play.[10]

Dodgson was not likely to wish to join their ranks but their antics distracted him by day and kept him awake by night. His first surviving letter home describes a fight between the gentlemen's dogs which took place outside his window:

> ... everything and everybody was fleeing from the scene of combat: six dogs went headlong down the steps, which lead into the quad, yelling at the very top of their voices, six sticks came flying after them, and after that came their six masters, all running their hardest, and all in different directions.[11]

Dining at Christ Church in those days seems to have been a rather rough and ready, not to say disorderly, business. Beneath the great hammer beam roof, in the Hall where Dodgson's portrait now hangs with those of Gladstone and Dean Liddell, separate tables were allocated to a 'mess' of some half dozen Commoners. They hacked unceremoniously away at a common joint, eating off pewter dishes with ancient silver cutlery and rising from the table whenever they pleased, without even waiting for grace. Dodgson's mess included the crippled Philip Pusey, the son of his father's old friend, and, according to Collingwood, a man who was said to have given his features to the Mad Hatter – though there were to be several claimants to that title. Another was George Girdlestone Woodhouse. Dodgson wrote to his widow in 1897:

> Of all the friends I made at Christ Church, your husband was the very first who spoke to me – across the dinner table in Hall. That is 46 years ago, but I remember, as if it were only yesterday, the kindly smile with which he spoke.[12]

From the beginning of the Easter Term of 1852, Dodgson and Woodhouse shared rooms on the Cloister staircase. George Woodhouse was, like Dodgson, the son of a clergyman. His father was Vicar of Albrighton in Shropshire, where Dodgson went to stay with his friend while they were undergraduates and where he heard for the first time the song, 'Mary Call the Cattle Home', 'a wild and beautiful bit of poetry'. Dodgson commemorated his friendship with Woodhouse in verse: a mock heroic epic entitled the 'Ligniad' which he wrote in 1853. 'Lignum' is Latin for wood, which accounts for the title, but it is Woodhouse's passion for Greek which the poem celebrates:

> *Small taste had he for toys of infancy;*
> *The coral and the bells he set aside;*
> *But in the cradle would soliloquise,*
> *And hold high commune with his inner man*
> *In Greek iambics, aptly modified –*[13]

But a great shadow casts itself across Woodhouse's life, the realisation that of the plays of Euripides, 73 have been lost:

> *'Homer may come, and Homer may go,*
> *And be shifted, like lumber, from shelf to shelf,*
> *But I will read no Greek, no Greek,*
> *Until the lost dramas I've found for myself!'*
> *Thus, all unconscious, rhymed his agony,*
> *Adapting to the anguish of the hour*
> *A fragment from our Poet Laureate.*[14]

In the second 'book' of his mock epic, Dodgson turns from Woodhouse's classical attainment to his achievements on the cricket field, with a passing glance at Coleridge's 'Christabel':

> *The wickets pitched, the players ranged around;*
> *And he, the hero, in his glory there;*
> *A sight to dream of, not to write about!*[15]

It is an affectionate parody in which Dodgson is constantly delighting in his own ingenuity, high-spirited and light-hearted. It is one of the few glimpses we have of his undergraduate years. Curiously, it is the only one of his poems addressed to a man, and one of the very few to an adult. The stories which were circulated about Dodgson in his later years stressing his misanthropy, his austerity and his unapproachability have tended to obscure his very real gift for making life-long friendships, to which the 'Ligniad' bears witness. The poem was kept among his papers at Christ Church and given to Mrs Woodhouse after her husband's death.

> *Then fare thee well, greatest of little men,*
> *In Greek, in Latin, in the cricket field:*
> *Great as a bowler, greater as a bat,*
> *But as a 'short slip' greater yet than that.*[16]

On 23rd January, 1851, two days after Charles had taken up residence at Christ Church, news came from Croft of the death of his mother. It must have come totally without warning, or he would never have left home. The cause of her death was given as 'inflammation of the brain', which does not tell us very much. To judge from a letter written to the Archdeacon by his aunt, Mary Smedley, her last months seem to have been remarkably content.

The last walk we took together she spoke to me of her rare and
exceeding happiness ... she spoke most touchingly and feelingly of the
responsibility incurred by a lot of so much happiness – and that it
really was at times 'alarming' to look round her and feel that she had
not a wish unfulfilled.[17]

The family were in a state of profound shock. 'Only tell me what I can do
for you,' wrote Bishop Longley to the Archdeacon. 'My home will be open
to you and such of your children as would like to come, only let me have
the comfort of thinking I have been of some use to you in your hour of
need.'[18]

Since Dodgson's diary for this time has disappeared, we have no way of
gauging the extent of his grief. He rarely spoke of his mother's death. At
the birth of his sister Mary's first child, Stuart Collingwood, in 1870 he
wrote:

And may you be to him what our own mother was to her eldest son! I
can hardly utter for your boy a better wish than that![19]

It has been suggested that his mother's death was a blow from which he
never recovered. Two years later he wrote a poem entitled 'Solitude' which
has often been cited as an expression of his grief:

Kind nature to the aching heart
Brings sympathies of large relief:
Full gladly would she bear her part
In our dull load of grief.

So may the silent tears we weep
Lull the vexed spirit into rest,
As infants sob themselves to sleep
Upon a mother's breast.[20]

The problem is that, as with much of Dodgson's serious verse, it reads
more like conventional poetising than a statement of personal grief. In a
piece written much later – in 1876 – *An Easter Greeting to Every Child
who loves Alice*, he pictured a child waking on a summer morning:

And is not that a Mother's sweet voice that summons you to rise? To
rise and forget, in the bright sunlight, the ugly dreams that frightened
you so when all was dark?[21]

It is hard to see clearly through the mist of Victorian sentiment, but this
does suggest the recollection of a real experience. Undoubtedly his mother
was very dear to him and her death must have come as a terrible shock, yet
it was the death of his father, years later, that he would mourn as the
heaviest blow in his life. There are several loving fathers to be found in his

writing, but there is practically nothing in the way of a loving mother. Whatever the intensity of his grief, he must have thrust it firmly into the background of his consciousness. Yet this may have been the one thing which locked him for ever into his childhood.

Five weeks later, back in Christ Church, he was writing a thoroughly jaunty letter to his sister, Mary, hoping that she would imagine that he was present when her health was drunk on her birthday. He complains that he has left all his silk neckerchiefs behind at home and wonders why his father has not answered his question about a name-plate for his room in college. None of this sounds very much like inconsolable grief, but perhaps his relentless merry banter was his way of coping with it. Perhaps he felt that it was his duty to keep up his role as family jester and entertainer. Perhaps he was, quite simply, trying to keep at bay a deep-rooted horror of death.

Dodgson's cousin, Menella Smedley descended on Croft to help out the family. She was thirty-one and for a few weeks did her best to fill the void left by the death of Mrs Dodgson. She was a poetess of some repute, and the first real writer Charles had ever met. Her poems of watery religious sentiment appear very limp and pallid now, but they greatly appealed to the taste of the Victorians:

> *And shall I lie where sunsets drift,*
> *Or where the stars are born,*
> *Or where the living tints are mixt*
> *To paint the clouds of morn?*
> *Your mother's tones shall reach you still,*
> *Even sweeter than they were;*
> *And the false love that broke your heart*
> *Shall be forgotten there ...* [22]

Her verse was to have a deplorable effect on Dodgson's own. Serious verse was never his forte, and whenever he tried his hand at it he slipped into the Menella Smedley vein, producing verses every bit as vapid as hers:

> *'Peace dwells in those soft-lidded eyes.*
> *Those parted lips that faintly smile –*
> *Peace, the foretaste of Paradise,*
> *In heart too young for care or guile.* [23]

Menella left Croft early in February and her place was taken by Lucy Lutwidge, Frances Dodgson's younger sister. Lucy was forty-five and one of those devoted creatures who were destined always to serve and fill the place of others, to nurse elderly relatives and never to marry. Lucy had looked after her own invalid father for the last twelve years of his life and was now to devote herself to the Dodgson family for nearly thirty years.

> What a treasure you have in Lucy, [wrote Menella's mother to the Archdeacon,] that kind and excellent creature whose whole heart is wrapped up in you and whose whole life will be devoted to your children.[24]

Aunt Lucy had always been a great favourite with the children, and an honorary member of the Dodgson clan. Now she took her place at the centre of it, a fund of cheerfulness, affection and common sense. Charles, who always appears to have been more at ease with his Lutwidge relatives, found that she was a person in whom he could confide and whose advice he valued. He also saved up anecdotes for her entertainment. Aunt Lucy could not replace Frances Jane, but she could provide a practical stabilising force in the household at a time when the Archdeacon became more deeply preoccupied with the duties of his calling, and Charles himself began to discover other worlds beyond Christ Church and Croft.

6
'A child with a new toy'

Dodgson was by nature a hard worker. His vigorous pursuit of his studies at Oxford had nothing to do with fear of disappointing his father or subscribing to a Victorian sense of duty. All his life he would derive a kind of exhilaration from the prospect of a mound of work to be conquered. He would draw up long lists of books to be read, books to be written, and if he did not keep to them, it was only because something equally demanding had rushed into his mind. He was determined to fill every second of his life. 'I am uppe to mine eyes yn worke,' he informed his sister Louisa in a birthday letter written for her in his own particular brand of mock medieval English accompanying the gift of 'ane smalle boke, whilke I have hope ytte maie lyke thee toe possesse'.[1]

He seems to have survived his first year without mishap. His only fall from grace was to miss morning chapel (for which he would have been fined) through falling asleep after his early morning call. He might have benefited from an invention patented by Theophilus Carter, a former Christ Church pupil and furniture dealer, who was to be another candidate for the original of the Mad Hatter. This was an alarm clock which activated a mechanism for tipping the sleeper out of bed.

The bed was one of the many bizarre inventions on display at the 1851 Great Exhibition in Hyde Park which Dodgson rushed off to see at the beginning of the Long Vacation. Prince Albert's grand vision had opened in May and, despite predictions that the hundreds of foreign visitors would bring the bubonic plague or that Kensington Gardens would be turned into a 'bivouac for all the vagabonds of London', it was proving to be one of the wonders of the century. The Prince Consort had intended the Exhibition to present 'a living picture of the point of development at which the whole of mankind has arrived'.[2] The displays included a doctor's walking stick which contained an enema, a pair of false teeth fitted with a swivel so that the wearer could yawn without displacing both upper and lower plates, and a group of stuffed frogs from Wurtemburg, one of whom was holding an umbrella.

Dodgson escorted a party of assorted aunts: Charlotte, Henrietta and

Margaret Lutwidge and Elizabeth Raikes. 'I think the first impression produced on you when you get inside is of bewilderment. It looks like a sort of Fairyland,'[3] he told his sister Elizabeth. Only the works of living artists, or those less than three years dead, were on display. Dodgson was greatly impressed by August Kiss's monumental 'Amazon attacked by a Tigress'. 'The horse's face is really wonderful expressing terror and pain so exactly, that you almost expect to hear it scream.' There was an enormous figure of the crusader Godfrey of Bouillon on a horse 'a great deal larger than an elephant' and two plaster statues of a child being saved by a dog from a venomous snake:

> The body of the serpent is lying at one side and the head <u>Most</u> thoroughly bitten off, at the other. The dog seems to have quite chewed the neck of the serpent to make sure.[4]

What really took his fancy, however, were the mechanical toys:

> A tree (in the French Compartment) with birds chirping and hopping from branch to branch exactly like life. The bird jumps across, turns round on the branch, settles its head and neck, and then in a few moments jumps back again. A bird standing at the foot of the tree trying to eat a beetle is rather a failure ... the beetle is lying comfortably before it, but it never succeeds in getting its head more than a quarter of an inch down, and that in uncomfortable little jerks, as if it was choking.[5]

Dodgson took a childlike delight in mechanical toys. In later years he would entertain his little girl friends with 'Bob the Bat' which was powered by twisted elastic and which would fly round and round the room and which on one occasion flew right out of his window in Christ Church and alighted on a bowl of salad carried by a college servant who dropped it in horror.[6]

The visit to the Great Exhibition set the pattern for all Dodgson's future vacations. Instead of travelling directly back to Croft, it became his practice to spend the first few days of every vacation in London looking at the new paintings at the Royal Academy, or taking his aunts to see such wonders as the Diorama of Jerusalem in the Egyptian Hall in Piccadilly. In London there was no shortage of relatives to stay with and he frequently migrated from one set to another. There was a Raikes cousin in Gordon Square; his uncle Hassard lived in Wandsworth Lane, Putney; and his favourite uncle, Skeffington Lutwidge, lived in what was then called Alfred Place, South Kensington. Skeffington was Dodgson's mother's elder brother. In photographs he looks portly and benevolent, like a

Dickensian benefactor. He was a bachelor, a barrister and a Commissioner in Lunacy. The Lunacy Commission, set up in 1828, inspected and reported on conditions in asylums throughout the country. It was an exacting, depressing, and, as Skeffington Lutwidge was to find out, a frequently dangerous occupation. Even at the best of times, Uncle Skeffington seems to have been rather accident-prone. The first time we ever hear of him in his nephew's letters, he is recovering from a wound in the head, though whether this happened in the course of his duties is not clear.

Uncle Skeffington had a passion for new inventions and strange gadgets and at times sounds rather like the White Knight. The 'new oddities' he had acquired when Dodgson went to stay with him at the beginning of the 1852 Long Vacation included a lathe, a telescope stand, 'a beautiful little pocket instrument for measuring distances on a map' and a refrigerator. Together they observed the moon and Jupiter through the telescope, and 'animacula' through a microscope.

> This is a most interesting sight, as the creatures are most conveniently transparent, and you will see all kinds of organs jumping about like a complicated piece of machinery, and even the circulation of the blood. Everything goes on at railway speed, so I suppose they must be some of these insects that only live a day or two, and try to make the most of it.[7]

All the while, Dodgson was working away rather like one of his uncle's microscope creatures. He told his sister that, '25 hours *hard* work a day *may* get through all I have to do'. He was rapidly becoming a star performer in the academic circus. In 1851 he had won a Boulter scholarship and the following year he took a First in mathematics. He wrote off airily to Elizabeth: 'I am getting quite tired of being congratulated on various subjects: there seems to be no end of it. If I had shot the Dean, I could hardly have more said about it.'[8] Pusey, who up till then had been wary of promoting the son of his old friend, now felt that he could nominate Dodgson for a Studentship with a clear conscience. The Archdeacon wrote warmly and proudly to his son, telling him of the joy he had brought to the entire family:

> I cannot desire stronger evidence than <u>Pusey's</u> own words of the fact that you have <u>won</u>, and well won, this honour for <u>yourself</u>, and that it is bestowed as a matter of <u>justice</u> to <u>you</u>, and not of <u>kindness</u> to me.[9]

In 1852 the Archdeacon was appointed a Canon of Ripon. This new office required him to spend three months of every year there and he duly took a large house near the Minster for himself and his family. Ripon was an ancient town dating back to Saxon times where curfew was sounded every night at nine o'clock by blowing a horn in the market square – a custom that continues unchanged to this day. For Dodgson's sisters life in Ripon provided new interests and Fanny was recruited as fundraiser for the new East Window of the Cathedral. When she asked her brother what contributions he might be able to levy in Christ Church, Dodgson could not give her 'the smallest hope of any subscriptions' except from himself and his cousin Frank Hume Dodgson who had come up to Christ Church that year. The stained glass window of Christ and the Apostles which William Wailes created for Ripon with the help of the Dodgsons' contributions is a sadly pedestrian effort. That same year another stained glass window was placed in the Bishop's Palace at Ripon, – to the Reverend Dodgson himself. One hundred and eighty-five ordained clergymen had got together a subscription to commemorate 'The kindness, learning, piety and ability with which the Rev. Charles Dodgson MA Examining Chaplain, has discharged the duties of his office during 15 years.'

The new Canon soon found himself involved in a bitter religious dispute with the Dean of Ripon, Dr Goode. The Dean was a low church fanatic, a sniffer-out of heresy, who was antagonised by the elder Dodgson's High Church views. He formally denounced him to the Bishop for 'publicly preaching and teaching false doctrine contrary to that of the Church of England'. Neither the Bishop (the elder Dodgson's old friend Longley), nor the Archbishop of York would have any of it, and since Goode refused to argue his case in public, the Archdeacon blasted him in a pamphlet, accusing him of being motivated by 'EXCITEMENT OF PRIVATE AND PERSONAL FEELINGS'.[10] Dodgson undoubtedly relished the blow-by-blow accounts of the proceedings sent to him by his father. It gave him a taste for what Humpty Dumpty was to call 'a nice knock-down argument'.

At this point in Dodgson's career, following in his father's footsteps and taking Holy Orders was a comfortably distant prospect. It was, of course, one of the conditions of retaining his Studentship, as was not getting married, but neither of these matters seemed terribly important to Dodgson at that time. The whole course of his existence had been decided, he was entitled to lifetime membership of Christ Church, and yet in many ways he was still a schoolboy, anxious about how he was going to cope with dinner at the Deanery, writing enthusiastically to his cousin Frank Dodgson about the fortunes of the college boat and getting into trouble for failing to turn up to mark the absentees among the undergraduates attending chapel.

*

Dodgson was putting in long days and nights of incessant toil. His Studentship depended upon his passing his degree and he was frantically reading for 'Greats', the final examination in the honours school. He was working thirteen hours a day and on the eve of his *viva voce* he sat up all night reading. None of this seems to have helped him much. He was never very sympathetically disposed towards either philosophy or history as academic subjects and he did not put up a particularly distinguished performance.

> Herodotus was one of the subjects and the examiner questioned him without much success. At last he said, 'Well, Mr Dodgson, is there any fact mentioned by Herodotus which you do remember?' Then Dodgson brightened up. He remembered the name of a Libyan tribe of which Herodotus records nothing but that they painted themselves red and ate apes.[11]

For this unlikely piece of erudition on the subject of the Gyzantes, Dodgson was awarded a Third.

He thought it best to leave nothing to chance as far as the final mathematics school in October 1854 was concerned, and decided to spend a large part of the Long Vacation with a reading party in Whitby under the tutorship of Bartholomew Price. Price, later to become a great friend, was nicknamed the 'Bat' and it has been suggested that 'Twinkle, twinkle little bat' was composed in his honour. The reading party was an essential part of the Victorian university scene. A group of students would take themselves off to some picturesque spot and there, under the guidance of a tutor, would give themselves up to study. It was by no means all work. From time to time, the men would take a break to climb some nearby mountain or row in the local river. The weather in Whitby that summer seems to have been characteristically bracing:

> ... there is a strong wind blowing off shore, and threatening to carry Whitby and contents into the sea. There is sand and sharp shingle flying in the air, that acts on the face like the smart cut of a whip, and here and there the sight of an old lady being whirled round a corner in a paroxysm of dust and despair.[12]

Dodgson and his companions set out to take in one of the local attractions, a cascade which they were under the impression was called 'Mary Ann's Spout'. This earned them curious looks when asking their way since its name was in fact Mallyan's Spout. The spout itself was a great disappointment, 'a poor little feeble, fluttering thing' at the bottom of a steep and muddy road. Dodgson, most unusually for one so habitually unadventurous, elected to take a short-cut by climbing up the side of the cliff and soon found himself clinging for dear life to the roots of bushes. He made it to the top, muddy and exhausted. 'Such a scramble as I have rarely engaged in.' The most memorable thing about the reading party was that many years later, after Dodgson's death, one of the students present, Thomas Fowler, stated that:

> It was there that *Alice* was incubated. Dodgson used to sit on a rock on the beach, telling stories to a circle of eager young listeners of both sexes. These stories were afterwards developed and consolidated into their present form.[13]

This rather unlikely story proved something of a cat among the pigeons for Lewis Carroll enthusiasts who made strenuous efforts to work out which elements of *Alice* might have been told to the children at Whitby. Walter De La Mare suggested 'The Walrus and the Carpenter', Roger Lancelyn Green favoured 'She's all my fancy painted him' which was published the year after the Whitby reading party and which was to be pressed into service as 'Alice's Evidence'. The latter does not seem to be the kind of thing that anyone would choose for the entertainment of children on a windy beach. It is more probable that Fowler was being wise after the event. In the years that followed Dodgson's death, there were desperate attempts to scramble aboard the *Alice* bandwagon and to claim some kind of involvement with the inception of the work. That Dodgson sat on the beach telling stories to children is very probable. That the story told on this occasion was the germ of *Alice* was probably wishful thinking on Fowler's part.

The pursuit of Fowler's red herring has rather overshadowed the actual pieces which Dodgson did write at Whitby. They were published in the *Whitby Gazette* under the initials 'B.B.', with which he had signed some very slight pieces of verse in *The Rectory Magazine*. The first of them, 'The Lady of the Ladle' shows Dodgson in a very bright and breezy mood, and enjoying himself immensely:

> She called me her 'Neddy',
> (Tho' there mayn't be much in it,)
> And I should have been ready,
> If she'd waited a minute:
> I was following behind her
> When, if you recollect, I
> Merely ran back to find a
> Gold pin for my neck-tie.[14]

The other contribution was in prose and entitled 'Wilhelm Von Schmitz'. It is a rather thin tale, not unlike those with which he had filled the Rectory magazines, but it does have one sentence which seems to contain the essence of childhood (or, at least, Dodgson's childhood) and which, at the same time, looks forward both to *Alice's Adventures* and to 'The Hunting of the Snark'.

> Visions of his early days; scenes from the happy time of pinafores, treacle and innocence; through the long vista of the past came floating spectres of long-forgotten spelling books, slates scrawled thick with dreary sums, that seldom came out at all, and never came out right; tingling and somewhat painful sensations returned to his knuckles and to the roots of his hair; he was a boy once more.[15]

Dodgson returned to Oxford to find that cholera was raging in the poorer quarters of the city and there were 1,000 cases of smallpox reported. Robinson Duckworth, who was to accompany Dodgson on the 'Alice' river expedition nearly eight years later, walked to Headington Common through a yellow fog with Augustus Hare and came across a cottage where seven people had died. Special services were held in the churches and there was a great fear that the infection might spread. Fortunately, cholera didn't penetrate the colleges, and life at Christ Church went on much as normal. When the results of the first mathematical school were announced, Dodgson had come first. He wrote off an exultant letter to his sister Mary:

> I feel at present very like a child with a new toy, but I dare say I shall be tired of it soon, and wish to be Pope of Rome next.[16]

He gave his Scout a bottle of wine to drink to his First and on 18th December he took his degree. He had high hopes that he would be awarded a Senior Scholarship. Nothing now seemed to stand between him and the Mathematical Lectureship – all this within five years of arriving at Christ Church. It is small wonder that he felt 'very boastful'.

7
'I felt as if in a dream'

1855 is the first year for which we have Dodgson's diary. When Collingwood came to write his uncle's biography in the year following his death, he was able to draw on a series of diaries which covered Dodgson's life from the age of ten until his death, apart from the years at Rugby. By the time of the Lewis Carroll centenary in 1932, four of the thirteen volumes, covering the years up to January 1855, October to December of that year, and from April 1858 to May 1862 had disappeared. Derek Hudson, Dodgson's first biographer since Collingwood to have been allowed access to the diaries, said that 'probably their loss was accidental', but suspected that they might have been destroyed. In his preface to the 1969 edition of *Lewis Carroll, Photographer* Helmut Gernsheim said that Collingwood himself was responsible, but it seems more likely that it would have been one of Dodgson's sisters, who after his death came to look upon him as little less than a saint and became very jealous of anything that might affect his reputation.

Why should the diaries have been destroyed? To judge from the very substantial amount that remains, the diary was not a confessional. Dodgson rarely gives any indications of his deeper emotions – one suspects he rarely admitted them to himself. When he did record anything over which he had second thoughts, the entries have been scored through, or the diary has been cut and doctored. For the most part it is a dry, simple chronicle of events, not conscientiously set down day by day but frequently made up from his 'metallic' diary, a notebook containing brief details of appointments and events. The diary, now in the British Library, was written in quarto notebooks in Dodgson's clear, precise hand which changes very little from the first surviving entry to the last. There are pages covered with mathematical formulae and geometrical diagrams, there are plans of dinner table seatings and designs for postal orders, and there is an index. Unfortunately the lost diaries cover some of the most important periods of his life. While it is tempting to try to deduce scandals or major emotional upheavals, it is very possible, as Roger Lancelyn Green suggested, that the reason for the destruction of the missing volumes may have had nothing to do with the events of Dodgson's own life. The offending diaries may have simply contained details of the life of his family which the sisters considered ought not to be revealed.

What the diary tells us about the twenty-three-year-old Dodgson in the vacation of January 1855 is hardly exciting. The family were installed in Ripon, and he was finding it difficult to concentrate on any plan of work. He tried a little solid geometry and spotted a minor error in Bartholomew's *Differential Calculus*. He sketched a design for an illumination on the title page of his sister Mary's book of sacred poetry, heard a tedious recital on the handbells, attended a morning concert in Harrogate and studied the 'novel effect of Fountains Abbey in a mist'. At the same time he was reading steadily through Benjamin Haydon's autobiography: 'such perseverance and spirit under such difficulties as he met with, makes one's everyday trials shrink into nothing'.[1] Life at Ripon seems to have been very dull indeed. At the end of the vacation he reckoned that the work done 'must count as "nil"'. He had, however, managed one piece of original writing 'Ye Carpette Knyghte' which he thought sufficiently highly of to include in future collections of his verse, although it does not rise much above the level of the verse he was writing as a schoolboy:

> I have a horse – a ryghte good horse –
> Ne doe I envye those
> Who scoure ye playne yn headye course
> Tyll soddayne on theyre nose
> They lyghte wyth unexpected force
> Yt ys – a horse of clothes.[2]

When he returned to Christ Church everything seemed to combine to keep him from his studies. He was being coached by Bartholomew Price for the Senior Mathematical Scholarship but, at the same time, he was coaching pupils of his own for their 'little go'. He wrote to Henrietta and Edwin giving a lively account of his lessons with his first pupil. The important point, he told them, was that the teacher should keep a dignified distance from his pupil:

> So I sit at the further end of the room; outside the door (which is shut) sits the scout; outside the outer door (also shut) sits the sub-scout; half-way down stairs sits the sub-sub-scout; and down in the yard sits the pupil.
> The questions are shouted from one to the other, and the answers come back in the same way – it is rather confusing till you are well used to it. The lecture goes on, something like this.

TUTOR:	What is twice three?
SCOUT:	What's a rice tree?
SUB-SCOUT:	When is ice free?
SUB-SUB-SCOUT:	What's a nice fee?
PUPIL (TIMIDLY)	Half a guinea!
SUB-SUB-SCOUT:	Can't forge any!
SUB-SCOUT:	Ho for Jinny!
SCOUT:	Don't be a ninny!
TUTOR:	(looks offended, but tries another question ...)[3]

He had been appointed sub-librarian, a post which his old Daresbury friend Vere Bayne, who had been a Student of Christ Church since 1849, had just vacated. He calculated that it would add £35 a year to his meagre income, 'not much towards independence', but it did give him the opportunity to immerse himself in the Christ Church library. As befitted the future hunter of the Snark, he began with a bookcase labelled 'W–W'. In a Great Bible from the time of Henry VIII he came across a scrap of manuscript but was unable to decipher a single word. This was the year in which he was to write the first verse of 'Jabberwocky'.

Diversions crowded in from every side. He went out skating and cut his head, he took on more pupils. At the Town Hall Fanny Kemble was giving one of her readings from Shakespeare: the most famous Juliet of her time was reading Henry V. As a result of his father's ban on attending theatrical performances, Dodgson had never seen Shakespeare performed on stage, but there was nothing to prevent him attending a reading. He thought that Fanny Kemble delivered the lines with 'great spirit' but at times dwindled into mere recitation. He went back to his rooms inspired to read Henry IV again but found that even Shakespeare grew tedious without costume or scenery. The forbidden fruit of the theatre was beginning to prove a temptation that would become more and more difficult to resist.

Every day there was some news of the Crimean War which had broken out the previous year. The assault upon Sebastopol had begun and Florence Nightingale, destined to become one of Dodgson's personal heroines, had arrived at Scutari. Would the course of events be changed by the death of the Tsar? Had Tennyson really written a poem which contained lines as banal as:

> For up came an order, which
> Someone had blundered?[4]

Christ Church men began to leave for the war. The Mathematics Lecturer, Robert Faussett, went out to take a commission in the Commissariat. Dodgson had high hopes that he might inherit his post, but the Dean decided that no successor should be appointed. 'I fancy his real motive is his objection to appoint a B.A.'[5]

On 21st March Dodgson recorded, 'General humiliation on account of the war – services in all the churches'.[6] On the following day he suffered a great humiliation on his own account. In the examination for the Mathematical Scholarship he could only manage five questions in the morning paper and four in the afternoon. Worse was to come next day when there were only two questions he could finish. He made no attempt to sit the afternoon paper but went for a long walk with his friend Robert Mayo to Kidlington. There they could find no inn that would provide them with dinner and were forced to make do with bread and cheese in a public house. The Scholarship was won by Robert Bosanquet, who had come second to Dodgson the previous year. 'I might have got it, if only I had worked properly during the term, which I fear I must consider as wasted.'[7] He was not even optimistic about sitting the examination again, 'knowing how many similar failures there have been in my life already'. He was presumably thinking of his dismal performance in 'Greats' the previous year. 'Eheu fugaces!' (time rushes past) he wrote, quoting Horace. Time would always pass too quickly for him, leaving him lamenting a host of tasks undone.

He began the vacation in a determined frame of mind, reading Burton's *Lectures on Church History* and drawing up a plan for an essay on 'The Equation of the Second Degree', but after six days the temptation of the marionette theatre proved more than he could resist and he put on a special performance of *The Tragedy of King John* for the assembled family, the Webster boys and Harriet Chaytor, the daughter of Archdeacon Dodgson's late adversary.

The play went off so successfully that he began to wonder whether he might put his plays for marionettes to some commercial use. There used to be a notion that Dodgson was an unworldly dreamer, but he was in fact gifted with a very shrewd business instinct. He rarely let slip an opportunity to exploit fully anything he produced and always made a point of trying to bring his work before as wide an audience as possible. On this occasion he thought of writing a Christmas book for children, explaining how to construct a marionette theatre and make puppets for it. The handbook would also include the plays he had written for the Rectory theatre.

> All existing plays for such objects seem to me to have one of two
> faults – either (1) they are meant for the real theatre, and are therefore

not fitted for children, or (2) they are overpoweringly dull – no idea of fun in them. The three already written for our theatre have at least the advantage of having been tested by experience and found to be popular.[8]

Nothing came of the project but he continued to work on plays for the puppet theatre, sketching out scenes for *Alfred the Great* and setting his sister Mary to work on the scenery – 'I am convinced now that sized calico is the best material for painting on.' But that is the last we hear of it.[9]

By the Easter Term of 1855, Dodgson was taking on more pupils, fourteen in all, whom he was instructing in Algebra, Conics, Trigonometry, Euclid and Arithmetic. This was not an official arrangement. The pupils had been sent to him by his friend, George Kitchin, the Mathematical Examiner. But it was a way of augmenting the meagre allowance he received from his father and of demonstrating his abilities as a teacher. His tactics paid off. Dean Gaisford awarded him the Bostock Scholarship – 'This very nearly raises my income to independence – Courage!'[10]

It was during the Easter Term that Dodgson made the acquaintance of Elizabeth Siddal, if we are to believe her first biographer, Violet Hunt. Two years older than Dodgson, the pre-Raphaelite model whose face gazes out of so many of Rossetti's paintings, was trying to establish herself as an artist. Her patron, John Ruskin, was concerned for her health and had persuaded her to consult his old friend Henry Acland, the Radcliffe Professor of Medicine at Oxford. Acland decided that it would be best if she were to stay in Oxford for a while and engaged rooms for her in George Street. Dante Gabriel brought her down by train and then promptly departed, leaving her alone and miserable. The Warden of New College did his best to entertain her by showing her an engraving by Dürer of a black beetle and suggesting that they should compare it with a live one from the kitchens. She was not amused. Mrs Acland took against her and the dons were cold and inhospitable. The only person she did get on with, according to Violet Hunt, was Charles Dodgson:

> 'Lewis Carroll' sketched Gabriel for her when she came down, and made her and the chimney sweeps laugh and the undergraduates thaw: but she was too old for him.[11]

It is difficult to know what to make of all this. There is no mention of her in Dodgson's diary, but the most likely time for a meeting to have taken place, the middle of June, is a blank – 'Nothing remarkable occurred during the rest of the term.' He was not acquainted with Acland at this time but he may have met Lizzie Siddal through a daughter of Dr Pusey

with whom she seems to have struck up a sort of friendship. If Dodgson did
draw a picture of Rossetti for Lizzie, it can only have been the kind of wild
caricature that he drew for his sisters. That could certainly have amused
her.

Violet Hunt was not the most reliable of biographers, but she did seek
out all the relevant people who were still living when she wrote her
biography of Elizabeth Siddal in 1932, and her account may well be based
on someone's personal reminiscence. After all, there is no reason to
suppose that she invented the encounter and there is no reason why it
should not have taken place. Many things happened to Dodgson which he
did not mention in his diary and it does seem quite likely that he would
have done his best to entertain a sick and lonely, rather neurotic girl who
was so close to the centre of the enchanted realm of pre-Raphaelite
romance. Dodgson, who made it his business to keep up with everything
that was happening in the London art world, would certainly have
recognised Lizzie as the girl who had lain in a tin bath of cold water as
Millais' *Ophelia*.

On 2nd June, Dean Gaisford died at the age of seventy-six. His death came
as a surprise, both to the college and to Dodgson, who only the previous
week had been helping the old man put the new books up onto the library
shelves. Gaisford had been the incarnation of the old Oxford, stubbornly
opposed to change of any kind, resisting to the last the Royal Commission
that had been empowered to usher the university into the nineteenth-
century.

> As to the commission itself, [wrote Gaisford] I feel, in common with
> almost everyone both at Oxford and Cambridge, that it is a measure
> which can be productive of no good, and may eventually breed
> discord and disunion, and destroy the independence of those bodies.[12]

These words were addressed to Henry Liddell, the Headmaster of
Westminster, on the occasion of his being made a member of the
Commission. Liddell was a former pupil of Gaisford's, and was now the
man chosen to be his successor as Dean of Christ Church. The prime
minister, Lord Palmerston, wrote to Liddell telling him of the great cheer
which had greeted the news of his appointment in Parliament, but there
were few cheers at Christ Church. 'Nothing but what is evil is threatened,'
growled Pusey when the first rumours of Liddell's appointment reached
him. It would, he said, be the end of the old Christ Church. 'The selection
does not seem to have given much satisfaction in the college,' noted
Dodgson drily.[13] Christ Church represented all that was most solidly and

unrepentantly conservative in Oxford. The prospect of being subjected to the rule of a man who was totally committed to reform and the abolition of many of the traditions that the old dons held dear, can only have filled them with dismay.

It was the beginning of the Long Vacation and Dodgson travelled up to London with Vere Bayne. The accident-prone Uncle Skeffington was laid up with a leg injury, but this did not interfere with Dodgson's plans to make the most of the days he had in London. Exactly when he had decided to contest his father's ban on attending stage performances we do not know, but in the first week of that vacation, after seeking the advice of his friend Henry Liddon, he went to the theatre four times. Accompanied by Ranken, one of the Whitby reading party, he saw Madame Arga in Bellini's *Norma* at Drury Lane. Although presumably he had never seen the opera before, some of the music would have been familiar to him from Croft. One of the arias had been hijacked for Mrs Muddle to sing in *La Guida di Bragia*:

> *Oh dear! Whatever am I to do?*
> *Dear, whatever am I to do?*
> *Here's all my luggage is gone,*
> *I haven't the least idea where to!*
> *There was three trunks and an oblong box*
> *And none of them had got any locks.*[14]

The performance was followed by a Grand Ballet, which Dodgson loathed:

> Talk of the poetry of motion! The instinctive grace of cottage children dancing is something far more beautiful: I never wish to see another ballet.[15]

The following day, after a morning at the Royal Academy and an afternoon at Lord's cricket ground watching the Oxford and Cambridge match, he went to see *Norma* again, or at least, the first act of it. This time it was at Covent Garden and the singer was the legendary Giulietta Grisi, 'in appearance red-faced and coarse, though wonderfully young looking for sixty'.[16] This was followed by *The Barber of Seville*, an opera unknown to Dodgson, which he found tedious.

It was on the third day that Dodgson enjoyed 'the greatest theatrical treat I ever had, or ever expect to have', a production by Charles Kean's company of Shakespeare's *Henry VIII* at the Princess's Theatre. It was a performance which transformed his life and turned him into an inveterate theatre-goer. For the first time he realised the power of the stage to conjure up beautiful aery visions and to fill his whole being with wonder. It was an experience which he was to try to repeat again and again.

The Princess's, which was to become Dodgson's favourite London theatre, was at that time beginning to rival Drury Lane and Covent Garden. Until 1843, under the terms of exclusive patents granted by Charles II, these two theatres had enjoyed a monopoly of full-length classic drama and, most importantly, Shakespeare. Other theatres were obliged to introduce songs and divertissements, so that their bills offered a weird mixture of Shakespearean fragments, sketches, farces, operatic excerpts and ballets. This curious state of affairs came to an end when the patents were revoked and all theatres were allowed to put on whatever plays they chose. Under the management of Charles Kean, son of the legendary Edmund, the Princess's Theatre was one of the first to take advantage of this new freedom. It was not a prepossessing place. It was hemmed in between a furrier's and a tobacconist's at the unfashionable east end of the unfashionable Oxford Street, but Dodgson held it in great affection. The memorable evening of 22nd June began with John Maddison Morton's farce, *Away with Melancholy*, which Dodgson was to convert into a one-man show for himself. And then came *Henry VIII*. It was not Kean's performance as Wolsey, which Dodgson thought 'magnificent', nor his wife as Queen Catherine – 'a worthy successor to Mrs Siddons' – that bowled him over, but the 'exquisite vision' which appeared to the Queen as she lay dying:

> I almost held my breath to watch; the illusion is perfect, and I felt as if in a dream all the time it lasted. It was like a delicious reverie, or the most beautiful poetry. This is the true end and object of acting – to raise the mind above itself and out of its petty everyday cares – never shall I forget that wonderful evening. . .[17]

He watched with wonder as a troop of angels floated down through sunbeams to hover over the sleeping Queen.

The last thing he would ever have wanted to see in the theatre was anything approximating to the miseries and splendours of life as it is actually lived. The theatre of realism would have filled him with horror and revulsion, as it did most of his contemporaries. What he sought to recapture over and over again was his child-like rapture at the dream spectacle – angels floating through sunbeams. 'I never enjoyed anything so much in my life before – and never felt so inclined to shed tears at anything fictitious, save perhaps at that poetical gem of Dickens, the death of Little Paul.'

Four days later he was back again at the Princess's with a family party which included Uncle Hassard and Menella Smedley. If anything, he enjoyed *Henry VIII* more than the first time. It was highly characteristic of Dodgson that if something had given him pleasure he would try to repeat the experience over and over again, and now that he had tasted the forbidden fruit of the theatre he would never let an opportunity slip to take his seat before the bright lights and let the 'delicious reverie of the theatre' work its spell on him.

'The difficulty of teaching'

The school which Dodgson's father had built shortly after his arrival in Croft was now in its tenth year, busy and flourishing with 120 pupils and a permanent staff of two, Mr Hobson and his wife, Sarah. Much of the teaching there was still carried on by the Archdeacon and his elder daughters, and Dodgson had not been home for the Long Vacation of 1855 more than a few days before he too was conscripted. To his surprise he found he rather enjoyed it. He gave scripture lessons to the boys, assisted Mr Hobson in Latin and mathematics and gave private coaching to James Coates, the son of one of the employees of the Rectory. One day, when there was nothing for him to do in the boys' school, he decided to take the second class of girls, and suddenly found himself in his element.

'I ... liked the experiment very much. The intelligence of the children seemed to vary inversely as their size. They were a little shy this first time, but answered well nevertheless.'

He was soon spending most of his time in the second class of the girls' school, making maps of the Holy Land for them and drawing plans of Jerusalem. This was the summer when, perhaps for the first time, he realised how much he was at home in the company of little girls. It helped him to recreate for himself something of the old atmosphere in the Rectory when his sisters were still children.

That August he went with his sisters to stay with his Wilcox cousins at Whitburn, on the coast a few miles north of Sunderland. At that time there were thirteen children, from twenty-year-old William Edward to newly-born Clara Menella, and over the years they would all crowd into his life. He did his best to find jobs for them, to subscribe to their enterprises, to pay for their children's education, to publish their books, to make them welcome in Oxford. They formed what was virtually an extra family for him.

While staying with there Dodgson met the seven-year-old Frederika Liddell: 'Each time I see her confirms in me the impression that she is one of the most lovely children I ever saw, gentle and innocent looking, not an inanimate doll-beauty.'[2]

This was the quality he would look for in all his child-friends and which would be most perfectly realised in Frederika's second cousin, Alice. Dodgson sought out Frederika whenever he had the opportunity and drew a sketch of her sitting on a stile – 'dear, sweet, pretty little Frederika'.

The Wilcoxes were eager to make an attempt at charades. The game was, at that time, little short of a full scale theatrical entertainment with costumes and disguises, with each charade rarely running less than three-quarters-of-an-hour. Dodgson wanted to introduce a degree of professionalism and discipline into the performance – like Dickens, he fancied himself as author, stage manager, producer and performer. He began by reading aloud the 'play' to be performed, rather like a Victorian actor-manager, while the rest of the company went through their performances in dumb show, occasionally working out details of their dialogue and what Dodgson called 'gag' – theatrical slang of the day for improvised additions. The actors would then have a clear idea of what they were doing and would not spoil the overall effect by continually falling about with laughter. Dodgson was highly pleased with the results of his rehearsal and the company performed such enigmas as 'Den-Mark'. He took the opportunity to try out for the first time his own solo rendition of the farce he had seen at the Princess's, *Away with Melancholy*, which became part of his repertoire. The Wilcoxes concluded the evening with their version of *Box and Cox*. Dodgson marked the day in his diary with a 'white stone', a Latin tag for a memorable day, though this may have been to mark his first getting to know little Frederika Liddell, rather than the Wilcox charades. The next 'white stone' in his diary commemorated his acquaintance with Frederika's younger sister, Gertrude, who had 'the most lovely face I ever saw in a child'.[3]

At Whitburn, Dodgson received a long letter from his father. Now that the Mathematical Lectureship seemed certain, the Archdeacon had drawn up a plan for his son's future. Dodgson would hold the lectureship for ten years or so (thus avoiding the trap into which the Reverend Dodgson had fallen) and then leave Christ Church and marry when a suitable living became available. He had also worked out details of his son's future finances: how much he should put aside for a library, what he needed for a 'nest egg', what should be invested in an insurance policy. All of this must have seemed too much like growing up to his son. Dodgson had no thoughts of marriage, even in ten years' time, he was uncertain about his suitability for the priesthood and, in any case, he was beginning to see his future for himself. There was a chance that his writing might reach a larger audience than the inhabitants of Croft Rectory.

Earlier in the year he had given various short pieces, including a Tennyson parody, 'The Three Voices', to his cousin Menella Smedley for her to show to her cousin, the novelist and humorist Frank Smedley. Smedley thought very highly of them and offered Dodgson his help in getting them into print. He also wanted him to become a regular contributor to *The Comic Times*, a new magazine which his friend Edmund Yates was about to launch. Yates, who was to play an important part in the publication of Dodgson's early work, was a bumptious, assertive man of the world. He had been one of the group of ambitious young men with whom Dickens had surrounded himself, and had a finger in many journalistic pies. *The Comic Times*, for which he had recruited Dickens's renowned illustrator, Phiz, was intended to rival *Punch* and Dodgson sent off to Smedley some pieces which *Punch* had turned down. 'The Dear Gazelle, arranged with Variations' was published in the second number of Yates's magazine.

At the end of the first week of September, Uncle Skeffington arrived at Croft with his latest curiosity, a camera. Dodgson had already acquired some knowledge of the mysteries of photography through his friend Reginald Southey at Christ Church and had admired a picture he had taken of the Broad Walk, but now he had a chance to observe every stage of the process at first hand. None of Skeffington's attempts at Croft appears to have been very successful. His pictures of the church and the old bridge were failures. Dodgson took his uncle over to Richmond but they had no better luck there. Uncle Skeffington's first photographic attempts may have proved a fiasco but they kindled his nephew's enthusiasm for the uncertain craft and had set him thinking. He watched with fascination the changes which came over the image as it was developed, emerging from a dim, milky impression to a more deeply defined reality. What would happen if this process were applied to writing? He sat down and dashed off a piece for *The Comic Times* entitled 'Photography Extraordinary'. The article never quite lives up to the originality of its conception, but it does illustrate the weird and wonderful way in which his imagination was working.

A young man 'of the very weakest possible physical and mental powers' is mesmerised and his thoughts are captured on a photographic paper. The first treatment reveals a product of the 'milk and water school': 'The eve was soft and dewy mild; a zephyr whispered in the lofty glade, and a few drops of rain cooled the thirsty soil.' This is rejected as unsaleable. 'The paper is dipped into various acids and at its next development is transformed into the 'strong-minded or Matter-of-Fact School'. 'The evening was of the ordinary character, barometer at "change", a wind was getting up in the wood, and some rain was beginning to fall; a bad look-out for the farmers.' Development to the highest possible degree results in 'the Spasmodic or German School', with furious torrents of rain and precipitous mountain gorges with a horse 'snorting fire from its distended nostrils'. When the process is applied to some passages of Byron, the paper bursts into flames.

The diary for Dodgson's Michaelmas term is missing. We know that this must have been a period of bitter disappointment. At the end of the vacation he had heard from Kitchin that he was not going to be Mathematical Lecturer: the post had gone to Charles Lloyd and Dodgson would be expected to carry on as before. By the end of the year, however, all had come right again. Rather in the manner of a new king declaring an amnesty for his criminal subjects, Liddell had celebrated his installation as Dean by conferring certain honours and appointments. As a result Dodgson was made Master of the House, a privilege which effectively removed any further obstacle to his taking up a mathematical lectureship. On the last day of the old year (in a passage preserved in Collingwood's biography) he could write in his diary with some satisfaction:

> It has been the most eventful year of my life: I began it a poor
> bachelor student, with no definite plans or expectations; I end it a
> master and tutor in Christ Church with an income of more than £300
> a year, and the course of mathematical tuition mapped out by God's
> providence for at least some years to come. Great mercies, great
> failings, time lost, talents misapplied – such has been the past year.[4]

Did he include his creative writing in the 'talents misapplied'? It had been almost as remarkable a year for that as for his academic achievements. The series of contributions to *The Comic Times* had confirmed him as a humorist of a highly original talent – the mind that would create *Alice* was already beginning to mark out its own territory. In the last of the family magazines, *Misch Masch*, he wrote out a poem which Yates had refused, 'The Palace of Humbug', a fascinating and highly erratic piece which veers wildly between the kind of parody he had written as a bright schoolboy –

> *I dreamt I dwelt in marble halls,*
> *And each damp thing that creeps and crawls*
> *Went wobble-wobble on the walls.*

and passages which in their intense simplicity recall William Blake:

> And one, a dotard grim and gray,
> Who wasteth childhood's happy day
> In work more profitless than play.
>
> Whose icy breast no pity warms,
> Whose little victims sit in swarms,
> And slowly sob on lower forms.[5]

He included another poem in the magazine which he had entitled 'Stanza of Anglo-Saxon Poetry' (Facsimile of the 'original inscription'). He had composed it during a verse-making game with the Wilcoxes at Whitburn that December. This curious fragment reads thus in modern characters:

> TWAS BRYLLIG AND THE SLITHY TOVES
> DID GYRE AND GYMBLE IN THE WABE:
> ALL MIMSY WERE THE BOROGOVES:
> AND THE MAME RATHS OUTGRABE.

With Jarrow and Monkwearmouth only a few miles away, the Wilcoxes lived in the heart of Anglo-Saxon territory, but nothing could be less like Anglo-Saxon verse (which Dodgson had probably never read) or more like Lewis Carroll. Dodgson appended a list of meanings which were designed as much to confuse as to elucidate:

> Borogove. An instinct kind of Parrot. They had no wings, beaks
> turned up, and made their nests under sundials: lived on veal.

By the beginning of Michaelmas Term 1855, Henry Liddell had been installed as Dean of Christ Church. It was a position of considerable power in Oxford, combining the prestige of head of the grandest and wealthiest college with that of administrator of the Cathedral. Liddell looked as if he had been cast for the part; austerely handsome, he had all the noble gravitas of a leader of ancient Rome.

Liddell had earned a formidable reputation for himself at Westminster. On his arrival he had sacked the entire staff and had succeeded in restoring the school to something of its former glory. His standing was further enhanced by his appointment as Domestic Chaplain to the Prince Consort. Albert, dismayed by the religious controversies which raged throughout the 1840s, was anxious to attach to himself 'One who has kept the even tenor of his way amid the perils by which his path at Oxford was beset'.[6] In the year of his arrival at Westminister Liddell had married the strikingly handsome Lorina Reeve. During their time at the school she bore five children: Edward Henry, known as Harry, in 1847; Lorina Charlotte in 1849; James Arthur, who died of scarlet fever at the age of three; Alice Pleasance in 1852; and, two years later, Edith Mary. Westminster was no place to bring up a family. Whatever Liddell may have achieved at the school academically, he was fighting a losing battle with the school's insanitary and pestiferous surroundings and, by the time Edith was born, the Liddells were desperate to get away. The Mastership of Sherburn Hospital at Durham fell vacant, but Mrs Liddell, who led an ambitious social life and who had been judged 'certainly one of the loveliest and most beautifully dressed of the guests' at the Queen's Ball in June 1847, was not going to waste her charms in a bleak northern bishopric. Gaisford's death gave them the opportunity they had been looking for. Within four days, Palmerston had put Liddell's name before the Queen.

The Liddells did not move their family into the Christ Church Deanery immediately. It had grown rather shabby during Gaisford's long occupation and did not measure up to the kind of lifestyle which they envisaged for themselves. The drawing room and the hall were to be panelled in oak, the long gallery opened out as an additional reception room, and a stately staircase installed, with lions on the corner posts, to lead up to the first floor where Mrs Liddell would receive her guests. It was known as the 'Lexicon' staircase, since it was paid for out of the profits of Lidell's celebrated dictionary. The lions became a subject of horrified fascination for the Liddell children. 'When we went to bed we had to go along this gallery,' Alice remembered in old age, 'and we always ran as hard as we could along it, because we *knew* that the lions got down from their pedestals and ran after us.'

As soon as the Liddells took up residence, they launched themselves and their newly panelled Deanery with two musical evenings. Dodgson was invited to the second. The music seems to have made little impression on him, but he did take the opportunity to make friends with six-year-old Lorina. Mrs Liddell quickly made her mark on Christ Church, and Oxford soon made up its mind about her:

> I am the Dean and this is Mrs Liddell,
> She plays the first and I the second fiddle.

So ran the rhyme in 'The Masque of Balliol'. Mrs Liddell was popularly supposed to be the dominant partner in the marriage. She was a formidable personality and Liddell, for all his eminence, was a deeply sensitive man who avoided argument and direct confrontation whenever possible. One suspects that he frequently let his wife have her way in the interests of peace and quiet, an aspect of their marriage which Dodgson was cruelly to exploit in his anti-Liddell squibs.

Dodgson had begun the new year reading Kingsley's *Alton Locke*. This was something of a new departure for him. Much of his reading was given over to trivial or undemanding works. *Alton Locke* was a thoroughly harrowing, relentlessly lurid and at times quite savage account of the sufferings and deprivations of the poor. Surprisingly, Dodgson found it 'a powerful and grandly written book', but he wished that Kingsley could have proposed some remedy for the miseries he had described.

> If the book were but a little more definite, it might stir up many fellow-workers in the same good field of social improvement. Oh that God, in his good providence, may make me hereafter such a worker! But, alas, what are the means? Each has his own nostrum to propound and in the Babel of voices nothing is done. I would thankfully spend and be spent so long as I were really sure of effecting something by the sacrifice, and not merely lying down under the wheels of some irresistible juggernaut.[8]

Dodgson was beginning to have doubts about taking up his religious calling, but was unsure as to what role he would fill in life.

> How few seem to care for the only subjects of real interest in life, – What am I to say so? Am I a deep philosopher, or a great genius? I think neither. What talents I have, I desire to devote to His service, and may He purify me, and take away my pride and selfishness. Oh that I might hear 'Well done, thou good and faithful servant!'[9]

Just at the point where Dodgson seems about to engage in a little self-questioning, he takes refuge in conventional piety. This is not to say that the piety was any the less sincere, but he shared a common nineteenth-century affliction of letting religion stand as a barrier to deeper thinking, a way of closing the door when speculation becomes too risky. If Dodgson was incapable of emulating Kingsley's dour hero, he felt he could at least contribute something by continuing at Oxford the kind of teaching he had practised at Croft. Maurice Swabey ran a school attached to the ancient church of St Aldate's just outside the walls of Christ Church, and was desperately hard-pressed for teachers. He arranged for Dodgson to give lessons in elementary mathematics to a small class of boys. At first, all seemed to go well and Dodgson found it pleasanter than he had anticipated:

> The contrast is very striking between town and country boys; here they are sharp, boisterous, and in the highest spirits – the difficulty of teaching being, not to get an answer, but to prevent all answering at once. They seem tractable, and in good order ...[10]

Their tractability was not to last. The boisterousness and high spirits began to get out of hand. To make matters worse, he was asked to take the first class of girls in with the boys, and found that the girls could not keep up. He wanted to form a class consisting only of the brightest boys and girls, but with the resident master already trying to conduct three lessons at once, this was out of the question. Swabey persuaded Dodgson to soldier on. He scored a brief victory over the class by threatening to banish the rowdy and inattentive element altogether and then began to wonder if there was any point in going on. 'The novelty of the thing is wearing off,' he admitted. Instead of being able to open up to his pupils a mathematical world which he himself found endlessly fascinating, he found himself reduced to setting sums and trying to shout down a rising tide of disorder. On the last day of February he left word that he would not be returning. 'I doubt if I shall try again next term: the good done does not seem worth the time and trouble.'[11]

He was having little better success with his older pupils at Christ Church. He began his career as Mathematical Lecturer with a request to all the men he was to teach to attend a meeting in the lecture hall. Out of sixty, only twenty-three turned up. He posted a notice in Hall asking the remainder to come and see him. They did not come. In desperation he went to Dean Liddell to ask for his help. A compromise was reached 'whereby the men who undertook to get their work up by themselves may do so, and are to be examined from time to time during term'.[12]

At first he seems to have had great difficulty in coping with his classes. He was only a little older than the men he had to teach and his nervousness and diffidence, coupled with his concern over his speech impediment, forced him to assume a 'dry and perfunctory manner'.

> In dealing with we undergraduates he never smiled or showed the smallest sign of his pent-up humour. I had the distinction of being set to write out 50 lines for not attending his lectures, which were unspeakably dull.[13]

Part of the problem was that very few of the men would have been even remotely interested in the finer points of the subject. Most of them were not reading for honours in mathematics, but were only concerned to acquire the minimum knowledge necessary for Responsions. Once over that hurdle they would put the subject out of their minds for ever. It is little wonder that so many of them found Dodgson's lectures 'as dull as ditchwater'. According to A. S. Russell, a round robin was got up by some of the students asking to be transferred to another teacher.[14]

Yet when Dodgson chose, he could enliven his classes with flashes of humour. 'What is a corollary?' he asked Watkin Williams. His pupil could not supply the answer.

'Do you ever play billiards?'

'Sometimes.'

'If you attempted a cannon, missed, and holed your own and the red ball, what would you call it?

'A fluke.'

'Exactly. A corollary is a fluke in Euclid. Good morning.'[15]

When he sought to put mathematics into a wider context he could be disturbingly provocative. He put a standard question: 'If it takes so many men so many days to build a wall, how long would it take 300,000 men?' When the answer, mathematically impeccable, was given Dodgson would retort:

> You don't seem to have observed that that wall would have gone up like a flash of lightning, and that most of those men could not have got within a mile of it.[16]

It is not surprising that he was not popular.

Within the year, Dodgson found himself worn down by the unremitting drudgery of it all:

> I am weary of lecturing and discouraged. It is thankless, uphill work, goading unwilling men to learning they have no taste for, to the inevitable neglect of others who really want to get on.[17]

But teaching was the price he had to pay for remaining at Christ Church and, as the years wore by, Dodgson protested less and less. He was to continue as Mathematical Lecturer for the next twenty-five years.

'The camera of rosewood'

The Comic Times, which had printed at least five of Dodgson's earliest pieces, had come to the end of its not very remarkable existence in November 1855. Yates, with George Augustus Sala, another Dickens *protégé*, and the ever loyal Frank Smedley, lost no time in setting up a new monthly publication to be called *The Train – a First Class Magazine*. Dodgson read the first number and did not think much of it – 'only average in talent, and an intense imitation of Dickens throughout'. He did not reckon it would survive the year. This did not prevent him from submitting 'The Palace of Humbug', which Yates did not care for, and the more conventionally sentimental 'Solitude', which he did. The poem was published in March 1856 with an illustration by William M'Connell of a man sitting on the edge of a wood, looking extremely uncomfortable.

> Ye golden hours of Life's young spring,
> Of innocence, of love and truth!
> Bright beyond imagining
> Thou fairy-dream of youth!
>
> I'd give all wealth that toil hath piled
> The bitter fruit of life's decay,
> To be once more a little child
> For one short sunny day.

Dodgson seems to have attached great importance to the poem, since he carefully revised it in its subsequent appearances. For all the banality of the verse there is no doubting his absolute sincerity. His childhood was the most precious thing he possessed and he wanted somehow to preserve it intact. The difficulty lay in keeping the outside world from breaking in.

Contributions to *The Comic Times* had been anonymous, but Yates wanted pieces in *The Train* to be signed. What was Dodgson to call himself? He favoured 'B.B.' which he had used for the family magazines and for the *Whitby Gazette*, but Yates wanted something more definite. Dodgson suggested 'Dares', linking him to his birthplace, but Yates considered this too like a newspaper signature. Dodgson then put forward four alternatives. Two were anagrams of Charles Lutwidge: Edgar

Cuthwellis and Edgar U. C. Westhill and two were based on Lutwidge Charles: Louis Carroll and Lewis Carroll. Dodgson had played with the latinisation of his name ever since his school days at Richmond when he had inscribed one of his books: 'Hic liber ad Carolum Ludvigum Dodsonum pertinet.' Yates took his time considering the matter, but in the end settled for Lewis Carroll. 'Solitude' was the first of his works to carry the name. 'Ye Carpette Knyghte', published in the same number, bore no signature.

Dodgson had been working for a long time on a poem about Florence Nightingale which he now thought of completing for Yates. On 26 March 1856, he went to see an exhibition of photographs of the Crimean War by Roger Fenton in Ripon. Five days later the bells of the Cathedral rang out all day to commemorate the signing of peace. All this must have spurred Dodgson on to finish 'The Path of Roses'. It is one of his few serious poems that can be read without embarrassment. It relies heavily on Tennysonian effects, so that at times it reads almost like a parody:

> And, so it seemed to her, an awful light
> Pierced slowly through the darkness, orbed and grew,
> Until all passed away – the ancient room –
> The sunlight dying through the trellised vine –
> The one tall window – all had passed away,
> And she was standing on the mighty hills.

During the Easter vacation he went to see a woman who was to become an equally important member of his private gallery of heroines as Florence Nightingale. This was Jenny Lind, who was singing in *The Messiah* at Exeter Hall in the Strand. The 'Swedish Nightingale' was then thirty-six and Dodgson was surprised at how old she looked:

> her settled expression seems severe, but this changed as she sang into a beautifully sweet smile, and she seemed to abandon herself to the glorious music with almost a child's delight.[1]

Jenny Lind was an ardent supporter of worthy causes and frequently donated her fees to charity. The story of how she once sang to an old woman in her Manchester cottage –

> Then and there, in that poor little cottage, the great Singer sang three or four of her sweetest songs and gave the old woman the desire of her heart –[2]

was to join the tale of Florence Nightingale's dog in a sermon for children which he composed many years later. Dodgson marked the day of *The Messiah* with a white stone. It was also on that day that a far more important event took place. Dodgson bought his first camera. We cannot be sure which event merited the white stone.

Ever since his photographic expeditions with Uncle Skeffington the previous September, Dodgson had been determined to acquire a 'photographic apparatus' of his own. 'I want some other occupation here, than mere reading and writing.' Until 1852 photography had been jealously guarded from amateurs by Henry Fox Talbot, the pioneer of the Calotype, or, as he preferred to style it, the Talbotype. The process was protected by a patent and to practise it the would-be photographer had to take out a licence from its inventor. Photographs were not allowed to be circulated without Fox Talbot's permission and it was expressly forbidden to sell them.

In March 1851 Fox Talbot's monopoly was broken by the invention of a new process, the collodion or wet-plate method, by Frederick Scott-Archer. That same year photography had been given a considerable boost by the Great Exhibition when some seven hundred photographs had been put on view and the general public were keen to try their hand at the art. Fox Talbot fought doggedly to try to extend his rights to cover the collodion process as well as his own, but failed. Photography was open to anyone who could afford to buy the cumbersome apparatus.

One also needed patience and dexterity. The collodion process was quite remarkably difficult, messy and accident-prone. In a parody written in 1857 of Longfellow's 'Hiawatha', Dodgson described, as accurately as the metre would allow, exactly what was involved:

> *First a piece of glass he coated*
> *With collodion, and plunged it*
> *In a bath of lunar caustic*
> *Carefully dissolved in water –*
> *There he left it certain minutes.*
> *Secondly my Hiawatha*
> *Made with cunning hand a mixture*
> *Of the acid pyro-gallic,*
> *And of glacial-acetic,*
> *And of alcohol and water –*
> *This developed all the picture*
> *Finally he fixed each picture*
> *With a saturate solution*
> *Which was made of hyposulphite,*
> *Which, again, was made of soda.*[3]

The whole process required calm nerves and a very steady hand. The glass plate had first to be carefully polished to make sure that it was perfectly clean. The photographer then balanced the plate on his thumb and fingers and poured the collodion solution over it, ensuring that it was covered evenly. The plate was then dipped into a bath of silver nitrate and put into the camera while it was still wet. When the photograph had been taken – and an exposure could take up to one-and-a-half minutes while the subject made heroic attempts to keep still – the plate had once again to be precariously balanced while a developing solution was poured over it. It then had to be rinsed, fixed in hyposulphite of soda, washed, dried and varnished. It was vital that at every stage dust was kept off the plate. A dark-room was needed for the beginning and the end of the operation. The practitioner constantly had to cope with the most improbable handicaps. It is not surprising that so many of Skeffington Lutwidge's early attempts had ended in disaster.

On 18th March, with Reginald Southey to advise him, Dodgson visited Ottiwell's in Charlotte Street, a little way off the Caledonian Road, to choose a camera. He calculated that it would cost him about £15, but this did not take into account all the rest of the apparatus, the plates and the chemicals. A serious photographer would need to carry with him the camera, its lens and tripod, a chest containing bottles of various chemicals and solutions including collodion and silver nitrate, dishes, glass plates, funnels, beakers, scales and weights, a stirring rod and a sensitising bath, and a portable dark-tent.

Dodgson was eager to start as soon as possible, but by the beginning of the Easter and Act Term his camera had still not arrived from Ottiwell's. Reginald Southey needed little persuading to take out his own camera and on 25th April the pair of them descended on the Deanery garden to try to take a photograph of the cathedral.

> From his shoulder Hiawatha
> Took the camera of rosewood,
> Made of sliding, folding rosewood;
> Neatly put it all together.
> In its case it lay compactly,
> Folded into nearly nothing;
> But he opened out the hinges,
> Pushed and pulled the joints and hinges,
> Till it looked all squares and oblongs,
> Like a complicated figure
> In the second book of Euclid.

Hiawatha's first attempt 'failed entirely' and so did Southey's, yet Dodgson marked the day with a white stone, for this was the occasion when he made friends with the little daughters of Dean Liddell.

*

He must have noticed the children playing from the windows of the Old Library which overlooked the Deanery garden, and he had already made the acquaintance of Lorina at the Liddells' musical evening. He had encountered the eight-year-old Harry at the 'Torpids', a curiously Carrollean name for the bumping races which took place in the Hilary Term, and he had been very impressed by him. As a rule he did not care at all for boys – 'Boys are not in my line. I think they are a mistake.' – but he was prepared to make an exception in the case of Harry Liddell: 'He is certainly the handsomest boy I ever saw.'[4]

The Liddell girls, dressed by their mother to look like elegant little fashion plates, were, by general consent, quite remarkably pretty. Alice Pleasance, who was nearly four, was described by her mother's old friend Lady Pleasance Smith, from whom she received her second name, as looking like: 'one of Raphael's Holy Family strayed out of the picture –

> *The crisped locks of pure refulgent gold*
> *The lambent lightning of the angelic smile*[5]

quite enchant me when in her daily visits she sits by my side and opens her lovely mouth for a few grapes.' Dodgson unconsciously echoed Lady Smith when he wrote:

> *Red lips for kisses pouted warm –*
> *And elf locks tangled in the storm.*[6]

but he would not have had much faith in her powers of observation. Alice was dark haired with blue eyes.

Lorina, Alice and the two-year-old Edith Mary were all playing in the garden the day of the photographic experiment, but Dodgson, at this first meeting with his future heroine, was largely preoccupied with technical problems. He tried to group the children in the foreground of the picture, but they could not be persuaded to keep still.

The following week the two enthusiasts decided to try again and set up the camera in the garden in the hope of taking a prospect of Merton. The children played happily around them, but,

> *All was fruitless, as the picture*
> *Ended in an utter failure.*

The following two days brought no better results. Southey concluded that the fault lay with the collodion and they decided to give up until a supply of better chemicals could be obtained.

In the first week of May Dodgson's own camera arrived at last. Chemicals – iodised collodion, glacial acetic acid and pyro-gallic acid –

were obtained from London and they set up the camera in Southey's room. Dodgson himself was photographed, as was his friend Faussett, looking rather wild-eyed in his determination to keep still. Dodgson was so pleased with the results that he called Harry Liddell from the garden. The result was a 'fair profile'. Dodgson carried it off in triumph and showed it to the Dean and his wife. Mrs Liddell was highly delighted and pressed him to take further pictures of Harry. Dodgson was invited to stay for luncheon. For the first time he had discovered that a photograph could be a useful passport.

All this time Dodgson should have been working on a paper on the life of Richard Hakluyt, the Elizabethan geographer. It was customary to commemorate the worthies of Christ Church by a reading on the life and achievements of one of them in Hall on the night of the Gaudy, the College feast, and Liddell had asked Dodgson to undertake the task. It was not an attractive prospect. Such occasions were regarded as a kind of blood sport by the College rowdies. On the night before the reading, Dodgson sat late writing up what little he had been able to prepare on the life of the industrious cosmographer. 'He was born, as the learned Anthony Wood informs us, of an ancient and honourable family at Yetton or Yatton in Herefordshire: the date of his birth does not seem to have been accurately ascertained, but it was very nearly in the middle of the sixteenth-century.'[7] The only aspect of Hakluyt's collection of voyages that really aroused Dodgson's interest were the accounts of early journeys to Russia, and he revelled in the wonder and eccentricity of it all. When the time came for him to read out his essay, 'the noise was tremendous'. Several men were ejected from the hall, but somehow he struggled through to the end.

Dodgson was spending more time at the Deanery, and was getting on famously with the children. On the day after the Gaudy, he took Harry and Lorina, along with his cousin Frank Dodgson, on a boat trip on the river and treated the children to biscuits and ginger beer. Harry insisted on rowing stroke.

> ... fortunately, considering the wild spirits of the children, we got home without accidents, having attracted by our remarkable crew a good deal of attention from almost everyone we met.[8]

The children had at last met an adult with whom they could be themselves. Out on the river they could play and shout and misbehave, and Dodgson was there to supply them with songs and stories and biscuits. He described that first boating expedition as a *Dies Mirabilis*. One cannot help wondering whether, on the many river trips before the famous Alice voyage, there had been tales for Harry and for Lorina that were never written down. Would Alice's story have been utterly forgotten if she had not insisted that he wrote it out for her on paper?

Frank Dodgson, who had accompanied Dodgson, Harry and Lorina on their maiden voyage, was the son of Uncle Hassard. He is probably 'F' who figures in one of the two surviving extracts from Dodgson's missing diary for that time:

> Spoke to the Dean about F, who had brought an imposition which his tutor declares is not in his writing, after being expressly told to write it himself.[9]

His cousin had come up to Christ Church the previous year and Dodgson clearly felt it was his responsibility to keep an eye on him. He was, after all, now the family's representative at Oxford, and the head of a growing clan. His brother, Skeffington, now nineteen, and Wilfred, a year younger, were expected to matriculate to Christ Church later that year. 'His being there will be in many ways a comfortable thing for you and Wilfred,'[10] the Archdeacon told his second son.

The path of Skeffington's and Wilfred's education had been rather less fraught than that of their elder brother, and they had not been obliged to follow him through the miseries and persecutions of Rugby – they had both been sent to Twyford in Hampshire. Skeffington's Greek and Latin were giving him trouble. He had nothing of his elder brother's easy aptitude for learning, and made slow progress, carried forward only by his dogged refusal to allow himself to be defeated. The Archdeacon saw that he would need private tuition if he were to matriculate that year, and Skeffington, along with Wilfred, was sent off to Crosthwaite in the Lake District to study with Alexander Webster, who had been a curate at Croft. The brothers enjoyed their sojourn in the Lakes so much that their father thought it wise to send them a few words of warning:

> For instance it is necessary to be particularly on your guard with regard to young ladies into whose company you are introduced – it is perfectly well understood in society that ladies may shew to youths in the position of Private Pupils a sort of kindness and attention, which they would not think of shewing if those youths were a little older and more out of the world ...[11]

The brothers successfully avoided the charms of the maids of Crosthwaite and passed the matriculation examination at Christ Church on 15th May 1856. Skeffington, always a lover of fine scenery, suggested to Dodgson that he return with them to Keswick that summer and see the splendours of the Lakes for himself.

Dodgson took his time. First there were London theatres to be visited, with Frank as his companion. At the Adelphi they saw *The Flying Dutchman*, not Wagner's music drama, which Dodgson would have found incomprehensible, but a nautical drama by Fitzball. At the Princess's Theatre the Keans were presenting *A Winter's Tale*: '... the visions were gorgeous, but did not please me nearly as much as Queen Katherine's dream'.[12] Nothing would ever efface that experience, but there was one performance he especially admired, that of the eight-year-old Ellen Terry as Mamilius, 'a beautiful little creature who played with great ease and spirit'. Ellen Terry's memories of what was in fact her theatrical début were not so happy. Charles Kean had decided to give her a little go-cart to trundle about the stage, imitated from a toy on a Greek vase. On her exit she tripped over the handle and fell on her back. Since she was performing not just before Charles Dodgson, but the Queen, Prince Albert and the Princess Royal, she was certain that her career as an actress was finished. She went on to play the part for 102 performances. Dodgson delighted in everything that she did, but he was not to meet her for eight-and-a-half years.

Dodgson had brought his camera with him to Putney where he was staying with Uncle Hassard. Some friends of Hassard, the Murdochs, presented themselves to be photographed. A picture of their youngest daughter, aged four, has survived. She looks sadly small and overawed, almost on the edge of tears. Dodgson wrote an extempore poem to her, picturing her little hand opening a door to the undiscovered land of the future.

As with many of Dodgson's poems written for children, he allows his mind to go into a kind of free fall. As he ventures into the 'darkness blank and drear' of the 'realms of love and hate', he compares his quest to a boat 'laden with flickering fire' launched into the subterranean streams of a cavern and floating away until the flames are swallowed up in the distant darkness. It is a chilling and disturbing poem, and a very strange one to dedicate to a four-year-old child. In its unrelenting nihilism it anticipates that other bleak and hopeless voyage, 'The Hunting of the Snark'.

On the coach from Croft to Keswick, Skeffington and Dodgson had to spend part of their journey perched perilously on top of the luggage on the roof. The first sight of the distant mountains came as a disappointment. Nowhere could Dodgson see the grandeur his brothers had led him to expect. He had invited an old college friend, John Martyn Collyns, to be his companion on the tour. As they tramped through rain and mist, everything seemed to contrive to let them down. The Falls at Lodore, immortalised by the poet Southey, were not 'hurrying and scurrying' or 'thundering and floundering' but totally inactive. They ascended Great Gable but the mist came down and they could see nothing and the icy wind gave Dodgson a swollen face. They did have a brief glimpse of a rainbow at Bassenthwaite but the falls at Rydal, which Dodgson watched swathed in waterproofs against the pouring rain, he thought 'not imposing in height and breadth'. At Penrith the 'insufferable vulgarity and overbearing manner' of a couple of American tourists in the coffee room of *The Crown* drove the travellers to take refuge in their bedroom.[13] Dodgson had intended the holiday to be a photographic expedition, but the camera went no further than Keswick. The bad light and the foul weather gave little chance for landscape pictures, but he probably soon realised that scenic photography was not in his line. Dodgson was really only interested in human beings and he liked to have his subjects firmly under control. Landscape photography left far too much to chance, as the hero of his story 'A Photographer's Day Out' was to discover:

> Trees rather misty – well! the wind had blown them about a little; that wouldn't show much – the farmer? well, he had walked on a yard or two, and I should be sorry to state how many arms and legs he appeared with – never mind! call him a spider, a centipede, anything – the cow? I must however confess that the cow had three heads, and though such an animal may be curious, it is not picturesque.[14]

In Keswick Dodgson had met Wordsworth's eldest son, John, but he does not seem to have said anything worth recording. However, the encounter set his thoughts running on a parody of Wordsworth's 'Resolution and Independence', a poem called 'Upon the Lonely Moor', which he completed on his return to Croft:

> *I met an aged, aged man*
> *Upon a lonely moor;*
> *I knew he was a gentleman*
> *And he was but a boor.*
> *So I stopped and roughly questioned him,*
> *'Come tell me how you live!'*
> *But his words impressed my ear no more*
> *Than if it were a sieve.*

These verses, revised and modified, were to become the song which he gave to the White Knight in *Through the Looking Glass*, thinking that it rather suited his character. Dodgson rarely wasted anything he had written. There is very little of his published writing that he did not choose to reprint in later collections of his work, and he had a kind of genius for fitting the most unlikely pieces into a new structure. 'She's all my fancy painted him', which Yates had published in *The Comic Times*, was cut and reshaped to provide Alice's 'evidence' at the trial of the Knave of Hearts, and the 'Stanza of Anglo-Saxon Poetry' resurfaced after seventeen years as 'Jabberwocky'. Dodgson was able to manipulate the nonsense element in his work with a mathematician's precision.

Before returning to Oxford, Dodgson proposed to write a 'long intended essay on Nursery Songs'. Of all Dodgson's might-have-beens, this is perhaps the one whose loss is most to be regretted. It was forgotten in his eagerness to get back to what was to become his favourite and most obsessive photographic subject, the children of the Deanery.

'No present likelihood of marriage'

On 10th October, 1856 the three Dodgson brothers arrived at Christ Church for the start of the Michaelmas Term:

> ...the threefold luggage, all marked with one name, put down at Tom-Gate, caused the wildest scene of confusion I ever witnessed here, and after all we found that no rooms had been allotted to my brothers, who accordingly had to spend the night at the Mitre.[1]

Rooms must have been found for them in the next few days, since the Archdeacon wrote, 'Now that they have once let you in, they cannot turn you out again...' He instructed his sons to keep strict individual accounts, and arranged for their allowance to be paid into their elder brother's account.

To judge from the rare appearances they make in his diary, Dodgson left his brothers very much to their own devices. In any case, there were other matters to claim his time and attention. Henry Liddell had been confined in Torquay with a severe cold for the first weeks of term and when he returned to Christ Church in November he was still far from well. But Dodgson still pressed him for an agreement to allow him to continue the photography in the Deanery garden. In his enthusiasm, etiquette was thrown to the winds and he enlisted the children's governess as his helper and go-between.

Miss Prickett, known to the children as 'Pricks', was, according to Alice's son, Caryl Hargreaves, 'far from being the highly educated governess of today'.[2] She was the daughter of James Prickett, the butler of Trinity College, a more exalted position than the title suggests, since he was the general administrator. She was responsible for the children's general education. For 'extras' such as French and German, 'Drawling, Stretching and Fainting in Coils', specialist outside teachers were brought in. Dodgson asked her to arrange for the Dean's children and Dr Acland's children to be in the garden. As soon as Mrs Liddell heard of his plans she decided to take evasive action. He arrived at the Deanery on a fine November morning only to see the whole Deanery party driving off in their carriage. Anyone but Dodgson would have admitted defeat. But a few days later, he was back at the Deanery photographing the children and, when the light failed, playing with them up in the schoolroom with Miss Prickett, showing them how to make paper boats. When he turned up again on the Deanery doorstep at the end of the week following a request from Harry to take pictures of himself and Lorina, he was met with a firm refusal. Mrs Liddell put her foot down. The children were not to be photographed until they could be taken together as a group. 'This may be meant as a hint that I have intruded on the premises long enough: I am quite of the same opinion myself.'[3] Dodgson took offence and decided that he would not waste any more time over portraits 'at such a bad season of the year' and that he would not go to the Deanery again without invitation.

A few days later an invitation did arrive, asking him to come to the Deanery to meet the Dean's father. Mrs Liddell asked Dodgson's advice about sending Harry to Twyford and showed him some of the boy's sums and Latin exercises. Dodgson eagerly offered to give Harry extra lessons in arithmetic, but this was not at all what Mrs Liddell had had in mind. She had no intention of giving Dodgson *carte blanche* to come round to the Deanery whenever he wished.

At the end of term Liddell's health showed no improvement and Dr Acland suggested that he should leave the 'extinct air' of Oxford for the balmier climate of Madeira. Mrs Liddell decided that she must accompany him, leaving the children at the Deanery in the care of Miss Prickett. Nothing now stood in Dodgson's way. He would be able to see the children as often as he pleased.

Dodgson made a brief trip to London, but was soon back at Christ Church, ostensibly to give one of his pupils some last-minute coaching, but he had also brought Christmas presents for the children: a copy of *Mrs Rutherford's Children* for Lorina and a mechanical tortoise for Harry. He lingered on at Christ Church waiting until the Liddells, accompanied by Acland, drove away on the first stage of their long voyage to Madeira. As soon as the coast was clear, he descended on the Deanery, delivered his gifts and stayed for the children's dinner. The following day he set off on the twelve-hour train journey back to Croft for Christmas, having spent the previous night packing – always a lengthy and complicated operation with him, since every item had to be wrapped individually in paper.

Dodgson's energy at this time was inexhaustible. Within a few days of his arrival at the Rectory, he had got up an elaborate magic-lantern entertainment for New Year's Eve, which he performed before an audience of eighty children. It lasted two hours, and included thirteen songs, six for himself and seven for the children. He managed to include some of the Mooney and Spooney dialogues from *La Guida di Bragia* and recited what was now his party piece, 'Away with Melancholy'. The whole performance was repeated the following day.

He always seems to have reserved his really serious reading for Ripon, perhaps feeling that it accorded with the atmosphere of the place. This year he settled down to Kingsley's *Hypatia*, a novel of ponderous seriousness, occasionally enlivened by bursts of sexual sadism. He found it powerful and even beautiful in parts, but, like many other readers, thought it 'outrageous to taste in some parts'. He was distressed by the sneers against Christianity which Kingsley had put into Hypatia's mouth, and, like Tennyson, he was shocked by the scene in which she was stripped naked and hacked to death with oyster shells. He followed this with Orsini's *Austrian Dungeons in Italy*, which can scarcely have enlivened the prevailing gloom.

The moment he was back in Christ Church he made straight for the Deanery. He ignored Mrs Liddell's instructions and arranged with Miss Prickett for Harry to come for three days a week to learn arithmetic. Mrs Liddell had, however, taken the precaution of warning her mother, Mrs Reeve, who wrote to Miss Prickett expressing her alarm at Harry's learning 'mathematics' with Dodgson, fearing the effect of over-work on his brain. Dodgson blithely brushed aside her objections, sending a message back to Mrs Reeve telling her that she need have no fears on the score of Harry over-taxing his brain. Dodgson had rather overestimated the enthusiasm of his pupil. After a few days Harry began to grow weary of arithmetic, and would do nothing. Dodgson appealed to Miss Prickett for help, and she did manage to persuade him to take a little interest. Miss Prickett had obviously taken to Dodgson. She fell in eagerly with all his schemes for the children and even began to show him Mrs Liddell's letters from Madeira. Together with Harry and Lorina, they went to look at the pictures in the Taylor Gallery and on most days Dodgson would walk with Miss Prickett and the children in Christ Church meadow. This happy state of affairs came to an abrupt end when Harry came round to tell Dodgson that there had been an outbreak of scarlet fever in the next house and that Dr Acland, who had returned from Madeira, had ordered the children off to Lowestoft to stay with their grandmother. It had been scarlet fever that had claimed the life of little Arthur Liddell six years earlier and Acland was not going to take any risks.

With the Liddells far away at Lowestoft Dodgson was able to devote a little more time to Skeffington and Wilfred with walks and expeditions up the Cherwell. Alice and Edith Liddell ran in to him on 1st April to tell him that the scarlet fever scare was over and that they were all back from Lowestoft. The Dean and his wife were not expected in England before the beginning of June and Dodgson was reluctant to miss the chance of having the children all to himself. He decided that instead of returning to Croft for the Easter vacation, he would stay on at Christ Church.

Life with the Liddell children soon fell into a regular routine. Every day they would meet in the meadow; Harry resumed his arithmetic lessons and Dodgson photographed the girls at every opportunity. One evening the Aclands were invited to dinner at the Deanery and he entertained them with yet another recital of 'Away with Melancholy'. Dodgson even started to take Harry to Chapel, but he was soon worn down by the boy's all too obvious indifference to the proceedings.

On 5th May for the first time, Alice had an entry to herself in the diary. It was her birthday, and Dodgson called at the Deanery with a present for her and stayed for tea. His frequent visits there were beginning to excite the attention of the undergraduates and a rumour spread around the college that, under pretext of seeing the children, he was paying court to Miss Prickett. Dodgson was horrified. Miss Prickett was no beauty; formidable is the word that springs to mind from the surviving photographs, and Dodgson had no desire for his name to he linked with that of the daughter of the butler of Trinity. He had a hasty conference with his friend Sydney Joyce and decided that it would be inconsiderate to Miss Prickett to expose her to any further gossip. 'I shall avoid taking any public notice of the children in future, unless any occasion should arise when such an interpretation is impossible.'[4]

His determination lasted all of ten days, during which he walked with Skeffington to Godstow, sang part-songs with the Choral Society, photographed Dr Acland's skeleton of a tunny fish in the anatomy school, and was enchanted by a little girl he saw at a choral concert, 'with the most perfect little face I ever saw – like one of the French beauties one sees painted on enamel'.

He was soon back with his camera in the Deanery garden. One evening he took Harry down to the river to see the races from the College barge, 'but I did not like staying long as some of the men there were very undesirable acquaintances for him'. His friendship for Harry was rapidly being overtaken by his delight in the company of the 'two dear little girls', Lorina and Alice. All too soon, the Liddells returned. Either Mrs Reeve or Miss Prickett must have told them about all the photographic carryings on while they were away, as Dodgson was quickly invited to present himself at the Deanery with his pictures. For once, all was sweetness and light. Mrs Liddell was so delighted with the pictures he had taken of the children that it was arranged that Dodgson should take a picture of the Dean:

> *He would contemplate the distance*
> *With a look of pensive meaning,*
> *As of ducks that die in tempests.*

Despite many attempts, which continued until the time came for Dodgson to return home to Croft, all his pictures failed. He did, however, manage to have a splendid time with the children, playing with them on the swing and teaching them to play backgammon. He marked the day with a special white stone.[5]

It had been Dodgson's longest stay at Oxford: five months during which, by his own account, he had 'learned almost nothing, taught not much more, and forgotten a great deal'.[6] Yet the time had not been altogether wasted. In the course of his many sessions with the children he had discovered how to make photography into a creative art through which he could express not just the personalities of the children, but his own. His achievement as a photographer was made possible not so much by his increasing technical competence, but because he understood children, and loved them and could gain their perfect confidence. He learned how to find ways of getting them to behave naturally in front of the camera and as spontaneously as long exposure would allow. 'Being photographed,' remembered Alice, 'was a joy to us and not a penance as it is to most children.'[7]

He had also begun to explore ways of making his expensive hobby pay. Quentin Twiss, an undergraduate at Christ Church, was a popular amateur actor. Dodgson photographed him in a sailor's costume and as *The Artful Dodger* and *Tom the Pot Boy* and sold prints of his pictures at Ryman's. Now, when he went to a gallery or to an exhibition of new paintings, he would take a notebook with him or make sketches in the margin of the catalogue so that he could record groupings or attitudes that might be of use to him in posing his sitters, or details such as the arrangement of hands.

Dodgson had a fascinating ability to turn his mind to the most unlikely subjects. That year he sent off to *Bell's Life in London and Sporting Chronicle* a scheme for making betting fool-proof, 'giving an instance (the Derby odds of the other day) of a certainty-winning book made by taking odds in the proper proportion'. There is a charming absurdity in the notion of a mathematician and a prospective candidate for holy orders listing the odds on such runners as 'Skirmisher, Saunterer, Loyola, Bluejacket and Beeswax.'

Dodgson returned to Croft with Skeffington on 4th July. He was at a loss what to do with himself without the Liddell girls and passed his time reading Mrs Clive's *Paul Ferrol* in which a desperate man murders his violent and domineering wife. This can hardly have been an appropriate preparation for a long discussion with his father about insurance, which may have been the Archdeacon's roundabout way of inquiring about his eldest son's matrimonial intentions. Dodgson told him that, so far as he was concerned, he saw no need to take out insurance:

> It is unadvisable to insure unless with the prospect of marrying some day, and even <u>with</u> that prospect it seems better to save at present, and only insure when the prospect becomes a certainty ... If at any future period I might contemplate marriage (of which I see no present likelihood), it will be quite time enough to begin paying the premium then.[8]

How could he have been so certain? He was twenty-seven, without, as far as we know, having ever ventured in the direction of sexual experience and, with the possible exception of Elizabeth Siddal, never having enjoyed a close friendship with a woman. Yet he had decided that there was no 'present likelihood' of marriage. Not that he was alone in this – of Charles and Frances Dodgson's eleven children, only Mary, Wilfred and Skeffington would ever get married. The other sisters, with the exception of Henrietta, were to remain together as a family unit for the rest of their lives, and Edwin was to plunge into voluntary exile in some of the remotest spots on the globe. The Victorians would not have seen anything unusual or disturbing in Dodgson's decision. They might, as Dodgson's sisters in fact did, conclude that the person had been crossed in love, or that the 'shadow of some disappointment'[9] lay over his life, but they would have seen nothing unusual in his decision to remain a bachelor. Emotional considerations aside, marriage for Dodgson would have carried with it the obligation to go out into the world and leave his cloistered life at Christ Church behind him, which he was not prepared to do. He was surrounded by men who, like him, do not appear to have questioned the prospect of a lifetime of celibacy; Vere Bayne, Henry Liddon, Robert Faussett, Edward Sampson were all to live out their lives as bachelors.

Although every year that passed removed him further from it, Dodgson never entirely closed his mind to the idea of marriage. There was always the tantalising possibility that it might somehow be made to happen, even though what he really sought was not marriage with a living woman, but with his own childhood. The companion he needed was someone with whom he could recreate the 'fairy-dream' of those first years at Croft, when his younger sisters were little girls in pinafores and he was their entertainer and enchanter. The problem was that this person could not be an adult, but a little girl – who would in time grow into a woman and expect a real marriage and a real sexual relationship. There Dodgson feared he could not follow. Yet this did not prevent him from continuing to hope that somewhere, somehow, he might find a girl who would help him cross that impossible threshold.

'A strange, shaggy-looking man'

One day during the Long Vacation of 1857 the Chaytors brought over to the Rectory a little girl whom they hoped to persuade Dodgson to photograph. Agnes Grace Weld was the daughter of Tennyson's sister-in-law and was staying at Clervaux Castle. This was the closest that Dodgson had yet come to the Laureate and he could not resist the temptation to bombard Mrs Weld with a barrage of questions about Tennyson and his family. He learned that his sons were called Lionel and Hallam and were said to be remarkably beautiful and that a new poem was to be expected shortly.

Tennyson was the person in England that Dodgson most wanted to meet. He had worshipped the poet for years and had read every poem by him that he could get hold of, enthusiastically discussing them with his sisters and friends. He had also paid the poet the rather back-handed compliment of producing a parody of Tennyson's dialogue on suicide, 'The Two Voices'. Dodgson called his poem 'The Three Voices' and it had been published by Yates in *The Train* in 1856. It is a curious, uneven and, at times, incomprehensible poem: it is difficult to catch Dodgson's overall intention and to decide how much of the poem is intended to be funny. It begins in his brightest and breeziest style with an encounter between a man and a woman on a beach. His hat blows off and she pins it to the ground with the tip of her umbrella.

> *A while like one in dreams he stood,*
> *Then faltered forth his gratitude*
> *In words just short of being rude:*
>
> *For it had lost its shape and shine,*
> *And it had cost him four-and-nine,*
> *And he was going out to dine.*[1]

In the dialogue that follows Dodgson moves into an affectionate parody of Tennyson's gloomy exchanges, and hits off some of his funniest lines:

> *The man that smokes – that reads The Times –*
> *That goes to Christmas pantomimes –*
> *Is capable of <u>any</u> crimes!*

Dodgson was delighted to learn that his idol had a new poem in the pipeline, but Mrs Weld had also divulged an even more interesting piece of information about the poet. Tennyson was interested in photography. A plan of action began to take shape in Dodgson's mind. He would take a photograph of Agnes Grace and send it to Tennyson, using it as a kind of letter of introduction. Little Agnes was not a beautiful child, but she had a curious and striking face. Dodgson dressed her up as Little Red Riding Hood and posed her, soulful and hollow-eyed, carrying a basket. The picture was sent off to the Laureate, who told Mrs Weld that he thought it a 'little gem'.

The opportunity to put his plan into practice came later that year when, after a singularly damp and dismal holiday in Scotland with his brothers, Dodgson returned by way of Ambleside, in the Lake District. He had discovered that Tennyson was staying six miles away at Tent Lodge overlooking Coniston Water, and decided that the time had come to put his plan into action. He sent Skeffington off to climb Coniston Old Man, while he carried out a reconnaissance of Tent Lodge. The painfully sensitive Tennyson could be very unpredictable about any invasion of his privacy but Dodgson was confident that his stratagem would succeed. He sent in his card with a note, 'Artist of *Agnes Grace* and *Little Red Riding Hood*'. As it happened, Tennyson was out, but Mrs Tennyson welcomed him in. He met Hallam and Lionel and found them every bit as handsome as Mrs Weld had told him. Emily Tennyson said that he would be quite free to take pictures of them and even hinted that the Bard himself might be tempted to sit. She also promised him an autograph. It is not surprising that Dodgson marked the day with a white stone. He had already arranged for his photographic equipment to be sent to Ambleside. On 22nd September he again presented himself at Tent Lodge and was shown into the drawing room. After a short time a 'strange shaggy-looking man'[2] with wild, neglected hair entered and shook hands with the shy stammering photographer don.

Tennyson proved to be surprisingly affable, but to Dodgson's dismay he announced that they were leaving Tent Lodge the following day and would be away until the end of the week. However he did not want to let the photo opportunity pass by and suggested that they should go over together to the Marshalls' splendid house at Monk Coniston Park and ask if Dodgson could set up his camera there. The Marshalls happily gave permission for Dodgson to take his photographs in their house and he went back to have dinner with the Tennysons. That evening the poet was in high good humour and had apparently taken a liking to Dodgson. They all looked through the albums which he had brought with him on the off chance that he might persuade Tennyson to sit for him. A picture of Skeffington in a fishing costume afforded great amusement. Tennyson said that his expression seemed to say, 'Well! I've come down here to catch trout, and if I don't catch a trout this season, the great business of my life will be gone.'³ He then took up one of Dodgson's anatomical photographs of a monkey's skull and remarked that 'a young monkey's skull is quite human in shape and gradually alters – the analogy being borne out by the human skull being at first more like the statues of the gods and gradually degenerating into human.' After making this startling contribution to evolutionary theory two years before the publication of *The Origin of Species*, he turned to Emily and said, 'There, that's the second original remark I've made this evening.' Sadly, Dodgson does not record what the first one was.

On the Tennysons' return to Tent Lodge, Dodgson spent two days taking pictures of them and their children. This was long before Tennyson fell under the thrall of Julia Margaret Cameron – photography was still a novelty to him and he wanted to see how it was done. He looks singularly patient in most of the photographs, although in a group picture taken with the Marshalls at one of the windows of Monk Coniston, he is slumped in a chair with Hallam sprawled across his lap and looks as if he is wondering whether the ordeal will ever end. However, the pictures were judged to be a great success. Dodgson had learned the power of the camera as a lionising instrument, but he profited from the visit in more ways than one. He persuaded Joseph Cundall of Bond Street to publish one of the photographs of the Laureate commercially, though it does not seem to have occurred to him to ask for Tennyson's permission. Later that year, he received a strange letter from Emily Tennyson asking him to destroy the pictures he had taken of herself and Tennyson, except for those in the family album at Croft and the one he had given to Reginald Southey. Since his photograph of Tennyson was by then on sale to the public, there was little he could do but preserve a discreet silence.

The Long Vacation of 1857 had seen the descent of the pre-Raphaelites on Oxford. Rossetti had offered to decorate the walls of the Debating Chamber of the Union with scenes from the *Morte D'Arthur* and he had co-opted various members of the brotherhood to share the task with him. William Morris, when not paying court to Jane Burden, was working on *Tristram and Iseult*; Rossetti's own subject was *Sir Lancelot's Vision of the*

Holy Grail; Burne Jones contributed to *The Death of Merlin* and Arthur Hughes, shortly to become a friend of Dodgson, *The Death of Arthur*.

They all had a high old time, splashing paint about all over the place and over one another. Despite the fact that all this communal activity exemplified his expressed notions about medieval craftsmen, the great Ruskin watched it all in some bewilderment. Although he thought Rossetti's painting 'the finest piece of colour in the world', he wrote to Rossetti's brother, William, 'The fact is they're all the least bit crazy and it's very difficult to manage them.'[4] Unfortunately their craziness extended to a total ignorance of the techniques of fresco painting and their glorious vision faded rapidly and irrevocably away into the Union walls. The only part of the grand scheme that survived was a bas-relief of King Arthur over the door by the sculptor Alexander Munro, who was to prove Dodgson's passport to the world of London theatre and art.

The Morte d'Arthur paintings must inevitably have been a topic of conversation when Dodgson met Ruskin for the first time at a Common Room breakfast at the beginning of term. He found him rather disappointing – 'a general feebleness of expression, with no commanding air, or any external signs of deep thought, as one would have expected in such a man'. Although they were to see one another frequently over the years, their acquaintance never grew into friendship. Ruskin was the high priest of art appreciation in Oxford and Dodgson cannot have been greatly heartened by being told by him that he lacked the talent to make it worthwhile devoting any attention to drawing.

It was 1875 before Dodgson managed to get Ruskin to sit for a photograph: 'With some difficulty I persuaded Ruskin to come and be photographed, and to stay to luncheon with us.'[5] The difficulty is clearly reflected in the picture. Ruskin looks as if he had been tied to the chair prior to being shot by a firing squad. Dodgson did not have much trust in Ruskin's judgement: 'I think he is rather hard to please: and is *not* omniscient as an Art critic,' he told the painter Frederick Shields. The one thing that the two men had in common was their admiration for Alice Liddell, although she did not come into Ruskin's life until the point at which she was leaving Dodgson's.

Whatever plans Dodgson may have had for Alice and her sisters that autumn were doomed to disappointment. The Liddells decided to take the girls with them to winter in Madeira. Even Harry was to be denied him – he was to be taken away and looked after by his Uncle Charles, before entering Twyford, 'an arrangement anything but satisfactory', Dodgson commented morosely. On the day before the Liddells left, Dodgson called in at Ryman's to take a look at Landseer's painting of *Titania*. He thought that there were 'wonderful points' in it and there was a white rabbit which caught his eye. He spent nearly an hour at the Deanery saying goodbye to the 'dear loving little children'.[6]

As soon as term finished he went down to Twyford school on the pretext of visiting his old friend George Kitchin, who was now Headmaster, and his cousin Jimmy Dodgson, another of Uncle Hassard's sons who was a pupil.

It seems likely that Dodgson's real reason for visiting Twyford was to see how Harry Liddell was settling in, and through him, to maintain a fragile link with 'his little sisters beyond the seas'. It was, however, to be the Liddells' last winter on the island. Dean Liddell's absence was causing endless discontent at Christ Church, and he was obliged to transfer his affections from Funchal to Llandudno.

Dodgson still seemed to be incapable of settling down. The Hilary Term of 1858 drifted away without there being very much to show for it. His picture of Agnes Weld was shown at the Photographic Exhibition at Kensington, he started to read George Eliot's *Scenes from Clerical Life*, he devised a plan for scripture reading but does not seem to have continued with it. He began to read physiology and anatomy. He invented ciphers and called on the Aclands to show them his photograph albums, possibly hoping for news of the Liddells. He wrote nothing, although he did work out the rules for a new card game, 'Court Circular', which he published as a pamphlet in 1860, his first printed work to appear outside a magazine or newspaper. A 'Court Circular' was a line of four court cards, and may well have been invented for the Deanery children. It is not very demanding, but in laying out the cards for them he may have given them characters of their own, preparing the ground for the arrival of the King and Queen of Hearts and their family.

At the end of April he accompanied his brother Edwin down to Twyford. At this point the diary disappears and the next surviving volume is not until May 1862. If the diaries were in fact destroyed, it is just possible that they contained an account of serious differences between Dodgson and his father on the subject of whether he was to take up a religious vocation. Dodgson's doubts over this must have been all too apparent. He could not bring himself to seal that 'irrevocable bond of self-resignation' which his father regarded as an essential preliminary to ordination. Wilfred was not falling in line with the Archdeacon's plans either: his chief interests lay in shooting and fishing. Only Skeffington, still making slow progress with his studies, had declared his intention of entering the church. For his father this more than compensated for any academic shortcomings:

> You have much in you which would make you a blessing to many in the most blessed of all professions, that of a Clergyman in which great knowledge is not the point – but a simple desire to serve God, for God's sake.[7]

However, the Archdeacon's disappointment in his eldest son's reluctance to go into the priesthood seems an inadequate reason for destroying two years' of diaries. The remainder of 1858 is virtually a complete blank. There are no letters, no contributions to *The Train* or any other publications, not even a letter to a newspaper.

We know a little more about 1859 because in the spring Dodgson went to see Tennyson again, this time at his home at Farringford near Freshwater on the Isle of Wight. Dodgson had gone down to Freshwater to stay with John Martyn Collyns, his companion on the Lakeland tour. Wilfred told everybody that his brother had gone down there on a lion hunt, but Dodgson indignantly denied this. In a letter to William Wilcox, he told him that he did not even know that Tennyson lived nearby, but as soon as he found out he asserted 'the right of a freeborn Briton to make a morning call'.[8] At the house he came upon a man painting a fence and asked whether the Laureate were at home. 'He's there, sir,' replied the man, and there, sure enough, was the Bard himself in a wideawake hat, wearing his spectacles and mowing the lawn of his 'careless-ordered garden'. Tennyson was too short-sighted or too forgetful to recognise his caller, but once Dodgson had identified himself he welcomed him in and showed him round the house. Dodgson was gratified to see that the pictures he had taken two years earlier were hung 'on the line'. He was invited to stay and returned again for dinner and again the next day, with his photograph album. He showed Tennyson the picture he had taken of Alice Liddell as a beggar girl with a torn dress exposing her bare shoulders. Tennyson said it was the most beautiful photograph he had ever seen but later put Dodgson firmly in his place by suggesting that where he, Tennyson, dreamed poetry, Dodgson must dream photographs.

The absence of diaries means we only have odd glimpses of Dodgson at this time. He surfaced again in 1860, when he wrote a review of the Photographic Exhibition for the *Illustrated Times*. This was his only review, formal and to the point. Some of his criticisms reflect on difficulties he had himself experienced, particularly in giving his subjects something to do with their hands:

> ... if the artist attempts the arrangement himself, he generally produces the effect of the proverbially bashful young man in society who finds for the first time that his hands are an encumbrance, and cannot remember what he is in the habit of doing with them in private life.[9]

Dodgson soon learned to make sure that the hands of his sitters were gainfully employed. Aunt Lucy Lutwidge holds a needle and thread, Tennyson a copy of his poems, Rossetti his hat, while George MacDonald's arms are resolutely folded as if to prevent them flying away.

Dodgson had met the poet and novelist George MacDonald in 1859 when he was consulting a speech therapist, Dr James Hunt. Hunt lived at Ore House, conveniently close to Hastings, where Dodgson's Lutwidge aunts lived in Wellington Square. Hunt's *Stammering and Stuttering, Their Nature and Treatment* was considered a landmark for the methods which it advocated. In the past all kinds of weird and wonderful cures had been suggested. The Romans advised gargling and massage. Francis Bacon thought that speech difficulties were caused by the refrigeration of the tongue and recommended hot wine. Johann Dieffenbach, a Prussian surgeon, took the rather drastic view that people stuttered because their tongues were too large and proceeded to slice those of his patients to what he considered a suitable size. Dodgson found Hunt's system beneficial and even stayed for a week at Ore House. MacDonald was a fellow sufferer, and the two men quickly became great friends. MacDonald was a clergyman, of the evangelical variety, and the author of *At the Back of the North Wind* and *The Princess and the Goblin*, strange and highly individual tales written for children. Dodgson rapidly became a favourite with MacDonald's wife Louisa, and with their children, who called him 'Uncle Dodgson'. He first met the eldest son, Greville, in the studio of Alexander Munro, sculptor of the figure of Arthur at the Oxford Union, where the boy was posing for the statue of the *Boy with a Dolphin*. Dodgson did his best to persuade Greville to exchange his head for one of marble, telling him that it would save him the trouble of having to brush and comb his long hair. He was to become one of the few boys whom Dodgson accepted as a friend.

Edwin was about to follow in Dodgson's reluctant footsteps and go to Rugby. While Dodgson was in London waiting to meet him, and see him safely installed, he heard that Holman Hunt's new painting *Christ in the*

Temple was on private view. He had met Holman Hunt in the Christ Church Common Room three years earlier, so sent in his card. He was admitted and found that there were so few people there that he was able to corner Hunt and discuss the painting with him. 'It is about the most wonderful picture I ever saw.'[10] Dodgson was fortunate to see the picture in such calm surroundings. It was the sensation of the year and at the Bond Street gallery where it was on show, a thousand visitors a day clamoured to be admitted. The Prince Consort could get nowhere near it and the picture had to be temporarily removed to Windsor so that the Queen could see it for herself. A few weeks later, at a party, Hunt met Charles Dickens, who anticipated a certain tea party with the words: 'You have caused my hatter to be madder than ever. He declares that you have choked up Bond Street with the carriages for your exhibition so that none of his established customers can get to his shop.'[11]

Dodgson was deeply moved by the painting and tried to express his feelings about it in a poem, 'After Three Days'. It was written in his worst religioso style and was either flatly descriptive or conventionally pious. Like so much of his writing, the poem takes the form of a dream in which the poet is drawn from the crowd of people in the gallery into the heart of the picture itself. But the dreamer is woken by a 'sudden lark' and lies in the gathering light,

> *lovingly clinging to the skirts of night*
> *For that sweet vision's sake.*

Clinging to dreams, clinging to childhood, constantly trying to revisit or re-enact things which had brought him pleasure or delight, was a central element of Dodgson's personality. The gaiety and high spirits which had marked his youth were to be subdued by a steadily pervading inner melancholy for which there is no simple explanation. In all the photographs taken of Dodgson, there is not one which betrays the least hint of a smile. Although he had managed to preserve somewhere inside him the essence of his childhood, he became increasingly obsessed by the passage of time and by the brevity of human existence. By the time he was fifty he considered himself to be an old man, even though there were moments when he felt no different from his twenty-one-year-old self. He did not make life any easier for himself by concentrating all his emotional energy on children whose affection for him could at best be transient. A few of his friendships survived into adult life, but, for the most part, he grew accustomed to them fading away, leaving him lonelier than ever.

12

'Practically a layman'

On December 22nd, 1861, 'Charles Lutwidge Dodgson, Master of Arts, Student of Christ Church in the University of Oxford (of whose courteous and pious life, conversation and competent learning and knowledge in the Holy Scriptures we were well assured)', was admitted by Bishop Wilberforce into the Holy Order of Deacons of the Church of England. Taking Deacon's Orders was a compromise between being in the Church and being out of it, the outcome of a struggle that had been going on within Dodgson ever since he had come up to Oxford.

In his 1838 Ordination sermon, Dodgson's father had stressed that the Church required those who sought admission to sacred orders to examine and 'prove their own selves'.

> She carries her enquiries into the sanctuary of the conscience, and calls upon the still small voice to respond to the awful question, 'Do you trust that you are inwardly moved by the Holy Ghost to take upon you this office and ministration to serve God for the promoting of His glory and the edifying of His people?'[1]

The still, small voice within Dodgson could only question his worthiness and suitability for taking priest's Orders at all. One of his New Year's resolutions for 1858 had been to begin reading for Ordination by the end of the year and to settle 'the subject finally and definitely in my mind'. Others had no difficulty. His brother Skeffington was still intent on entering the priesthood; his friend Henry Liddon, ordained in 1853, had worked as a priest in the parish of Wantage. Another close friend, Robert Faussett, became Vicar of Cassington, a village a few miles outside Oxford. But Dodgson simply could not see himself working as a parish priest. He gave himself various reasons for this, but none of them is entirely convincing. There was his stammer, which he feared would be an impediment to carrying out his clerical duties. It was an obstacle certainly, but he had never let it stand in his way when delivering a recitation or performing in charades; however, there is no denying the terror which the prospect of delivering a sermon or reading the lesson aroused in him. He had a very deep and very real fear of being seized with a fit of stammering before a large congregation, and was afraid he might make Holy Things laughable. A second reason was that it would involve giving up the study and teaching of mathematics. As his diary shows, contemplation of algebraic and geometric problems was part of his daily pattern of thought. 'I found myself established as the Mathematical Lecturer, and with no sort of inclination to give it up and take parochial work,' he told his cousin William Wilcox, many years later, 'and I had grave doubts whether it would not be my duty <u>not</u> to take Orders. I took advice on this point (Bishop Wilberforce was one that I applied to) and came to the conclusion that, so far from educational work (even Mathematics) being unfit for a clergyman, it was distinctly a <u>good</u> thing that many of our educators should be men in Holy Orders.'[2] His chief obstacle was his own conviction of his unworthiness to work as a parish priest. He was particularly concerned about being able to answer and combat the religious problems of his parishioners. He was not prepared to fob them off with easy or specious answers. During the time when the question of his ordination was weighing heavily on his mind, he had a long and rather fruitless argument with his brother Wilfred on the subject of the need to respect college discipline.

> This also suggests to me grave doubts as to the work of the ministry which I am looking forward to. If I can find it so hard to prove a plain duty to one individual and that one unpractised in argument, how can I ever be ready to face the countless sophisms and ingenious arguments against religion which a clergyman must meet with?[3]

He seems somehow to have managed to sustain a deeply sincere religious belief while being, in another region of his highly complex self, a hopeless nihilist. His diaries bear witness to a conventional, simple, unquestioning religious devotion, while the books which he was to write, and on which his fame now chiefly depends, seem to suggest a completely different mind and a wholly different world where God has ceased to exists: where Alice wonders what it would be like to be snuffed out like a candle and where the Baker, confronted by his Boojum, vanishes into nothingness.

Dodgson's was not a deeply reasoned faith, although in later life he would try to use his formidable powers of logic as a weapon against disbelief. He quite simply accepted the faith which his father had taught him and followed it with a rather evangelical piety, but this could never entirely enable him to conquer an instinctive horror of the void. In later years he could always sympathise with anyone afflicted by religious doubt. In 1886 he wrote to Edith Rix, about a friend of hers who was an agnostic:

> The Moral Science student you describe must be a beautiful character,

and if, as you say, she lives a noble life, then, even though she does not, as yet, see any God ... I don't think you need be unhappy about her ... I have a deep dread of arguments on religious topics: it has many risks, and little chance of doing good.[4]

His other problem was that he was ill at ease among working class people. He knew that he could not work as a pastor to artisans and share their life. It was not in his nature.

Dodgson was also reluctant to give up the life he was living. If he proceeded to full Holy Orders one of the first things he would have to sacrifice would be the theatre. Bishop Wilberforce had declared that the 'resolution to attend theatres or operas was an absolute disqualification for Holy Orders'. Henry Liddon was of the same opinion:

Speaking for myself, there is no form of entertainment which I should so entirely enjoy, as good acting. But I have never been inside a theatre since I took orders in 1852, and I do not mean to go into one, please God, while I live ... There can ... be no doubt that a clergyman who goes to theatres forfeits moral influence to a certain extent with all classes and quite irretrievably with some.[5]

The objection, however, extended only to those working as parish priests. If Dodgson could find some way of not proceeding to full Holy Orders he could continue to go to the theatre as often as he wished. There would be other sacrifices, too. Teaching may have bored and dispirited him at times, he may have become irritable with the college servants and weary of the conversation and company of his fellow dons, but his existence at Oxford was life as he wished to lead it. The atmosphere of Christ Church itself, the afternoons on the river, his photography, his little girl friends, his mathematical problems, his puzzles and conundrums, his visits to London's galleries and exhibitions – what could the life of a parish priest have to offer in compensation for the loss of these? Had he been born a hundred years earlier he would not have had to make the choice. He could have lived like Gilbert White, freely pursuing his own interests with his clerical duties as an undemanding background to his life. In the 1860s this was no longer possible. 'He was not prepared,' wrote Collingwood, 'to live the life of almost puritanical strictness which was then considered essential for a clergyman.'

However, if he wished to avoid being deprived of his Studentship, Dodgson had to take up Holy Orders of some kind. He began to consider those which did not involve any direct ministerial duty:

I asked Dr Liddon whether he thought I should be justified in taking Deacon's Orders as a sort of experiment, which would enable me to try how the occupation of a clergyman suited me, and then decide whether I should take full orders. He said 'most certainly' – and that a Deacon is in a totally different position from a priest: and much more free to regard himself as <u>practically</u> a layman. So I took Deacon's Orders in that spirit.[6]

So Dodgson's lifestyle continued exactly as it had been before, but the mere fact of his ordination undoubtedly had a profound effect upon his inner self. He became more aware than ever of living out his life in the continual presence of God, which involved him in agonised bursts of soul-searching, though fortunately it did nothing to make him change his ways.

His trips to the theatre became more frequent than ever, as did his visits to art galleries and popular exhibitions. He devoted more and more time to his child-friends and to devising puzzles, tricks and stories for their entertainment. Every year he would lament time wasted, every year he would resolve to devote more time to the church and to works of religion, every year seemed to confirm him in his simple evangelical piety and yet every year would be lived out in the same old worldly pattern.[7]

'A grave and gentle maid'

At the beginning of 1860 Dodgson published a poem entitled 'Faces in the Fire', in Dickens's magazine *All the Year Round*. It is a highly personal poem and it is tempting to read some kind of autobiographical significance into it. Dodgson was always prone to exaggerate the effects of age – by his late forties he was already referring to himself as an elderly man. In 1860 he was twenty-eight with the prospect of a full life ahead of him. Yet 'Faces in the Fire' is a poem of might-have-beens and lost love:

> *The night creeps onward, sad and slow:*
> *In these dead embers' dying glow*
> *The forms of fancy come and go.*[1]

The poet gazes into the fire and pictures 'the happy spot where I was born'. The vision fades and another takes its place, the face of a child, a little girl of course, with locks of jet like Lorina or Alice –

> *That might have been my own, my dear,*
> *Through many and many a happy year –*
> *That might have sat beside me here.*

He pictures the child growing into:

> *A grave and gentle maid,*
> *At her own beauty half afraid*

and then as

> *A matron with her boys,*
> *Dear centre of domestic joys.*

What happens in the course of the poem to the 'little childish form' would happen to Alice Liddell and to all the other little girls that he would fall in love with. Three years earlier he had put aside the idea of marriage as a likely possibility – he was now assessing the consequences of this, a lifetime of loving little girls who would grow up and leave him sitting alone looking at the ashes in the grate.

Even though his diary for this time is lost to us, we can trace the course of Dodgson's love affair with the Liddell children and his relationship with

Alice through the photographs he took of them. His experience of taking pictures of the girls turned Dodgson from a well-meaning amateur to one of the most sensitive Victorian photographers of children. He went to endless trouble to make sure that the girls enjoyed the experience as much as he did. Miss Prickett would bring her charges up to Dodgson's rooms, and the girls would settle down on the sofa on either side of him. He would start to tell them stories, illustrating them with drawings as he went along: 'He seemed to have an endless store of these fantastical tales, which he made up as he told them, drawing busily on a large sheet of paper all the time.'[2] When the children were happy and relaxed the photographing would begin.

'Imperious' Lorina at first looks indignant and resentful at the idea of being photographed at all, but gradually succumbs to Dodgson's persuasive charm, coolly poised in a Chinese costume, wistfully forlorn with a very ugly doll. Edith, small and demure, seems to be living in a world of her own, gazing vaguely out of the picture or looking down. But Alice, even in the earliest pictures, seemed to strike up a very personal relationship with the camera. In a picture of the three girls posed on Dodgson's sofa Alice is eyeing the viewer coquettishly. Each of the photographs reflects a very definite personality. Alice, deeply serious, beneath a hat garlanded with flowers; Alice sitting on a table by a pot-plant – 'a grave and gentle maid'; Alice sitting on a chair in profile, looking vulnerable and very small; Alice in her beggar girl's rags and tatters in photographs which, to modern eyes, but not to Tennyson's, seem to come perilously close to pornography. Alice lies on a rug with a large black hat across her white dress; she has been told to pretend she is asleep, but is not at all convincing. She stands in a corner of the Deanery garden, with a slightly nervous smile beginning to form on her lips – 'at her own beauty half afraid'. Mrs Liddell always saw to it that if her daughters were to be photographed they should be turned out like fashion plates. 'The three girls stand together, playing miniature guitars, wearing white dresses with frilly pantaloons peeping from under their skirts. Lorina is making a conscientious attempt to look as if she is playing her guitar, Edith, as always, is gazing out of the picture, Alice, making no pretence of music-making, stares directly at the camera. In the most carefully structured of all the pictures, *Open your mouth and close your eyes*, a determined looking Lorina dangles a bunch of cherries over Alice's open mouth, while Edith sits quietly by. Dodgson's camera evokes a telling childish sensuality. The pictures tell us, if nothing else, that he is in love with Alice.

*

In February 1861, the young Liddells all contracted measles. Alice looked 'awfully melancholy' and Dodgson found it almost impossible to make her smile. He did his best to cheer up the children with 'A Sea Dirge', a poem he had written for the university magazine, *College Rhymes*:

> *There are certain things – as, a spider, a ghost,*
> *The income-tax, gout, an umbrella for three –*
> *That I hate, but the thing that I hate the most*
> *Is a thing they call the sea.*[3]

He then goes on to enumerate all the things which he pretends to detest about the seaside: thousands of nurse-maids leading children with wooden spades, the fleas that infest seaside lodgings, sand in coffee, a fishy taste in eggs, wet feet. Since Dodgson was to spend virtually every summer of his life in watering places round the south coast, the poem was clearly intended to annoy the little Liddells and to evoke from them the response which it did – 'Not true'. They had themselves recently become seaside addicts as a result of their first visits to Llandudno.

Llandudno was totally unlike the typical resort Dodgson described in his poem. The Dean and his wife had spent their honeymoon there, and Penmorfa, the house they built on the rocks at the foot of the Great Orme, became their holiday home for the next nine years. It must have seemed a wildly romantic spot. The house they built was a rather extravagant and ungainly gothic structure – in old photographs it has something of the air of the Bates Motel in Hitchcock's *Psycho*. The house soon attracted a series of eminent visitors. Matthew Arnold came and praised the sunsets, Gladstone had a fit of vertigo on the Great Orme, George Richmond painted the Liddell sisters among the rocks. The one person who did not visit was Charles Lutwidge Dodgson.

This is rather a tragedy for a town which has always prided itself on its association with Lewis Carroll. George Richmond claimed in 1907 that in the evenings, while he was painting the Liddell sisters, Dodgson would read aloud parts of *Alice in Wonderland* which he had been writing there during the day. The legend rapidly grew, and the rabbit warren not far from the beach was claimed as the origin of the one down which the White Rabbit popped. During the Lewis Carroll centenary celebrations in 1932, Llandudno threw all discretion to the wind and erected a statute of the White Rabbit at the West Bay, a little way from Penmorfa, now the Gogarth Abbey Hotel. The inscription beneath the statute read:

> *On this very shore*
> *During happy rambles with*
> *little Alice Liddell*

> LEWIS CARROLL
> *was inspired to write that*
> *literary treasure*
> ALICE IN WONDERLAND
> *which has charmed children*
> *for generations.*

Alice herself, by then a widow of eighty, was invited to unveil it, but refused. According to her son, Caryl, she said she did not have the faintest memory of Dodgson ever visiting Penmorfa, but in her reply declining the invitation, she was carefully ambiguous:

> I still have the happiest memories of Penmorfa, as my father's house at Llandudno was then called, and of the rambles over the Great Orme's head and among the Llandudno sand hills. I wish I could come personally in gratitude for those joyous days, and for the joyous days spent with Mr Dodgson.[4]

Shortly after his ordination, Dodgson called in at the Deanery with a Christmas present for the three little girls, *Holiday House*, by Catherine Sinclair. It was probably the most original and unusual book written for children before *Alice*. Although in the end it had its conventional moral to make, it positively encouraged children to be 'noisy, frolicsome and mischeivous'. The dedicatory poem with which Dodgson accompanied the book was the first literary fruit of his friendship with the Liddell children. It is rather a limp performance, and very far from the lively anarchy of Miss Sinclair's book:

> *Never think that hours of play*
> *Are your only HOLIDAY,*
> *And that in a HOUSE of joy*
> *Lessons serve but to annoy ...*[5]

However, it is one of Dodgson's earliest attempts at an acrostic and the first letters of each line spell out LORINA.ALICE.EDITH.

There was a side to Dodgson that at times seemed to be encouraging children to behave as dangerously as possible. It was all in fun, of course, but there were alarming undertones. In March 1861, he sent Kathleen Tidy, another of his little child friends, a miniature penknife as a birthday present. He suggested that she should eat her meat at dinner with it – 'in this way you will be safe from eating too much, and so making yourself ill'. But his gentle teasing took a rather sinister turn:

> Whenever you wish to punish your brothers, you will find it very convenient to do so by running the knife into their hands and faces

(particularly at the end of the nose): you will find it gives a good deal of pain if you run it in hard enough.[6]

This kind of sadistic humour is common enough in Victorian children's writing but it seems to bring out a rather sickening and uncharacteristic relish in Dodgson. In an even more disturbing letter to Tennyson's ten-year-old son Hallam he wrote:

> I am glad you liked the knife, and I think it a pity you should not be allowed to use it 'till you are older'. However, as you are older now, perhaps you have begun to use it by this time: if you were allowed to cut your finger on it, once a week, just a little, you know, till it began to bleed, and a good deep cut every birthday, I should think that would be enough, and it would last a good time so. Only I hope that if Lionel ever wants to have his fingers cut with it, you will be kind to your brother, and hurt him as much as he likes.[7]

Doubtless, Hallam and Lionel found this very funny. Most children would. It is this grim teasing that gives the Alice books their particular quality – the black humour, the death jokes, Humpty Dumpty's sinister aside about Alice growing older. For all Dodgson's love and patience and kindness, there were times when he could not restrain a streak of sadism which led him to tease children to a point where they became hurt or bewildered. But at times like this Dodgson had ceased to be an adult. He was a child playing with other children.

In April 1862 Dodgson spent a few days at Plumbley's Hotel at Freshwater in the hope of cornering Tennyson, but he had to be content with the poet's sons, whom he initiated into the game of 'elephant hunter'. The boys took him to meet Julia Margaret Cameron, who, like Dodgson, was a Tennyson fanatic, and had bought a house next door to Farringford in order to be near the great man.

Mrs Cameron had not yet begun her photographic career, but she and Dodgson would both be highly critical of one another's work. Dodgson was brusquely dismissive of her 'large heads, taken out of focus', and she told Sir Henry Taylor that the photograph taken of him by Dodgson had been described as looking like a 'sea monster fed upon milk'. Dodgson and Mrs Cameron frequently stalked the big game to persuade them to sit for photographs. Both bagged Tennyson and Ellen Terry, but Dodgson's friendship with the Terry family debarred him from snaring Ellen's estranged husband Watts, who reluctantly yielded to Mrs Cameron. She caught Browning, who failed to turn up for Dodgson, but Dante Gabriel Rossetti, who posed several times for Dodgson, refused to speak to her. The great betrayal was to occur in 1872 when not only Dean Liddell but Alice and her sisters were persuaded to sit by Mrs Cameron.

The one person Dodgson hardly saw at all that spring was Tennyson himself. In January he had published an index to 'In Memoriam', for which most of the spade work seems to have been done by his sisters; Mary in particular was a great enthusiast. Each separate clause in the poem is referred to by the most important names or nouns, or occasionally verbs, contained in it:

> ARTHUR.
> 9.1   My lost Arthur's loved remains.
> 9.5   My A whom I shall not see.
> 88.2 My A found your shadows fair.[8]

Although the Index was published anonymously, Tennyson can scarcely have been unaware that Dodgson had compiled it, since he had given his permission for it to be printed. He may have been deliberately keeping away from his admirer but he did have graver problems on his mind. Prince Albert had died in the December of the previous year and on April 14th Tennyson had been summoned to Osborne to give what comfort he could to the desolate Queen. Embarrassed and somewhat at a loss for words, he had blurted out, 'He would have made a great king,' and instantly regretted it. To his surprise and considerable relief, the Queen was deeply moved and grateful.

Tennyson's guest and companion on his visit to Osborne was his great friend, Benjamin Jowett. Jowett had been the subject of a lampoon written by Dodgson the previous year, 'The Endowment of the Greek Professorship'. It was published anonymously and Dodgson does not suggest that in the course of his various encounters with Jowett during his stay at Freshwater, he gave him any hint that he had written it, or that Jowett suspected him. He would be one of the principal butts of Dodgson's university satires over the coming years.

Benjamin Jowett, silvery-tongued, with the appearance of a rather pawky cherub, was considered one of the finest minds in Oxford. In 1854 he had been appointed by Lord Palmerston to the Regius Professorship of Greek. As a result of one of Oxford's more curious anomalies, the salary for the post remained as it had been when the chair was founded in the reign of Henry VIII, at the none too princely sum of £40 per annum. Everyone was agreed that Jowett's stipend must be increased and it seemed a simple measure to carry through Congregation, but there was one major obstacle. Jowett had published an article in *Essays and Reviews*, a collection of studies on Christianity, in which he had advocated that the Bible should be open to examination and criticism like any other major text of literature or philosophy. Jowett's article, along with the rest of

Essays and Reviews was received with consternation by the Anglican establishment and denounced by the Archbishops of Canterbury and York, backed by no less than twenty-four other Bishops. There were those in Oxford who would cheerfully have seen Jowett burned at the stake.

As in many an Oxford controversy some of the protagonists found themselves fighting for both sides. Archdeacon Dodgson's old friend Dr Pusey was outraged by Jowett's religious opinions but nevertheless tried to put forward a measure by which the stipend of the Regius Professor should be increased, with a clause which dissociated the establishment from 'any theological views the Professor held or ever would hold'. This met with the approval of both Palmerston and Gladstone, but Oxford would have none of it. Dodgson felt compelled to speak out on the debate in Congregation:

> The speaking took up the whole afternoon, and the two points at issue, the endowing a Regius Professorship, and the countenancing Jowett's theological opinions, got so inextricably mixed up that I rose to beg that they might be kept separate. Once on my feet, I said more than I at first meant, and defied them ever to tire out the opposition by perpetually bringing the question on (Mem: if ever I speak again I will try to say no more than I had resolved before rising).[9]

Once again he had allied himself firmly with the conservative die-hards. He did not show the least sign of contrition but rushed into print two days later the first of his Oxford squibs on the subject of the endowment, making sport of such phrases as 'that the Corpus element be omitted':

> ... a condition never before annexed to a Professorship, and which indicates but too clearly the wide influence which the so-called 'spiritualist' views have attained both in America and in this country.[10]

and he went on to suggest that 'none but a member of All Souls can possibly fulfil the stringent requirements here proposed'. The joke would have more point for those acquainted with Jowett, for he was nothing if not portly.

The pamphlet is far from being one of Dodgson's more memorable utterances, but it marks his entry into a field where he could translate the dry academic joke into an instrument of satire and allowed the Humpty Dumpty in him to let rip. From this point on he could never resist an opportunity to use the long running tale of Jowett's endowment as a means of sharpening his wit.

From 9th May, 1862, until a few days before his death, Dodgson's diary has survived intact. What is immediately noticeable since the last surviving diaries is a change in tone. Up to the point where the previous journal breaks off, prayers and self-questioning had been almost entirely confined to his annual New Year assessments. The entry for 31st December, 1856, is a representative example:

> I do trust most sincerely to amend myself in those respects in which the past year has exhibited the most grievous shortcomings, and I trust and pray that the most merciful God may aid me in this and all other good undertakings – Midnight is past: bless the New Year, oh heavenly Father, for Thy dear Son Jesus Christ's sake![11]

The tone is calm and measured, almost complacent, but when the diary resumes, the prayers occur every few weeks, sometimes every few days, and their tone is now immediate and urgent: 'I pray God help me to lead a new life,' 'Oh God help me to live a better and more earnest life.' This is not a formal, dutiful response. He really is asking for God's help. As the weeks go by and the prayers grow more frequent and more urgent, a more anguished and hysterical note begins to creep in. After turning down a request for him to preach, he writes:

> till I can rule myself better, preaching is but a solemn mockery – 'thou that teachest another, teachest thou not thyself?' God grant this may be the last such entry I may have to make! that so I may not, when I have preached to others be 'myself a castaway'.[12]

The following year he wrote that he repented of his past life, '...the spirit is willing: help thou the weak flesh'. He asks God to 'break down the trammels of evil habits', beseeching God on his knees 'to help me put away my old sins and lead a new life'. He prays to be delivered from the 'chains of sin' and hopes that his life 'may not be sullied with the sins that have clouded these 6 months and so much of my life hitherto'.

And yet this was the happiest and most creative period of his life, the blissful, carefree time of the river expeditions with the Liddell children, the 'golden afternoon' when he told the story of Alice's adventures. What kind of personal crisis is being chronicled? The most obvious explanation is that this a record of his failure to overcome the Victorian demon of masturbation. In the preface to *Pillow Problems*, written many years later, Dodgson writes of 'unholy thoughts, which torture, with their hateful presence, the fancy that would fain be pure', the 'unclean spirit' is always close by, waiting to take advantage of the unoccupied mind. There is, after all, no evidence that Dodgson was impotent. It would not be very surprising if he sometimes succumbed to temptation. It would, in fact, make him more human.

But with a personality as complex as Dodgson's, nothing is ever simple.

Without the advantage of the missing diaries, it is impossible to say when these entries first begin, but it is likely that they grow more and more frequent after his ordination as Deacon. Even though he was only enrolled in the church as 'practically a layman', he had taken an irrevocable decision and he was a priest of God. The diary entries may well chronicle his pangs of conscience for wasting his time in worldly frivolities and not devoting enough of his energies to the service of God. These, as much as auto-erotic malingering, may well be the sins he is recording.

Despite his misgivings, Dodgson did manage to deliver at least one sermon at this time. At the request of his friend William Ranken he agreed to preach at his church at Sandford-on-Thames, some five or six miles outside Oxford. Dodgson, considering how nervous he could be when delivering sermons in later life, seems to have approached the ordeal with remarkable *sang froid*. He was to preach his sermon on 7th June, 1862. The previous evening he had a dinner party with Ranken and Vere Bayne and was too sleepy to do anything about the sermon, but the following morning he lay in bed, working it out, wrote down the headings, went to morning service in Iffley, walked on to Sandford and preached at evensong. 'I found I had to refer to the headings constantly: it lasted, I should think, about half-an-hour.'[13] He took for his text the blessing at the end of the Second Epistle to the Corinthians: 'The grace of the Lord Jesus Christ and the love of God, and the communion of the Holy Spirit be with you all.' His theme was the mystery of the communion between God and man, and how man could be separated from his Creator by sin. He quoted Bunyan's *Pilgrim's Progress*, one of the books which his mother had read to him as a child, and his notes refer, rather obscurely, to 'Children in Garden' which sounds like an archetypally Dodgsonian theme.

In the summer of 1862 he published in *College Rhymes* a poem with the title 'Stolen Waters' which is heavily laden with scriptural reference, and his only poem on the theme of sexual temptation and the loss of innocence. It leans very heavily on Keats's 'La Belle Dame Sans Merci', and tells of a knight who yields to the allure of a tall, fair enchantress. She tempts him into drinking the juice of a forbidden fruit:

> 'Drink of this juice, Sir Knight.' she said:
> 'Tis good for knight and maiden.'[14]

Under the influence of the 'stolen draught' he kisses her. There follows a very strange passionate exchange, ending in a line which owes a great deal to Tennyson:

> 'True love gives true love of the best:

> *Then take', I cried, 'my heart to thee!'*
> *I plucked, I gave it willingly:*
> *Her very heart she gave to me –*
> *Then died the glory from the west.*

In the post-coital return to reality which follows, the knight sees that the lady's face is 'withered, old and gray' and he flees from her like a 'hunted deer'. He longs for death but is consoled by the vision of:

> *A rosy child*
> *Sitting and singing in the garden fair.*

He realises that he can no longer reach out to the happy childhood innocence of which she sings:

> *Be as a child –*
> *So shalt thou sing for very joy of breath –*
> *So shalt thou wait thy dying*
> *In holy transport lying –*
> *So pass rejoicing through the gate of death,*
> *In garment undefiled.*

He had failed to keep his vow and now the 'garland' of lost innocence can only be attained through tears and pain.

It is a curiously interesting poem, especially as it was written at this time of self-doubt and remorse. It is unlikely that Dodgson actually fell for the wiles of a witchy lady, but it does seem that he may be conjuring up for himself a vision of what might happen if he did. He is telling himself that if he were to engage in a real-life physical love affair, the gates of the garden of childhood would be closed to him for ever. The delights he found in the company of children were more important to him than the uncertainties of sexual reality.

14

'There ought to be a book written about me'

Boating excursions with the Liddell children were a well-established tradition long before the voyage which gave birth to *Alice's Adventures*. Alice herself remembered them happening 'four or five times every summer term'. Sometimes they would set out for the whole day and row downstream to Nuneham, taking a large basket packed with cold chicken and salad, and stop for a picnic luncheon at one of the huts, thoughtfully provided by Lord Harcourt (later to become a member of Gladstone's administration) on his estate by the river. Alice recalled:

> To us the hut might have been a Fairy King's palace, and the picnic a banquet in our honour. Sometimes we were told stories after luncheon and transported into Fairyland. Sometimes we spent the afternoon wandering the more material Fairyland of the Nuneham woods, until it was time to row back to Oxford in the long summer evening.[1]

If the children were only free for the afternoon, Dodgson and one of his companions would take the boat up river to Godstow. The children were not chaperoned on their river excursions, and Dodgson would be accompanied by one of his brothers or by a fellow don. The girls' favourite was Robinson Duckworth, a fellow of Trinity, who had a good voice and was always ready to oblige with a song. The river trips were a rare chance for the Liddells to let off steam. Away from the sober confines of the Deanery and free from the restraining hand of Miss Prickett, they could make as much noise as they wished. Songs and games and story-telling were an essential part of the day. Dodgson later remembered:

> Many a day we had rowed together on that quiet stream – the three little maidens and I – and many a fairy tale had been extemporised for their benefit ... yet none of these many tales got written down: they lived and died like summer midges, each in its own golden afternoon.[2]

Not all afternoons were golden. On 17th June, Dodgson, Duckworth and the three girls set out for Nuneham to take luncheon there and walk in the park. With them came Dodgson's elder sisters, Fanny and Elizabeth, and they seem to have cast something of a damper over the usual light-hearted atmosphere. According to Alice, 'they seemed to us rather stout, and one might have expected that, with such a load in it, the boat would have been swamped'.[3]

To judge from photographs neither of the sisters was particularly stout, but they were in the habit of wearing dresses that were unusually heavy and voluminous even by the standards of that time. 'This was a serious party,' Alice remembered, 'no stories nor singing: we were awed by the "Old ladies".' Fanny and Elizabeth were in their early thirties.

They had got a mile above Nuneham when it began to rain seriously. They stuck it out for a while and then Dodgson suggested that they should leave the boat and walk. Everyone was very wet indeed and they took refuge in a house at Sandford where Dodgson's friend William Ranken had lodgings, 'and if the Dodo hadn't known the way to that nice little cottage, I don't know when we should have got dry again'.[4] The ladies did their best to dry themselves by the fire, while Dodgson and Duckworth walked back to Iffley and sent off a 'Fly' to Sandford to bring back the rest of the party. The day ended with music and singing in Vere Bayne's rooms.

The excursion must have registered firmly in everyone's minds since Alice was to remember it clearly when she was in her eighties. But then, it did provide Dodgson with one of the key incidents for the story which he was to improvise for Alice nearly three weeks later. For the wetting on the river became Alice's ordeal in the Pool of Tears, in which the stammering Do-do-Dodgson became the Dodo, Duckworth the Duck, Lorina the Lory and Edith the Eaglet. No specific characters were invented for Fanny and Elizabeth. They were ranked, rather dismissively, as 'several other curious creatures', although Mavis Batey has suggested that Fanny, as the eldest person present, might have been the Mouse, 'who seemed to be a person of some authority among them'.

It rained again on 3rd July when Dodgson took a Cambridge acquaintance, Francis Atkinson, over to the Deanery, intending to go down to the river with the children. Atkinson was a contributor to *College Rhymes* and was assured of Dodgson's attention since he had been a tutor for a while in the Tennyson household. The weather ruled out any prospect of a boating trip and Dodgson and Atkinson stayed on at the Deanery to listen to the children sing. One of their songs was a 'nigger minstrel' number, 'Sally Come Up', which Dodgson was to transform into the song 'Salmon Come Up!' which the Mock Turtle and the Gryphon sing for the Lobster Quadrille.

> *All in the golden afternoon*
> *Full leisurely we glide* ...

begins the poem which prefaces *Alice's Adventures in Wonderland*. Alice

Hargreaves remembered 4th July, 1862, as a 'blazing summer afternoon'. According to Meteorological Office records, the weather in the Oxford area that afternoon was 'cool and rather wet' and 0.17 inch (4 mm) of rain fell between 10 a.m. on 4th July and the same time the following day. Yet it is most unlikely that Dodgson would have set out on the river in rainy weather – he had cancelled the previous day's expedition because of the rain. Even accounting for their sentimentalising that memorable day after the event, the weather could scarcely have been as bad as the report suggests, or the tale would never have got told at all. Dodgson remembered: 'the cloudless blue above, the watery mirror below, the boat drifting idly on its way, the tinkle of drops as they fell from the oars, as they waved so sleepily to and fro ...'[5] Even Duckworth, who had no need to sentimentalise the event, referred to it as a 'beautiful summer afternoon'.[6]

And so, on what we must accept as an idyllic summer day, Dodgson went over to the Deanery with Duckworth to collect the little girls. He would have been wearing his boating clothes, white flannel trousers and a straw hat instead of his habitual black costume and top hat. 'Of course, he retained his black boots,' Alice remembered, 'because in those days white tennis shoes had never been heard of. He always carried himself upright, almost more than upright, as if he had swallowed a poker.'[7]

Salter's boatyard was by Folly Bridge. Later in the century it was a thriving concern operating river steamers which offered 'delightful summer trips through ninety miles of Thames scenery' but in those days it was simply a place from which boats could be hired, a picturesque and rather down-at-heel spot. Dodgson would have been a familiar figure in the boatyard but finding a suitable boat would not have been an easy matter. It would have to be impeccably clean so that the little girls' dresses would not be dirtied, and large enough for all of them (Alice had been frightened that the Dodgson sisters would sink the boat on the Pool of Tears voyage).

Once Dodgson had found a boat which satisfied all his requirements, the girls were handed to their seats and made comfortable with cushions. Dodgson rowed bow and Duckworth stroke. As they pulled away and set off up the Isis, with Alice doing her best to steer them on their course:

> While little hands make vain pretence
> Our wanderings to guide ...

the children began their usual refrain of 'tell us a story':

> Imperious Prima flashes forth
> Her edict 'to begin it' –

In gentler tones Secunda hopes
'There will be nonsense in it!' –
While Tertia interrupts the tale
Not more than once a minute.

Prima was Lorina, Secunda was Alice and little Tertia, Edith. The children's interruptions formed a vital part of the story-telling, as Gertrude Chataway remembered:

> One thing that made his stories particularly charming to a child was that he often took his cue from her remarks – a question would set him off on quite a new trail of ideas, so that one felt that one had somehow helped to make the story, and it seemed a personal possession. His vivid imagination would fly from one subject to another, and was never tied down in any way by the probabilities of life.[8]

Duckworth remembered the story being told while they were moving along:

> ... the story was actually composed and spoken over my shoulder for the benefit of Alice who was acting as 'cox' of our gig. I remember turning round and saying. 'Dodgson, is this an extempore romance of yours?' and he replied, 'Yes, I'm inventing it as we go along.'[9]

Alice herself remembered most of the story being told in the shadow of the haycocks near Godstow where they had landed to take shelter from the blazing sun.

Every now and then, Dodgson would pretend to fall asleep, or he would tell the girls, 'That's all till next time,' which was the cue for them all to chorus, 'It is next time!' Over the river, beyond Port Meadow, the spires and towers of Oxford glittered on the horizon, as Alice pursued her curious adventures. The world of Christ Church Deanery was never far away from Dodgson's tale. The edifying, moralising poems which the children had learned and recited were subtly transmogrified and anar-chised – Isaac Watts's 'How doth the little busy bee?' and Southey's 'An Old Man's Comforts'. Then there were Miss Prickett's constant reproofs to the children, and to Alice in particular, who was not her favourite: 'You ought to be ashamed of yourself, a great girl like you to cry in this way! Stop this instant I tell you!' And there were private jokes for Alice herself – her ignorance of geography, not knowing latitude from longitude and being very confused about the capitals of Europe: 'London is the capital of France and Rome is the capital of Yorkshire.'

But there are scores of references to which we have lost the key. Who is poor Florence who lives in the 'poky little house and has no toys to play with ...'? She must have been a real person or Dodgson would not have changed her name to Mabel when *Alice's Adventures* were published so that she would not be recognised. Was she a friend of the Liddells or the daughter of one of the servants? And was there a maid called Mary Anne? And were Pete and Bill familiar at the Deanery? As for the gardeners, was Mrs Liddell in the habit of going on the warpath when her instructions were not carried out? Was she the Queen of Hearts, Dodgson's 'embodiment of ungovernable passion – a blind and aimless Fury'?[10] And was Dean Liddell her timid, unassertive King? Dodgson was not above ridiculing the parents of his little friends and the Liddells became frequent butts of his satire.

The party set off back to Christ Church and reached the college at a quarter-to-eight and went to Dodgson's rooms in the Great Quadrangle to look through photographs, reluctant to see the day end. Alice was highly delighted with being the centre of attention and the subject of a story:

> I used to read fairy tales, I fancied that sort of thing never happened, and now here I am in the middle of one! There ought to be a book written about me, that there ought!

Alice was determined to see her own story preserved and not go the way of all the other tales. Duckworth remembered Alice turning to Dodgson, when they had escorted the children back to the Deanery, and saying, '"Oh, Mr Dodgson, I wish you would write down Alice's adventures for me."[11] He said that he would try, and he afterwards told me that he sat up nearly the whole night committing to a MS book his recollections of the drolleries with which he had enlivened the afternoon.'

The following morning Dodgson and Atkinson caught the 9.02 for London and discovered that the Liddells were travelling by the same train. Alice Hargreaves recalled 'going on' at Dodgson, and she would not have let the opportunity slip of asking him how he was progressing. Dodgson spent the journey setting down the heads of his story, and wondering where he should go next: 'I had sent my heroine down a rabbit hole, to begin with, without the least idea of what was to happen afterwards.'[12]

The story progressed by fits and starts through the summer. On 1st August Dodgson called at the Deanery with Augustus Harcourt, a senior student of Christ Church, to ask if they could take the children on a river excursion the following day. The girls were singing J.M. Sayles's 'Beautiful star in heav'n so bright' which must have immediately set Dodgson's mind working. The following day, with the daughters of the Professor of chemistry, Margaret and Ida Brodie, and with Harcourt as fellow oarsman, Dodgson and the Liddell girls took to the water again. In the evening they all played croquet in the Deanery garden. Dodgson should have been marking examination papers and it took him a day and a night's solid work to catch up. On 6th August, Dodgson and Harcourt took the trio once more to Godstow. The girls insisted that he went on with 'my interminable fairy tale of Alice's Adventures'. Dodgson recorded the Godstow trip as Lorina's fourteenth expedition with him on the river, '– the last I should think, to which Ina is likely to be allowed to come'. Lorina was thirteen, but looked to be already a young woman. She had been the first of the sisters to become Dodgson's friend and already she was beginning to grow away from him. In the epilogue to *Alice's Adventures*, Dodgson portrayed Lorina as older and wiser, dreaming of 'an ancient city, and a quiet river winding near it' and a boat 'with a merry party of children on board' and of Alice grown up, telling tales to her own children. This is one of Dodgson's most beautiful and evocative passages of prose, and it must have been difficult to cut it in favour of a less personalised sequence in the published book – where the inhabitants of Wonderland pass in review and their sounds and voices melt into the natural sounds of the river bank and the farmyard which had grown in the ruins of Fair Rosamund's nunnery.

Two days later Dodgson caught sight of the Liddells driving out of the Deanery on their way to Llandudno. The Wonderland voyages had come to an end.

Dodgson continued to tell himself that he 'must try and get into regular habits and a life of more direct preparation for the Ministry', but he was still very reluctant to enter the priesthood and on 21st October 1862, he asked Dean Liddell whether he thought he was 'in any way obliged to take Priest's Orders'. To his astonishment and dismay, Liddell informed him that since he had been ordained a Deacon he now ranked as a Clerical Student and should have taken priest's Orders within four years of becoming an M.A. Since it was five years since Dodgson's M.A. this was clearly impossible and Liddel rubbed salt in the wound by telling Dodgson that he had probably already forfeited his Studentship and that he was 'at least bound to take priest's Orders as soon as possible'. It is difficult to avoid the suspicion that Liddell was not acting without a degree of malice. Dodgson refused to allow himself to be panicked, and he told the Dean that he did not agree with his interpretation. Liddell threatened to 'lay the matter before the Electors'. For twenty-four hours Dodgson saw his whole comfortable existence hanging in the balance. But Liddell gave in and told Dodgson that he proposed to take the matter no further. Dodgson was determined to try and extend his clerical activities as far as he could without actually becoming a priest.

Having recovered from the shock of a brush with one member of the Liddell family, Dodgson discovered that he was in hot water with another. He called on Mrs Liddell to discuss with her an idea that he had of asking the artist at Shrimptons, the printers of *College Rhymes*, to colour some of the photographs he had taken of the children. He met with an icy reception. Mrs Liddell did not wish to discuss the matter. 'I have been out of her good graces since Lord Newry's business,'[12] he commented.

Francis Charles Needham, Lord Newry, was an undergraduate at Christ Church and, as heir to his grandfather, the Earl of Kilmory, a highly eligible young bachelor. Newry wanted to hold a ball but this was not permitted by the regulations of Christ Church. Newry, no doubt, claimed special privileges and was backed by Mrs Liddell. Dodgson, for reasons best known to himself, pointed out to Newry that the ball was against the rules, privileges notwithstanding.[14] Dean Liddell avoided trouble as usual, and plans were halted. Newry bore no malice towards Dodgson over the matter, but Mrs Liddell emphatically did.

For the next three weeks Dodgson was barred from the Deanery and saw very little of the children. Occasionally he would come across them in the Quadrangle, but their meetings were formal and constrained. The girls evidently missed Dodgson as much as he missed them, and eventually they devised a stratagem to get him re-admitted. He had been collecting crests of various members of the nobility from calling cards and envelopes for Alice and Edith, and had made books to mount them in and had written out the names of the families to whom the crests belonged. The children somehow managed to convince their mother that they could not put in the crests without Dodgson's guidance and she was reluctantly obliged to send for him. She was not, after all, likely to stand in the way of her daughters familiarising themselves with the names and titles of the aristocracy into which she hoped they would marry. Dodgson and the girls managed to spin out this activity for several days with 'games and story-telling' taking up more time than the crest books.

Dodgson had hoped to present Alice with her story at Christmas, but it was progressing very slowly. Although the dialogue 'came of itself' he refused to force the story along. He could not, as he put it, 'set invention going like a clock', and inspiration had a way of coming at the most inconvenient times:

Sometimes an idea comes at night, when I have had to get up and strike a light to note it down – sometimes on a lonely winter walk, when I have had to stop, and with half-frozen fingers jot down a few words which should keep the new-born idea from perishing – but whenever or however it comes, <u>it comes of itself</u>.[15]

The pictures, however, did not come of themselves. The problem was that, as he would have been the first to admit, Dodgson's skills as an illustrator were very limited. He had always been in the habit of accompanying his stories with lively if grotesque drawings and in the family magazines he had developed an astonishing aptitude for matching text to picture. The book he was making for Alice had to have illustrations. After all, Alice's very first words in the book are, 'what is the use of a book, without pictures or conversations?'

The Dodo presented no problem since there was a painting of one in the university museum, but where was he to find a gryphon, and how was he to contrive a mock-turtle? The difficulty was that the bizarre creations he had conjured out of his imagination had somehow or other to be recreated by his unskilled hand.

> To please a child I loved (I don't remember any other reason) I printed
> in manuscript and illustrated with my own crude designs – designs
> that rebelled against every law of Anatomy or Art (for I had never had
> a lesson in drawing) ...[16]

Dodgson's pictures offer something that is far closer to the spirit of the text than Tenniel's superbly finished drawings. Dodgson catches the anarchy and subversiveness and sheer danger of the story. The characters he draws have a raw, grotesque energy and a life of their own that is quite frightening. The Mock Turtle and the Gryphon really do bound in the air with a terrible manic gaiety during the Lobster Quadrille. Alice grows to fill every centimetre of the frame when she drinks from the bottle in the 'tidy little room' and the effect is disturbingly claustrophobic. When Dodgson writes that Alice looks down on an 'immense neck which seems to rise like a stalk out of a sea of green leaves', that is exactly what he draws. It is small wonder that the pigeon takes Alice for a serpent, for that is what she looks like, a medieval picture of the serpent in the Garden of Eden, with a human head. The gardeners in the Queen of Hearts episode are quite simply playing cards with arms and legs. They have no heads, which gives an extra point to the soldiers telling the Queen, 'their heads are gone'.

Dodgson's Alice bears no resemblance to Alice Liddell. She has long fair hair in the manner of the pre-Raphaelite beauties Dodgson so much admired, particularly those painted by Arthur Hughes, fragile child-women who carry no sexual threat. In 1863, when Dodgson was still working on the drawings, he bought Hughes's painting *Girl with Lilacs*, which he hung over his fireplace at Christ Church. It bears such a close resemblance to his drawing of Alice putting down the bottle and saying 'I hope I shan't grow any more. I wish I hadn't drunk so much!' that Dodgson must have used the painting as a model.

He seems only to have attempted one picture of Alice Liddell – the little girl with sharp eyes and jet black hair who looks directly out at us at the end of the manuscript of *Alice's Adventures Underground*. Dodgson cannot have thought very highly of it, for he pasted over it a photograph of Alice and the drawing remained hidden until Morton Cohen persuaded the keeper at the British Museum to lift the photograph and find out what lay beneath it.

That Christmas, on Boxing Day, Alice went out for a ride on the Liddells' new pony. On the Abingdon road the pony fell, taking Alice with him. 'I was on my back for six weeks with a broken thigh,' she remembered. 'During all these weeks Mr Dodgson never came to see me.'[17] Since this was the time when Dodgson was at work on *Alice's Adventures Underground* and when his love for her was supposed to be at its height, why did he not visit her? He makes no mention of the accident, and yet on 16th February he was dining at the Deanery with the philologist Max Müller and the children remained with them through the whole evening. Was it in fact the following Christmas that Alice broke her leg? At the time Dodgson was involved in a vigorous dispute with Dean Liddell which could have accounted for his absence. If it did happen in the Christmas of 1862 it was an unfortunate omen for what was to happen the following year.

'Not all days are marked with white stones'

The turn of 1862 found Dodgson trying to compose a comic song 'Miss Jones', while at the same time drawing up plans for his future life. He was 'grievously neglecting means of grace' and resolved to begin daily reading and meditation on the Bible, catch up with lecture work and deny himself the luxury of sleep in the evenings.

> 'I long to do better: the spirit is willing: help Thou the weak flesh for Jesus Christ's sake.'[1]

And yet a few days after this diary entry he was back in London watching *The Trial of Effie Deans* at Westminster Theatre.

Oxford was in an uproar of religious controversy and once again Jowett was at the centre of it. Williams and Wilson, two of the contributors to *Essay and Reviews* which had so scandalised the religious establishment, had been prosecuted and found guilty of heresy by the Court of Arches, the ecclesiastical court of the Archbishop of Canterbury, and Pusey was determined to make Jowett stand trial. By some curious oversight, when Jowett was summoned to account for his opinions, his case was brought not before the Court of Arches, but that of the Vice-Chancellor of Oxford–

> *A Court obscure, so rumour states,*
> *There is, called 'Vice-Cancelarii',*
> *Which keeps on Undergraduates,*
> *Who do not pay their bills, a wary eye.*[2]

There was considerable doubt as to whether this court had any jurisdiction in matters of heresy and the Vice-Chancellor declined to carry the matter any further. Dodgson composed a cheerful satire on the whole affair, mocking both Jowett and the system that could find a man guilty in one court, but not in another. It was called *The Majesty of Justice* and subtitled with a gentle jibe at Matthew Arnold, *An Oxford Idyll*. An undergraduate, in conversation with Jowett, is trying to find out why Justice is not so majestic in the Vice-Chancellor's court:

> *Is't only when the Court is large*
> *That we for 'Majesty' need hunt?*

> Would what is Justice in a barge
> Be something different in a punt?

Oxford's concern for Jowett's heretical opinions was diverted by the celebrations for the wedding of the Prince of Wales to Princess Alexandra. The Liddell girls had an important role to play in the festivities. Lorina, Alice and Edith each planted a tree by the Cherwell: 'Long live this tree,' they cried, 'and may it prosper from this auspicious day.' Alice had sent a note to Dodgson asking him to escort her round the illuminations and that evening they set out into the town with Edwin who had come over from Rugby. Somehow they contrived to lose Lorina, Edith and Miss Prickett and Alice had the brothers all to herself. For two hours they roamed the streets together:

> The mob was dense, but well conducted – the fireworks abundant, and some of the illuminations very beautiful. It was delightful to see the abandonment with which Alice enjoyed the whole thing.[3]

The excitement of it must have had a profound effect upon the ten-year-old girl, for she remembered it all vividly seventy years later:

> The crowd in the street was very great, and I clung tightly to the hand of the strong man on either side of me.[4]

One of the illuminations caught her eye, 'in which the words "May they be Happy" appeared in large letters of fire'. The next day Dodgson drew a caricature of it for her, yet another of his acts of *lèse-majesté*, in which underneath those words appeared two hands holding very formidable birches with the words 'Certainly not'.

It is not surprising that Dodgson marked the day with a white stone. His feelings about Alice were becoming more complex and confused. He tried to set down his thoughts in a poem 'in which I mean to embody something about Alice'. He called it 'Life's Pleasance' after her middle name:

> Child of the pure unclouded brow
> And dreaming eyes of wonder!
> Though time be fleet, and I and thou
> Are half a life asunder ...

Alice was within two months of her eleventh birthday, and approaching an age which, Dodgson knew all too well, frequently heralded the beginning of the break-up of his relationships with his little girl friends. He saw that he would soon have no part to play in her life and it obviously affected him deeply:

> No thought of me shall find a place

> *In thy young life's hereafter ...*

And in a deeply ambiguous verse, he envisaged the end of her maidenhood:

> *Come hearken then, ere voice of dread,*
> *With bitter tidings laden,*
> *Shall summon to unwelcome bed*
> *A melancholy maiden!*

Dodgson is careful to suggest that this could mean both death and a child's bed-time, but the possibility of the marriage bed is inescapable. In which case 'unwelcome' for whom? Was it at this time that the remote possibility of marriage to Alice first occurred to him? The poem first saw the light of day in *Through the Looking Glass*.

Mrs Liddell was expecting a baby at the beginning of April and her daughters were to stay with the Dean's mother at Hetton Lawn, her house at Charlton Kings. Dodgson walked with them and Miss Prickett to the station 'to get a few minutes more of the society of my little favourites'. The girls rapidly became bored with life at Charlton Kings and on April 3rd he received a note from imperious Lorina, summoning him to have lunch at Hetton Lawn the following day. Lunch extended itself for three days. Dodgson reached Cheltenham at 11.30 am where he was met by Alice and Miss Prickett and they all spent the day at the Iron Age fort on Leckhampton Hill. The children were 'in the wildest of spirits'. The following day it rained steadily and Dodgson spent most of the time with the girls in their schoolroom, looking at photographs, telling stories and playing games.

Hetton Lawn is generally supposed to have been the original of Looking Glass House. The view from Leckhampton over fields divided into squares by hedges is said to have inspired the chess-board landscape of the book, and Roger Lancelyn Green once noted that the railway line from Gloucester to Didcot passes over six brooks. However, the chequered ditches of Otmoor, north of Oxford, have also been claimed as the source of the Looking Glass terrain. Miss Prickett herself also contributed to the story. The Rose (Alice's younger sister, Rhoda, who was not, however, at Hetton Lawn) refers to the Red Queen as 'one of the thorny kind' and Miss Prickett's nickname was 'Pricks'. As if to confirm this identification, Dodgson, years later, referred to the Red Queen as 'pedantic to the tenth degree, the concentrated essence of all governesses!'[5] All this was years ahead in the future, but since story-telling for the Liddells was soon to come to an end, Dodgson must have kept his memories of the last precious months with them intact.

Back in Oxford the holiday mood continued. There was a boating expedition with the sixteen-year-old Harry and the girls, but Mrs Liddell insisted that Miss Prickett accompanied them. It must have been a very crowded boat and Harry 'managed to be always in the way, and generally spoiled what would otherwise have been a very pleasant expedition'.[6] Disenchantment began to cloud over the spring days. Alice was laid up with a sprained ankle. Dodgson went to sit with her for an hour but for once she was very far from being the 'child of the pure unclouded brow'. Dodgson's entry in the diary is heavily scored over but it is just possible to make out 'Alice was in an unusually imperious and ungentle mood and by no means improved by being an invalid.'[7] Perhaps this was why he gave her as her birthday present Charlotte Mary Yonge's rather ponderous *Scenes and Characters* which she seems, nevertheless, to have treasured.

Within a few days Alice was herself again and the river excursions resumed, with Dodgson giving recitals of *Miss Jones* and the children, and perhaps even Miss Prickett, singing songs of their own. Then in the Deanery garden there were games of Croquet Castles, which Dodgson had invented and which proved even more difficult than Alice's experiences with the flamingo and the hedgehog. The croquet hoops were arranged as castles. Four of the balls became soldiers and four sentinels. It was, like all Dodgson's games, incredibly complicated, but presumably it was great fun once one got the hang of it. There was another 'white stone' day on 9th June, a river excursion to Nuneham with the children and Miss Prickett, but on the following day Dodgson noted gloomily, 'Not all days are to be marked with white stones' and prayed 'that here, at this milestone on my way, I may begin a new life'.[8]

Suddenly there was no time for gloomy introspection or mourning and probably not much time for prayer. The Prince of Wales and his new bride announced their intention of descending on Oxford and they were to stay at the Deanery. Dodgson had met the Prince during the time he had been an undergraduate at Christ Church three-and-a-half years earlier, and had done his utmost to persuade the Prince to sit before his camera: 'if ever impudence and importunity deserved to succeed, I did'. He harassed the Prince's governor relentlessly, and had even managed to corner his royal victim during a reception at the Deanery.

> The Prince shook hands graciously, and I began by apologising for having been so troublesome about the photograph. He looked perhaps a little ashamed of himself and said something about the weather being unfavourable.[9]

If the Prince positively would not allow himself to be photographed, would he at least give Dodgson his autograph? The Prince had assented. Dodgson then offered to present him with copies of his own photographs. The Prince mumbled a vague reply and 'did not seem inclined to go on'. Dodgson's first royal audience came to an end.

On the occasion of the royal couple's visit in 1863, Dodgson was not considered of sufficient consequence to be invited to the formal reception, and took his telescope up to Vere Bayne's room to obtain a decent view of the proceedings. In the afternoon he looked in at the charity bazaar in St John's garden, hoping that the Liddell children might want him to help out at their stall, and stayed with them until the royal party made their appearance. The children were selling kittens but Alice could not pluck up the courage to offer hers to Princess Alexandra. Dodgson had no such fears and asked the Prince whether his bride would not like to buy a kitten. The Sea King's daughter told him that she had already purchased one, 'which I record as the only remark *she* is ever likely to make to me'.[10] She had, in fact, been sold a kitten by Lorina.

Later, the children were whisked away to play croquet with their royal visitors, providing Dodgson with another scene for his story. There were banquets and a boat procession on the river. All Oxford was *en fête* and Dodgson had a long argument with a cab driver who demanded to be paid double in honour of the royal visit. After the Prince and Princess had left, he took his camera up to the royal chamber and photographed the royal bedstead with Alice and Lorina sitting demurely in the window. That evening, with Miss Prickett in attendance, they all went to see Sanger's Circus.

Two days later came what was to be the last of the river expeditions. It was an astonishing epilogue, particularly after all the excitement of the royal progress, for not only were Alice, Edith, Lorina and Rhoda on board, but the Dean and Mrs Liddell as well, and, rowing sturdily all the way, Viscount Newry. They all took tea together under the trees at Nuneham and then the Liddells drove back with Newry in their carriage, leaving Dodgson to return by train with the little girls and, 'mirabile dictu' as he put it, an unchaperoned Lorina.

Two days later, without any warning, it was all over. There was a quarrel with Mrs Liddell which was so serious that it effectively brought Dodgson's friendship with the children to an end and parted him from Alice for ever. Dodgson's diary has been drastically doctored at this point. His entry for 27th June reads:

> Photographed the young Owens in the morning, and looked over the

The Archdeacon as a young man

Silhouettes of Dodgson's parents

Daresbury Parsonage

'The children of
the north' outside
Croft Rectory

Dodgson's sisters

The garden at
Croft Rectory,
with the
'railway station',
drawn by
Dodgson's sister
Louise

left Dodgson's Aunt
Lucy Lutwidge

above Dodgson's sisters
with Edwin, at Croft Rectory

below left Skeffington Lutwidge

below right Wilfred on his bicycle

The only sister who would write to her brother, though
the table had got "folded" done! The other sisters are de-
-picted "sternly resolved" to set off to "Halnaby & the Castle,"
tho' it is yet "early early morning," ——— *Rembrandt.*

'The only sister who *would* write to her brother'
Drawing by Dodgson at Croft

The Rectory Umbrella

Dodgson as a young man

The Liddell children: Alice, Lorina, Harry and Edith,
photographed by Dodgson
around 1859

Four studies of Alice, taken by
Dodgson at Christ Church

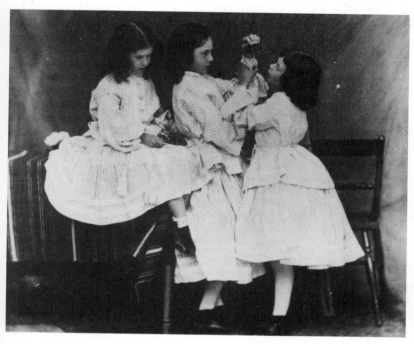

Edith, Lorina and Alice Liddell

Alice Liddell
as a beggar girl

Reginald Southey

Thomas Vere Bayne

Henry Parry Liddon

Robert Godfrey Faussett

Euclid papers from the Ladies' College at Cheltenham. Wrote to Mrs Liddell urging her either …

'Either' has been crossed out and a harmless sentence has been cobbled together (probably by Dodgson himself) to make it look as if the page ends there:

… to send the children to be photographed.[11]

The next page has been torn out and we hear nothing more of the Liddells until 30th June, when they depart for Llandudno and Dodgson is apparently more concerned about trying to get Mrs Acland to persuade the Duchess of Marlborough to let him photograph her children. Dodgson did not speak to the children again until the end of the year. On 5th December, he attended the Christ Church theatricals and noted that he 'held aloof from Mrs Liddell and the children, as I have done all this term'.[12]

There seems to have been a temporary cessation of hostilities on 19th December when Dodgson was allowed to visit the children at the Deanery and stayed until eight in the evening 'making a sort of dinner of their tea'. He marked the day with a white stone, perhaps expecting a resumption of their friendship, but it proved to be only a Christmas truce and he was soon involved in an acrimonious dispute with Dean Liddell.

There is no mention of another meeting with the children until May of the following year when he came across Lorina, Edith and Alice walking by the river with Miss Prickett and they remained together to watch the boat races. But when Dodgson applied to the Deanery for permission to take the girls on a boating excursion, he met with a firm refusal. On 26th November, 1864, when at long last Dodgson presented Alice with the books of *Alice's Adventures Underground* on which he had worked for two years, he did not even bother to record the event in his diary.

What had happened? What was the alternative that Dodgson 'urged' on Mrs Liddell? It must have been a matter of some seriousness, since we know that Mrs Liddell subsequently destroyed all Dodgson's letters to her daughter. The explanation most frequently brought forward is that Dodgson asked for Alice's hand in marriage. This would not have seemed quite so preposterous at the time as it does now. Alice was eleven and Dodgson thirty-one. Although, with twenty years between them they were 'half a life asunder' they were still quite a possible match in Victorian terms. E.W. Benson, the future Archbishop of Canterbury, asked for the hand of his wife when she was little more than Alice's age. Ruskin was contemplating marriage to Rose de la Touche when she was twelve. The heroine of Henry James's early novel, *Watch and Ward*, is all of ten when

Richard Lawrence decides that he will adopt her and bring her up to be his wife. The evidence for Dodgson's offer of marriage, however, is decidedly slim. In the preface to the second edition of *Lewis Carroll, Photographer*, Helmut Gernsheim wrote:

> I learned soon after the publication of my book from Alice's son, Wing Commander Caryl Hargreaves, that Lewis Carroll had wanted to marry his mother but had been rejected by her parents.[13]

But Caryl Hargreaves himself never confirmed this and in fact once asserted exactly the opposite.

In *The Fortnightly Review* in 1941, Margaret Woods, the daughter of G.C. Bradley, Master of University College, wrote:

> When the Alice of his tale had grown into a lovely girl, he asked, in old world fashion, her father's permission to pay his addresses to her. The Dean might reasonably have refused him permission on the grounds of the girl's youth and inexperience, and the discrepancy in age between her and their friend. But Dean Liddell, whose manner was always haughty, rebuffed Mr Dodgson's appeal in so offensive a way, that all intercourse between them ceased.

This sounds little more than a report of Oxford gossip. By the time Alice 'had grown into a lovely girl' she was far beyond Dodgson's influence. In any case, Margaret Bradley did not come to Oxford until 1870 and only met Dodgson twice, once when her mother brought her to have lunch in his rooms, and once at Reading station when he decided that it was not suitable for a young lady to travel alone in a third-class compartment and kept her company trying to entertain her with a series of mathematical puzzles which she found incomprehensible.

Oxford gossip was also the source of the last and most fragile piece of evidence, John Howe Jenkins's satirical masque *Cakeless*, in which Dodgson is depicted as a suitor not for Alice but for Lorina. There is a pencil note in the manuscript in the British Museum which states, '-dgs-n had been rejected'. *Cakeless* was written in 1874 and can no more be considered as 'evidence' than the verse read out at the trial of the Knave of Hearts. Rumour had got its facts wrong again, as when Dodgson was popularly supposed to be paying court to Miss Prickett. Even so, Dodgson had been seen often enough in Lorina's company to set tongues wagging. She seems to have considered him almost as her private property, sending for him whenever she wanted assistance or amusement, and even when she was nearly fourteen she was running races with Dodgson on the reservoir bridge. But he would never have thought of marriage to anyone as mature as Lorina.

If Dodgson really contemplated marriage with Alice it was because she was a child. Like Ruskin he seems to have been alarmed by the sexual reality of mature women. But he may well have considered it possible to slide gradually into matrimony through a long engagement to Alice and somehow cross the yawning gap of adulthood with her and conquer his fear of a real sexual relationship.

It is more than likely, however, that the whole story of his proposal is no more than a myth. What we do now know, thanks to a letter discovered in the Hargreaves papers, is the immediate cause of the quarrel with Mrs Liddell. In 1930, Lorina, then eighty-one, gave an interview to Florence Becker Lennon who was working on her Lewis Carroll biography, Victoria Through the Looking Glass. Mrs Lennon had been trying to find out whether Dodgson had ever wanted to marry Alice, and Lorina was worried that she might have said the wrong thing. She wrote to her sister Alice, the widowed Mrs Hargreaves, who was then seventy-eight:

> I suppose you don't remember when Mr Dodgson ceased coming to the Deanery? How old were you? I said his manner became too affectionate to you as you grew older and that mother spoke to him about it, and that offended him so he ceased coming to visit us again, as one had to give some reason for all intercourse ceasing ... Mr Dodgson used to take you on his knee. I know I did not say that! Horrible being interviewed if your words are taken down.[14]

This does not altogether solve the problem, nor does it entirely rule out the possibility of a proposal, but it goes some way to accounting for what happened. From the outset, Mrs Liddell seems to have been suspicious of Dodgson. Although she was happy enough for him to take charming photographs of her beautiful daughters in their elegant dresses, her patience must have been stretched to breaking point by Dodgson continually haunting the Deanery, arriving at all hours and rushing backwards and forwards with the dirty collodion plates. There were the endless games and stories and songs and the river trips which went on until late into the evening. There was always a fair amount of kissing and cuddling and climbing upon knees in Dodgson's relationships with little girls and he even asked Alice to give him a lock of her hair:

> Mr Dodgson wrote and asked me (for fun) if I would send him a piece of my hair, wrote Alice to her mother in Lowestoft, ... so I sent him really a piece and he told me I was stupid.[15]

Something must have triggered an alarm bell in Mrs Liddell's mind. Dodgson, who always regarded his conduct with children as beyond reproach, would quite naturally have taken offence and remained aloof.

From that point on, Dodgson's relationship with the Dean and his lady moved steadily towards total war.

'Perfectly ladylike'

Dodgson's immediate response to any major disaster in his life was to close his mind to it and seek out something that would occupy all his energies. Melancholy, introspection and self-doubt must be kept at bay. In the summer of 1863 he turned to photography for consolation and to prevent him brooding about Alice Liddell and the rebuff he had received from her parents.

He needed new faces, stimulating company, some kind of challenge. His experiences with Tennyson had proved that the camera could easily open doors to the great lions of the day, and Dodgson left Oxford in search of prey. At the top of his list came the pre-Raphaelites, but at the same time he was eager to establish contact with the theatre and with the Terry family, especially Ellen. He cast about for someone who might be able to provide him with suitable introductions.

In London, on 18th July, he put up at the Old Hummums Hotel, calling on the Almighty for strength to 'leave old sins behind me'.[1] He had decided that the man who might be able to help track down his photographic victims was Arthur Munro, the sculptor he had met at the Oxford Union. Munro would be able to provide him with access to Rossetti and his family, and he was also a friend of Tom Taylor, who might be able to introduce him to the Terrys. Taylor knew everybody and had a finger in most of London's literary and dramatic pies. He was a Scot, a fellow of Trinity, Cambridge, a barrister, Professor of English at University College, London, Secretary to the Board of Health and a prolific writer of popular drama. By way of preparation, Dodgson went to see Taylor's most successful play, *The Ticket of Leave Man*, at the Olympic and a new play of his, *A Lesson for Life*, at the St James's, in which both Ellen Terry and her sister Marion were appearing.

Dodgson had planned to use Munro's house as a base for his photographic activities and to arrange for his various sitters to call there. He arrived at Munro's house in Wandsworth at the rather unworldly hour of 1.30 a.m. but, despite ringing and knocking for the best part of half an hour, he failed to get anyone to open the door. When he returned the following day with George MacDonald's ten-year-old daughter, Mary, as his companion, he was rather put out to find that Munro and his wife were leaving that evening for Inverness.[2] This was only the first in a train of disasters. Dodgson went to meet Arthur Hughes, but the painter had just left for Brighton. When he presented himself at Tom Taylor's with Munro's letter of introduction he was informed that Taylor had been out of town for some time. Since Dodgson did not even know where the Terrys lived, there seemed no point in pursuing his subjects any further. He gave up and went home to Croft.

Better fortune awaited him in London when he returned at the end of September. 'All my photographic victims seem to be available, but the Terrys who are acting in Bristol.' Munro conducted him round to Cheyne Walk where Rossetti received him with great cordiality and offered him the use of his house and garden for 'picture taking'. He also arranged to bring over his mother and his sister Christina for the sitting.

Rossetti had moved into Tudor House, 16 Cheyne Walk, in October 1862, several months after the death of Lizzie Siddal. There was nearly an acre of garden, growing wild, with a vast mulberry tree, planes and limes. Through a wilderness of weeds roamed a motley menagerie of creatures, including armadillos, rabbits, hedgehogs, salamanders, kangaroos and Rossetti's favourite, the wombat, or the 'uomobatti' as his sister called it.

> With such inhabitants [wrote Christina] Tudor House became a sort of Wonderland; and once the author of Wonderland photographed us in the garden. It was our aim to appear in a family group of five; but while various others succeeded, that particular negative was spoilt by a shower, and I possess a solitary print taken from it in which we appear as if splashed by ink.[3]

Dodgson and Christina were to remain friends for the rest of their lives. They had, after all, much in common. Both were shy, withdrawn, over-sensitive creatures who shared a love for children's stories. Both were haunted and hampered by their religious commitment. 'She seemed a little shy at first, and I had very little time for conversation with her,' he noted, 'but I very much liked the little I saw of her.'[4] The photographs Dodgson took of Christina have a quality and understanding which no other picture of her even remotely matches.

Dodgson did his best to persuade Christina to come to Oxford and see her brother's murals at the Union, but Christina reluctantly turned down the offer.

> Delightful it would be, that visit to Oxford. We contemplate it in a spirit of vague approbation. Stirred up by the kind offer of such a

Showman, and by a wish to see the sights of Oxford in general and Gabriel's work in particular: weighed down by family immobility; – we tremble in the balance, though I fear the leaden element preponderates. It is characteristic of us to miss opportunities. A year or two ago I had a chance of seeing Cambridge and of course I missed it.[5]

In the meantime, Dodgson had managed to track down Tom Taylor who received him 'very cordially' and carried him off to see *The Ticket of Leave Man* again. Dodgson, never a man to be easily overawed, lost no time in pointing out to Taylor a whole series of errors in the action of the play. Nevertheless the genial Taylor promised that he would do all that he could to persuade the Terrys to sit for him.

There was another matter in which he hoped that Tom Taylor could help him. He wanted someone to provide him with an introduction to the cartoonist and illustrator, John Tenniel. The artist whose name was to be linked so inseparably with Dodgson's was then at the height of his fame. A reserved and gentlemanly man with the features of an army colonel whose old world courtesy concealed a degree of stubbornness and intransigence, he was forty-four and blind in one eye as a result of an accident when fencing with his father. Appropriately enough, the future illustrator of 'The Slaying of the Jabberwock' had begun his career as a political cartoonist with a picture of Jack the Giant Killer in which John Henry Newman figured as the Giant and Lord Russell as Jack. He was at *Punch* for thirteen years, but was also well known as a painter and book illustrator. He had drawn pictures for Edgar Allan Poe's 'The Raven' and Moore's 'Lallah Rookh' but it was probably his illustrations for Aesop's *Fables* which drew Dodgson's attention to him as a possible illustrator for *Alice's Adventures*.

Dodgson had been considering the publication of the book he was preparing for Alice shortly after he had completed the text in 1863. The situation has been somewhat confused by Robinson Duckworth claiming that after Dodgson had presented the book to Alice it was:

> often to be seen on the drawing-room table at the Deanery ... One day Henry Kingsley, when on a visit to the Dean, took up the MS., and read it through with the greatest delight, urging Mrs Liddell to persuade the author to publish it. On hearing this, Dodgson wrote and asked me if I would come and read *Alice's Adventures* and give him my candid opinion on whether it was worthy of publication or not, as he himself felt very doubtful, and could not afford to lose money over it. I assured him that, if only he could induce John Tenniel to illustrate it, the book would be perfectly certain of success.[6]

This story is almost wholly apocryphal. Henry Kingsley, Charles Kingsley's brother, knew nothing about the book until it was published, when he spoke of it as 'like gathering cowslips in springtime'. Dodgson may well have shown the manuscript to Duckworth, since he passed it to several of his friends, but this was long before the finished book was delivered to the Deanery. The friends who positively made up his mind in favour of publication were the MacDonalds, who received the manuscript in the spring of 1863. MacDonald had passed the story on to his six-year-old son George, who was most enthusiastic, saying that 'there ought to be sixty thousand volumes of it'.[7]

Dodgson first met Alexander Macmillan, who was to publish so much of his writing, in October 1863, through Thomas Combe, the director of the Clarendon Press at Oxford, who was printing Blake's *Songs of Innocence* for him to distribute among his friends. The Macmillan brothers, Alexander and Daniel, had set up first as booksellers and then as publishers in 1843. Thomas Hughes's *Tom Brown's Schooldays* and Kingsley's *Westward Ho!* had brought the firm a wide popular audience and by the time Dodgson met Macmillan the house had acquired a considerable reputation. Dodgson was exceptionally fortunate to have chosen such a far-sighted and energetic publisher. He was not in the least in awe of Macmillan – on the contrary he saw his publisher as a businessman who was obliged to carry out his instructions to the letter. As their relationship developed so did a guarded respect for Macmillan's shrewdness and integrity, and Dodgson would even occasionally accept his advice. Macmillan for his part soon realised that behind Dodgson's constant nagging and obsessive attention to detail lay absolute professionalism.

Macmillan was taking something of a leap into the dark with a totally unknown author, but the terms of the agreement with Dodgson placed the company in a position of no financial risk. The author was to bear all the costs of publication; he would pay for the illustrations and the advertising. All Macmillan was required to do was bring the book out and sell it on a commission basis. Dodgson had complete control and authority over the whole process; Macmillan was simply his publishing instrument.

On Dodgson's first meeting with Tenniel, he found the artist 'very friendly', and seeming 'to think favourably of undertaking the pictures'. Tenniel had, however, a good deal of work on his hands. Dodgson left the manuscript with him and heard nothing for the next two months. He bore the long wait with uncharacteristic patience and restraint and on 5th April Tenniel agreed to accept the commission. The chapters were sent off to him after they had been printed up in galley proof. It is not certain at what point Dodgson decided to expand the 18,000 words of *Alice's Adventures Underground* to 35,000 words, but by now two major new episodes, 'Pig and Pepper' and the Mad Tea Party, had been inserted to follow the encounter with the Pigeon, and the Trial Scene was extended to include Alice's 'Evidence' and the inquisition of the Mad Hatter. Some of the private and personal details which related specifically to the Liddell girls were removed, as was the Dodo's suggestion that the collection of drenched creatures should move 'to a house nearby where we could get the young lady and the rest of the party dried', since this was a private joke about a disastrous river trip with the Dodgson sisters. To take its place the 'Caucus Race' was substituted, perhaps because American politics were much in everyone's minds due to the Civil War. Although the new additions probably had their roots in tales told to the Liddells, they changed the character of the story, transforming it from a private act of obligation to Alice to something more universal, wilder, more exuberant, more deeply anarchic.

There remained the matter of a title. On 10th June, 1864, Dodgson wrote to Tom Taylor, asking for his advice on what he should call the book:

> The heroine spends an hour underground, and meets various birds, beasts, etc. (no fairies), endowed with speech. The whole thing is a dream, but that I don't want revealed till the end. I first thought of *Alice's Adventures Underground* but that was pronounced too like a lesson book, in which instruction about mines would be administered in the form of a grill; then I took *Alice's Golden Hour*, but that I gave up, having a dark suspicion that there is already a book called *Lily's Golden Hours*.[8]

He suggested a number of titles for Taylor to consider, including *Alice's Adventures among the Goblins*, and *Alice's Doings in Elfland*, but said that he himself preferred *Alice's Adventures in Wonderland*. Fortunately, Taylor agreed with him.

Dodgson had hoped that the book might be published before Christmas, but he had reckoned without Tenniel, who was a notoriously slow worker. When he called on him on 20th June, he discovered to his great dismay that Tenniel had not even started. His mother was seriously ill and he was sunk in a fit of morbid depression, since his mother's condition had recalled to him the death of his beloved wife Julia ten years before.

Dodgson did his best to divert himself with photography. During the weeks when he had been waiting for Tenniel to make up his mind, he had secured a letter of introduction from Holman Hunt to Millais, whom he hoped to add to his collection. Millais received Dodgson cordially enough, but does not appear to have greatly taken to him. They did not meet again that year, but Dodgson did call again in April 1865 when he met Mrs Millais whom he thought 'very pleasing and ladylike', which seems a rather curious thing to say. Perhaps he had expected Effie, who had fled from her unconsummated marriage with Ruskin into the arms of Millais, to be some kind of scarlet woman. That July he persuaded them both to be photographed but his subsequent encounters with the painter were not very fortunate. When he presented himself at their home the following year he was told that the painter was 'at home but busy with a model, and said he would be for another week'.[9]

Fortunately there were sitters who were only too happy to receive Dodgson. In 1864 Charles Longley had reached the top of the ecclesiastical tree and become Archbishop of Canterbury. Dodgson was invited to set up a studio and a dark room in Lambeth Palace, which he used as a base to photograph the new Primate, as well as groups of little girls who were invited there. The previous year Dodgson had scored a notable photographic coup when George Kitchen brought over Prince Frederick of Denmark. Now Dodgson decided that he would try and contrive for the Queen herself to look at his photographs, and devised a subtle but extremely roundabout route. He left a number of his pictures with Mrs Read, the daughter of the Dean of Ripon, 'to show to friends'. Among her 'friends' was her aunt, Lady Maria Dawson, who in turn showed them to Lady Augusta Stanley, wife of the Dean of Westminster and a member of the Queen's court. Lady Stanley showed Dodgson's pictures to the Queen who asked her to tell the photographer that 'Her Majesty admires them very much. They are such as the Prince would have appreciated very highly and taken much pleasure in.' To Dodgson's great disappointment the Queen declined to keep any of his pictures nor was Lady Stanley able to arrange a sitting for Victoria's youngest daughter, the seven-year-old Princess Beatrice, known as 'Baby' or the 'Little Butterfly'.

In August, he received news from Tom Taylor that the Terry family were all together at home and would be happy to see him. The house in Stanhope Street stood between a public house and a pawn shop; it was the first permanent home they had ever had. Ben Terry and his wife Sarah had spent nearly twenty years travelling up and down the country with various troupes of strolling players, but now that their children were enjoying a success beyond their wildest expectations, they had decided to settle down in London. Kate, their eldest daughter, had won universal praise for her performances as Cordelia and Ariel for the Keans. Dodgson thought her 'exquisitely graceful and beautiful'. He had adored her younger sister Ellen since he had seen her first appearance on the stage as Mamillius in *The Winter's Tale*. She was, by her own account, 'vain and cocky', boisterous and high-spirited. Sarah had hoped that her youngest daughters, Marion and Florence, might be shielded from the stage and had sent them off to boarding-school to be brought up as young ladies. But she had underestimated the Terry spirit, for both found their way into the theatre.

The Terrys' plans for their children had been blown violently off course by the marriage in February 1864 of the sixteen-year-old Ellen and the finicky, pampered forty-seven-year-old painter George Frederick Watts. This disastrous union had been contrived largely by Tom Taylor who was convinced that it would be a 'wonderful match' for Ellen and a 'most advantageous connection' for the Terrys. 'I was delighted,' wrote Ellen, 'and my parents were delighted ... It all seemed like a dream – not a clear dream, but a fitful one which, in the morning, one tries in vain to tell.'[10] Watts was noticeably less enthusiastic: 'To make the poor child what I wish her to be will take a long time, and most likely a great deal of trouble, and I shall want the sympathy of all my friends.' The marriage was doomed from the start. If gossip is to be believed, it was never consummated and the bride spent her wedding night weeping on the staircase. She was never treated as Watts's wife, but more as an adopted child, and consequently began to behave like one. Eventually considered unworthy of Watts's genius, she was packed off back to Stanhope Street.

Dodgson came into the Terrys' life at the moment when Ellen was about to be expelled from her 'paradise'. Somewhere at the back of Dodgson's mind there lurked a suspicion that consorting with actresses was perhaps not entirely proper, but his scruples were soon forgotten. He found that the Terrys were a family with whom he could feel perfectly at home – with theatrical people he was in his element. He called several times on the Terry family that autumn, telling tales, including *The Three Pixies*, to the children, but it was not until 20th December that he met Kate – 'one I have so long admired from a distance'. He soon met Ellen Terry at the house in Stanhope Street:

> I was very much pleased with what I saw of Mrs Watts – lively and pleasant, almost childish in her fun, but perfectly ladylike.[11]

The day was marked with a white stone.

Ellen Terry has acquired a disproportionate importance in Dodgson's life story as the consequence of the family belief that 'he had had a disappointment in love, and that the lady in question was Ellen Terry'.[12] There have been attempts to build up some kind of love affair, but Ellen

Terry, already sexually mature at sixteen, was a highly unlikely match for Dodgson. Langford Reed, who seems to have read a passage from the diary which has since disappeared, quotes a comment made by Dodgson when he heard that Ellen Terry was engaging a companion to read to her and to brush her hair: 'I can imagine no more delightful occupation than brushing Ellen Terry's hair!'[13] but this is scarcely the proof of an ardent passion. Ellen Terry came closer to the truth herself when she wrote: 'He was as fond of me as he could be of anyone over the age of ten …'[14]

17
'An hour underground'

Dodgson can scarcely have been unaware of the alarming originality of the tale which he had composed, and perhaps we should not be taken in by his casual, almost dismissive, description to Tom Taylor:

> The heroine spends an hour underground and meets various birds, beasts, etc. (<u>no</u> fairies) ...

He had created something that was very distinct from the children's literature that had preceded it by the fact that he had given the incidents no moral: 'I can't tell you just now what the moral of that is, but I shall remember it in a bit.' Even Mrs Sinclair tempered the high spirits of *Holiday Home* by insisting that 'Punishment is as sure to do us good as physic when we are ill.' Dodgson would have none of this. His contemporaries might see children as little savages to be tamed and civilised, but he saw childhood as a paradise to be treasured and enjoyed and safeguarded. He did not wish them to be pressed into becoming little adults; he did not, in fact, want them to grow up at all. Dodgson wanted to share in childhood, to prolong it, and he was determined that his heroine:

> should have that eager enjoyment of life that comes only in the happy years of childhood, when all is new and fair, and when sins and sorrow are but names, empty words signifying nothing.

In Wonderland it is the adult world, as represented by the weird array of characters that Alice encounters, which is badly behaved. Alice does her best to preserve her good manners and to set an example, though she does not always succeed.

The very individual way in which the story is presented owes almost everything to the way in which it was told in the first place. Because it was improvised for the benefit of three little girls whom he knew very well, a whole series of private jokes could readily be integrated into the story:

> 'Once upon a time there were three little sisters,' the Dormouse began in a great hurry; 'and their names were Elsie, Lacie and Tillie; and they lived at the bottom of a well ...'

And because the Liddell sisters knew Dodgson as well as they did, they felt perfectly free to interrupt his story-telling whenever they pleased and ask him questions which would often lead the narrative off in the most unlikely directions, and this too Dodgson wove into the pattern of his story:

> 'What did they live on?' said Alice, who always took a great interest in questions of eating and drinking.
> 'They lived on treacle,' said the Dormouse, after thinking a minute or two.
> 'They couldn't have done that, you know,' Alice gently remarked; 'they'd have been ill.'
> 'So they were,' said the Dormouse; '*very* ill.'

Although the story was told *to* three little girls, it was told *for* only one of them, and what gives the *Adventures* their remarkable flavour is the way in which Dodgson so absolutely identifies with Alice as to become her. Because of the intensity of his feelings for Alice Liddell, Dodgson assumed something of her personality, while at the same time the Alice of his story assumed his. The dream child and the child-adult merge into one personality – the personality of Alice. The story-teller entwines his narrative with Alice's internal monologue, and only makes the occasional sympathetically ironic comment:

> 'Curiouser and Curiouser!' cried Alice (she was so much surprised, that for the moment she quite forgot how to speak good English); 'now I'm opening up like the largest telescope that ever was! Good-bye feet!' (for when she looked down at her feet, they seemed to be almost out of sight, they were getting so far off).

Alice's running commentary on the experiences maintain her, and our, equilibrium throughout her story. If her successive changes of shape and size were baldly narrated they would be as alarming and repulsive as Strewwelpeter. As it is, Alice's cheerful chatter to herself keeps the story within Dodgson's comic framework.

If Dodgson is Alice, he is also Wonderland and in telling his story he is lining up two elements of his personality against one another. Dodgson/Alice is being taken on a tour of Lewis Carroll's imagination. On the one hand we have the spinsterish, meticulous, nervous don who, even when in a state of free-fall down a rabbit hole, would always take the precaution of putting an empty marmalade jar where it could not fall and hurt anyone; on the other we have the anarchic, subversive eccentric who rejoiced in setting improbable conundrums for his colleagues (rather like the Mad

Hatter posing the riddle of the Raven and the Writing Desk) or delighted in running the risk of offending Mrs Grundy.

At the time of writing *Alice*, Dodgson was still going through the spiritual crisis which had accompanied his taking up Deacon's orders and he was constantly tormented by his own sense of unworthiness, haunted by 'anxious thoughts, worrying thoughts, uncharitable thoughts' which flew at him like the malicious sprites from whom the old gentleman shielded himself with the Rectory Umbrella. Dodgson spent much of his life precariously balanced on the edge of the void and it is hardly surprising that he sometimes brings his heroine close to this nightmare world. Alice wonders what it would be like to be snuffed out like a candle and twice comes near to shrinking out of existence. Since Alice was both heroine and audience, she was provided with a kind of safety net, but I suspect there were times when Alice Liddell became justifiably alarmed at the prospect of what was going to happen to her next.

Alice's Adventures is the story of the little girl's quest to find a way into 'the loveliest garden you ever saw' and, though the shape-changing vicissitudes she endures are not altogether unlike those of the heroes of the tales of the Arabian Nights, the creatures she encounters are quite unlike anything else outside the pages of Lewis Carroll.

In the conventional fairy quest story the monsters and gnomes and mysterious old men that the protagonist encounters generally have some positive role to play, challenging, threatening, advising, helping. In Wonderland the characters have no particular axe to grind; they have nothing to gain or lose from Alice, and they are only marginally interested in her. The Duchess's household and the Mad Hatter's tea-table can manage perfectly happily without her. The Caterpillar, it is true, does give Alice some not very helpful advice, and the Mock Turtle sees in her a potential audience for his sad history, but that is all. Moreover, Alice is never in any real physical danger. She has moments of doubt as to whether the Queen of Hearts may really be serious about the general removal of heads, but she can always rest on the assurance that '"they're only a pack of cards, after all. I needn't be afraid of them."'

The dangers which do beset Alice are more subtle and much more unsettling. Alice is an inquisitive, lively, highly self-possessed little creature who is very much the product of the Deanery and of Miss Prickett's instruction. Whenever she finds herself in a perplexing situation, she turns for support and reassurance to what she has learned in the nursery. What Wonderland does is to subvert and undermine the Miss Prickett world and to threaten not only Alice's but the reader's belief in the accepted normalities of existence. Alice keeps up her spirits throughout her long fall down the rabbit hole by babbling cheerfully away to herself what little she can remember from her geography lessons or with thoughts of her cat, Dinah, but once she has arrived 'thump! thump!' in Wonderland and drunk from the little bottle, her fragile confidence deserts her: 'London is the capital of Paris, and Paris is the capital of Rome ...'. Nor can she remember her arithmetic, and her multiplication tables are slyly subverted by Dodgson into what may be for him an abstruse technical joke, but which to her is rather unnerving. Even the sanctimonious improving rhymes she has learned at Miss Prickett's knee begin to take on a wholly individual new existence of their own when she tries to recite them and busy bees become gently smiling crocodiles.

As the story progresses she begins to lose grip on all the elements of her previously stable world. Words no longer behave in the way they are supposed to. When the Mouse in his history lesson (probably taken from one of Alice's primers) comes to the phrase:

> '... and even Stigand, the patriotic Archbishop of Canterbury, found it advisable –'
> 'Found *what?*' said the Duck.
> 'Found *it,*' the Mouse replied rather crossly: 'of course you know what "it" means.'
> 'I know what "it" means well enough, when *I* find a thing,' said the Duck: 'it's generally a frog or a worm. The question is, what did the archbishop find?'

Even Alice gets caught up in the linguistic disfunctioning:

> 'I had *not!*' cried the Mouse, shortly and very angrily.
> 'A knot!' said Alice, always ready to make herself useful, and looking anxiously about her. 'Oh, do let me help to undo it!'

The Mad Hatter and March Hare bring 'madness' into Wonderland, and cheerfully tear up any notion of the working of time which Alice may possess, rather as Dodgson plagued his sisters with the problem of the two clocks, and in their discussion about moving round the table because it is always tea-time, we come perilously close to the problem of existence itself, hanging helplessly in the void:

> 'But what happens when you come to the beginning again?' Alice ventured to ask.
> 'Suppose we change the subject,' the March Hare interrupted, yawning.

At first, Alice allows her situation to get the better of her, but while

Dodgson exposed his heroine to his own vertiginous doubts, he came to her rescue by endowing her with a determined spirit and a rather useful shortness of temper. In her encounter with the Caterpillar:

> Alice said nothing: she had never been so much contradicted in all her life before, and she felt she was losing her temper.

She is furious with the March Hare for offering her wine when there is none, and it is with a final explosion of temper that she at last bursts out of the dream.

Being the high-spirited, lively child that she is, she rapidly learns to take on Wonderland on its own terms and even begins to enjoy herself when she enters into the spirit of the thing:

> 'I know something interesting is sure to happen,' she said to herself, 'whenever I eat or drink anything; so I'll just see what this bottle does.'

In the beginning, Alice is rather overawed by the creatures she encounters. She approaches the Caterpillar 'shyly' but, discomfited by his repetitions of 'Who are you?', she turns on him with: 'I think you ought to tell me who you are first.' When she eventually manages to get into the Duchess's house, Alice questions her, 'a little timidly, for she was not quite sure whether it was good manners for her to speak first', but she is soon proudly airing her not very extensive knowledge of the rotation of the earth. By the time she reaches the Mad Hatter's tea party she is confident that she has the measure of Wonderland and marches straight up to the table and sits herself down, despite the cries of 'No room! No room!' She is determined to hold her own through all the wilfully subversive arguments which ensue, but eventually the wild logic-chopping and the sheer rudeness of the Hare and the Hatter prove too much for her and she stalks off in disgust. She has so little patience left for the Queen of Hearts that, although she replies politely enough to the Queen's first question, when she is asked about the Gardeners she replies: 'How should I know ... It's no business of *mine*.' And when the Queen, whom Dodgson once described as 'a sort of embodiment of ungovernable passion – a blind and aimless fury', predictably screams 'Off with her head!' Alice shouts back, 'Nonsense!' She has all but conquered Wonderland.

When Alice rejects Wonderland and fights her way out of her dream to find herself on the bank with her sister brushing the dead leaves from her face, Lewis Carroll wakes to find that he is, after all, Charles Lutwidge Dodgson, and a gentle sentimental mist begins to steal over the story, blurring its uncompromising clarity. Alice returns to the comfortable, secure world of the nursery tea, and Lorina begins to drift into a dream, glimpsing Wonderland, but remaining safely outside it.

> So she sat on with closed eyes, and half believed herself in Wonderland, though she knew she had but to open them again, and all would change to dull reality ...

Dreaming was, for Dodgson, a metaphor for human existence 'Life, what is it but a dream?' is a theme to which he constantly returns, particularly in his acrostic poems. Part of him believed that the dreamer would wake to eternity in the presence of Christ. In a letter to Gertrude Chataway he told her that the sufferings her mother was undergoing as the result of a paralytic stroke would 'seem like a bad dream of last night' when she and her daughter met again 'in a bright world'. There was also a part of him that feared that at the end of the dream he would be snuffed out like a candle. In *Alice's Adventures* he brought together all the discordant and contradictory elements of his personality into a work of astonishing comic genius. He would never again manage to achieve this singular harmony.

18
'The pictures are so badly done'

On 26th November, 1864, Dodgson finally sent to Alice Liddell the book of *Alice's Adventures Underground* which he had been working on devotedly since 5th July, 1862. It was months since he had spoken to Alice and what might once have been an occasion for celebration was little more than an agreement fulfilled. His inscription 'Christmas gift to a Dear Child in Memory of a Summer Day', carried undertones almost as melancholy as Tennyson's 'In Memoriam A.H.H.'.

The larger work which had grown out of the little book was progressing painfully slowly. In October, Tenniel had at last begun work on the first of the thirty-four pictures, Alice sitting by the Pool of Tears with the White Rabbit scurrying away into the darkness. Scarcely had he begun when he heard of the death of John Leach, his predecessor at *Punch*. A few days later his mother died, and all thoughts of Alice were swept aside. Dodgson wrote to Macmillan:

> I fear my little book *Alice's Adventures in Wonderland* cannot appear this year. Mr Tenniel writes that he is hopeless of completing the pictures by Xmas. The cause I do not know, but he writes in great trouble, having just lost his mother, and I have begged him to put the thing aside for the present. Under these circumstances what time should you advise for bringing out the book? Would Easter be a good time or would it be better to get it out before then?[1]

One thing at least had been settled with Macmillan. The cover of the book would be bright red, 'not the best, perhaps, artistically, but the most attractive to childish eyes'.

Tenniel eventually took up his pencil again and Dodgson went off to spend Christmas with the Wilcoxes in Whitburn. His mind was wandering off in all kinds of weird and wonderful directions. He put in some work on geometrical sections, attended trials for sheep-stealing and indecent assault, experimented with 'a photograph of a new kind, where one person is repeated twice in the same picture' and wrote to the management of Covent Garden with a scheme for organising the arrival of carriages to collect their passengers after a performance.[2]

Easter 1865 came and went, but still the illustrations for Alice were not complete. However, it was now Dodgson as much as Tenniel who was responsible for the delay. He scrutinised every stroke that Tenniel drew with a highly critical eye and was constantly asking him to revise his drawings. Dodgson gave very specific instructions as to the shape, dimension and content of each illustration and its exact place on the page in relation to his text and provided his own drawings as a guide. Tenniel was simply required to contribute his professional skills as a draughtsman. He had never been treated like this in his life, and, very naturally, he resented it. In the past, he had for the most part been given *carte blanche*. Even the mighty Dickens, who could be highly critical of the efforts of his illustrators, had accepted without quibble Tenniel's drawings for *The Haunted Man*, yet here was an obscure and eccentric don whose practical experience of book illustration had been confined to diagrams in mathematical text books, telling one of the leading artists of the day how to carry out his work.

Of course, it was not as simple as that. Dodgson's immediate experience may have been limited but his knowledge and understanding were considerable. He knew most of the leading artists of the day, photographed or copied their work, and was particularly sensitive to the problem of book illustration. He had carefully studied the way in which other stories for children had been illustrated, and in producing his own drawings for *Alice's Adventures Underground* he had seen exactly how text and picture could be most effectively integrated. However infuriatingly petty and pedantic his criticisms may have seemed to Tenniel, however much he confined his celebrated artist in a straitjacket, he was invariably right, even if he was obsessed by the jealousy of error of which his headmaster at Richmond had once spoken. Tenniel would have been deeply mortified had he known that it is only through Dodgson that posterity remembers him.

The one point on which Tenniel and Dodgson never agreed was the question of drawing from life. Dodgson was insistent that Tenniel use a model for Alice and was even prepared to find one for him. After the quarrel with the Liddells, Alice herself was clearly out of the question, and in any case, she was too old, being nearly thirteen. The question of who actually served as Tenniel's model is another illustration of the way in which mythology has often taken over from reality in the Lewis Carroll story.

According to Williams and Madan, who published the first handbook to his work, Dodgson came across a picture of the daughter of the Dean of

Ripon, a fair-haired and very determined little girl named Mary Hilton Badcock, and persuaded Tenniel to make the journey north to draw sketches of her. A rival candidate to little Miss Badcock was Kate Lemon, the daughter of the Falstaffian editor of *Punch*. She would have been a familiar figure to Tenniel and had long fair hair falling down to her shoulders and an appropriate expression of childish wonder. She even remembered how much she hated the striped stockings she had to wear when posing for Tenniel and how she 'stuffed them through a hole in the staircase'. It all sounds a highly plausible story, except that Alice does not wear striped stockings in *Alice's Adventures*, but in *Through the Looking Glass*, by which time Kate would have been fourteen and out of the running. Another girl who has been suggested as Tenniel's Alice is his niece, but the simple fact is that Tenniel didn't use a model. Dodgson wrote to his friend, the artist Gertrude Thomson:

> Mr Tenniel is the only artist, who has drawn for me, who has resolutely refused to use a model, and declared he no more needed one than I should need a multiplication table to work out a mathematical problem! I venture to think that he was mistaken and that for want of a model, he drew several pictures of 'Alice' entirely out of proportion – head decidedly too large and feet decidedly too small.[3]

By 8th May, Dodgson had received a blank copy of *Alice's Adventures*, bound in red cloth. The last three proofs from Tenniel (there were now forty-two illustrations) arrived a month later. By 15th July, 2,000 copies had been printed and Dodgson spent a happy morning at Macmillan's inscribing presentation copies to various friends. Forty-eight copies were despatched to a cross-section of Dodgson's acquaintances which included Tennyson, Christina Rossetti, Tom Taylor, Edmund Yates and the Christ Church Common Room, not to mention many little girl friends and Robinson Duckworth, his companion on the Alice voyage. Alice Liddell's own copy, bound in white vellum, had already been sent to the Deanery to reach her by the third anniversary of the Golden Afternoon.

Dodgson had spent the previous day with the Terrys, photographing them all in the garden of the house at Stanhope Street. He now considered himself a kind of honorary Terry and interestingly when he participated in the children's tea he used exactly the phrase he had used about the Liddells: 'I made a sort of dinner of their tea.' He spent three days with the family and marked each one with a white stone.

On 19th July, Tenniel suddenly struck back. He declared himself 'entirely dissatisfied with the printing of the pictures', and demanded something be done. He had been suspicious of entrusting the printing to the Clarendon Press at Oxford in the first place, and now his doubts had proved to be well-founded. It is difficult not to see in his abrupt reaction some kind of revenge for all the humiliations he had been obliged to suffer at Dodgson's hands. He never gave his *Punch* illustrations so much as a second glance and the pictures for the first edition of *Alice* do not appear to have been anything like the disaster he made them out to be. Nine of the pictures were lighter than those in the printing he subsequently passed and nine were heavier. The remainder seem to have been much the same.

Dodgson was understandably horrified and rushed off to Macmillan. There seemed to be no course open to him but to bring out a second edition. This would be at considerable cost to himself, but he felt bound to respect Tenniel's wishes. Millais, whom Dodgson was photographing when Tenniel threw his thunderbolt, prudently suggested that Dodgson should keep back the remaining 2,000 copies to sell as a second edition. By the beginning of August Dodgson had decided to honour his obligation to Tenniel and his readers and scrap the whole edition. He calculated the cost of drawing the pictures, cutting, printing, binding and advertising a new printing at £600. If he could make £500 on the sale of the new edition he reckoned that he would only be out of pocket by £200. If Macmillan could manage to sell a second 2,000 copies this would cost him a further £300 but he would make £500 and the accounts would be square. 'But that,' he added, 'I can hardly hope for.'[4]

Tenniel wrote triumphantly to the Dalziel Brothers who had cut the wood blocks for his illustrations, 'Mr Dodgson's book came out months ago; but I protested so strongly against the disgraceful printing that he cancelled the edition.' Once he had made up his mind Dodgson was determined that no trace of the first printing should survive. Lesser mortals would have resigned themselves to the fate of the forty-eight presentation copies, but Dodgson would not rest until he had got them all back. A standard letter, though not circular, was sent out to the majority of the recipients:

> I write to beg that, if you have received your copy of *Alice's Adventures in Wonderland* you will suspend your judgement on it until I can send you a better copy. We are printing it again as the pictures are so badly done.[5]

In the end thirty-four of the presentation copies were recovered and these were given to hospitals in Oxford, Margate, Walton and London, including the Children's Hospital in Great Ormond Street.

There remained the problem of the as yet unbound sheets. At Croft

Dodgson considered the possible alternatives. To follow Millais' suggestion might bring down on him the wrath of Tenniel. Could he sell them in
the provinces or abroad? Should he offer them at the reduced price of five
shillings (the edition was priced at 7s. 6d.)? Should he try to salvage 'all
such sheets as appear to be well printed?' or should he dispose of the whole
lot as waste paper? His final decision was cynically commercial.

> To Macmillans ... I saw Mr Craik, who told me they had an offer
> from America, the man wanting to know what they would charge for
> one or two thousand. He proposed sending out the Oxford
> impression.[6]

Dodgson hastily consulted Tenniel who had no objection. The copies were
bound up with a new title page and sold to Messrs Appleton of New York
as the 'second issue' of the first edition.

Alice's copy had been returned so that the new edition could be bound
up in the special white vellum cover. She was drifting further away from
him than ever, 'Alice seems changed a good deal,' he noted, 'and hardly for
the better – probably going through that usual awkward stage of
transition.'[8] Puberty inevitably brought the majority of Dodgson's child-
friendships to an end. 'About nine or ten' he wrote 'of my girl friendships
got wrecked at the critical point "where the stream and river meet".'[9] But
that October he was forced to look at his friendships in a different light.
His brother Wilfred announced that he wanted to marry Alice Donkin, the
daughter of a Wiltshire land agent. She was fourteen and Wilfred was
twenty-seven. Dodgson wrote his brother a long letter urging him to keep
away from her for the next two years. Reluctantly Wilfred took his
brother's advice and agreed to 'put aside the thought of Alice for the
present'.[7] Dodgson was very much aware of the degree to which his
brother's situation mirrored his own. He dined with his uncle Skeffington
at the Randolph and 'had a good deal of conversation about Wilfred and
about A.L. – which is a very anxious subject'. 'A.L.' can only have been
Alice Liddell and Dodgson must have been haunted by the spectre of what
he had lost.

Dodgson received his first copy of the new 'first' edition of Alice on 9th
November. The printing had been entrusted to Richard Clay of Bread
Street in London. It had cost nearly twice as much as the Clarendon Press
printing but Dodgson considered it 'very far superior to the old, and in fact
a perfect piece of artistic printing'. Tenniel was satisfied and Dodgson's
copies were sent out again.

There is no record of how Alice's Adventures was received by Dodgson's
family or by his close friends. According to Langford Reed, who consulted

as many of Dodgson's surviving relatives as he could track down, 'no one was more surprised at its success than Archdeacon Dodgson ... It is not too much to say that at the outset the good man was absolutely flabbergasted.'[10] The nearest we can get to a reaction from the rest of the family (and it is not very near) comes in the form of two letters from friends of Aunt Lucy Lutwidge. Miss Poole wrote to her: 'The poetry caught my eye at once, and it is just to my taste ... I had no idea Charles aspired to be a poet.' Poetry was also the word which occurred to Miss Hartshorne:

> One could hardly have expected so much imagination and such graceful flowing lines from a mathematician: He must possess a great deal of poetic talent besides, and he proves that they are not incompatible with one another.[11]

Of Dodgson's recently acquired circle of famous friends, Christina Rossetti wrote to tell him that she was delighted with the 'Funny pretty book':

> My mother and sister as well as myself made ourselves quite at home yesterday in Wonderland, and (if I am not shamefully old for such an avowal) I confess it would give me sincere pleasure to fall in with that conversational rabbit, that endearing puppy, that very sparkling dormouse. Of the Hatter's acquaintance I am not ambitious, and the March Hare may fairly remain an open question.[12]

Only Christina Rossetti would have described the Dormouse as sparkling. Her brother, Dante Gabriel, came across the book on his sister's table and found himself 'still childish enough to enjoy it very much ... the wonderful ballad of Father William and Alice's perverted snatches of school poetry are among the funniest things I have seen for a long time'.[13]

Sadly, there is not a single comment from any of the child-friends who received a copy.

Dodgson approached the question of reviews of his book with some caution, as if uncertain that anyone would take the trouble to comment on it at all. 'In case any papers or magazines should notice the book,' he wrote to Macmillan, 'I should wish to have copies to keep of the numbers containing the notices.' Most of the reviewers had a large pile of children's books to wade through for Christmas, but all of them singled out *Alice*. There is a tradition that it was roughly handled or underestimated by the critics, but they were, in fact, remarkably appreciative. The *Guardian* spoke of 'nonsense so graceful and so full of humour that one can hardly help reading it through'. The *Illustrated London News* thought it 'a very elegant piece of fancy-work wrought by a clever brain for the amusement and even instruction of children'. 'This is the book for little folks,' declared the *Spectator*, 'and big folks who take it home to their little folks will find themselves reading more than they intended, and laughing more than they had any right to expect.' Only the *Athenaeum* struck a sour note:

> This is a dream-story; but who can, in cold blood, manufacture a dream, with all its loops and ties and loose threads, and entanglements and inconsistencies, and passages which lead to nothing, at the end of which Sleep's most diligent pilgrim never arrives ... Mr Carroll has laboured hard to heap together strange adventures, and heterogeneous combinations; and we acknowledge the hard labour. We fancy that any child might be more puzzled than enchanted by this stiff over-wrought story.

The critic could not even find a good word to say for Tenniel, describing his illustrations as 'grim and uncouth'.

Word of the author's real identity seems to have filtered through. Dodgson told Tom Taylor that the critic of *John Bull* seemed to have some private information,

> ... as he says that Lewis Carroll is 'of course a nom de plume' and adds that the book furnished evidence that Mathematics are not inconsistent with writing works of imagination – hinting that, though in Cambridge men may be dried up by Mathematics, the 'classic atmosphere of Oxford' has something in it which neutralises the evil influence which overshadows the Sister University.[14]

Did Taylor admit the distinction? he wanted to know. Taylor was, of course, a Cambridge man. *Aunt Judy's Magazine* was evidently also in on the secret and heavily hinted as much:

> For the author (Mr Lewis Carroll, of course – you see his name on the title page, do you not?) has a secret, and has managed his secret so much better than any author who has ever 'tried out' a secret of the same sort before that we would not for the world let it out.

The editor of *Aunt Judy's Magazine* was Mrs Gatty, who knew Dodgson well. She herself was a great *Alice* enthusiast and wrote to a friend: 'If you want to have a good hour's smiling do beg, borrow or steal *Alice's Adventures in Wonderland* ... It is the only dreamy dream I ever read.'

The book had scarcely been in print before Dodgson was eagerly asking how sales were going. He had, after all, invested a considerable amount of his own money in the project. 'I shall be very much interested to hear whether you think the sale has made a good start,'[15] he wrote to Macmillan on 19th November. 'I shall be happy to hear how the sale progresses' he wrote on 27th December. He called in on 30th December and learned that more than 500 copies had been sold.

Despite the excellent notices in the Christmas reviews, the book sold slowly at first. By March 1866, Dodgson was lamenting that it was not doing any better – 'Is it likely to sell at all at Easter?' He was concerned that the book was not being sufficiently advertised. Macmillan assured him that the book would not 'drop out of sight'.[16] After two years he had recovered his initial outlay on the book and had even made a modest profit of £250. By the time of his death the book had sold 180,000 copies.

Spurred on by the publication of *Alice*, Dodgson determined to make his first venture into drama since the plays he had written for the Marionette Theatre at Croft. On 17th January, 1866, he took the Terry children, Polly (as Marion was generally known), Flo and Charlie, to see *Little King Pippin* at Drury Lane. Dodgson thought it the most beautiful spectacle he had ever seen in a pantomime, but the 'gem of the whole thing' was the acting of little Percy Roselle. 'Miss Terry tells me he is eighteen or nineteen – he looks about eight.'[17]

Dodgson immediately sat down to sketch out 'a domestic drama, for Percy Roselle to play the chief part in'. After he had drafted the outline he talked it through with his old friend Robert Faussett. 'The main plot is his being stolen away at the instigation of his father's younger brother – his mother (a widow) to be played by Miss Terry.'[18] It has generally been assumed that Dodgson intended the role for Ellen Terry, but there can be no doubt that it was Kate whom he had in mind. Kate was 'Miss Terry'. Ellen at that time was always scrupulously referred to as 'Mrs Watts'. Dodgson plunged into an incoherent account of the drama he had in mind, beginning with detailed sketches of two of the scenes, following this with a synopsis of the general plot and concluding with a scene-by-scene breakdown. The outline of the general plot which was sent to Tom Taylor is so dreadful that it is worth quoting in full. It gives an idea of the kind of sentimental drama to which the London stage (and Dodgson) had become addicted by the mid-1860s.

> An old baronet has two sons. The eldest has died, leaving a widow and two children, girl and boy (the latter of course heir to the title and estate). The younger is the villain of the piece, and an associate of coiners and thieves; but he keeps all this in the background, and acts the upright and affectionate son. He steals the boy, and hands him over to a gang of thieves, on condition of their keeping him out of the way, and assists with a great show of zeal in trying to find him again. The widow sees through his hypocrisy, but conceals her feelings and watches him. When the boy has been missing for years, and is given up – the old man failing – and the villain's plans nearly reaching their

goal, the gang try a burglary on the house, not knowing that their old 'pal' is there. And they put the boy in at a window to open the door for them. The uncle recognises him, and his first idea is to shoot him (under the pretext of defending the house), but the widow interposes and strikes down the pistol, from mere motives of humanity at first, but directly afterwards she finds it is her boy whose life she has saved. I have no distinct idea what is to become of the villain.[19]

Dodgson even had plans for a 'comic element' involving a 'Private Enquiry Office' which sounds more promising than the rest.

Tom Taylor was a highly experienced theatrical practitioner, who had plays running all over London. Dodgson's synopsis was neither better nor worse than many of the plays running at the time and he agreed to pass it on to Kate Terry. In the meantime, Dodgson had decided upon a title, *Morning Clouds*.

Kate Terry did not share Taylor's favourable view of the play. In reporting back to Dodgson one suspects that Taylor was trying to break the news to him as gently as possible. Miss Terry thought the play 'impracticable. The public taste demands more sensation.' Besides, Percy Roselle was not to be had. Some days later, Dodgson tackled Kate herself about it, after a game of castle croquet at the Terrys with Ellen, Polly and Flo. 'She said her opinion of it was that it was weak throughout – not enough action in it for this sensational age – but that it might possibly be compressed into an actable Vaudeville.'[20]

Never a man to be easily discouraged, Dodgson was not prepared to accept this as the final word. The following year he got to know the actor and manager Thomas Coe and he showed the outline to him. Coe professed to be most enthusiastic about the idea and urged Dodgson to 'do a bit of dialogue'. He also suggested (and this was what really interested him) that they should work on an 'extravaganza' based on *Alice's Adventures*. Dodgson never wrote the dialogue for *Morning Clouds* and this seems to have been the end of the play, but, although he did not pursue it with Coe, the notion of a stage entertainment based upon *Alice* was a will o' the wisp which he was to follow for the next twenty years.

'Hypercritical and unnecessary'

However much he sought to conceal it, the quarrel with the Liddells and the strain imposed upon his relations with the children had deeply injured Dodgson. His resentment of the humiliating way in which he considered he had been treated for showing 'too much affection' for Alice began to show itself in a hardening of his attitude towards anything associated with the Dean and his wife. He had always been an instinctive conservative and now he started to put himself forward as a defender of the old order against the changes which Liddell was conspiring to bring about.

Since his appointment the Dean had been steadily trying to dismantle what he saw as the abuses and anomalies which clung like ancient ivy to the regulations of the college. Servitors were no longer obliged to support themselves by waiting at table in Hall, the sacred number of 101 members of the college, commemorated by the nightly tolling of the bell, was abolished. The term 'Student' was superseded by 'Senior Student' and 'Junior Student'. The former very roughly corresponded to a 'Fellow' in other colleges. Students of both Senior and Junior persuasion were no longer to be nominated (as Dodgson had been by Pusey) but were elected in open competition.

In January 1864, Dodgson found himself involved in another bitter personal feud with the Dean. Liddell had announced, without consulting him, that one of the junior studentships would be 'adjudged to the candidate who shows the greatest proficiency in Mathematics'. Dodgson fired off an indignant letter of protest. Liddell told Dodgson that he thought his objection 'hypercritical and unnecessary' but promised to modify future notices.[1] This was not good enough for Dodgson, who wanted the present notice rescinded, and when Liddell declined to do this, he refused to act as assessor. The gap between Dodgson and the Deanery was steadily widening.

Of all Oxford's sacred cows none was closer to Dodgson's heart than the compulsory study of classics. In February 1864, a statute was put before Convocation proposing that classics should no longer be compulsory after their first year examinations for degree candidates proposing to graduate in science. The status of learning in the university was to be further undermined by the institution of a Third Class degree in every school and even the introduction of a Fourth Class, which Dodgson considered 'degrading'.

His first response to the new examination statute was a light-hearted squib which he concocted with Vere Bayne, listing in alphabetical rhyming couplets some of those who would be voting when the measure came up in Convocation. The names were left blank when the squib was printed but no great wit was needed to identify them:

> *A is for (Acland) who physics the masses,*
> *B is for (Brodie) who swears by the gasses ...*

He himself was included as were two of his favourite satiric victims:

> *I am the Author, a rhymer erratic –*
> *J is for (Jowett) who lectures in Attic:*
> *K is for (Kitchen), than attic much warmer,*
> *L is for (Liddell) relentless reformer.*[2]

The zeal of the reformers carried the day, and Dodgson began to have more serious misgivings. On 4th March a letter appeared from him in the *Morning Post* officially announcing his resignation:

> I much regret the necessity under which the new examination statute has placed me, of resigning my present office of Public Examiner in Mathematics ...

The determined, uncompromising tone of the letter is highly reminiscent of his father, the Archdeacon. The abandonment of the study of classics for scientists:

> ... involves a partial surrender, and so is a step towards total surrender of the principle, hitherto inviolate, that the Classics are an *essential* part of an Oxford education.

The hardy perennial of Jowett's endowment came before Congregation yet again and was turned down. It was not until 17th February, 1865 that, after ten years of wrangling, a way was found to give Jowett a decent stipend, and his salary was raised from £50 to £500. Dodgson marked the occasion with one of the most brilliant of his satires, a 'sham mathematical paper' entitled *The New Method of Evaluation as applied to* π.[3] It was the first time he had enlisted mathematics in the service of one of his squibs and it proved to be a highly effective weapon. The paper is prefaced by a nursery rhyme, appropriate to the 'portly don':

> *Little Jack Horner*

> *Sat in a Corner*
> *Eating his Christmas Pie.*

How is Jowett's Pie or 'π' to be evaluated?

> The following are the main data of the problem:
> Let U = the University, G = Greek, and P = Professor.
> Then GP = Greek Professor; let this be reduced to its lowest terms and call the result J. Also let W = the work done, T = *The Times*, p = the given payment, π the payment according to T, and S = the sum required, so that π = S. The problem is, to obtain a value for π which shall be commensurable with W.

The New Method shares Humpty Dumpty's taste for black humour, particularly in a reference to the attempts to indict Jowett for heresy:

> In an earlier age of mathematics J would probably have been referred to rectangular axes, and divided into two unequal parts.

But the paper is essentially good-humoured, and even benevolent. It must have been snapped up eagerly by the Common Rooms of Oxford, for Dodgson swiftly followed it up by another pamphlet in the same vein, *The Dynamics of a Parti-cle*, in which Gladstone's election defeat as Member for Oxford was described in terms of an elaborate theorem. He even managed to introduce an Euclidean romance telling the love of two parallel lines:

> They had lived and loved: fate and intervening superficies had hitherto kept them asunder, but this was no longer to be: a line had intersected them, making the two inferior angles less than two right angles.[4]

It must have given Dodgson considerable satisfaction that no one could have felt the humiliation of Gladstone's defeat more acutely than Dean Liddell who had been his ardent supporter in the campaign. In Dodgson's next university squib, the Dean himself was to be one of his victims.

Liddell's reforms may have been far-reaching in many respects, but they were yet to reach the Senior Students of Christ Church whose position was markedly inferior to that of the Fellows in other colleges. On 11th February, 1865, Thomas Prout, one of the censors, invited the Senior Students, Dodgson, Vere Bayne, and Henry Liddon among them, to a meeting in his rooms. 'We agreed on the necessity of Students being raised to the position of Fellows,' wrote Dodgson, and they drew up a proposal to that end for the Dean and Chapter. A committee was formed to look into the Students' 'considerable dissatisfaction'. It consisted of the Dean, the sub-Dean, the Treasurer and Dr Pusey, the men most likely to resist any change in the constitution of the college.

It occurred to Dodgson that the whole proceedings could be parodied in terms of the Civil War in America, and on the night of 15th February, he began work on *American Telegrams*. The Students' proposals became the *Confederate Platform* to be put before President L, Liddell. The Butler, or general administrator of Christ Church, was Henry Grant, who appears both as General Butler and as General Grant:

> (I) That the almost dictatorial power, held by General Grant, shall be largely curtailed, if not altogether abolished. It is understood that the President himself is so entirely under his influence as to be an agent in name only: a state of things which, it is urged, cannot but be highly prejudicial to the Union.[5]

There is much carefree punning on 'battels' (college bills) and on the 'roar of the canons' and on the name of the Under Treasurer, Alfred Blott:

> That the Treasury shall be placed under the control of Confederates and Federals alike: the Confederates urge that their party is 'inadequately represented under the present administration', and that the Secretary in particular, 'would be a blot in any conceivable form of government.'

Liddell had altered the hour of Chapel in the summer term from 7 a.m. to 8 a.m. and this gave Dodgson the opportunity to introduce another character into his *Telegrams*, General Early, who was hoping for advancement for the services he had rendered;

> This proposal, however, is said to be distasteful to the Federals, and the President himself is so opposed to the very idea of Early rising that there is little hope of its being agreed on.

At the end of February the Dean and Chapter pronounced themselves 'in opposition to the wishes of the Students. They are not prepared to take steps towards promoting constitutional changes of the kind desired.'[6] The Students began to dig in for a long battle. The Dean and Chapter had greatly underestimated the opposition. Christ Church men from all over the country rallied to their support. Arbitrators were called in, Gladstone himself took up the Students' cause and the matter eventually reached Parliament. Throughout the two years which elapsed between the Students' first meeting with the Dean and Chapter and the Christ Church Ordinance (Oxford) Bill which was passed by Parliament in 1867, Dodgson was a voice for moderation and common sense. His particular concern was, as he put it in *American Telegrams*, 'improving the condition of the lower classes'. He may have complained endlessly about the failings and misdeeds of the college servants, but he was the first to stand up for their rights. The problem was that the Butler, the Manciple and the Cook were appointed by the Dean and Chapter and received only nominal salaries and relied on the profits which they made on selling food and drink. This was passed on along the line, so that all the servants were trying to carve a living out of what was supplied to the members of the college. Matters came to a head in March 1865, when the Christ Church commoners presented a petition to the Dean and Chapter protesting at the prices charged by the Butler for, among other things, bread and butter, a state of affairs perhaps reflected by the Mad Hatter when he complained about 'the bread and butter getting so thin'. The 'Bread and Butter row', as it was called, rapidly spread to the columns of *The Times* and soon became inextricably entangled with the campaign for representation. It was to be two years before either issue was satisfactorily resolved.

By the end of 1866, Dodgson and the Liddells seem, as far as outward appearances went at least, to have patched up their feud. Dodgson was invited to dine at the Deanery – 'one of the pleasantest evenings I have had there for a long time'.[7] He had a 'good deal of talk' with Mrs Liddell, sat next to Lorina at dinner and, 'mirabile dictu', enjoyed a 'long chat' with Mrs Liddell's mother, Mrs Reeve.

But he was still brooding about Alice. He was nearly thirty-five and felt that life was running away from him. 'As the years of my life pass away,' he wrote on New Year's Eve, 'the looking back on each, with its wasted time and opportunities, its follies and its sins, grows sadder every time.'[8] Yet he had rarely been more fully occupied. That year he published *Condensation of Determinants* and was hard at work on its successor, *An Elementary Treatise on Determinants* which was giving him 'more trouble than anything I have written: it is such entirely new ground to explore'.[9] He was also writing to the *Pall Mall Gazette* with a proposal for the 'Organisation of Charity', which involved a central clearing house for all charitable causes giving information as to where and how to give for those 'having abundance'. At the same time he was turning over in his mind 'a floating idea of writing a sort of sequel to Alice' drawn from the scraps of stories he had told to the Liddell girls which had not found their way into *Alice's Adventures*.

By January 1867, the 'floating idea' had progressed far enough for him to want to tie down an illustrator. Tenniel immediately pleaded overwork, though it was obvious that he didn't want to be harnessed to Dodgson again. He suggested one of his predecessors at *Punch*, Richard Doyle. Doyle had turned Dodgson down when he made a tentative approach over

Alice's Adventures, but now his growing reputation made him a writer not lightly to be discounted. Dodgson called on Doyle on 24th January: 'He seems willing to undertake it, but not certain that he could get them done by next Christmas. We left the matter unsettled for the moment.'[10] Since Macmillan was not to receive the first chapter of *Through the Looking Glass* until 1st January, 1869, Dodgson's time schedule was characteristically optimistic. He let the idea bob about in his mind, while wrestling with the problem of Determinants and composing a verse satire on a proposal to turn part of the University Parks into cricket grounds. He was coming to see himself as the self-appointed custodian and laureate of the old Oxford, and yet, for the first and only time in his life, he was about to leave its spires and domes behind him and venture out into the wide world.

20
'Gilded domes'

'Received my passport from London,' wrote Dodgson on 11th July, 1867. 'During last few days Liddon has informed me that he can go abroad with me, and we have decided on Moscow!'[1] Liddon seems to have thought it was his idea, for the previous week he had written in his diary:

> Proposed to Dodgson that we should go together to Russia. He was much taken by the idea.[2]

For Dodgson it was an 'ambitious undertaking' since the furthest he had been out of England was across the Scottish border. Liddon, on the other hand, was a hardened and experienced traveller. It was his principal form of relaxation and for some years the country he had chiefly desired to visit had been Russia.

Three years older than Dodgson, Henry Parr Liddon was destined for the priesthood from birth. As a child his favourite game was to preach, wrapped up in a sheet of *The Times*. At sixteen, when Dodgson was writing plays for his marionette theatre, Liddon was already composing sermons and, unlike Dodgson, he had no hesitation in taking priest's Orders, which he did when he was twenty-four. At a time when most of the old tractarians were drifting away from the Oxford Movement, Liddon embraced its principles with fervour. Pusey was by then the most distinguished survivor and Liddon became his most ardent supporter and disciple. Dodgson would have been all too familiar with Liddon's opinions on such matters as the importance of ritual in church worship and of the real presence in the sacrament, since they coincided entirely with those of another Pusey enthusiast, Archdeacon Dodgson. Dodgson's friendship with Liddon dated back to his earliest days at Christ Church. They would walk together, go boating on the river, take tea and talk long into the night. Dodgson even managed to entice Liddon into occasional visits to the theatre despite the latter's assertion that he never entered a theatre after he took Orders. For Liddon the journey to Russia was a mission on behalf of the Anglican Church. One of the underlying objectives of the Tractarian movement had been to try and establish the Church of England on a firmer historical basis, to demonstrate that it derived directly from the teaching of

Christ and the early fathers and was not merely a schismatic offshoot of the Church of Rome. It was therefore of the greatest importance to the English Church to forge links with other churches that were similarly independent of the Pope, and of these none was more important than the orthodox churches of Greece and Russia. Contact with the Russian Church had been established as early as 1843, by William Palmer, a fellow of Magdalen, and in 1863 the Eastern Church Association had been founded. The Bishop of Moray and Ross had visited Russia in 1866 and made valuable contacts with leading church members, including the Grand Duke Constantine and the Metropolitan, Philaret. The purpose of Liddon's mission was to cement these relationships and establish further contacts. Dodgson, on the other hand, saw the trip as a holiday, and had no particular aim in view other than simple curiosity. Like Alice down her rabbit hole he was prepared to encounter anybody and anything, even 'people that walk with their heads downwards'. He was curious to discover whether Russia was still the weird and wonderful world he had discovered in Hakluyt.

The journal which Dodgson kept on his travels is not the best of his writing, but it does demonstrate his customary eagle eye for absurd detail, particularly in the behaviour of waiters. At The Lord Warden at Dover it took thirty minutes for the chops to arrive at breakfast, while the waiters 'hid themselves behind sideboards and dish covers. We agreed that of all a waiter can display, that of a retiring disposition is quite the least desirable.'[3] The Channel crossing was smooth but uneasy. The passengers' luggage was piled up into 'a very successful imitation of the Great Pyramid' and Liddon and Dodgson sought the refuge of their private cabin. Liddon recorded that he was 'nearly sick but not quite', while Dodgson simply noted:

> The pen refused to describe the sufferings of some of the passengers during our smooth trip of 90 minutes: my own sensations – it was not for *that* I paid my money.

At Calais he discovered a simple but effective way of dealing with the natives. This was to answer firmly '*Non*' to any offer of services or advice. 'It was probably not strictly applicable in all cases, but it answered the purpose of getting rid of them: one by one they all left me, echoing the "*Non!*" in various tones, but all expressive of disgust.'

On the train to Brussels a family party boarded the train and Dodgson was highly delighted with a little girl of four who 'hardly ceased talking a moment the whole way'. He made a drawing of her, 'which was inspected by the family and freely (and I think favourably) criticised by the original'.[4]

The family got off at Tournai and the little girl was sent back to bid the English gentleman '*bon soir*' and to be kissed.

In Brussels they attended the Fête du Miracle du Saint Sacrément at the church of Saint Gudule. The service was not at all to Dodgson's liking:

> ... there were generally two things going on at once: the choir were generally singing anthems &c. while the priest went on, quite independently, with his part of the service – and the whole body of priests &c., were continually going up in little processions, kneeling for about a second before the altar (quite too short a time for any act of devotion) and returning to their places.[5]

This was Dodgson's first encounter with a Roman Catholic service. Beautiful though he found the music, and picturesque the scarlet and white vestments of the thurifers, 'it was very difficult to realise it was a service for the congregation to join in – it all seemed to be done *for* them'.

Dodgson's unease and disapproval were to increase as their travels progressed. On 15th July, they set off for Cologne. 'No adventures by the way,' noted Dodgson, but Liddon complained of 'Great difficulty in saving the train at Verviers owing to Dodgson's delay about the tickets.' At Cologne Dodgson lost his umbrella, the first in a series of similar mishaps. In the cathedral at Cologne he had one of his very rare lapses into letting his feelings get the better of him. According to Liddon:

> Dodgson was overcome by the beauty of Cologne Cathedral. I found him leaning against the rails of the choir and sobbing like a child. When the verger came to show us over the chapels behind the Choir, he got out of the way: he said that he could not bear to hear the harsh voice of the man in the presence of so much beauty.[6]

'If one could imagine the spirit of devotion embodied in any material form,' wrote Dodgson, 'it would be in such a building.'

The following day they went the round of the city's churches – 'the effect of which is that I have no definite idea of any of them'. Throughout the whole of their tour Liddon would observe the details of rituals and vestments in the places they visited, while Dodgson only had eyes for the people who worshipped there. He noticed three women confessing at once while a priest held a handkerchief in front of his face because there was no curtain. During a wedding he watched the way in which the children 'ran about the church as they liked, but quietly and very unlike English children'.[7] They had decided to take the overnight train to Berlin, a twelve-hour journey during which Liddon failed to get any sleep. They stayed in Berlin five days, systematically visiting the galleries and churches. Considering the many changes of train that their journey involved, it would have been impracticable for Dodgson to have taken his camera and all its accompanying equipment with him, but he did want to keep some kind of photographic memento of the places they visited. Liddon notes, with just a hint of impatience – 'Spent the greater part of the morning in going about to shops for photographs for Dodgson.'[8]

He was irritated again a few days later by Dodgson's persistence in trying to track down the Great Reform Synagogue, which had been completed the previous year. Dodgson was so enthusiastic about it that they returned first thing the following day. He thought the richly decorated building 'gorgeous' (his favourite word on that tour), but as always, it was the behaviour of the congregation which fascinated him:

> We followed the example of the congregation in keeping our hats on. Many of the men, on reaching their places, produced white silk shawls out of embroidered bags, and these they put on square fashion: the effect was most singular ...[9]

On their way back from visiting the Synagogue, Liddon and Dodgson had the first of many arguments about religious observance. Liddon insisted on the necessity of saying the daily Morning and Evening services. Dodgson 'fiercely contested' it. As if to prove his point on the following day, which was a Sunday, Dodgson went off in the morning to an English service, while Liddon was attending mass in St Hedwig's cathedral, and in the evening declined to go to church at all. He strolled alone in the Lustgarten, watching the children playing, singing and dancing:

> Once they found a large dog lying down, and at once arranged their dance around it, and sang their song to it, facing inwards for that purpose: the dog looked thoroughly puzzled at this novel form of entertainment, but soon made up his mind that it was not to be endured, and must be escaped from at all costs.[10]

They caught the train to Königsberg, but when they reached their destination, Liddon was in a miserable state, suffering from stomach ache and diarrhoea. Dodgson went out in search of a doctor and found a man whom Liddon thought looked like an 'intelligent Chinese'. Blotting paper soaked in mustard, morphia powder and endless cups of camomile tea relieved Liddon's sufferings a little and the following evening Dodgson took himself off to the theatre to see a play called *Anno 66*. He could make out very little of the plot, but was greatly entertained by the antics of a character supposed to be the correspondent of an English newspaper. 'He said "morning" as a general remark, when he first came on, but afterwards talked what I suppose was broken German ... he ended his career by falling in a drum.'[11]

By 26th July, Liddon was well enough to travel and they set off for St Petersburg. A journey of twenty-eight-and-a-half-hours lay ahead of them. They reached St Petersburg at 5.30 in the afternoon of 27th July. Even in the late 1860s Russia was largely unknown to English tourists. Dodgson would have known the principal rivers, mountains and towns of Russia and a little of its history. But of Russian culture it is safe to say that he would have known practically nothing. The only Russian literature that Dodgson might have encountered would have been fairy stories and folk stories – ice palaces and bears and wolves and brave young men called Ivan. The first person Dodgson encountered on Russian soil could only have confirmed his fairy-tale expectations:

> At one station where we paused for lunch, there was a man playing a guitar with panpipes fixed at the top and bells somewhere about it, all of which he managed to play in tune and in time.

Dodgson's first reaction to St Petersburg was one of childlike delight. It was the wonder and novelty of it all that excited him and which shone through everything he wrote about it:

> The enormous width of the streets ... the little droshkys that went running about, seemingly quite indifferent as to running over anybody ... the enormous illuminated signboards over the shops, and the gigantic churches, with their domes painted blue and covered with gold stars – and the bewildering jabber of all the natives – all contributed to the wonders of our first walk in St Petersburg.[12]

On the Sunday after their arrival the pair set off to morning service in St Isaac's Cathedral. Liddon was overwhelmed by the splendour of the ceremony and by the devotion of the people, but Dodgson was not in the least impressed. 'A long argument with Dodgson', noted Liddon. Dogson was prepared to admit that the singing was wonderful and the dresses were splendid, 'but the more one sees of these gorgeous services, with their many appeals to the senses, the more I think one learns to love the plain, simple, (but to my mind far more real) service of the English church'.

However it was Russia, not its churches, that Dodgson had come to see and he was determined to get to grips with it. He had already acquired a working knowledge of the alphabet and with the aid of a map and a vocabulary book, he set out to conquer the city. But first, he must not allow himself to be browbeaten by the local *droshky* drivers:

> MYSELF: *Gostonitia Klee* – (Klee Hotel)
> DRIVER: *(utters a sentence rapidly of which we can only catch the words) Tri groshen* – (Three groshen – 30 kopecks?)
> M: *Doatzat Kopecki?* (20 kopecks?)

D: *(indignantly) Tritzat! (30.)*
M: *(resolutely) Doazat.*
D: *(coaxingly) Doazat piat? (25?)*
M: *(with the air of one who has said his say, and wishes to be rid of the thing) Doatzat.*
(Here I take Liddon's arm and we walk off together, entirely disregarding the shouts of the driver. When we have gone a few yards, we hear the droshky lumbering after us: he draws up alongside, and hails us.)
M: *(gravely) Doatzat?*
D: *(with a delighted grin) Da! Da! Doatzat! (and in we get.)*[13]

Liddon's plans to spend his time in St Petersburg cementing church unity were dashed when he discovered that Stuart, at the British Embassy, had gone back to England. Since he had been counting on Stuart to introduce him to the various leaders, and since nobody else was able to perform this function, there was nothing whatever he could do. His misery was made more complete by breaking his glasses and his aneroid barometer.

Everything combined to frustrate the travellers. They were refused admission to the Hermitage because they were not carrying their passports and when they were eventually allowed in they fell into the hands of a guide who insisted on showing them all the treasures of his own department, the sculpture gallery, leaving them time only to pass through the picture galleries at a brisk trot, catching glimpses of the Titians, Murillos and Raphaels.

On the 2nd August they set off on the nineteen-and-a-half hour journey to Moscow. Dodgson stayed up until one o'clock in the morning on the observation platform of the carriage, gripping the handrail as the train clattered and roared its way through the countryside. He was even more delighted by Moscow than he had been by St Petersburg and reported on it with the same childlike wonder.

> ... a city of white and green roofs, of conical towers that rise out of one another like a fore-shortened telescope; of bulging gilded domes, in which you see as in a looking-glass, distorted pictures of the city; of churches which look, outside, like bunches of variegated cactus (some branches crowned with green prickly buds, others with blue, and others with red and white) ... and finally of pavement that goes up and down like a ploughed field, and droshky drivers who insisted on being paid 30 per cent extra today, 'because it is the Empress' birthday'.[14]

Liddon was still unable to embark upon his mission since his letters of introduction had not yet reached Moscow, but they did run into two men from Oxford, Edward Ware and his brother. The great annual fair, reputed to be the largest in Europe, was in full swing at Nishni Novgorod, and they decided to pass a little time there. Their hotel in the Holy City was a 'truly villainous place', but again it was the waiters who caught Dodgson's eye, even though he was unable to catch theirs. The men, dressed in white tunics and white trousers,

> ranged themselves in a row and gazed in a quite absorbed way at the collection of strange animals that were feeding before them ... Now and then a twinge of conscience would seize them, that they were not after all fulfilling the great object of life as waiters, and on these occasions they would all hurry to the end of the room, and refer to a great drawer, which seemed to contain nothing but spoons and forks.[15]

The city swarmed with Greeks, Jews, Armenians, Chinese and Persians, 'with their gentle intelligent faces'. Dodgson was utterly fascinated by his visit to the Tartar mosque which overshadowed 'all the novelties of the day'. The Muezzin's call to prayer was, he told his sister Louisa, 'the strangest, wildest thing you can imagine ... It ended in a prolonged shrill wail, which floated overhead through the still air with an indescribably sad and ghost-like effect: heard at night it would have thrilled one like the cry of the Banshee.'

In the evening, in company with Edward Ware, Dodgson went to the theatre – what else would one do in the evening in Nishni Novgorod? They saw a performance of *Aladdin and the Wonderful Lamp* which they managed somehow to follow with the aid of Dodgson's pocket dictionary. Back in Moscow, Dodgson lost no time in going to the theatre again, this time with Ware's elder brother. They saw *A Woman's Secret* and *The Burgomaster's Wedding* but neither was as entertaining as *Aladdin*. 'It was all in Russian,' Dodgson commented rather superfluously.

Dodgson and Liddon were beginning to weary of one another's company, or at least Liddon was. He was forever complaining of his companion's late rising (which constantly held him up, especially since his letters of introduction had arrived) and probably did not much share his taste for roundabouts and Tyrolean singers. They argued continually – about prayers for the departed and about the character of Russian religion which Dodgson found 'too external'. When the day came for them to visit the Monastery of the New Jerusalem at Kryukovo, Liddon took no chances, and had Dodgson woken at 6 a.m. Even then their journey was delayed, partly because the railway line had not been completed, and partly because Dodgson insisted on sketching a peasant's hut. By the time they eventually reached the monastery there was no hope of them being able to return to Moscow that night, and they were forced to spend the night at an inn. Their landlord 'who seems to be a little the worse for drink, and a good deal out of his mind', kept on coming in during dinner and at intervals throughout the night to shake their hands and assure them of his undying friendship. Since they had to rise at 3 a.m. to return to St Petersburg, they can have had very little sleep.

They journeyed home through Warsaw, and Breslau, where Dodgson lingered outside the playground of a girls' school wishing he had brought his camera. At Dresden he was so sated with sight-seeing that 'two hours gazing' in the picture gallery was enough for him. Only the Sistine Madonna seems to have awakened any interest at all. At Giessen he found another waiter to add to his collection:

> 'Coffee!' he exclaimed delightedly, catching at the word as if it were a really original idea, 'ah, coffee – very nice. And eggs. Ham with your eggs? Very nice.' – 'if we can have it broiled,' I said. 'Boiled?' the waiter repeated with an incredulous smile. 'No, not boiled,' I explained, 'broiled.' The waiter put aside this distinction as trivial, 'yes, yes, ham,' he repeated, reverting to his favourite idea. 'Yes, ham,' I said, 'but how cooked?' 'Yes, yes, how cooked,' the waiter replied with the carelessness of one who assents to a proposition more from good nature than from a real conviction of its truth.[16]

They journeyed down the Rhine by steamer to Bingen where they caught a train for Paris. Dodgson was captivated by Paris. After seeing the Tuileries and the Champs Elysées, he could 'wonder no more that Parisians call London "triste".' He went to the Théâtre Vaudeville where he was entranced by 'Mdlle. Camille, who could not have been more than 6 years old', and the Opéra Comique where he saw Thomas's *Mignon* – 'a very pretty spectacle, with charming music and singing – the heroine Mdme Galli-Marie, contributing a very large share to both departments of beauty'. Liddon, meanwhile, was having long discussions on the Pan–Anglican Synod with colleagues at the Hotel Chatham.

The passage home was smooth, uneventful and moonlit. 'Not a single person was ill,' observed Liddon. Dodgson spent most of his time in the bow, chatting with the sailors and watching the lights of Dover drawing nearer, 'as if the old land were opening its arms to receive its homeward bound children'. His first tour abroad was also to be his last, which seems a pity. He had shown a natural aptitude for travel, coping cheerfully with uncomfortable trains and dirty hotels, tedious guides and intransigent *droshky* drivers. He had also seemed at ease with foreign languages. Yet he was never again to venture further than Jersey. There is really no satisfactory explanation for this. The duties he was to assume the following year as head of the family would have initially ruled out foreign travel, and then, as the years passed, his growing affection for the English seaside put all thoughts of crossing the Channel out of his mind. The Isle of Wight and Eastbourne offered him all that he needed by way of a holiday: a place where he could concentrate on his writing and where he could observe and collect little girls. Travelling abroad constituted too much of a distraction and got in the way of what he really wanted to do:

> It would be a very pleasant thing to do: but I can see no prospect of ever going outside England again [he told Mrs MacDonald in 1892, when she invited him to join the family in Bordighera] and more and more I grudge the hours that _must_ be given to so many other things, when I would like to work 24 hours a day, at the books that I have on hand, nearly done, or half done, or only begun.[17]

'A tale begun in other days'

While they were in Moscow Dodgson had prevailed upon Liddon to write to his old friend W.M. Capes asking him whether he could check through the proofs of the French edition of *Alice's Adventures*, for Alice was about to follow in her creator's footsteps and make her first venture into the Continent. The idea of putting *Alice* into French and German had first occurred to Dodgson in August 1866:

> The verses would be a great difficulty, as I fear if the originals are not known in France, the parodies would be unintelligible.[1]

The great problem was how to find a sympathetic translator. Macmillan was unable to come up with any useful suggestions, and it was Dodgson himself who discovered Henri Bué, the son of the Taylorean Teacher of French at Oxford. Bué completed the work in two months. Dodgson was all too well aware that his own meagre understanding of French would not be up to the task of assessing the translation, which was why Capes had been called in. He took the additional precaution of sending a set of proofs to George du Maurier, the illustrator and cartoonist, for his opinion of the songs.

It was Dodgson's aunt, Caroline Hume, who found a German translator for him. Antonie Zimmermann was a teacher and proved more than equal to the task. 'I think there will be no name to alter other than the name of the Lizard which I wanted changed from 'Bill' to some German name,'[2] wrote Dodgson. 'Bill' eventually became 'Wabbel' and Father William – for fear of giving offence to the Kaiser – was transformed into 'Vater Martin'.

For the Italian version, Dodgson approached a cousin of the Rossettis, Teodorico Piettracola-Rossetti, who had made a translation of Christina's *Goblin Market*. *Le Avventure d'Alice Nel Paese Delle Meraviglie* appeared in 1872 with even the ticket in the Mad Hatter's hat rendered into Italian: 'Prezzo fisso L12'.

While Alice was improving her geography and discovering that Paris was not the capital of Rome, Dodgson was himself exploring new territory.

Before setting out for Russia he had written a little story called 'Bruno's Revenge' which Mrs Gatty, who had written such a gushing review of *Alice's Adventures*, published in *Aunt Judy's Magazine*. She was even more enthusiastic about 'Bruno's Revenge' than she had been about *Alice*. She told Dodgson that it was:

> BEAUTIFUL and fantastic and child-like ... Some of the touches are so exquisite, one would have thought nothing short of intercourse with fairies could have put them into your head.[3]

She wanted the story to be the first of a series. 'You have great mathematical abilities,' she informed him, 'but so have hundreds of others. This talent is peculiarly your own, and as an Englishman you are almost unique in possessing it.' Dodgson himself suspected that the piece might serve 'as a nucleus of a larger story' but for the moment he did nothing. It would be twenty years before the story resurfaced as part of the vast, incoherent assembly that was *Sylvie and Bruno*.

At the same time as he was writing his sentimental little fairy tale, Dodgson was engaged in *Through the Looking Glass* and he seems to have been utterly incapable of distinguishing between the merits of his two projects. Self-criticism was not his strong point at the best of times but over everything concerned with *Sylvie and Bruno* he seems to have had an absolute blind spot. What Mrs Gatty had described as 'intercourse with fairies' had a disastrous effect upon his writing. 'I don't much care about fairies, as a general rule,' he told his friend Helen Feilden. But once the notion of fairy-writing had taken hold of him, there was no stopping it. Dymphna Ellis, the ten-year-old daughter of the Vicar of Cranbourne, received, with her copy of *Aunt Judy's Magazine*, a letter, written in microscopic handwriting from 'your affectionate little fairy-friend, Sylvie'. Sylvie took up her tiny pen again to write to Dolly Argles, daughter of the Rector of Barnack, who had written to Dodgson asking what he looked like. Sylvie told her that she was enclosing a photograph –

> ... so that you needn't wonder any more what he is like, and he hopes you will send him one of *yourself*. (He says I oughtn't to have put in that last bit: he meant the sentence to end at 'is like'). Next, he wants very much to know how old you are. I told him it was rude to ask a lady's age, but he only said, Oh, she's very young, and she won't mind.[4]

Dodgson was working on a new book of verse, *Phantasmagoria*, a collection (intended for adults) of his comic and serious poems, most of which had already appeared in *The Train* and various other periodicals. The title poem is one of Dodgson's most attractive and light-hearted productions. It is the story of a haunting. Ghosts held an irresistible appeal for Dodgson – he was one of the original Charter Members of the Society for Psychical Research and accumulated a collection of books on the subject, Lee's *Other World*, Christmas's *Phantom World*, Home's *Light and Shadows of Spiritualism* and the *History of Apparitions*. The poem abounds in Carrollean touches. Houses are classified by ghosts on a Good Haunt Guide principle and there is even an 'Inn-Spectre' who reports on the standard of accommodation and the quality of the wine and food:

> You'll find the bread improved, I think,
> By getting better flour:
> And have you anything to drink
> That looks a little *less like ink*,
> And isn't quite *so sour?*

Through the Looking Glass was making slow progress, but Dodgson was still bogged down over the question of who should do the pictures. Doyle was no longer 'good enough', he told Mrs MacDonald, 'and Arthur Hughes has not, so far as I know, any turn for the grotesque'. 'Bab' (W.S. Gilbert) was certainly not lacking in his talent for the grotesque, 'but I have seen no symptoms of his being able to draw anything pretty and graceful'.[5] Fortunately he did not pursue the idea – the prospect of a collaboration between the irascible Gilbert and the inflexible Dodgson is too horrific to contemplate. Macmillan suggested Noel Paton, who had provided the frontispiece for *The Water Babies*, but Paton was too busy – 'my cup of occupation is already filled to the brim'. Eventually Dodgson decided to call Tenniel's bluff. If *Punch* really was claiming all of his time, Dodgson would buy him out for five months at a cost of £200. Tenniel reluctantly gave way. He would do the pictures, but only in his own time. 'He thinks it possible (but not likely)' Dodgson noted in his diary, 'that we might get it out by Christmas 1869.'[6]

Meanwhile, the 'bits and pieces' of the story were gradually becoming a book. The composition of *Through the Looking Glass* has fallen victim to the mythologising process which dogs so much of the Lewis Carroll legend. In 1932, Alice Theodora Raikes, a distant cousin, staked her claim to the origin of the story:

> As children we lived in Onslow Square and used to play in the garden behind the house. Charles Dodgson used to stay with an old uncle there, and walk up and down, his hands behind him, on the strip of lawn. One day, hearing my name, he called me to him, saying, 'So you are another Alice. I'm very fond of Alices. Would you like to come and see something which is rather puzzling?'[7]

He took her into the house and stood her near the tall mirror which stood in the corner of a room opening out onto the garden.

> 'Now,' he said, giving me an orange, 'first tell me which hand you have got that in.' 'The right,' I said. 'Now,' he said, 'go and stand before that glass, and tell me which hand the little girl you see there has got the orange in.' After some perplexed contemplation, I said, 'The left hand.' 'Exactly,' he said, 'and how do you explain that?' I couldn't explain it, but seeing that some solution was expected, I ventured, 'If I was on the *other* side of the glass, wouldn't the orange still be in my right hand?' I can remember his laugh. 'Well done, little Alice,' he said. 'The best answer I've had yet.'

This, she claimed, was what gave Dodgson his first idea for *Through the Looking Glass*, but his final remark suggests that this was a test to which he had subjected several little girls. In any case, he records his first meeting with Alice Raikes as taking place in the gardens by Uncle Skeffington's house in Onslow Square on 24th June, 1871, by which time he had already handed the complete text of the book to Macmillan. It is just possible that Dodgson made her acquaintance much earlier. Skeffington Lutwidge moved into the house in the spring of 1866 and Dodgson stayed there for the first time two years later, when Alice Raikes would have been eight. Even if this were so, it would still have been a very late stage for their meeting to have such a fundamental effect on a book which was already sufficiently advanced for him to have had discussions with several illustrators.

The story belongs unquestionably to Alice Liddell. By 1870 he was already exploring the possibility of binding her presentation copy with an oval piece of mirror glass let into the cover. The book evolved from memories of stories told to her and her sisters on those far-away days on the river, of bringing chessmen to life when he was teaching the sisters how to play the game, of rowing lessons calling 'Feather! Feather!' and jokes about catching dear little crabs. The two younger Liddells also found their way into the Garden of Live Flowers, Violet as the flower which bore her name – 'I never saw anybody that looked stupider', she said of Alice and Rhoda as the Rose – 'Her face has got *some* sense in it, though it's not a clever one!'

Behind the Looking Glass and what Alice found there, as the book was then called, is a winter story:

> *Without, the whirling wind and snow,*
> *The storm-wind's moody madness –*
> *Within, the firelight's ruddy glow,*
> *And childhood's nest of gladness.*

However much individual episodes of the book stem from memories of past happiness, they are clouded over by the melancholy which had overtaken his relationship with his 'dream child'. The poem which he had written while she was still a child and which now prefaced the book had proved all too prophetically true. They were now 'half a life asunder' and the lines:

> *I have not seen thy sunny face,*
> *Nor heard thy silver laughter*

had come to describe their situation exactly. Alice had other admirers now. Ruskin was her drawing master and Benjamin Jowett made frequent portly calls at the Deanery.

Images of decay, mutability and fading beauty haunt the pages of the book. Insects fly into candles, rushes fade and lose their beauty when they are plucked, Alice loses her own identity in the wood 'where things have no names' and is told by Tweedledee that she may not exist at all, that she may be only 'a sort of thing' in the Red King's dream.

Dodgson wanted restored to him the little girl he had fallen in love with when she was not yet ten. No one girl appeared to take Alice's place. In her stead were dozens of child-friends, daughters of Oxford dons or friends from Croft or Ripon whom he entertained with games and stories and invariably photographed. Not that all of Dodgson's little friends were the daughters of dons or clergymen. Occasionally he would be confronted with perfectly charming children from the lower-middle classes or even those whose parents were in trade. He was prepared to play with them and take their photographs, but they were not likely to be taken to the theatre or receive letters from him. Dodgson was excessively class-conscious and he became increasingly so as he grew older. He had a strong sense of the Victorian hierachy, and felt ill at ease in company with what he considered to be the lower classes. He had to set strict limits to his friendship with little girls who were liable to drop their 'h's. But there was one area where he could happily put aside distinction of class, and that was in the theatre. It was the little Terrys who had introduced him to the wonderful world of stage-children, but in 1867 Thomas Coe, the theatre manager to whom he had shown *Morning Clouds*, invited him 'behind the scenes' at a performance of *Living Miniatures*, in which all the players were children. Such an opportunity had never come Dodgson's way before and he cancelled three lectures so that he could make the most of it.

He was given the freedom of the theatre and found himself perfectly at home, elated at being backstage for the first time, finding his way to the green room, watching the little actresses being carried downstairs from their dressing room – 'I suppose to keep them from the dust of the narrow stairs'. He was taken under the stage and shown the working of the theatrical machinery. He watched the children rehearsing their songs and dances and was charmed by the 'picturesqueness' of the little fairies in their muslin and spangles 'wandering about among the carpenters and scene shifters'.[8]

He was so enthusiastic about the 'sperience' that he sat down and wrote a long letter to his brother Edwin describing it all in excited detail, even though, somewhere in the back of his mind there lurked the suspicion that this was not the kind of thing a man of the cloth, even though only in Deacon's Orders, ought to be doing:

> I did not try to make acquaintance with the children (except the smallest 2 fairies), thinking that, as they are only poor children, and not in the profession, they would not be the better for being noticed and made to think much of themselves – though certainly I never saw such clever little things – the sharpest of the sharp race of London children. They had very nice manners, and talked extremely well. In fact you might introduce most of them into a drawing room without anyone guessing their lowly birth.[9]

It was the ambiguity of the children's social position which intrigued him. In many ways stage children were ideally suited to be Dodgson's companions. It was their vigour of life which appealed to him, 'the intensity with which they enjoyed everything, great or small, which came their way'. And there were other advantages. Their parents were not likely to object if the author of *Alice's Adventures* took them out unchaperoned, or occasionally put them upon his knee. The closest there ever was to a successor to Alice – though she was not to put in an appearance for another twenty years – was to be one of the enchanted race of theatre children.

By the beginning of 1868, Dodgson had evidently begun to come to terms with himself. His New Year entry in his diary reveals a new confidence and assurance:

> A year of great blessings and few trials, of much weakness and sin; yet I trust I have learned to know myself better, and have striven (yet how feebly and ineffectually) to live nearer to God.[10]

The diary contains no more cries of anguish or prayers to be delivered from the sins of the flesh. A calmer, more self-possessed Dodgson had come into being. It was just as well, for trials lay ahead.

Dodgson was so preoccupied with his life in London and Oxford that year that he did not go back to Croft at Easter, but spent his time pottering about the London galleries. A splendid set of rooms had become available at Christ Church and he was planning what alterations might be necessary before he moved in. Would it be possible to erect a 'photographing room' on the roof above?

On 21st June, 1868, the work of the summer term being ended and the Moderation examination list drawn up, he went off to see a burlesque of *Romeo and Juliet* at St John's College. That evening his father died of a sudden illness at Croft, so unexpectedly that his sisters had no time to send a message to Christ Church to summon their brother home.

> This was a terrible shock for him [wrote his nephew] his father had been his ideal of what a Christian gentleman should be, and it seemed to him at first as if a cloud had settled on his life which could never be dispelled.[11]

The fact that he had not gone back to Croft that Easter must have weighed heavily on his conscience, as he set out on the long journey northward, and the realisation that at the hour of his father's death he was laughing at a college burlesque can only have increased his guilt. He had disappointed the Archdeacon by his refusal to take up the priesthood and the gap between them must have been widened by his growing antipathy towards those High Church attitudes of which his father was the embodiment.

The Archdeacon had come to put all his hopes on Skeffington who, after a long and determined struggle to get his degree, had been ordained at Ripon in 1865 and had worked as his father's curate at Croft. 'He is my chief present care,' the Archdeacon had written to his aunt Mary Smedley in 1866, 'and I feel that I wish to live for him more than for any of the others.'[12]

The Archdeacon had died as the result of a severe attack of diarrhoea, which carried him off in a few hours, but there are signs that he had already lost much of his earlier vigour and determination, and in photographs he appears melancholy, weary and rather crumpled. Dodgson described his father's death as 'the greatest blow that has ever fallen on my life', but at least he was able to put his grief into words. Confronted with the death of his mother he had been incapable of facing it and had taken refuge in the everyday trivialities of college life, behaving as if nothing had happened. At his father's death he was able to mourn openly, and even managed to derive some comfort, as the Archdeacon himself might have done, from a religious text.

> In those solemn days, when we used to steal, one by one, into a darkened room, to take yet another look at the dear calm face, and to pray for strength, the one feature in the room that I remember was a

framed text, illuminated by one of my sisters, 'Then they are glad, because they are at rest; and so he bringeth them into the heaven where they would be.'[13]

The text was carved upon the Archdeacon's tomb by the south wall of the chancel where he was buried beside Frances Jane.

Scarcely had the family begun to recover from the shock of the death of their father, than they received news of the death of his defender and benefactor, Archbishop Longley. 'No one could have known him who is thus suddenly removed from us without loving him,' Dodgson wrote to the Archbishop's son. 'One ground of sympathy I can claim – our own recent loss – which to *me* had brought the unseen world more near, and made death less awful, than I have ever felt before.'[14]

But although the Christian in Dodgson may have come to terms with the horror of death, the man who lay awake through the night wrestling with doubt and temptation had not. Death had only been driven underground.

'Inclining to the neighbourhood of Guildford'

'May God help me to be a real comfort to the dear ones around me!' Overnight Dodgson had become the head of a family which was not only very large, but which was almost wholly without the means of supporting itself. Very little had changed in the lives of the family since they had first moved into Croft Rectory in the autumn of 1843. The seven sisters, from Fanny who was forty, to Henrietta who was twenty-five, had occupied themselves running the house, teaching at the school, paying calls and carrying out works of charity as if life at Croft would never have an end. Mary spent much of her time trying to colour photographs, Louisa was a talented mathematician, but none of the sisters was capable of earning her own living, nor would they have considered it proper to do so.

The youngest son, Edwin Heron, twenty-two at the time of his father's death, had not yet settled upon a career and he too was a permanent resident at the Rectory. Skeffington had failed to find a suitable curacy outside his father's parish. And there was Lucy Lutwidge, now sixty-five, who had lived with the family since the death of her sister. Apart from Dodgson himself, only Wilfred Longley, thirty, still waiting for Alice Donkin to be old enough to marry him, and working in estate management, was entirely self-supporting.

None of them could have anticipated that the Archdeacon would die so suddenly and with so little warning. To make matters worse, the Rectory had to be vacated as soon as possible to make way for the new incumbent, Mr Law. There was no hope of Dodgson finding them all a 'common home', however humble, by the end of August, and it was decided that Elizabeth, Caroline and perhaps Fanny should take lodgings in Croft, while the rest of the family went off to stay with their numerous relations in Whitburn and Scarborough.

Dodgson's first concern was to find a position for Edwin. Always prepared to make use of anyone of whom he had the least acquaintance, he wrote to the Home Secretary, Gathorne Hardy, whose photograph he had taken at Christ Church the previous year, in the hope that he might smooth the path for his brother to put down his name for an examination for a

Clerkship in the Board of Trade. A suitable curacy for Skeffington would have to wait until his sisters had chosen where they wanted to live.

Fanny and her sisters came to a revolutionary conclusion: they would leave the north for good and set up a new family home together somewhere in the home counties. Their thoughts were 'inclining to the neighbourhood of Guildford'.[1] The town was relatively easy to reach by train from both Oxford and London. It was not so close to Oxford as to threaten Dodgson's privacy, but close enough for holidays and emergencies. Surbiton, where there were Wilcox cousins, was not far. Uncle Hassard lived in Putney, Menella Smedley in Ealing and in London there was Uncle Skeffington, so that the sisters would still be close to the Dodgson, Lutwidge and Wilcox family network.

Dodgson, accompanied by Wilfred, set off for Guildford on 13th August. At that time it was a relatively small market town on the North Downs with some 10,000 inhabitants. It had an ancient castle, a Tudor hospital, a Tudor grammar school and five large coaching inns, and within a few hours Dodgson had come across two properties 'which would suit the party very well'. The first, The Chestnuts, he described as semi-detached and 'close to Guildford'. It was in fact detached and a few hundred yards from the High Street, standing beneath the castle on a steep slope over the river Wey with a 'splendid view' across the river towards the Hog's Back. The house, which had never been occupied, had been built in 1861 on the site of the old town gaol, close to the thirteenth-century castle gate. The second property was at Merrow, two miles outside the town, 'an even better house, and a much better garden'. From Merrow, Dodgson walked 'through some very picturesque lanes arched over with trees' until he came to Albury where the Reverend George Portal invited him to stay for the night. Satisfied with the progress of his house-hunting, Dodgson sent off a telegram to Fanny at Croft, telling her to come down without delay.

Skeffington's curacy was still very much on his mind. Portal suggested that he should approach Robert Trimmer, the vicar of St Mary's, Guildford. The church, which dated back to Saxon times, was in Quarry Street, only a stone's throw from The Chestnuts. It would be the family parish church if they decided to take the house and on Sunday 16th August, Dodgson tried out the service and had lunch with the Reverend Trimmer. Trimmer was happy to consider Skeffington as a possible curate and Wilfred was deputised to send off a telegram telling him to come down as rapidly as he could. Another telegram was sent to Edwin announcing that, thanks to the good offices of Gathorne Hardy, an examination for a clerkship in the Post Office had been arranged for him – 'a splendid prospect if he can get in'.[2]

Dodgson returned to London to collect Fanny and Aunt Lucy who had taken up residence in Uncle Skeffington's house in Onslow Square. They were so pleased with The Chestnuts they did not even trouble to look at the house in Merrow. After a hasty family council with Uncle Skeffington back in London, it was decided to take the house on a long lease at £73 per annum. The Dodgsons were to stay there until 1919.

On 1st September 1868, the clan said their last farewells to Croft. All that remained to bear witness to those happy years was the cache of little objects beneath the nursery floor – the thimble, the white glove, the lobster shell, the tiny penknife and all the other curious relics of their childhood, including the lines about wandering through the wide world and chasing the buffalo. Dodgson returned to Guildford to set up headquarters from which he could supervise the necessary alterations to The Chestnuts. He was immediately plunged into a state of hopeless Carrollean confusion as to which his headquarters were. He had announced that the hotel he intended to stay in was The White Hart, opposite Quarry Street, and had booked a room and arranged for all his mail to be sent there. Unfortunately the hotel opposite Quarry Street was The White Lion. Dodgson paid his bill at The White Hart, collected his luggage and moved into The White Lion. He soon found that the hotel was not at all to his liking – 'a very commercial inn', and so, having made a trial of breakfast at The White Hart he decided that he would move back there – 'but to avoid the unpleasantness of moving from one hotel to another, I sent my things down to the Railway and got a ticket for them, and in the evening had them taken to The White Hart'.[3]

The Dodgson sisters moved in piecemeal between October and early December, but there was one sister for whom The Chesnuts would not be a permanent home. Mary married the Reverend Charles Collingwood, who later became Vicar of Southwick, near Sunderland. Dodgson wrote a belated letter of congratulation to his future brother-in-law from The White Hart – 'I have been so hurried about between here and London that I have been, and am, a mere waif and stray, quite unfit for writing …' On 14th November the whole family assembled at The Chestnuts to celebrate the engagement. After all the jollifications were over Dodgson managed to miss his connecting train at Reading by going to the wrong platform, the first of many such mishaps that were to befall the creator of *La Guida di Bragia*.

*

Dodgson would now make use of the railway more than ever before as he travelled regularly between Oxford and London and Guildford. He never seems to have wearied of his frequent journeys, rapidly perceiving the potential the train offered for making friends with little girls, and it became a kind of hunting ground for him. The intimacy of the railway carriage created an etiquette all of its own, where an acquaintance could be struck up within seconds, without formalities or introductions, and although these frequent encounters were not premeditated, Dodgson was always prepared for them, carrying with him a bag stocked with tricks and novelties.

His meeting with the Drury children in August 1869 is typical of dozens of others. They were sitting in a train with their nursemaid, engrossed in a story she was telling them, when a man with unfashionably long hair entered their compartment. He apologised for interrupting their story and went on to finish it himself.

> Afterwards he took off his grey and black gloves, opened his bag and found inside it three puzzles he had made himself, he told them, and he gave one to each of them to find out. When they were tired of this game he produced three little pairs of scissors and paper so that they could cut out patterns. There were many other surprises in that wonderful bag.[5]

Afterwards he noted down their names and their addresses so that he could send them, as was his custom, 'a children's book that I have written', and in due course a brown paper parcel arrived containing a copy of *Alice* with a poem he had composed for them written on the fly-leaf:

> *Three little maidens weary of the rail,*
> *Three pairs of little ears listening to a tale,*
> *Three little hands held out in readiness*
> *For three little puzzles very hard to guess.*
> *Three pairs of little eyes open wonder-wide*
> *At three little scissors lying side by side.*
> *Three little mouths that thanked an unknown Friend*
> *For one little book he undertook to send.*
> *Through whether they'll remember a friend, or book or day*
> *For three little weeks is very hard to say.*[6]

This is all very coy, not to say mawkish, but it does give a glimpse of the kind of pleasure which these not-so-chance encounters gave Dodgson. On the surface it is all delightfully innocent – the little hands reaching out for his puzzles, the wide eyes looking at the scissors, the polite words of thanks. What is disturbing is the way in which it is all so carefully calculated, and this kind of scene was to be repeated over and over again.

The children would be added to Dodgson's collection. There would be charming letters and tea with the parents and trips to the theatre – all of it perfectly harmless, and providing the children with memories which they would treasure all their lives. But Dodgson was to become increasingly dependent on it all, as though the company of little girls was a kind of addictive drug.

Without *Alice* none of this could have happened so easily. There had been many child-friendships before this time but the success of *Alice's Adventures* had assured Dodgson of a ready way of getting children's affection. It added enormously to the excitement of these railway friendships if the slightly eccentric stranger could throw off his cloak and reveal himself as the creator of the most remarkable children's book of the century. A time would come when Dodgson would go to absurd lengths to conceal his dual identity, but he never hid it from children. With them he used it as a kind of trump card, eagerly anticipating their delighted reaction.

The long wait between trains at Reading, where Dodgson changed trains for Guildford, gave him the opportunity to add even more little girls to his collection. Close to the station were the Forbury gardens and it was there that he met Maud and Isabel Standen playing under the eye of their governess. Within minutes he had scooped Isabel up onto his knee and out came the puzzles and the little scissors. His good friend Lewis Carroll – 'we are the same age of course' – was prevailed upon to send them a copy of *Alice's Adventures* and over the years there were photographs and stories, and visits to The Chestnuts and to Christ Church. For once their friendship survived beyond the point 'where the stream and river meet' and they continued to see one another for the next twenty years.

It was not long before Dodgson began to find child-friends at Guildford. The first were Edith and Ethel Haydon, the daughters of a local solicitor. At his first meeting with Edith, he found her in a state of utter misery on account of a woollen dress of blue-and-grey check which she had been forced to wear. Dodgson sat her down on a stool and produced a square drawing board which he told her to put under her skirt.

> He also produced a set of draughts. The little girl sat on one stool and he on another, and together they played a novel game of draughts on the grey and blue squares of her dress.[7]

He photographed the Haydon girls in the garden of their house wearing their seaside dresses, tunics and knickerbockers – 'some of the prettiest photographs I have done for some time', and Ethel subsequently had the honour of having her picture taken 'undraped'.

His other great Guildford girl friends were the Watson girls, Harriet, May and Georgina, whom he addressed as a portmanteau compound, 'Harmarina'. Dodgson took great delight in sending them puzzles, games and conundrums. Georgina received one of his most charming 'rebus' letters in which pictures were substituted for words, and an ingenious maze which she was to find her way through by following clues spelling out the names of her sisters. The following year he tried to coach the girls in their roles as fairies in a play at Guildford, but found them 'quite deficient in theatrical talent'.[8] Nevertheless their friendship continued well into the eighties.

For a person renowned for his shyness, Dodgson had a remarkable talent for making friends – with adults as well as little girls. Within a few weeks of the family's arrival at Guildford he had formed a network of acquaintances upon whom his sisters might call and who were happy to join in evenings and croquet parties, although it was not until a year later that the Dodgsons gave their first dinner party. As soon as Dodgson had seen the family securely housed and settled at The Chestnuts, he began to move into his newly acquired rooms at Christ Church – 'perhaps the most spacious and beautiful suite of rooms to be found in Oxford',[9] according to his friend Ethel Arnold. He was to live there for nearly thirty years.

Most of the descriptions of the rooms come from the reminiscences of the little girls whom Dodgson entertained there and for whom the suite undoubtedly constituted a kind of Wonderland:

> ... the climb up the winding, wooden staircase in the corner of Tom
> Quad; the unlocking of the great oak door with The Rev. C.L.
> Dodgson painted in white letters over it ...[10]

The door opened into a lobby with doors to the scullery and a small dining room with bookcases full of books. This led to a small bedroom with a 'japanned sponge bath'. Beyond the bedroom was the large sitting-room, with windows giving onto St Aldate's to the west and the Archdeacon's garden to the north. On the St Aldate's side were two tiny turret corner rooms. Isa Bowman recalled that:

> He always used to tell me that when I grew up and became married he
> would give me the two little turret rooms, so that if I ever disagreed
> with my husband we could each retire to a turret until we had made
> up our quarrel![11]

The wallpaper was green; the sofa, the chair-covers and the brocade curtains were red. The walls were hung with photographs of little girls (some of them coloured), and with the painting which he had commissioned from Arthur Hughes, *The Lady with the Lilacs*, with her half-open mouth and her hand raised in a gesture of languid farewell. In one of the windows overlooking St Aldate's was a pane of glass with a semi-circular flaw in it, and Dodgson used to get his little friends to peer through it, so that they could watch the curious effect it had on the progress of the horse-drawn buses as they made their way along the street.

'I do not think there was ever such a fairy land for children,' wrote Isa Bowman. In many ways the room was like an enlarged version of the bag which Dodgson carried with him on his railway journeys. Under the bookcase were cupboards which Dodgson would unlock with his 'special key':

> Musical boxes, mechanical performing bears, picture books innumerable, toys of every description, came forth in bewildering abundance before the child's astonished eyes ...[12]

Some of the musical boxes had glass tops through which his little guests could observe the workings. One of Dodgson's favourite tricks was to tinker with the machinery so that the tunes would emerge backwards, or 'standing on their heads', as Father William's creator put it. He was also the proud possessor of an 'organette' which would produce music from a series of perforated cards.

The room was not just a children's Eldorado, but Dodgson's work-place, with a mahogany writing-desk (one of whose drawers was inhabited by 'Bob the Bat') and another desk at which he could stand to write if he chose. Everywhere there were scrupulously labelled and catalogued boxes and files of manuscripts, letters and photographs. Dodgson kept a register of every single letter received and sent with a brief record of its content. Every photograph was listed and numbered – including a sketch of Elizabeth Siddal: '1151 Drawing ... head leaning against pillow (late Mrs D.G.R.)'. There were even notes, carefully filed, on what food had been served in his rooms when he entertained, so that the same menu should not be repeated.

There was hardly an aspect of Dodgson's existence that was not governed by method. His tea had to be brewed for precisely ten minutes before it was allowed to come out of the teapot:

> The idea of the grave professor promenading his book-lined study, and carefully waving a tea-pot to and fro may seem ridiculous, but all the minutiae of life received an extreme attention at his hands.[13]

Every parcel which he sent by mail was elaborately done up with string and sealing-wax and carefully weighed on his own scales so that he could affix the proper stamps before taking it down to the post office. On one memorable occasion a clerk weighed one of his packages and told him that it was insufficiently stamped. Dodgson snatched up the parcel in a rage, carried it back to his rooms, checked the weight and returned to the counter with not only the parcel but his own scales and weights. The clerk, whose determination for accuracy seems to have matched Dodgson's own, examined the weights and pointed out that one of them was slightly chipped. 'From his look of annoyance,' the postmaster observed, 'it was evident that Mr Dodgson felt his reputation for accuracy had been tarnished.'[14] Nothing must ever be left to chance. Whenever Dodgson set out on a railway journey he would calculate in advance exactly what sums of money would be needed for his rail fare, tips to porters, for cabs and for refreshments and the coins for each transaction would be put into different partitions of the two purses he always carried.

This rigorous exactitude ran through all his life. The great disadvantage of his rooms was that they were extremely draughty, but he had a theory that 'there could be no draughts if the temperature were equalised all over the room'. Thermometers were therefore located at various points around his rooms next to oil stoves. Dodgson would prowl round the rooms, checking the readings on the thermometers and adjusting the stoves accordingly. The other serious problem was mice. Dodgson was determined to dispose of them in as humanitarian a fashion as possible. He constructed a square wooden box-trap which contained a small wood and wire compartment with a sliding door which would trap any mouse rash enough to enter. The compartment would then be removed and plunged into water, minimising the death throes of the unfortunate intruders. Even so, Dodgson was considerably less generous than Anton Chekhov, who would carry the trap some distance outside his dacha and then release the mice, counting on their sense of fair play not to return.

On the upper floor of Dodgson's rooms there was his main bedroom, a bathroom and lavatory and a cubby hole which he used as a dark room. In 1871 he had a photographic studio built onto the roof and there, over the years, dozens of little girls were photographed costumed as beggar-maids, or as Chinese children or fisher-girls or sometimes in nothing at all. Then they would perch on a box by Dodgson's side to watch the plates slowly, mysteriously, take on life as they were developed. If the weather were fine they would be taken out onto the leads, to watch the traffic wending its way along St Aldate's or play at hide and seek among the chimney stacks.

*

Dodgson still cherished the hope that he might somehow manage to add members of the royal family to his list of photographic victims, but his prey eluded him. The story that Queen Victoria had been so delighted with *Alice's Adventures* that she invited Dodgson to send her his next book and had duly been presented with a copy of *Condensation of Determinants* is, sadly, apocryphal, and for the time being he had to content himself with make-believe. For the amusement of his railway acquaintances, the Drury girls, he concocted an invitation from Buckingham Palace:

> Dear Mr Dodgson,
> I hope you will be able to come to my Garden Party on Friday afternoon.
> Yours truly,
> Victoria R.[15]

If Dodgson had been invited to a royal garden party he would almost certainly have turned it down, but in fact, it does seem that the Queen had had *Alice* drawn to her attention. Walter De La Mare recounted the story of a little girl who was sitting reading *Alice's Adventures* 'while a favourite and favoured aunt conversed with the Queen and her ladies at an adjacent tea-table. Noticing the child's total absorption in the book, the Queen wanted to know what she was reading. The little girl carried the book over to the Queen and showed her the picture of Alice swimming in the pool of her own tears. '"Do you think, please," she asked, "you could cry as much as that?"'[16] The reply of the Widow of Windsor, still in deepest mourning, is not recorded, but the little girl did receive a locket containing the Queen's portrait.

If Alice had not yet unlocked the gates of the palace, she was rapidly making Dodgson into a celebrity, and he was constantly receiving admiring letters from scores of enthusiastic child admirers. Dodgson could not bear to think of all these happy children whose faces he would never see and he conceived the wild idea of inserting a notice in all future copies of *Alice* asking for his little fans to send in their photographs. Macmillan was horrified:

> Cartes! I should think so, indeed – cart loads of them. Think of the postmen. Open an office for relief at the North Pole and another at the Equator ... But it's no use remonstrating with you.[17]

Reluctantly Dodgson abandoned his scheme, but an idea had taken root. He was becoming increasingly aware that the readers of *Alice* constituted a vast audience of children with whom it would be possible for him to communicate:

> The thought of the many English firesides where happy faces have

smiled her a welcome, and of the many English children to whom she had brought an hour of (I trust) innocent amusement, is one of the brightest and pleasantest thoughts of my life.[18]

He would turn his fame as Lewis Carroll to good effect by using it as a means of advancing the causes and the faith to which he was committed. Accordingly pious little homilies began to find their way into copies of his books dedicated 'to every child who loves Alice' and letters on a wide variety of increasingly improbable topics reached the newspapers signed with his pseudonym. Dodgson's awareness of his own fame and his conviction that his fame carried with it a measure of moral responsibility eventually had a disastrous effect upon his style and would, in the long run, undermine and diminish his achievement. Sentimentality tinged with evangelism was Dodgson's Achilles' heel and would have a numbing effect upon his creativity.

'Don't think me brutal'

Robert Cecil, 3rd Marquess of Salisbury, was installed as Chancellor of the University on 25th June, 1870, and Dodgson enlisted Liddon's help in persuading him to sit for his photograph in full regalia. The resulting picture is a rather uneasy looking affair with Salisbury crouching on the corner of Dodgson's sofa looking like a fugitive money-lender, protected by his two apprehensive sons in their pages' uniforms. A picture of his daughters, Maud and Gwendolen, taken the same day, is more successful. Maud sits with her arm round Gwendolen looking at a book of photographs. Dodgson was delighted by the ease with which all this had been effected and by the courtesy with which he had been received. 'I fancy Wonderland had a great deal to do with my gracious reception,' he noted, 'and the children are very charming.'[1] Their visit was followed by an even more astonishing event. Mrs Liddell arrived with Lorina and Alice in tow and asked him to take their photograph. Clearly, if Dodgson were good enough for Lord Salisbury, he was good enough for them. *Alice* was beginning to accomplish marvels.

However, one person was not influenced by Dodgson's new-found fame, and that was Tennyson, for in March their acquaintance came to an abrupt and angry conclusion. Dodgson's part in the whole wretched business seems to have been blameless: his only fault was his habitual conscientious punctiliousness and his undue reverence for the Laureate's wishes. Dodgson had always been a keen collector of everything Tennyson produced. Some years earlier 'a young lady, a cousin of mine', had lent him a copy of *The Lover's Tale*, a long rambling piece, which had been written when the poet was nineteen and which he had withdrawn. Dodgson, knowing Tennyson's aversion to his unprinted work being circulated, wrote and asked his permission to keep it. He was instructed to destroy it, which he reluctantly did. Now another work had come into Dodgson's hands, *The Window*, a sequence of poems which Tennyson had printed privately in 1866 and which had been set to music as a song-cycle by Arthur Sullivan. Again Dodgson wrote to ask for permission to keep it and to show it to his friends: 'I have not even read it yet, and shall do so with much greater pleasure when I know that you do not object to my possessing it.'[2] He went on to point out that since many copies of the poem were already in circulation, his having a copy was not a matter of great consequence. What followed must have totally astonished him. Tennyson himself did not deign to reply, but he instructed Emily to write on his behalf. She despatched a brusque, sour and utterly unmerited letter of rebuke in which she took him to task for troubling the Laureate with a request which could only annoy him, and informed him that 'a gentleman should understand that when an author does not give his works to the public he has his own reasons for it'.

It must be admitted that Tennyson had good reason for wishing to suppress the poems. Verses like:

> Mens' love and birds' love,
> And women's love and men's!
> And you my wren with a crown of gold,
> You my queen of the wrens!
> You the queen of the wrens –
> We'll be birds of a feather,
> I'll be King of the Queen of the wrens,
> And all in a nest together.

were not likely to enhance his waning reputation. To add to his problems he was breaking with his publisher, Moxon, Son and Co., which was causing considerable irritation and bitterness. However, Dodgson was not prepared to accept the imputation in Emily's letter that he was not a gentleman and he wrote a firm but temperate letter to Tennyson:

> It is by no act of mine that this poem is now in circulation and that a copy of it has come into my hands. Under these circumstances I may fairly ask you to point out what I have failed to do that the most chivalrous sense of honour could require.[3]

The appeal to Tennyson's chivalry failed to produce the expected response. The fragment of his reply that does exist suggests it was far from apologetic:

> … no answer to that request reached her, whereupon I was naturally disgusted and believed that whether I liked it or not, you were resolved …[4]

In reply Dodgson send a brief resumé of the words which had passed between them couched in the form of a dramatic dialogue, accompanied by a letter that, under the circumstances, was remarkably generous:

My dear sir,

Thus it is, as it seems to me, that you first do a man an injury, and then forgive him – that you first tread on his toes, and then beg him not to cry out!

Nevertheless I accept what you say, as being in substance, what it certainly is not in form, a retraction (though without a shadow of an apology or expression of regret) of all dishonourable charges against me, and an admission that you had made them on insufficient grounds ...[5]

Nine months later Tennyson gave his permission for the poems to be published with Sullivan's music, thereby rendering his conduct more inexplicable than ever. Dodgson, unlike Tennyson, was not a man to bear a grudge. On 22nd December 1871, he sent the poet a copy of *Through the Looking Glass* bound in morocco, as a peace offering. It was 'rewarded by a note of thanks from himself ... and I am quite pleased with the result of my experiment'.

The quarrel with Tennyson put an end to Dodgson's days of lion-hunting and, in any case, he no longer needed to pursue the great and famous. There were more important matters to attend to, in particular, those which concerned his own family; an oculist to be found for Aunt Lucy, another curacy for Skeffington and an occupation for Edwin. The Post Office had not proved to be the solution Dodgson had hoped for. 'I am getting more and more down-hearted about my brother,' he told Macmillan, 'his present life of "nothing to do" is so very bad for him, that I would gladly see him in *work* of any kind.' So great was his desperation that he was even prepared to see his brother go into publishing. 'Couldn't you try him (if only temporarily) as a sort of clerk?'[6] Macmillan would have none of it. One Dodgson in his life, one suspects, was quite enough. The problem was solved, at least for the time being, when in October 1870, a post was secured for Edwin as an accountant in the firm of a Mr Ball.

The beginning of the year had seen the birth of the next generation of the family. In January, Mary had borne a son, Stuart Dodgson Collingwood, who would become his uncle's first biographer. Dodgson was already godfather to five children, but he was prepared to take on just one more:

Though I am intending to decline, in all *other* directions, any addition to my quite sufficient family of godchildren, I cannot possibly refuse to gratify *your* wish in such a matter.[7]

Then, there was Louisa, now thirty, whose 'strength needs recruiting'. A holiday by the sea would be the answer and Dodgson set out to examine the comparative virtues and attractions of Margate and Eastbourne. Rather surprisingly, he chose Margate. At that time the resort had the reputation of being a raffish, noisy kind of place, whereas Eastboure was considered, in the words of Augustus Sala, 'the quietest and gentlest watering place I have beheld'. 'Margate seems to be the place,' Dodgson noted and Louisa's indisposition became the occasion for a family holiday with Fanny, Margaret, Dodgson himself and, 'mirabile dictu' (as he would have put it), Miss Goode, the daughter of his father's implacable adversary, Dr Goode, the Dean of Ripon, who happened to be staying at The Chestnuts when the holiday was mooted.

Margate was to set the pattern for all Dodgson's seaside summers:

> I made very many pleasant acquaintances, chiefly on account of being attracted by their children: very few turned out to be above the commercial class – the one drawback of Margate society.[8]

Dodgson discovered that the seaside, like the railway and the stage, was a place where rules normally governing society could be relaxed or ignored. If you were helping children to build a sandcastle there was no need to question overmuch whether their parents were in trade. With Catherine and Frederika and Florence from Tulse Hill he climbed the lighthouse and explored the shell-encrusted grotto 'supposed to be three hundred years old and probably the work of a hermit'.

In December, Wilfred at long last announced his engagement to Alice Donkin, who was now nineteen. Alice and her sister Eleanor were invited to The Chestnuts for a family celebration, but Dodgson, nursing a bad cough, stayed on at Christ Church until the latest possible moment, reluctant to face the railway journey and the inevitable stay at The White Lion, since The Chestnuts was, as usual, full to overflowing. Wilfred and Alice were married the following year. Wilfred had been made agent for the lands of Lord Boyne in Shropshire and could now comfortably set up a house of his own. Dodgson gave a little dinner party for the happy couple in his rooms at Christ Church and took them over to the Deanery where there was croquet and music. Was Alice Liddell one of the croquet party, and did Dodgson look enviously at his brother's happiness? He still recorded Alice's birthday in his diary. She was nineteen and had grown far away from him.

> *Still she haunts me phantomwise*
> *Alice moving under skies*
> *Never seen by waking eyes*

he wrote in the epilogue poem to *Through the Looking Glass*.

By January 1870, Tenniel had managed only eight sketches for *Looking*

Glass House as it was then called. The book's title was still giving Dodgson trouble; should it perhaps be *Looking Glass World*? Macmillan was not enthusiastic, he thought that the first title 'harmonises with your particular humour'. Dodgson consulted Henry Liddon, who suggested *Through the Looking Glass*, which instantly removed all doubt. 'You'll never beat it,' was Macmillan's comment.[9]

On 4th May he heard from Tenniel that he hoped to have all the pictures finished by the end of July. Like all Tenniel's forecasts, this turned out to be highly optimistic, but the book was at long last beginning to move steadily forward. Dodgson had completed the text at the beginning of the year and had noted, when the slips were dispatched to Tenniel, 'it all now depends upon him, whether we get the proofs out by Easter or not'.[10] Part of the difficulty was that there were no drawings for him to follow or to react against (as there had been for *Alice's Adventures*), and for this reason he had great difficulty in accommodating himself to some of the characters in Dodgson's story. Dodgson, for once, showed remarkable patience and understanding. When Tenniel 'remonstrated against the walrus and the carpenter as a hopeless combination and begged him to have the carpenter abolished', Dodgson obligingly offered him as alternatives a butterfly or a baronet, since either would fit his rhyme scheme. Confronted with these two even more unlikely concepts, Tenniel opted for the carpenter although he said that he could not see his way to drawing them 'walking hand-in-hand'. Dodgson, still eager to oblige, changed the line to 'walking close at hand', considerably weakening it. In the illustration of the railway carriage in the third chapter, there were originally three passengers in the compartment with Alice, a goat, the man in white paper and a white haired old lady. When the carriage rose into the air to jump over the brook (the kind of incident which might have taken place on the Croft railway) Dodgson had intended Alice to catch hold of the old lady's hair, but Tenniel objected to this both on the grounds of propriety and design: 'I think that when the jump occurs in the railway scene you might very well make Alice lay hold of the goat's *beard* as being the object nearest at hand – instead of the old lady's hair. The jerk would actually bring them together.'[11] So, out went the old lady.

Tenniel even managed to persuade Dodgson to remove an entire episode. In the original text, at the point where Alice is about to spring across the last brook and become a Queen, she notices 'something like a very old man', leaning against a tree, which turns out to be a wasp wearing a bright yellow wig 'all tangled and tumbled about like a heap of seaweed'.

'Don't think me brutal,' wrote Tenniel, 'but I am bound to say that the "wasp" character doesn't interest me in the least, and I can't see my way to a picture. If you want to shorten the book I can't help thinking – with all submission – that *there* is your opportunity.'[12]

Dodgson had been concerned for some time that the book was too long. When he had first approached his illustrator on the subject of cuts, Tenniel had suggested getting rid of the Railway Scene which had never struck him as being very strong. 'I think it might well be sacrificed without much repining.' Dodgson was not prepared to see the scene go, but it is likely that he already had his own doubts about the wasp. He may have considered it too similar in tone to the episode of the White Knight; an encounter with a querulous old wasp following hard on the heels of the gallant but accident-prone old inventor would considerably interfere with the story's onward movement. It might have been this, as much as a desire to defer to Tenniel's wishes, which caused him to jettison the bewigged wasp without a struggle. It has to be admitted that the standard of writing is not equal to that of the rest of the work, but even so, the wasp himself is a considerable character and the episode does have that hard edge and sense of menace which pervades so much of *Through the Looking Glass*:

> '... the top of your head is nice and round'. He took off his own wig as he spoke, and stretched out one claw towards Alice, as if he wished to do the same to her, but she kept out of reach, and would not take the hint.[13]

In Tenniel's hands it was the Jabberwock who summed up the terror which lurks beneath the surface of *Looking Glass* world, and the drawing presented Dodgson with something of a problem. It was a magnificent monster, but what was he do to with it? He had originally intended to use the picture as a frontispiece, but various friends told him that it was 'likely to alarm nervous and imaginative children' and that he should preface the book with a 'pleasanter subject'. Reluctant to take the decision upon himself, and wary of offending Tenniel, he decided to put the question to a panel of about thirty of his married lady friends and circulated a questionnaire among them along with a print of the loathly beast.

> We have three courses open to us:
> (1) to retain it as the frontispiece;
> (2) to transfer it to its proper place in the book (where the ballad occurs which it is intended to illustrate) and substitute a new frontispiece;
> (3) to omit it altogether.
> The last-named course would be a great sacrifice of the time and trouble which the picture has cost, and it would be pity to adopt it

unless it be <u>really</u> necessary.[14]

In the end it was the White Knight who was chosen to lead readers into the book and the Jabberwock did not come 'whiffling through the tulgey wood' until page twenty.

This is not to say that Tenniel was the only one who created difficulties. Dodgson took exception to Tenniel's drawing of the Mad Hatter in prison which showed him in profile, when he had wanted him full-face. In his picture of the chequer-board landscape Tenniel originally showed Alice in the foreground: Dodgson insisted that she be removed. In examining the drawing of the slithy toves under a magnifying glass he came across something which disturbed him. Tenniel wrote to the Dalziel brothers in some exasperation:

> Will you please clear away the ear of the centre animal according to the enclosed proof. Mr Dodgson sees a second face, the ears forming the snout. Be so good as to send a rubbing of the head when you send the other proofs.[15]

In later years, Dodgson would say that he liked none of Tenniel's illustrations, except for Humpty Dumpty, but then, this was the only character for whom he had provided a sketch. Dodgson evidently felt a certain kinship with his oviform creation, since he once signed himself, in a letter to his friend Gertrude Thomson, 'Humpty Dumpty'.

As the drawings crawled towards a finished state, Dodgson realised it would, after all, have to be a Christmas book. Determined to make the best of the situation he set to work on a seasonal address 'To All Child-Readers of *Alice's Adventures in Wonderland*' which was to be enclosed in all future copies of both books, in which he thanked them for the kindly interest they had taken in his 'little dream-child'. He sent it off to Menella Smedley for her approval.

By November, *Through the Looking Glass* was at long last printing rapidly. Macmillan had already received orders for 7,500 copies and was printing 6,000 more. On 6th December, Dodgson received his first copy and two days later, despite being a 'prisoner' with a sore throat and a headache, he sent off ninety-nine presentation copies. Alice had to be content with a morocco binding since it had not proved possible to incorporate a mirror into the cover, and Tennyson and Ellen Terry's younger sister Florence also had morocco. All seemed to be going at 'railway speed' as he might have put it when, suddenly, on 17th December, he called a halt. Once again, Tenniel had protested about the quality of the printing of the pictures, this time because of the 'inequality' of their finish. Dodgson told Macmillan that this was because the pages were being dried by being pressed between two sheets of blank paper. This practice must cease at once. Macmillan insisted that the 6,000 copies he was then printing must be out by Christmas:

> Why, half the children will be laid up with pure vexation and anguish of spirit … Darkness will come over all the hearths, gloom will hover over the brightest boards …

But Dodgson was not to be swayed, nor did he want any more complaints from Tenniel:

> You will think me a lunatic for thus wishing to send away money from the doors; and will tell me perhaps that I shall thus lose thousands of would-be purchasers, who will not wait so long, but will go and buy other Christmas books. I wish I could put into words how entirely such arguments go for nothing with me … the only thing I <u>do</u> care for is, that all copies that <u>are</u> sold shall be artistically first rate.[16]

Macmillan gave way and told him that he was not prepared to press his own interests 'against your high aim'.

Tenniel had triumphed again, but for him that was the end of the affair. Not only was it the last book he would illustrate for Dodgson, it was the last he would illustrate for anyone. 'It is a curious fact,' he commented wryly, 'that with *Through the Looking Glass* the faculty of making drawings for book illustration departed from me, and notwithstanding all sorts of tempting inducements, I have not done anything in that direction since.'[17]

24
'That blots the fair heavens above'

One damp, dreary afternoon in the autumn of 1871, Dodgson was taking his favourite walk through the University Parks when he was spotted by a 'number of little girls, bursting with youthful high spirits, and all agog for mischief'.[1] 'Here comes Mr Dodgson,' they cried and joined hands to form a barrier across his path. It was the kind of challenge that Dodgson found it impossible to resist. He advanced at the double and charged the little girls with his umbrella. Four of the little band clung on to him fiercely, but two of them hung back, uncertain whether this was the way to behave towards a 'tall, dignified gentleman in black broadcloth and white tie'. The two girls were Ethel and Julia Arnold, the daughters of Thomas Arnold, and the granddaughters of Arnold of Rugby.

Ethel always remembered the hours she spent in Dodgson's company as 'cases of brightness in a somewhat grey and melancholy childhood'. Their father, the celebrated headmaster's younger son and the younger brother of the poet Matthew Arnold, had effectively wrecked his career by converting to the Catholic church (a move which would have filled his father with horror) and had taken a post as Professor of English Literature at Newman's University of Ireland. His wife disapproved deeply of his conversion to Rome, and, according to Newman, used to 'nag, nag, nag him till he lost his senses. She preached against Catholicism to her children and made them most unmanageable.'[2] However in 1865 Arnold had been so distressed by the claim of the Church of Rome to infallibility that he had renounced the Pope and all his works and he had been reduced to eking out a rather miserable living as a private tutor in Oxford. Dodgson took pity on him, perhaps out of loyalty to the Arnold name, and helped him to a post as Assistant Charity Commissioner. All Dodgson's best efforts were, however, undermined when, in 1876, Arnold had yet another change of heart and returned to the Church of Rome.

Dodgson did his best to cheer the children's miserable childhood. He took them for walks, devised games for them, told them stories and lent them books, sometimes with unfortunate results:

What remarkably wicked children you are! I don't think you would find in all history, even if you go back to the times of Nero and Heliogabalus, any instance of children so heartless and entirely reckless about returning story-books.[3]

Like all his other child-friends, the Arnolds were frequently photographed and, though Ethel could not manage to hold a pose for longer than a few seconds, she was herself to become an enthusiastic amateur photographer. When the girls' elder sister, Mary, married Mr Humphrey Ward, Dodgson was so fascinated by the appearance of the bride and her sisters that he made them put on their wedding dresses again a few weeks later for 'a long photographic session'.

Dodgson's friendship with the Arnold girls underwent a severe trial when he was bitten by Ethel's dachshund, Bergman:

> Nothing would induce him to enter the house after this outrage [she recalled] though no real injury had been inflicted. Next day came a long letter containing an elaborate diagram of the rent which had been made in his left trouser-leg by Bergman's teeth, and announcing his determination never again to cross our threshold until the dog had been destroyed.[4]

Only Dodgson would have drawn a diagram. And yet this was the lover and champion of animals, the man who would become such a determined opponent of vivisection. Dodgson's sense of humour had severe limitations. The wretched Bergman survived, but Ethel was obliged to meet Dodgson henceforth only inside the park gates.

Ethel had dreams of making a career for herself on the stage: while still a child she and Julia put on a performance of the Mad Hatter's Tea Party which Dodgson attended, but her theatrical ambitions came to nothing. What is remarkable is that her friendship with him survived her committing what was for him the ultimate act of treachery, writing an article about him in a newspaper. Not content with telling the world that the author of *Alice's Adventures* was a Senior Student of Christ Church, she even went on to describe his rooms:

> As might be gathered from his books he is a genuine lover of children, and his beautiful suite of rooms in the north west corner of Wolsey's great quadrangle, looking over St Aldate's were at one time a veritable children's paradise.[5]

The person to whom Dodgson had applied when he was trying to secure an Assistant Charity Commissionership for Ethel's father was Lord Salisbury, whose support he tried to enlist in a bewildering variety of causes from anti-vivisection to electoral reform. There had been several invitations, which Dodgson had been forced to decline, for him to stay at the

Cecils' Jacobean mansion at Hatfield. There had been meetings with Salisbury's two daughters, Maud and Gwendolen, with visits to the Royal Academy, games and puzzles, but it was not until July 1871 that he finally arrived at Hatfield Station to be met by the Salisbury brougham.

It rained steadily all through the first day, and, under the guidance of Maud and Gwendolen, Dodgson 'lionised' the house which Robert Cecil had built in the first decade of the seventeenth-century for the then phenomenal sum of £40,000. After admiring the great hall, the staircase with its post crowned, as in the Liddells' Deanery, with lions, the long gallery, the Van Dyck Room and King James's drawing room, Dodgson was introduced to the not very distinguished company. Later in the day he went for a walk with the chaplain to the Duke of Northumberland. On the face of it, his visit sounds to have been extremely unexciting, but he considered it one of the 'pleasantest' he had experienced. The second day was 'Gwennie's' birthday and the rain held off sufficiently for them all to have a picnic in the vineyard. In the evening Dodgson was, presumably, expected to sing for his supper and duly produced some of his photographs as well as Tenniel's original drawings for *Through the Looking Glass*. The family, he noted in his diary, were really 'delightful' and 'kindness itself'. The feeling appears to have been mutual, for the following year Dodgson with Henry Liddon and Bishop Wilberforce was invited to the opening of the restored Hatfield church.

There was to be no summer holiday at the seaside for Dodgson that year. Instead he set off for Scotland, with the particular object of tracking down Sir Noel Paton. Paton had been one of the artists Dodgson had approached when he was looking for an alternative to Tenniel. The painter's refusal had in no way dampened Dodgson's enthusiasm to get to know his work and, if possible, to photograph it. In fact, the more difficult the meeting with Paton became, the more determined Dodgson grew to make it happen.

Paton was then at the height of his career. Prints of his most popular painting, *Home from the Crimea*, hung in hundreds of houses throughout the country. Dodgson was more drawn to Paton's fairy paintings and to rather sentimental subjects like *Who Lived Here*, a child looking at an old helmet. 'If you have seen none of them,' he told his sister Mary in that crushingly superior tone that had not altered since his childhood days, 'you had better simply regard him as the best painter of figure-paintings now living.'[6] He had also heard that Paton 'was said to have beautiful and charming children' who had posed for his frontispiece to *The Water Babies*.

Armed with a letter of introduction from George MacDonald, Dodgson called at Paton House in Edinburgh, only to discover that the painter was at his house at Lamlash on the Isle of Arran. Nothing daunted, Dodgson sent off a letter to Arran. After ten days he had heard nothing and decided that he would go on to Glasgow and take a boat from there to the island, where he was cordially received by Paton, 'a grand-looking man, tall and strong, looking much more of a soldier than an artist'.

He had some difficulty in 'taming' the children. They were, he told Mary, 'Quite unique in my experience, something like South Sea Islanders with the instincts of gentlemen and ladies.' His charm seems to have failed with the eleven-year-old Mona. 'He used to annoy me very much,' she remembered, 'by setting me puzzles, and I retaliated by making some paper stars and refusing to show him how they were done.'[7] Nevertheless, Dodgson marked the day with a white stone.

Dodgson could not resist the temptation to repeat the whole experience and returned a few days later with Uncle Skeffington who had arrived to join him on his Scottish tour. Paton gave him a note authorising him to have the key of his Edinburgh studio and three days later Dodgson spent an afternoon going through Paton's portfolios – 'such a treat as I do not remember *ever* having had in one day. The drawings are perfectly exquisite, and almost come up to *my* highest ideas of beauty.'[8]

His travelling companion, the accident-prone Skeffington Lutwidge, was going through a trying time. In August he had been hit by a stone thrown into his railway carriage and at the end of the year he was seized by a severe attack of erysipelas in the face and was 'quite invalided'. Dodgson went to stay with him for a few days in January; caring for the sick was something for which Dodgson had a great gift, whether his patient was a friend or relative or a college servant. While Skeffington Lutwidge remained a prisoner in Onslow Square, Dodgson discovered that Thackeray's daughter, Anne, whom he had met with the Synges at their house at Guildford, was living nearby in Onslow Gardens. He lost no time in calling on her and encountered two little girls, Gaynor and Amy Simpson, and was soon begging Anne Thackeray to get him their photographs 'for love or money' and added, 'as the Americans say, "I'm a whale at" photographs'.

Anne Thackeray drew on Dodgson's passion for photography in a novella she wrote five years later, *From the Island*. She was a close friend of Julia Margaret Cameron, and the book is set in a place closely resembling

'Dimbola', Mrs Cameron's house near Tennyson's Farringford. Mrs Cameron herself features in the novel as does Tennyson himself (as Lord Ulleskelf). Although Mr Hexham, the 'dark, close-cropped' amateur photographer, is totally unlike Dodgson in manner and appearance, Anne Thackeray has given him a selection of Dodgson characteristics. He is nervous, absent-minded and loses his way about the house. He describes his art as 'a game half of skill, half of chance ... When both these divinities favour me I shall begin to think myself repaid for the time and the money and the chemicals I have wasted.' Many of his pictures end in disaster through over-excitement. He adores children and plays a game of racing raindrops down a window pane. Like the hero of Dodgson's *A Photographer's Day Out*, he decides that the way to his beloved's heart is through the camera and when he is rebuffed falls into a very Dodgsonian 'haughty seclusion'.

By the middle of January Uncle Skeffington had recovered sufficiently for Dodgson to return to Guildford. However, in May of the following year, when he was seventy, Skeffington Lutwidge was attacked by one of the inmates of an asylum in Salisbury and died three weeks later. Characteristically Dodgson said very little about it. Of all the older generation his uncle had always been the person closest to him and the only member of the family in whom he had been able to confide. He had been invaluable when Dodgson was assuming his duties as head of the family. Now Dodgson had to shoulder those responsibilities alone.

Dodgson's fortieth birthday in 1872 was marked by a message from Macmillan's right hand man, George Craik (who had married one of Dodgson's favourite authors, Dinah Mulock,) announcing that *Through the Looking Glass* had already sold 15,000 copies and there were orders for 500 more. Even so, Dodgson continued to caution Macmillan against printing more copies than they could safely sell. He was in no hurry to put a new work before his public. He was working on a book of Symbols and Abbreviations in Euclid, but the only non-mathematical work to find its way into print that year (apart from the Italian version of *Alice*) was another of his squibs, signalling his return to the lists in the long tournament with Henry Liddell.

The Dean had moved on from reforming the constitution of Christ Church to reconstructing its fabric. His building works, which had begun with the transformation of the Deanery, had now progressed to the Cathedral which had remained largely untouched since the times of Charles I. The oak panelling of the choir stalls was thrown out and the screen which divided the choir from the main body of the church was taken down. George Gilbert Scott was called in to undertake a drastic 'restoration' at the then phenomenal cost of £24,000. In the course of rebuilding it was decided to open up the Norman tower, which necessitated the removal of the bells and their ringing chamber. They were rehung in a wooden, specially-constructed chamber above the Hall staircase. The ungainly structure in which the bells had been housed gave the conservative Dodgson the opportunity he had long been waiting for to attack Liddell's building programme. It was almost as if the Dean had delivered himself into his hands.

The New Belfry was written in two days and gives the impression of a man getting his ideas down on paper almost faster than he can think them. It is jumbled, occasionally incoherent, but undeniably funny. Dodgson begins with a flourish:

> The word Belfry is derived from the French bel, 'beautiful, becoming, meet', and from the German word frei, 'free, unfettered, secure, safe'. Thus the word is strictly equivalent to 'meatsafe', to which the new Belfry bears a resemblance so perfect as to almost amount to coincidence.'

Dodgson piles image upon image in an almost surreal extravaganza. Liddell's contribution to the Oxford skyline is compared to the Campanile of St Mark's reduced to a simple cube, to a gigantic copy of the Liddell and Scott Lexicon. Its shape has been imitated by bathing machines at Ramsgate, by bars of soap, 'and we are reliably informed that Borwick's Baking Powder and Thorley's Food for Cattle are now sold in no other shape'. At the approaching Gaudy each guest will be presented with a model of the new Belfry, 'tastefully executed in cheese'. Dean Liddell in his madness is compared to King Lear: 'The little dons and all, Tutor, Reader, Lecturer – see they bark at me!'

In the succeeding stages of Liddell's architectural improvements, an archway was cut through the old Canons' House to provide access from the Great Quadrangle to the Cathedral. Dodgson took one look at it and decided that 'it almost rivals the "Belfry" in ugliness.' He christened it 'The Tunnel' and immediately set to work on the second of his anti-Liddell squibs, *The Vision of the Three T's*. The 'Three T's' in question were the Tunnel, the 'Trench', a 'ghastly gash in the parapet, made during the removal of the bells from the tower, hacked as though by some wanton school-boy' and, of course, the 'Tea–Chest', the new belfry 'that blots the fair heavens above.'

The Vision is cast in the form of a dialogue between 'Piscator' and

'Venator' and is a parody of Walton's *The Compleat Angler*. They have come to fish in the circular pool in 'Thomas his Quadrangle' and are suitably appalled by the three architectural monstrosities. They endeavour to question various passers-by about them, but the men they ask are more concerned to get 'a great performance of music'. A lunatic, Jeeby – George Bodley, the architect of both the Belfry and the Tunnel – appears and tells them that the Quadrangle is to be the new railway terminus and that the line will enter through the tunnel, the design for which was inspired by a cheese scoop. A Tutor, also 'bound for music', delivers a highly Carrollean dissertation on the gateway which is, he says, an example of the Non-harmonic Mean, the Mean Absolute':

> But that the Mean, or Middle, is ever the safer course, we have a notable example in Egyptian history, in which land, (as travellers tell us) the Ibis standeth ever in the midst of the river Nile, so best to avoid the onslaught of the ravenous alligators, which infest the banks on either side: from which habit of that wise bird is derived the ancient maxim 'In medio tutissimus Ibis'.[10]

The 'music' to which the various passers-by are all hastening is Bach's *St Matthew Passion* (which Venator honours in a 'Bacchanalian Ode'). The performance actually took place in the Cathedral while Dodgson was composing his squib, and he deeply disapproved of the Dean's action in promoting it. 'I did not go. I think it is a pity churches should be so used.' To make matters worse, Alice Liddell had been greatly involved in selling tickets and in promoting the event. Ruskin had been delighted to buy a ticket from her. 'I am sure I shall like to hear you telling me about the music – or about anything else you like to tell me – much better than any music (unless you would sing it without all the organs and trumpets and showmen and things)' though he thought he would never come to feel Bach as more than the 'wonder of Wonderland'. As far as Dodgson was concerned, Liddell was using the house of God as a place for entertainment and, worse still, he was charging admission for it:

> A shilling a head for admission, and half a crown for every two-headed man ... and then, Sir, five shillings each for the care of your umbrella!

The tone of Dodgson's humour is that of the dry, academic, slightly laboured, common room joke, but he does allow himself one brief but vicious swipe at the Liddells' ambition for their daughters. Their desire to see Lorina, Alice and Edith handsomely, wealthily and, if possible, aristocratically married, was already notorious in Oxford. In Dodgson's

Vision, Piscator discourses on the variety of fish proper to the waters of Christ Church:

> I will now say something of the Nobler kinds, and chiefly of the Gold-fish, which is a species highly thought of, and much sought after in these parts, not only by men, but by divers birds, as for example, the King-fishers ...

If the Liddells were king-fishers, their wildest expectations came close to being gratified when in 1872, Prince Leopold, the youngest son of Queen Victoria, came to Christ Church as an undergraduate and promptly fell in love with Alice, an event which Dodgson could scarcely have failed to notice. The match was utterly out of the question, but Mrs Liddell may have been quietly gratified. Dodgson must have bitterly resented his Alice being used as royal bait.

Alice would soon be twenty-one, and a world away, but the Alice he had created was permanently locked in childhood, at the age of the little girl he had loved. He began to dwell more and more on the idea of recreating his 'dream child' by finding a little girl who could play Alice in a version for the stage. At an entertainment in Worthing he noticed a 'dear child of eight' called Lydia Howard, and thought that 'she would do well to act "Alice" if it should be dramatised'. The problem was how to go about it:

> Of course, if the thing were done, much would depend on the writer chosen, the actors and the properties. But the first question to settle is whether either book has sufficient dramatic element to warrant the attempt to exhibit it.[11]

The man he chose to advise him was Percy Fitzgerald, a member of the Dickens circle and a regular contributor to *Household Words*. Beyond advising against the play being acted by children, Percy Fitzgerald had very little positive to contribute, but he did urge Dodgson to take swift action to prevent the books being staged in pirated versions. Dodgson immediately wrote a letter to Macmillan:

> Will you kindly, with all reasonable expedition on receipt of this, engage a couple of copying clerks, and have all the speeches in Alice and the Looking Glass written out, with the names of the speakers, and such directions as Enter the White Rabbit, Exit the Queen, in the ordinary dramatic form, <u>and get them registered as two dramas</u>, with the same names as the books.[12]

Dodgson had been assured that this was the manner in which Wilkie

Collins protected his works, but in fact it did not secure him against piracy, which he could do very little to prevent.

Fitzgerald brought in Augustus Dubourg, a minor dramatist whom Dodgson had met several years before, to advise him on the dramatisation. By then it was Kate Logan, whom Dodgson had seen in a production of *Bella's Birthday*, who seemed to be the ideal Alice. 'I always think,' Dubourg commented, 'that any little girl of ten or twelve was potentially an "Alice" in his eyes.'[13] Dubourg was clearly disappointed to find that Dodgson was so unlike 'that exquisite humorist, Lewis Carroll' of popular imagination but he and Dodgson soon became great friends. Dubourg came to stay at Christ Church, but their discussions came to nothing, and Dodgson turned instead to Thomas German Reed, who had a reputation for providing 'respectable entertainments for the kind of audience who considered theatre-going rather scandalous'. At first Reed seemed excited about the possibility of putting *Alice* on the stage, talking of 'endless fairy versions of surpassing loveliness', but his enthusiasm soon cooled: 'I must now with regret resign the pleasure I had anticipated in being associated with charming little Alice in her dramatic introduction to the public'.

For the time being, Alice's theatrical début was indefinitely deferred, although she had achieved the ultimate Victorian accolade, a series of quadrilles, *The Wonderland Quadrilles*, by C.B. Marriot. The composer had offered to dedicate them to some member of Dodgson's family, but, for Dodgson, there was only one possible dedication: 'To Alice'.

'I knew not what it meant'

Dodgson never gave up hope that somehow he might find the means of deliverance from his speech impediment and, at the beginning of 1873, he made a determined attempt to cure not only his own stammer but those of his sisters. James Hunt, the therapist whom Dodgson believed had helped him considerably, had died and his practice had been taken over by his brother-in-law, Henry Rivers. Rivers was a clergyman and was particularly sympathetic towards Dodgson's plight. Dodgson came to have great faith in him, and wrote giving a detailed account of the family handicap. There was one sister who did not stammer at all, two who stammered slightly, and two moderate stammerers. The serious sufferers, apart from Dodgson himself, were Elizabeth and Caroline, and he was anxious for Rivers to see them as soon as possible. Accordingly, Elizabeth, Caroline and Dodgson went to Rivers for a course of lessons and reading together. By February, Dodgson began to find that he could speak with almost no hesitation, 'with the consciousness that the breath was flowing out in an unbroken stream'.[1] He became so enthusiastic that he even spent a week with one of Rivers' private classes at his home in Tonbridge, though he was distinctly put out to find that the rest of the group consisted entirely of young boys.

However, the best that Rivers could achieve was only a temporary relief, and despite Dodgson doing his best to work his jaw more vigorously and to keep the back of his tongue down in moments of crisis – 'I fear you might almost as well advise me to stand on my head'[2] – there were times when his affliction was as bad as ever. Years later, Isa Bowman recalled him trying to control his speech by reading aloud a scene from Shakespeare every day, while Mrs Stretton remembered his getting into difficulty telling a Sylvie and Bruno story: 'He'd suddenly stop and you wondered if you'd done anything wrong. Then you looked at him and you knew that you hadn't, it was all right ... He fought it very wonderfully.'[3]

It certainly did not prevent him from being appointed Court Story Teller at the Cecils' New Year parties at Hatfield where he would recount his favourite story of the Pixies or the Russian Tale of the Blacksmith and the

Hobgoblin – 'the appetite of the party for stories is insatiable'. He would also invent fresh episodes for Sylvie and Bruno, writing them down as soon as he had told them for fear of forgetting them.

Even so, 1874 was marked only by mathematical publications, a pamphlet on 'Suggestions as to the best method of Taking Votes where more than two issues are to be voted on' and the last and the most entertaining of his Liddell squibs, *The Blank Cheque*.

The ostensible reason for producing the pamphlet was a decision taken by Convocation to build new Examination Schools without laying before the University the expenses involved, or naming an architect (the building was in fact to be the subject of a competition). It virtually amounted, in Dodgson's opinion, to signing a blank cheque. In Dodgson's squib, the University is personified by Mr and Mrs Nivers, an extremely thinly disguised portrait of the Liddells at home. Mrs Nivers is vulgar and decidedly ignorant, cheerfully confusing asthmatic with aesthetic, and talks ten-to-the-dozen while her poor husband never manages to get a word in edgeways. Dodgson himself appears (initials reversed) as the mild-mannered Mr De Ciel, who happens to enquire where the family are intending to take their summer holidays. He is informed by Mrs Nivers that:

> We're certainly going somewhere, and we shan't even know the name of the place, till we find ourselves there![4]

They are as uncertain about finding a new school for their daughter Angela. It is finally decided that both the choice of holiday resort and of Angela's school shall be left entirely in the hands of the Nivers' maid, Susan, who is given a blank cheque to cover the whole of the expenses incurred. Dodgson was proved all too accurate in his prophecy about signing a blank cheque. Over £180,000 was spent on T.G. Jackson's grandiose Jacobean design and the University had to mortgage various properties in order to cover the cost.

The Blank Cheque was published three days before Lorina Liddell's wedding, and it can hardly have afforded her parents much amusement. In his diary for the day of the wedding, Dodgson begins to write 'Mrs L...' but then obviously thought better of it and crossed out the entry.

The undergraduates celebrated Lorina's nuptials with a firework display, but this was nothing to the fireworks which exploded over the publication of a squib by John Howe Jenkins, an undergraduate of Christ Church, which exposed the Liddells' ambitions far more ruthlessly than Dodgson had done in *The Vision of the Three T's*. This was *Cakeless*, mentioned earlier as identifying Dodgson as a rejected suitor for one of the

Liddell sisters, and it gives insight into an outsider's view of the Dodgson/ Liddell conflict.

Cakeless was designed to show that Lorina's match fell far short of the Liddells' matrimonial ambitions. It takes the form of a Grecian masque. Liddell appears as Apollo and his spouse as Diana, 'fond of hunting for husbands for her daughters', says a pencilled note. Like Mrs Nivers she can never stop talking. Apollo and Diana are about to celebrate a triple wedding of their daughters, Ecilia (Alice), Rose (Edith) and Psyche (Rhoda). Ecilia had been encouraged by her parents to 'aim high' and she has securely trapped 'Yerbua', Aubrey Harcourt, grandson of the Earl of Sheffield. (Harcourt was in fact a courtier at the Deanery but it was Edith he was interested in.) Rose's prize is 'Rivulus', Lord Brooke, the eldest son of the Earl of Warwick. Rhoda has outsoared them all, for she has trapped a 'Prince', Prince Leopold, who, as we have seen, was currently pursuing Alice.

Apollo enters, leading his three daughters, 'as a sacrifice to hymen', but before the ceremony can proceed, Kraftsohn (identified as '-dgs-n'), biting his nails, intervenes: 'I do protest against this match, so let me speak.' An irate Apollo orders the Scouts to strip the intruder and Kraftsohn protests in unmistakably Dodgsonian terms:

> *By circles, segments and radii,*
> *Than yield to these I'd liefer far to die.*[5]

The Scouts, led by Romanus, advance upon Kraftsohn, throwing their 'perquisites'. Romanus, incidentally, reveals that Kraftsohn 'never did to early temple go' nor tasted 'luscious steak' in hall but would never forsake his 'frugal luncheon', a reference to Dodgson's habit of taking only a biscuit and a glass of sherry. Romanus also supplies a summary of Kraftsohn's better known works:

> *Take him through trench and tunnel to the chest,*
> *Nor ever leave the cursed fiend at rest.*
> *Leave him in Wonderland with some hard hitting foe,*
> *And through the looking-glass let him survey the blow;*
> *Confine him in the belfry, not in Peck,*
> *And make him sign at pleasure your blank cheque.*

Diana is more concerned with the fact that the wedding cake has not arrived but Apollo is delighted that Kraftsohn has been imprisoned in the 'chest', the New Belfry. Romanus and his satellites seize the foe of the Scout and drag him off towards the 'plashing sea where the crocodile lives and the kedgeree', while Kraftsohn bids farewell to 'pamphlets and to angles round: I seek a shore where Euclid is not found'.

John Howe Jenkins may have had an uncertain ear for prosody, but he had a sharp ear for college gossip. He was well acquainted with Dodgson's eating habits, and knew that he had been paying court to one of the Liddell sisters. But what *Cakeless* demonstrates above all is the notoriety of Dodgson's pamphlets. *The Vision of the Three T's* had gone through three editions in one year, and had been reissued in 1874 with *The New Belfry* and *The Blank Cheque* (along with Dodgson's other Oxford squibs) as *Notes by an Oxford Chiel*. Far from being the shy, retiring don of legend, Dodgson was regarded as one of Oxford's more contentious figures. The unfortunate John Howe Jenkins was promptly sent down for his satire, but Dodgson remained at Christ Church for the rest of his life.

Three weeks after Lorina's marriage, Ellen Terry made her return to the stage. Six years earlier, while playing in a particularly dire little piece called *The Household Fairy*, she had committed the most defiantly dramatic act of her life and had run off with her lover, the flamboyant architect and theatre designer, William Godwin, to lead a life of idyllic rural bliss at Gustard Wood Common in Hertfordshire. There she bore two children, Edith and Edward 'and experienced exquisite delight from the mere fact of being in the country'.[6]

It was a long time before Dodgson learned anything of this. Kate never spoke of her sister and the doors of Moray Lodge were barred to her. Mrs Terry did her best to put a face of respectability on it all and told Dodgson that Ellen was 'staying in lodgings'. When at last he discovered the truth, he was predictably horrified: 'I felt that she had so entirely sacrificed her social position that I had no desire but to end the acquaintance.'[7] Not only had she set up house with a man who was not her husband, but she was still, technically, married to G.F. Watts.

But the more he thought about it, the harder he found it to dismiss Ellen Terry from his mind as a conventional 'fallen woman'. He admired her, to a degree even loved her, and he did his best to try and understand what had happened and to provide himself with an explanation for her 'mad conduct'. Even though he could not share her need for physical love, he did try to come to terms with it. In the process he surrounded her with a conventional Victorian picture frame, but he did at least try to understand her defiance of the moral code of the time. Years later he put his apologia into words for the benefit of the mother of one of his little girl friends whom he wanted to introduce to the great actress:

I honestly believe her position was, from her point of view, this:
'I am tied by <u>human</u> law to a man who disowns his share of what

ought to be a <u>mutual</u> contract. He never loved me and I do not believe, in God's sight, we are man and wife. Society expects me to live, till this man's death, as if I were single and to give up all hope of that form of love for which I pine and shall never get from <u>him</u>. This other man loves me as truly and faithfully as any lawful husband. If the marriage ceremony were *possible* I would insist on it before living with him. It is <u>not</u> possible and I will do without it.'[8]

Ellen Terry would, no doubt, have dismissed such pleading as pure hypocrisy. Marriage had never been a consideration. 'I have the simplest faith that absolute devotion to another human being means the greatest happiness,' was the way she put it. 'That happiness for a time was now *mine*.'[9]

Ellen's happiness, however, was coming to an end when Charles Reade, the novelist and playwright, came across her in a country lane when a wheel had just come off her pony cart. He did not have much difficulty in persuading her to give up the rural idyll and play the lead in his forthcoming play, *The Wandering Heir*. The play was conventional and unexciting, but it enabled Ellen Terry to make a triumphant return, despite the fact that her family boycotted the first night. Dodgson held out until 15th April, when he went to see the play with Dubourg. 'Her acting is simply *wonderful*,'[10] he wrote, but although he might admire her, he could not meet her. She was still living with Godwin in Taviton Street, and G.F. Watts was still legally her husband.

Dodgson had planned to spend the summer at Sandown on the Isle of Wight (on the opposite side of the island from Tennyson), working on his edition of the first two books of Euclid. As a diversion, he would take his camera with him and try some 'child subjects (in which the island abounds)'. He called in at The Chestnuts on 30th June where he found Aunt Lucy and Henrietta doing their best to care for his cousin and godchild Charlie Wilcox, who had developed inflammation of the lungs. As usual, the house was overflowing with people and Dodgson sought refuge in the Old Rectory with Edwin, who at long last had decided on his future. He would take Holy Orders and was studying at the Theological College in Chichester.

Dodgson returned briefly to Christ Church to pack up his photographic apparatus and to send off a note to Gathorne Hardy suggesting changes in the wording of money orders (always something of an obsession with him) but before he could set off for Sandown he received a message from Fanny telling him that Charlie Wilcox's condition was worsening. There was nothing for it but to return to Guildford and take a turn in the nursing, although there was still no room for him in the house.

On 18th July, Margaret Wilcox sat up with Charlie until three in the morning when Dodgson, who habitually took the night shift, came to relieve her. He watched over his godson until six in the morning, snatched a few hours' sleep at the Old Rectory and went out on to the North Downs to clear his mind of the sick chamber. While he was walking a single line of verse came unbidden into his mind:

> For the Snark was a Boojum, you see.

'I knew not what it meant,' he wrote many years later, 'I know not what it means now; but I wrote it down, and some time afterwards the rest of the stanza occurred to me, that being its last line.'[11] Within four days, in intervals between nursing Charlie, he had worked out what was to be the final stanza of 'The Hunting of the Snark':

> In the midst of the word he was trying to say,
> In the midst of his laughter and glee,
> He had softly and suddenly vanished away –
> For the Snark *was* a Boojum, you see.

What had happened before these lines was still a complete mystery to him, but he set to work to try and chart what series of events could possibly have led up to that chilling and awe-inspiring conclusion. Perhaps because he was spending his nights in Charlie Wilcox's sick room his mind went back to a Wilcox gathering years before at Whitburn in 1855 when the party had sat down to a game of verse making. It was then that the first stanza of Jabberwocky had come into his mind and this may have been why he set the final scene of his poem on the 'island that the Jabberwock was slain'.

On 31st July, a physician was called down from London who pronounced that one of Charlie's lungs was seriously diseased. The boy was not to move from The Chestnuts for at least six weeks, after which he might spend some time by the sea or go on a short voyage, but by the end of August Charlie seemed 'decidedly convalescent' and Dodgson returned to the Isle of Wight. At the end of the first week of September, Charlie was showing sufficient signs of improvement for him to be moved to the seaside and Margaret Wilcox came down from Guildford to find lodgings for him at Ventnor, five miles south of Sandown. Throughout the month the Wilcoxes began to arrive in droves and Dodgson, who had gone down ahead, tramped round the island trying to find rooms for them all. Menella Smedley, never one to miss a family crisis, took over half of Palmerston House. In between going back-and-forth to escort various groups of

Wilcoxes over from Portsmouth, Dodgson found time to take a few pictures of Florence, alias 'Birdie' Balfour, to tell stories to a girl called Kitty Napier and to delight in the antics of the Thresher children, 'who indulge in the rather unusual luxury of sitting in the sea, in ordinary dress'.[12]

By the begining of October virtually the whole Wilcox clan had assembled on the island together with a fair selection of Dodgsons including Wilfred and Alice Skeffington, Fanny, Louisa and Mary Collingwood, as well as the Hassard Dodgsons from Putney. They all went off together on expeditions round the island, visiting Bonchurch and the Landslip, perhaps marching shoulder to shoulder like the crew of the Snark. Poor Charlie suffered a serious relapse, and it seemed likely that he would be on the island throughout the winter. Dodgson found him warmer lodgings on Ventnor esplanade, but there seemed little more he could do and since Charlie was now surrounded by his entire family, he returned to Christ Church. On 11th November, after an illness which had lasted five months, Charlie Wilcox died at Ventnor.

'Surely the fittest day for it to appear?'

By the time of his godson's death in November 1874, Dodgson had already sketched out the first three cantos (or 'fits' as he had chosen to call them) of the poem which had come to him, unbidden, on the North Downs. Although it would be nearly a year-and-a-half before 'The Boojum', as he then titled it, would be complete, he lost no time in setting an illustrator to work; he wanted no repetition of the interminable frustrating delays which Tenniel had inflicted on *Through the Looking Glass*. From the first, Dodgson was determined that the pictures should be drawn by his old friend Henry Holiday, and as soon as the drafts of the first three 'fits' of 'The Boojum' were complete, they were sent off, and by November Dodgson was able to show the pictures to Ruskin, who was not impressed:

> He much disheartened me by holding out no hopes that Holiday
> would be able to illustrate a book satisfactorily.[1]

Dodgson decided to ignore Ruskin's misgivings and continued to send the 'fits' on to Holiday.

Henry Holiday is chiefly remembered now for his painting of Dante and Beatrice in the Walker Art Gallery in Liverpool, but in his lifetime he had a considerable reputation as a designer of stained glass, with windows in Salisbury, Westminster Abbey (commemorating Brunel), Boston, New York, Toronto and Philadelphia. Dodgson first met him in 1870 when they were introduced by Dr Kitchin, who had taken Dodgson to watch Holiday working on a frieze illustrating the Te Deum over the stalls of Worcester College Chapel.

'We became friends on the spot,' wrote Holiday, 'and continued so until his death.' Holiday frequently stayed in Dodgson's rooms at Christ Church and, in turn, Dodgson took over Holiday's various large houses in London where he would set up a photographic base-camp. A wide selection of his friends and acquaintances would be invited to pose or simply to watch while Holiday's pet gazelle, Psyche, pranced about the garden devouring everything within reach. Lord Salisbury came, as did his daughters Maud and Gwendolen, the Du Mauriers and the Terrys.

Dodgson was fascinated by a suit of chain mail which had been made for Holiday when he was painting a mural of the signing of Magna Carta for Rochdale Town Hall. (Since at least seventeen of the Barons are clad in chain mail it must have been put to good use.) Dodgson persuaded Marion Terry to put it on and photographed her lying uncomfortably on the lawn while Holiday sketched her. The painter shared Dodgson's preoccupation with naked children and made a number of sketches which Dodgson later used as the basis for poses in his own photographic compositions.

As a consequence of their friendship, Holiday was allowed a far freer hand than had ever been permitted Tenniel. He took what with any other artist Dodgson would have considered outrageous liberties. In the illustration for the crew pursuing their quarry with 'forks and hope', Holiday introduced a very un-Carrollean, voluptuous, thinly clad, bare-bosomed beauty. In the background was another classical intruder, seemingly in a gesture of despair. These, Holiday said, were intended to represent Hope and Care. When Dodgson told him that he had confused the two meanings of the word: 'with –

> *They sought it with thimbles, they sought it with care;*
> *They pursued it with forks and hope …'*

Holiday replied, '… precisely, and I intended to add a third – "in company with".' Dodgson, worsted by logic, gave way, 'so the ladies were allowed to join the hunt'.[2] Dodgson later became so enamoured of the intrusive beauties that he proposed an edition with the heads of Hope and Care bordered with forks and thimbles for the front and back covers.

Not that Holiday had it all his own way. Dodgson considered his first sketch of the Broker far too vulgar a specimen of his profession and Holiday was obliged to tone him down. One of the very first pictures which Dodgson asked him to undertake was of the Baker vanishing, the point of departure for the whole poem. Holiday introduced a most formidable Boojum, looking rather like a demented elephant seal. This was immediately vetoed by Dodgson, who told his illustrator that although it was a 'delightful monster' it was quite inadmissible. 'All his descriptions of the Boojum were quite unimaginable and he wanted the creature to remain so.'[3] The Boojum was the incarnation of Dodgson's profound horror of death, and must be left hidden in the remotest corner of his mind.

Holiday's contribution is of a quite different order to Tenniel's or to the pictures that Harry Furniss would provide for *Sylvie and Bruno*. His pictures do not so much illustrate the poem as provide a kind of commentary on it, underlining its anarchy, opening up its terrors and its unrelenting nihilism.

Originally Dodgson appears to have intended the poem to form part of *Sylvie and Bruno*, which was slowly beginning to piece itself together in his mind out of tales told to the Salisbury children, odds and ends of poems, fragments of sermons and anything else he thought might be fitted in. The framework for the insertion of the Snark was left in its place in the second part of the story, when the Professor asks his fairy friends if they know what a Boojum is and, finding that Bruno thinks it is a bootjack, begins to explain:

> 'Once upon a time there was a Boojum – ' the Professor began, but stopped suddenly. 'I forget the rest of the fable,' he said. 'And there was a lesson to be learned from it. I'm afraid I forget that too.'

In the ingeniously unhelpful introduction which Dodgson wrote for the completed poem he tantalisingly hints at the possibility of the fable's 'moral purpose', but says no more. In all his subsequent comments on the poems he went to great pains to state that if the poem had any meaning, he was wholly ignorant of it:

> Periodically I have received courteous letters from strangers, begging to know whether *The Hunting of The Snark* is an allegory or contains some hidden moral, or is a political satire; and for all such questions I have but one answer, I do not know!

That summer he went to stay again in Sandown with his old landlord, Mr Bignell. There he found many of his old friends, Kitty Napier and 'Birdie', and he rescued a kitten which had a fish-hook stuck in its throat. Next door were living a clergyman from Hampshire, James Chataway, and his family. His nine-year-old daughter, Gertrude, became immensely interested in their strange neighbour:

> He would come on to his balcony, which joined ours, sniffing the sea air with his head thrown back, and would walk right down the steps on to the beach with his chin in the air, drinking in the fresh breezes as if he could never have enough.[4]

He asked her why she always ran to her balcony when he came out. 'To see you sniff,' she told him. They were soon spending hours together on the beach, with Dodgson telling tales and, as usual, drawing pictures as he went along. 'His vivid imagination would fly from one subject to another,' she remembered, 'and was never tied down in any way by the probabilities of life.'

Gertrude's costume for the beach consisted of bathing drawers and a fisherman's jersey, 'a thing quite unheard of in those days'. Dodgson pronounced it eminently sensible, but he was clearly fascinated by it. He asked her to come round to his lodgings and made sketches of her in her beach attire. 'May she grow up,' he wrote wistfully to her mother, 'as delightful a woman as she is a child, and be the household treasure of some happy man, far on in summers that I shall not see.'[5] He began to compose an acrostic poem about Gertrude and her 'boyish garb'.

> Eager she wields her spade: yet loves as well
> Rest on a friendly knee, the tale to ask
> That he delights to tell.

At the same time the idea occurred to him to publish 'The Hunting of the Snark' that Christmas, dedicated to Gertrude. Macmillan had become a little wary of Dodgson's Christmas ventures and told him that the engraver could not possibly cut the blocks for the illustrations in less than three months. Would Dodgson be interested in publishing the poem without pictures in the forthcoming Christmas number of *Macmillan's Magazine*, 'to serve your purpose in keeping yourself fresh before the public?' Dodgson was unenthusiastic about the poem appearing in this way and considered publishing it with only one illustration, *The Landing*, as a frontispiece. He also thought of gumming in 'another little Christmas letter'[6] to his readers and had the distinctly odd notion of adding 'an advertisement for a house (and garden perhaps) in or near London, where I might put up a studio and take portraits for about a month each summer'.

None of these ideas came to anything and Dodgson resigned himself to publication the following Easter with his Christmas letter changed to an Easter Greeting and no advertisement. He continued to work sporadically and erratically on the poem but it was not until January that he completed the work. 'The Hunting of the Snark' finally made its appearance on 1st April, 1876 – 'Surely the fittest day for it to appear?' It marked a modest innovation in publishing, for Dodgson had invented the dust jacket. 'The advantage will be that it can stand in bookstalls without being taken out of paper (sic) and so can be kept in cleaner and more saleable condition.'[7]

Dodgson seized the opportunity of the poem's publication to compose a whole series of acrostic poems to girl friends of all ages to accompany their presentation copies. For Edith Denman, who was the daughter of a judge, he wrote:

> If the scales thou wield with care
> Truth and justice will declare
> Hunting Snarks is innocent and wise![8]

Curiously he persisted in regarding the Snark as a child's poem and wrote off merrily to Florence 'Birdie' Balfour asking if she could 'quite' understand it. 'If you do, please tell *me*: for I haven't an idea of what it is like.'[9]

The reviewers certainly had no idea of what it might be about. *The Athenaeum* spoke of the poem being 'inspired by a wild desire to reduce to idiocy as many readers, and more especially, reviewers, as possible'. *The Spectator* dismissed it as tiresome nonsense and *Vanity Fair* thought that it had little to recommend it beyond the name of the author. That alone, however, assured the book a steady sale, and the poem soon found enthusiastic, not to say fanatical, supporters. Collingwood heard of a little girl who had memorised the entire poem and who insisted on reciting it during the course of a long carriage drive. Dodgson continued to be besieged by readers wanting to know what he had meant by the poem, but he continued blandly to deny that it had any meaning at all.

Even if Dodgson did not know what his poem meant, there were plenty of people who believed that they did. Dodgson was prepared to accept a suggestion that it was an allegory of the pursuit of happiness, but he was understandably bewildered by readers who likened it to 'an unsound business venture' or the craving for social advancement or an expedition to the Arctic. Dante Gabriel Rossetti, his brain hopelessly impeded by his chloral addiction, believed that the poem was directed specifically against him and never spoke to Dodgson again.

If the poem has any meaning at all other than the story which it has to tell, it is not a satire on some abstract idea – Dodgson always made certain that his satires hit their targets in such a way that everyone would understand exactly what he meant. 'The Hunting of the Snark' is very closely bound up with the circumstances in which the concluding lines came into Dodgson's head. In his presentation acrostic to Ellen Terry's sister Marion, Dodgson writes:

> *Is it life of which it tells?*
> *Of a pulse that sinks and swells,*
> *Never lacking chime of bells,*[10]

which sounds very much as if he were dwelling on memories of looking after Charles Wilcox through the long night-hours. The boy's death had brought back to Dodgson all his own horror of being snuffed out like a candle, of softly and suddenly vanishing away like the Baker confronted with his own particular Boojum.

Dodgson, meanwhile, was pursuing a very determined personal crusade against what he believed to be one of the nineteenth-century's greatest evils: vivisection. 'I was once walking in Oxford with him,' his nephew remembered, 'when a certain well-known professor passed us. '"I am afraid that man vivisects,"[11] he said in his gravest tone.'

The use of live animals in experiments was regarded by its apologists as the means by which medical science might be most effectively advanced. Dodgson, despite his vexation at Ethel Arnold's dog and his desire to see it put down, saw himself as a champion of the animal world, and he regarded the knowing infliction of suffering as an abomination:

> Can the man who has once realised by minute study what the nerves are, what the brain is, and what waves of agony the one can convey to the other, go forth and wantonly inflict pain on any sentient being?

The argument that knowledge gained from animal experiments would benefit mankind was another instance of what Dodgson condemned as the 'worship of self' and, in a letter to *The Pall Mall Gazette* on 'Vivisection as a Sign of the Times', signed as 'Lewis Carroll', he went on to chart the path of Victorian 'advancement':

> The enslavement of his weaker brethren – the labour of those who do not enjoy, for the enjoyment of those who do not labour – the degradation of woman – the torture of the animal world – these are the steps of the ladder by which man is ascending to his higher civilisation.

In May 1875, Dodgson followed up his letter with an article for *The Pall Mall Gazette* on 'Some Popular Fallacies about Vivisection' which was declined by the editor on the grounds that the fallacies were 'unheard of'. Dodgson pointed out that the fallacies in question came from an article published by the *Gazette*, and passed his article on to *The Fortnightly Review*.

The authorship of the pamphlet in which Dodgson's article was reprinted has been called into question, and its tone is unusually robust. Nevertheless, the unrelenting logic of the argument is unmistakably Dodgsonian. The attack on man's cruelty to his fellow creatures is extended to field sports and bull fighting; it is not in the suffering caused to animals that the evil lies, but in the subsequent degradation of the human soul. Dodgson's bleak view of the consequences of this when the vivisector becomes 'a new and more hideous Frankenstein' comes close to anticipating the horrors of the Nazi concentration camps:

> the possible advent of a day when anatomy shall claim as legitimate subjects for experiment, first, our condemned criminals – next,

perhaps, the inmates of our refuges for incurables – then the hopeless lunatic, the pauper hospital patient, and generally him that hath no helper.[12]

He was by no means the only writer to take up the cause. Christina Rossetti got up a petition against 'that horror of horrors' and wrote a poem, 'Pity the sorrows of a poor old dog', for sale at an anti-vivisection bazaar. Ruskin resigned his Slade Professorship as a protest against the establishment of a vivisection laboratory in Oxford. Miss Francis Power Cobbe, an advocate of women's suffrage, applauded Dodgson's stand and paid him a visit at Christ Church in May 1875. Ironically, she was turned away by the porters because she had her dog with her.

Pamphlets and letters were not the only means by which Dodgson conducted his campaign. He tried to enlist Lord Salisbury's support when a measure bringing in restrictive legislation came before Parliament:

> It seems to me that there is a terrible need for legislation – not so much in the interests of the poor tortured animals as of the demoralised and brutalised medical students ...[13]

Dodgson's appeal to Salisbury may have been undermined by the fact that he was constantly seeking the great statesman's help on a wide range of interests – from finding employment for various members of the Wilcox family, to drawing his attention to a School for Drama which Dubourg proposed to set up.

Dodgson spent the New Year of 1876, as was now his custom, in the Jacobean splendours of Hatfield House with the Cecils. There was a ball for one-hundred-and-fifty children and charades and quadrilles and nursery rhymes and a six-mile walk with Lord Salisbury. This year, however, Dodgson refused to sing for his supper:

> I declined to undertake my usual role as story teller in the morning, and so (I hope) broke the rule of always being expected to do it.[14]

As he grew older, Dodgson became increasingly prone to refusing what he was asked to do or what was anticipated of him. He felt that he was being taken for granted by the Cecils and used as a kind of Punch and Judy man. The children were older now, Maud was sixteen and Gwendolen fourteen, and were not interested in tales of fairy babies. Dodgson did not return to Hatfield until 1884, even though Lady Salisbury made several attempts to persuade him to come and see them:

> Though you have forsworn children's parties perhaps grave old folks may tempt you. Will you come down on Dec 19th for a few days and

be old and serious?[15]

But on that occasion Dodgson was too absorbed in Euclid to be tempted.

He was growing increasingly high-handed in his dealings with the great and famous, and with royalty in particular. He was very keen to present Louise Victoria, the eldest daughter of the Prince of Wales, with a copy of 'The Hunting of the Snark', but everyone he consulted told him that this could only be accomplished 'through the hands of a secretary, or some other official'. Dodgson was not prepared to put up with nonsense from royalty any more than was Alice. In May 1875 he had met and photographed Prince Leopold. The picture had not been a complete success, since the Prince could not manage to keep still, but Dodgson had been invited to lunch, had been placed next to his royal host and had been treated with respect. Prince Leopold, Dodgson decided, would help him to cut through the absurdity of official protocol:

> If your Royal Highness could either present the book, for me, to the little Princess herself, or get permission for me to send it direct, I should esteem such an offer highly: but if the only available process is that the book should pass through the hands of a Secretary, I had rather not send it at all.[16]

The Prince could not offer much hope. He would approach his sister-in-law, the Princess of Wales. He told Dodgson, 'The amount of etiquette with which we are surrounded is indeed very tiresome ... but it is not in my power to diminish it.'[17] As far as is known, the book was never presented.

Memories of the book's dedicatee, Gertrude Chataway, continued to haunt Dodgson and in June 1876 he began to make arrangements for her to come and be photographed in the 'wading attire' which had clearly been something of an obsession. Now, however, he wanted to go a little further:

> If you should decide on sending over Gertrude and not coming yourself, would you kindly let me know what is the minimum amount of dress in which you are willing to have her taken?[18]

He would himself, he blithely informed Mrs Chataway, see no objection to photographing Gertrude, 'in Eve's original dress', provided that the girl were willing. If she were not, or if Mrs Chataway opposed the idea, he would of course give it up, 'though I do not once in a hundred cases, get so well-formed a subject for art'. What is disquieting is that he had evidently discussed the matter with Gertrude.

Dodgson's plans were thwarted by the sudden death of Gertrude's sister, Alice, and this was followed by another death, far closer to home. Edith Liddell had died suddenly on 26th June, of peritonitis. 'One of the three I have told you of,' he wrote to Mrs Chataway, 'the most intimate child friends I have ever had.'[19] Edith's death had come only one week after the announcement of her engagement to Aubrey Harcourt.

The Dodgsons had planned a family holiday together that summer at Sandown. His sisters came and went, as did Wilfred and Alice and their four-year-old daughter, Edith, but Dodgson continued to lament Gertrude's absence:

> Explain to me how I can enjoy Sandown without you. How can I walk the beach alone? How can I sit all alone on those wooden steps?[20]

There were of course compensations: a little girl called 'Boofy' who did her best to solve his wire puzzles, and Nellie da Silva, whom Dodgson rescued from an ugly scene after she had broken the peep-holes of a bathing-machine because she thought that the keeper mistreated his old horse. Kitty Napier and her sister played with Wilfred's daughter, but Dodgson took exception to the 'tribe of young roughs' who invariably accompanied Mrs Napier – 'they are hardly the sort that we want as our acquaintance here!'[21]

The five-year-old Lily Grey, daughter of a fellow of Exeter College, played on the beach with the Collingwood boys 'without an atom of shyness' and on his return to Oxford she came up to Dodgson's rooms to be photographed in the nude holding a wand in her hand. 'It is quite a privilege to have a subject for photography so entirely indifferent as to dress.'

Emboldened by his success with Lily, Dodgson wrote to Mrs Chataway telling her about the pictures he had taken of Lily Grey and suggested that Gertrude be photographed with her 'in the same way'. Mrs Chataway arrived with her daughter on 15 October and 'much against inclinations' she made concessions to Dodgson's 'rather *outré* and unconventional notions of art'. During a four-hour session, Gertrude was photographed in her beach attire, in her 'Swanage Costume' (whatever that may have been), in her nightdress and in nothing at all.

After her return to London, Mrs Chataway began to have misgivings and asked for the negatives to be erased. Dodgson had at first offered to do so, but now he grew characteristically stubborn:

> You speak of erasing a negative with a calmness which a photographer would not share with regard to any of his artistic offspring.[22]

Reluctantly he agreed to erase three of the pictures, but a negative of Gertrude and two other girls in their bathing drawers was locked up to be destroyed by his executors.

Dodgson's obsession with taking pictures of little girls scantily clad or 'in Eve's original dress' was threatening to become dangerous.

'I give you the Circumference!'

'My occupation,' Dodgson noted in his diary for the first day of 1877, 'is preparing my "Euclid" protest.'[1] Ever since he had begun teaching mathematics at Christ Church, geometry had been the subject of intense scrutiny, particularly in Germany (and consequently in Cambridge). A number of theories and interpretations had come into being in which Euclid had been subjected to the revisionary fervour of a host of rival geometers, Legendre, Cooley, Cuthbertson, Wilson, Pierce, Willock, all of whom offered alternative methods. Loyalty to Euclid was an essential part of Dodgson's mathematical philosophy – he had come to regard him almost as a personal possession and saw himself as his champion and prophet. What was needed, in his view, was a work which would conclusively demonstrate the necessity for retaining Euclid as the standard manual of geometry and would emphasise its superiority to the rivals who had challenged its authority. His difficulty was that he could not settle on a sufficiently effective way of putting his arguments across.

There were so many distractions, too. *Goody Two Shoes* was playing at the Adelphi with Connie Gilchrist – 'one of the most beautiful children, in face and figure, that I have ever seen' – playing Harlequin, and little Bertie Coote, one of the few boy actors to become a close friend, as the Clown. Ellen Terry was in a new play at the Court Theatre, *New Men and Old Acres*, jointly written by Dubourg and Tom Taylor. 'The gush of a light-hearted girl is beyond her now, poor thing!' he wrote. 'She can give a clever imitation of it, but that is all.'[2]

The old desire to see Alice take her place in the theatre stirred in him again, but his ideas had grown more ambitious. The previous year G.R. Buckland had put on *Alice's Adventures* as an entertainment for children at the Polytechnic in Regent Street, in a production consisting of dissolving slides of the illustrations, spoken narration and scenes acted out in dumb show. The songs had been composed by a very minor composer, William Boyd of Worcester College, who managed to persuade Dodgson to add two lines to ' 'Tis the Voice of the Lobster':

I passed by his garden, and marked, with one eye,

> How the owl and the oyster were sharing a pie,
> While the duck and the Dodo, the lizard and cat
> Were swimming in milk round the brim of a hat.

Dodgson went to see the performance with his sisters, Caroline and Henrietta, but took great exception to an interpolated song for a footman and housemaid, which Buckland was obliged to omit.

Dodgson had not been greatly impressed by Boyd's music, but never one to set limitations on his ambition, he approached the leading composer of the day, Arthur Sullivan. His first approach to Sullivan was cautiously non-committal, merely enquiring what were the possibilities of his accepting a commission. Sullivan replied that while he was always glad to 'get good words for music', he never accepted commissions. Dodgson reckoned that it would do no harm to push himself forward a little:

> I am the writer of a little book for children, *Alice's Adventures in Wonderland*, which has proved so unexpectedly popular that the idea of dramatising it has been several times started ...[3]

If this were ever to happen, it would have to be done 'in the best possible way' and one essential ingredient would be 'good music'. Would Sullivan be prepared to set two or three songs 'to be kept for the occasion (if that should happen) of its being dramatised'.

Sullivan was both charmed and baffled by this rather roundabout approach. He had no idea that he had been addressing *the* Lewis Carroll and had often thought that the story should be dramatised. When that happened he would be glad to enter into it, but he could not write a song and then part with it to Dodgson, 'except under conditions which would be thought absurdly extravagant'. Dodgson was not to be diverted from his singularly oblique approach – the existence of two or three song settings by Sullivan might well enable an Alice operetta to become a reality. There was also the possibility that by the time a dramatisation of Alice was complete, Sullivan might not be free to undertake it:

> what I know of your music is so delicious (they tell me I have not a musical ear – so my criticism is valueless, I fear) that I should like to secure something from you now, while there is leisure time to do it in.[4]

This delightfully ingenuous suggestion failed to get any response at all from Sullivan. Eventually he rather grudgingly agreed to apply his talents at the cost of thirty guineas a song. However, the song which he did attempt (sadly we do not know which) came to nothing since he said he could not cope with the irregular metre. So ended what might have been quite a remarkable venture. Considering the problems he was to encounter working with Gilbert, Sullivan might have found Dodgson an understanding partner.

What is curious is that Dodgson should have been so unusually reticent about attempting the dramatisation himself. Perhaps the failure of *Morning Clouds* undermined his confidence, or he felt that Alice could only be put on the stage by someone who could take an objective view of it. For the time being he put it out of his mind and turned his attention to *Sylvie and Bruno*. At this time *Sylvie and Bruno* consisted of little more than two published stories, *Fairy Sylvie* and *Bruno's Revenge*, and what he had managed to write down of the tales told to the children at Hatfield House. As yet Dodgson could see no way of stringing these together into a coherent story and he managed to convince himself that this was because he could not find a suitable person to illustrate it.

> I have some half-defined ideas, and a small amount of material for
> another tale [he told Luke Fildes] but I have been for some time
> discouraged from going on with it by the apparent hopelessness of
> finding an artist worthy to succeed Mr Tenniel.[5]

Luke Fildes, to whom Dodgson turned in July 1877, is probably best known for *The Village Wedding*. He was to achieve a considerable reputation and a modest fortune as a portrait painter, but it was his illustrations to *Edwin Drood* which first attracted Dodgson's attention to him.

Would Fildes be willing, at some time in the future, to illustrate a book, 'of the same general character as Alice's Adventures (if you do not know the book, I will send you a copy to look at)' and would he undertake to draw three or four pictures for a short tale?

> Such a book as I am hoping to write would require pictures of (1)
> children, (2) perhaps fairies, (3) grotesques like the Queen of Hearts in
> "Alice". It is true that neither children nor Grotesques occur in Edwin
> Drood, but I fancy I see in those pictures almost unlimited power of
> drawing and wonderful variety ...[6]

Fildes was rather disconcerted by the novelty of Dodgson's approach. His son suggests that he had probably not the least desire to draw fairies or grotesques, but the painter temporised. His last academy exhibit, *Playmates*, had not been a conspicuous success, and he was spending his time looking for a suitable location for his next subject, *The Return of the Penitent*. He told Dodgson that he would be unable to attempt anything for the next twelve months but that he had 'not positively decided to do no more wood-drawing'. In the end, however, nothing came of it.

Fildes was not the first illustrator that Dodgson had approached over

Sylvie and Bruno. Henry Holiday produced a charming sketch of the fairy pair but this was never followed up. Henry Paton was always too busy, and F. Gilbert's original picture for *Bruno's Revenge* had been dismissed by Dodgson as 'something like a blacksmith and a ballet-dancer'. In November 1877, Dodgson wrote to the painter Walter Crane, whose illustrations for Mrs Molesworth's *The Cuckoo Clock* encouraged him to think that here was the artist he was looking for. Crane wrote:

> Children's books ... are attractive to designers of an imaginative tendency, for in a sober and matter of fact age, they afford perhaps the only outlet for unrestricted flights of fancy open to the modern illustrator who likes to revolt against the 'despotism of facts'.[7]

An ideal partner, one might have thought, but Crane was very wary after receiving his first letter from Dodgson.

> His letters gave one the impression of a most peculiar person, and it is quite possible that he may have led Tenniel anything but a quiet life during the time he was engaged upon his inimitable illustrations.[8]

Having agreed to undertake one drawing, Crane was unable to summon up any enthusiasm for the story, and again, there was no result.

Unable to make progress on any of the projects closest to his heart, Dodgson produced very little that year. A proposal before the Hebdomadal Council to give a degree in Natural Science, conferring the same privileges as the M.A. degree, but requiring only one ancient language, provoked a predictable and highly entertaining response. In a letter to *The Pall Mall Gazette*, Dodgson rehearsed the whole history of science at Oxford. He pictured it sitting weeping at the gates, begging to be admitted:

> Why cram reluctant youth with your unsatisfying lore? Are they not hungering for bones; yea, panting for sulphuretted hydrogen?[9]

The motion was carried by 63 votes to 40, so that Dodgson at least had the consolation that a substantial minority agreed with him.

His lack of any constant occupation, other than teaching, that year and his need to find pastimes for his constantly restless mind, led him to devise a system for recalling dates and numbers, his 'Memoria Technica' as he called it. Mnemosyne, the goddess of memory and mother of the Muses, had a way of leaving Dodgson high and dry when it came to recalling faces and dates. On one occasion he went up to London to dine with a recently acquired acquaintance:

> The next morning a gentleman greeted him as he was walking. 'I beg

your pardon,' said Mr Dodgson, 'but you have the advantage of me. I have no remembrance of having ever seen you before this moment.' 'That is very strange,' the other replied, 'for I was your host last night.'[10]

Dodgson's system would have been of little use to him in such a situation, but it did enable him to remember such essentials as the foundation dates of the Oxford Colleges and the specific gravities of metals, provided that is, he could remember the rhyming couplet in which this information was preserved. Memoria Technica was based on a system devised in the eighteenth-century by Richard Gray. In Dodgson's version, each number is represented by one or more consonants:

> 1. 'b' and 'c' the first two consonants in the alphabet.
> 2. 'd' from 'duo', 'w' from 'two'.

Dodgson's choice of consonants is random and arbitrary in the extreme and very difficult for anyone to follow other than its wilful creator.

> Now suppose you wish to remember the date of the discovery of America, which is 1492: the '1' may be left out as obvious; all we need is '492'.
> Write it thus:
> 4 9 2
> f n d
> q g w
> and try to find a word that contains 'f' or 'q', 'n' or 'g', 'd' or 'w'. A word soon suggests itself – 'found'.
> The poetic faculty must now be brought into play, and the following couplet will soon be evolved:
> 'Columbus sailed the world around,
> Until America was FOUND'.[11]

All of which seems incredibly cumbersome compared with the old rhyme:

> *Columbus sailed the ocean blue*
> *In fourteen hundred and ninety-two.*

Dodgson wrote out his Memoria Technica with his 'electric pen', equipped with a tiny wheel instead of a nib, which made minute holes in the paper, so that copies of what had been written could be made by passing ink through the holes. Dodgson was very enthusiastic about his new toy but, as with Memoria Technica, it seems a highly elaborate way of going about a relatively simple task.

Two weeks after his electric account of Memoria Technica, Dodgson left for Eastbourne. He had been looking for an alternative to Sandown, which was becoming increasingly unsatisfactory, and had made a preliminary reconnaissance of the town in April when he had pronounced it 'a good seaside place'. On 31st July, Dodgson moved into new lodgings at 7 Lushington Road, Eastbourne, with Mr and Mrs Dyer. He described her as a 'good motherly creature'; Mr Dyer worked at the Post Office. Dodgson was to stay with the Dyers every summer for the next nineteen years, in fact, for the rest of his life.

Eastbourne had been a fashionable bathing place since the early years of the century and by the 1870s there was a mile-and-a-half of promenade stretching from the Wish Tower to the Redoubt. It boasted a pier, winter gardens, theatres, bandstands and pleasure gardens. The resort had a reputation for being select and respectable; excursionists were rare, as were the kind of young rowdies Dodgson had so disapproved of at Sandown. Outside the town was Beachy Head, 575 feet high, the haunt of puffins, guillemots and razorbills.

Louisa, Margaret and Edwin came down to join him, as did Elizabeth and Margaret Wilcox. Eastbourne was to be the family's holiday place as much as Dodgson's, but he was always careful to maintain his independence, using Lushington Road as his workplace and, from time to time, as a house where he could invite especially favoured little girls to come and stay. It was as a place for making child friends that Eastbourne was chiefly important to him. Every day he would stroll along the promenade and the beach, watching the children as they paddled in the sea, built sandcastles, screamed excitedly at the Punch and Judy show, played among the ubiquitous bathing machines, or sat demurely with their nursemaids. Every year, like a butterfly collector, he would list the names of the little girls he had met, and like a fisherman he would judge the success of his holiday by the size of his 'catch'.

Shortly after his arrival he wrote a letter to his eight-year-old cousin Menella Wilcox, describing a little girl who kept on running up to him when he was sitting on the parade and then running away again. She was carrying a piece of seaweed.

> So, when she had been about six times, I smiled at her, and she smiled at me and ran away again: and the next time I held out my hand, and she shook hands directly; and I said, 'Will you give me a piece of that seaweed?' and she said 'No!' and ran away again. And the next time I said, 'Will you cut off a little bit of the seaweed for me?' And she said, 'But I haven't got a pair of scissors!'[12]

So Dodgson took out his pair of folding scissors – and she carefully cut a tiny piece of seaweed and gave it to him, saying: 'I'm frightened that my mother won't like you to keep it!' So he gave it back to her and told her to ask her mother to sew the pieces together again.

There were lots of other little girls that summer. Margaret and Ruth Dymes were taken to morning service at St Saviour's. There was a little girl called Barbara who was pleasant, 'though not very bright'. There was Mabel Lucy Burton from Pentonville 'without an atom of shyness', and there were the Hull girls, daughters of a lawyer in the Temple, who were to figure largely and tempestuously in later Eastbourne holidays. 'It seems that I could, if I liked, make friends with a new set of children every day!'[13] His tally of little girls that year reached twenty-six. There was, however, one child that summer who resisted all Dodgson's attempts to make friends. He first caught sight of Dolly Blakemore, the daughter of a Birmingham businessman, on the pier, 'dancing incessantly' to the music of the band. So delighted was he with her that he left a little present for her at her lodgings, but her family teased her so about her admirer that whenever she met him she burst into hysterical tears. Dodgson told her mother, whom he blamed for too much petting:

> I have been nothing but a cause of grief and suffering to her. I will not even try to tell you how painful a thought that is to me, whose deepest and purest pleasures in the world have been in giving pleasure to children.[14]

In the end, largely due to the efforts of her mother, Dolly conquered her fears and Dodgson remained close friends with her and her family for many years.

A few days before leaving Eastbourne, Dodgson had had a sudden flash of inspiration about the Euclid 'protest'. He would write it as a series of dialogues between 'Geometer' and Euclid and some of his 'modern rivals'. 'The dramatic form will popularise it, and will make any "chaff" much less out of place than in a regular treatise.'

Dodgson set his drama in the study of a mathematical examiner, Minos (the Geometer). He sits between two gigantic piles of examination papers which he is trying to mark. What is making his task so exasperating is that the examinees will not confine themselves to geometry as defined by Euclid, but are continually suggesting solutions based on the work of modern geometricians. Eventually he falls asleep and is visited by the ghost of Euclid who demands, 'Now what is it you really require in a manual of geometry?' The only way in which this can be effectively answered is by an exhaustive examination of the claims and arguments of Euclid's modern rivals. This is 'weary work' for Minos to undertake alone, and Euclid obligingly enlists the assistance of the 'Phantom of a German professor, a great friend of mine. He has read all books, and is ready to defend any thesis, true or untrue.' His name is Niemand (Nobody) and he enters preceded by a cloud of tobacco smoke and a gigantic meerschaum (Dodgson was a militant non-smoker).

The German professor proceeds to make out a case for each of the rival geometers and Minos shoots them down one by one. The lengthy review is notable for Dodgson's ferocious 'jealousy of error', the unholy glee with which he trounces the arguments, and the grammar of Euclid's successors:

> The whole proposition is a grand specimen of obscure writing and bad English, 'is' and 'are', 'could' and 'would', alternating throughout with the most charming impartiality.

At times the tone resembles that of Dodgson putting down his sisters:

> Minos: ... You can't talk of 'one straight line' as 'these lines' you know.
> Niemand: We abandon the axiom.
> Minos: Better luck next time! Try another definition.

But there are rare moments when Dodgson allows Lewis Carroll to take over and the dry argument is transformed into something not far from Queen Alice's Banquet:

> Minos: 'A circumference is generally described in language by one of its radii.' Let us hope that the language is complementary – at least if the circumference is within hearing! Can't you imagine the radius gracefully rising to his feet, rubbing his lips with his table-napkin? 'Gentlemen! The toast I have the honour to propose is &c. &c. Gentlemen, I give you the Circumference!' And then the chorus of excited Lines, 'For he's a jolly good felloe!'[15]

(A 'felloe' being one of the curved pieces in the circumference of a wheel).

In his preface Dodgson spoke of the 'pitying friends' who had warned him of the perils of 'abandoning the dignity of a scientific writer' and there was even a rumour that he was about to produce a 'burlesque Euclid', but the book was generally well received. *Vanity Fair* commended the 'brightness and humour with which the ponderous stuff of geometry is handled' and *The English Mechanic* announced that the author had 'triumphantly proved' the superiority of Euclid's 'immortal elements' as an introduction to geometry. Only *The Saturday Review* considered that Dodgson, by using the dramatic form, had made his argument more difficult to follow.

'Little nudities'

In December 1878, Dodgson noticed two sets of Christmas cards by Emily Gertrude Thomson in Ackerman's premises in Regent Street, featuring naked fairy children with baby faces and tinted butterfly wings. Rightly sensing that he had found a kindred spirit in the artist, he wrote off immediately to Ackerman asking for her address. He received a rather cautious reply telling him only that Miss Thomson lived in Manchester and Dodgson felt obliged to explain his intentions:

> Photographing from life – and especially photographing children – has been his one amusement for the last twenty years. He has also made attempts (most unsuccessfully) at drawing them, but he has at least learned from his own failures to appreciate the difficulties of that line of art, and to enjoy such successful pictures as those of Miss Thomson.[1]

What he wanted to know, he told Ackerman, was what forms of drawing she had tried – oil, body-colour, chalk, pen and ink? Did she draw from life or 'out of her own head', had she drawn larger pictures that he might be able to purchase? He was so enthusiastic about the cards that he took them back with him to Guildford to show to his friends the Synges.

Gertrude Thomson was twenty-eight and the daughter of the Professor of Greek and Hebrew at Lancashire Independent College. She was a painter and illustrator and, like Henry Holiday, a designer of stained glass. Her particular speciality was the child nude, little fairy creatures hiding under sea shells or sitting on honeysuckle talking to bumble bees, all very much in the spirit of the times and all very innocent. Christina Rossetti, however, found it all rather distasteful and faintly disturbing:

> I think last night in admiring Miss Thomson's work, [she told the painter Frederick Shields] I might better have said less, unless I could have managed to convey more. I do admire the grace and beauty of the designs, but I do not think to call a figure a 'fairy' settles the right and wrong of such matters.[2]

At the end of December, Miss Thomson received her first letter from Dodgson, 'written in a rather boyish-looking hand' asking to see more of

her work. It was signed 'C.L. Dodgson', but she had already discovered
from Ackerman that he was the celebrated Lewis Carroll. Prudently she
decided to keep this to herself until he chose to reveal his identity.

He was not uncritical of the pictures she sent him. The knee and ankle of
one of the children were 'in excess of the truth', but perhaps her model had
been a 'country-peasant child'. He had come to believe, he informed her,
'in slender ankles as the normal standard of beauty'. He went on to
enlarge, in an uncharacteristically ostentatious way, on his acquaintances
in the London art world. Did she know his friend Ruskin? He was certain
that her work would interest him. Would she care to be introduced to
Frederick Leighton (whom he had in fact not yet met) or to Arthur
Hughes, or Holiday or Paton or Holman Hunt? 'I used to know Millais',
he added rather ruefully, 'but it is many years since, and he may have
almost forgotten me now.'[3] As it happened, he had just turned down a
request from *The Graphic* to supply a few lines to accompany a coloured
reproduction of Millais' *Puss in Boots* to be signed 'Lewis Carroll'. 'I have
no doubt the <u>name</u> is worth money by this time,' he wrote to Macmillan,
'but I don't care to make money by writing in periodicals.'[4] Dodgson
ended his letter with a flourish, revealing his identity rather like a conjurer
producing a rabbit out of his hat:

> As you like the books of child life, let me send for your acceptance one
> of two such books I have written, whichever you prefer (if you know
> them; if not I will send the first). Their names are <u>Alice's Adventures
> in Wonderland</u> and <u>Through the Looking Glass</u>.

Alice's Adventures was, of course, one of Gertrude Thomson's 'pet books'
and she knew it nearly by heart, but she told him that she would greatly
prize a copy presented by himself. She received copies of both books bound
in white calf – 'there is an incompleteness about giving only one'. He told
her that she could give her existing copy to a sick child. 'I have been
distributing copies to all the hospitals and convalescent homes I can hear
of, where there are sick children capable of reading them.' No recipient
could be more appropriate, he told her, 'than one who seems to have been
in fairyland herself and to have seen, like the "weary mariners" of old':

> *Between the green brink and the running foam*
> *White limbs unrobed in a crystal air,*
> *Sweet faces, rounded arms, and bosoms prest*
> *To little harps of gold.*[5]
> *(Tennyson: The Sea Fairies)*

'White limbs unrobed' were much on Dodgson's mind through the spring
and summer of 1879, for he was embarking on a series of photographs of

naked children which would make him a subject of gossip and scandal in Oxford, and which would eventually lead to his giving up photography altogether. He had been taking pictures of little girls in their 'favourite dress of nothing' for several years, but now it began to grow into a dangerous obsession. He seems to have been compelled by a desperate and irresistible desire to photograph his little girl-friends without their clothes on and what made the whole enterprise doubly hazardous was that these were not models or stage-children, but the daughters of highly respectable Oxford dons and clergymen.

At a dinner party in November 1878, he had met Anthony Lawson Mayhew, who was to become Chaplain and lecturer in Hebrew at Wadham. Thomas Arnold's wife had told him that Mayhew had a twelve-year-old daughter, Ruth, whom he 'ought to photograph', and her sister Ethel was equally attractive. It was not until May that the girls came to Dodgson's rooms, when he photographed each of them as the Comte de Brissac, one of the theatre costumes he frequently used. But what he really wanted was to pose Ethel in Gertrude Chataway's wading attire, and her little sister Janet in even less. For the latter he decided that he should ask Mrs Mayhew's permission:

> I should like to know <u>exactly</u> the minimum of dress I may take her in, and I will strictly observe the limits. I hope that, at any rate, we may go as far as a pair of bathing drawers, though for <u>my</u> part I should much prefer doing without them, and shall be very glad if you say she may be done 'in any way she likes herself'.[6]

He followed this up with a much more alarming request: could the same permission be extended to Ethel? He launched into a passionate plea on behalf of his art:

> Here am I, an amateur photographer, with a deep sense of admiration for <u>form</u>, especially the human form, and one who believes it to be the most beautiful thing God has made on this earth – and who hardly ever gets the chance of photographing it!

He could, of course, hire professional models, 'but first, they would be ugly, and secondly, they would *not* be pleasant to deal with: and so my only hope is with <u>friends</u>'.

For his part, he airily informed their mother, he would have no objection in photographing Ruth unclad as well (she was now thirteen) but he feared that there was no use in suggesting it. The pictures would be such as she might frame and hang up in her drawing room. He had seriously underestimated Mrs Mayhew. She was understandably unnerved by the tone of Dodgson's letter, and although her youngest daughter Margaret later dismissed her mother's objections as 'Victorian propriety', there is something rather disturbing about the way in which Dodgson tried to press his demands further and further.

In the event, Mrs Mayhew would only give permission for the children to be taken in bathing drawers and said that she was 'sure that the children themselves would decidedly object' to 'the entire absence of drapery'. Dodgson had taken the precaution of already canvassing the children themselves on this point and he was able to inform Mrs Mayhew's husband:

> both Ruth and Ethel seemed quite sure that Janet wouldn't in the least object to being done naked, and Ethel, when I asked her if she would object, said in the most simple and natural way, that she wouldn't object at all.[7]

He hoped that the Mayhews might reconsider their prohibition and at least allow a back view of Ethel without her drawers and to permit Janet to be taken naked – 'at her age, it is almost absurd even to suggest any scruple about dress'. He then added an unfortunate post script which he was to regret. If the three girls came to his rooms, there would be no need for Mrs Mayhew to chaperone them – 'that is, if you can trust me to keep my promise of abiding strictly by the limits laid down. If you can't trust my word, then please never bring or send any of the children again!'

Mrs Mayhew was not prepared to trust his word. The children were not to come without a chaperone and Ethel was not to be photographed without her drawers. Dodgson dashed off a furious response full of crossings out:

> I hope you won't think me very fanciful in saying I should have no pleasure in doing any such pictures, now that I know I am ~~not thought fit for~~ only permitted such privilege ~~except~~ on condition of being under chaperonage. I had rather do no more pictures of your children except in full dress: please forgive all the trouble I have given you about it.[8]

He told her that he wished to defer all further photography because of a 'distressing letter of domestic news'. The relevant page of his diary has been torn out. Was this to conceal the distressing domestic news, or the quarrel with Mrs Mayhew?

Dodgson could not forever be running the gauntlet of angry Oxford mothers. What he needed was a like-minded female friend who would share his enthusiasm and who would be an acceptable chaperone. Gertrude Thomson had come into his life at precisely the right moment. She arrived in London a few days after Dodgson's confrontation with Mrs Mayhew. Dodgson had been staying with Vere Bayne's mother, and had visited Henry Holiday to inspect his first full-size sculpture, a voluptuous sleeping female figure which Dodgson cautiously described as 'graceful'.

Dodgson had arranged to meet Gertrude Thomson at twelve by the Schliemann collection in the South Kensington Museum and had asked for two of his little theatrical friends, Beatrice and Maud Fearon, to chaperone him. Gertrude Thomson had been somewhat apprehensive that she might not be able to identify him in the crowded room, but the moment he arrived dead on the stroke of twelve, with a little girl clinging to either hand, there could be no doubt. Dodgson left it to one of his child companions to point out Gertrude Thomson. 'I told her I had come to meet a young lady who knew fairies, and she fixed on you at once. But I knew you before she spoke.'[9]

There is nothing remotely fairy-like about the face of the woman who stares out from the page in Collingwood's biography of his uncle. She has a firm jaw and a wide mouth and a slightly forlorn expression. She speaks of the 'close and happy friendship which gladdened and enriched my life for eighteen years' and it has been suggested that she may have been in love with him. Dodgson was to treat her with considerable generosity, but a certain cold firmness. She does not seem to have been under any illusion about the nature of their relationship in her description of an encounter with 'a lady friend of Mr Dodgson's':

'I hear that you spent the other day in Oxford with Mr Dodgson?'
'Yes, it was a most delightful day.'
'It's a very unconventional thing to do.'
'We are both very unconventional.'
'Mr Dodgson is not at all a ladies' man.'
'He wouldn't be my friend if he were.'
'He is a confirmed bachelor.'
'So am I, and, what is more, he is old enough to be my father.'
She steadily regarded me for a moment, and then said.
'I tell you what it is. Mr Dodgson doesn't think of you as a "young lady" or anything of that kind, he looks upon you as a sort of "old child".'[10]

When Miss Thomson 'defied Mrs Grundy' and came down to see Dodgson in Oxford in early July, she had with her a professional little model, Ada Smith. Dodgson took six nude studies of the girl 'in arranging which Miss Thomson was of great use'.

But in fact, Dodgson no longer needed professional models from London, for he had found a lady in Oxford who did not share Mrs Mayhew's scruples about her children appearing without their clothes. Mrs Patrick Henderson was the wife of a fellow of Wadham.

I had warned Mrs H that I thought the children so nervous I would not even ask for 'bare feet' and was agreeably surprised to find they were ready for any amount of undress and seemed delighted to run about naked.

The girls had overheard Dodgson talking to their father about photographing them in the nude and had promptly dived under the table and taken their clothes off.

It was a great privilege to have such a model as Annie to take: a very pretty face and a good figure: she was worth any number of my model of yesterday.[11]

The model of yesterday had been Ada Smith. Annie Henderson was an upper-class little girl, Ada Smith was not. Dodgson was still firmly convinced that only little girls from the upper classes had truly beautiful figures. 'It is very pleasing to me to think that the children are so absolutely at their ease with me,' he told Mrs Henderson, and, no doubt with Mrs Mayhew in mind he added:

I assure you I take it as a great compliment and privilege that you are willing to trust me with them so entirely.[12]

Gertude Thomson's presence made it far easier for Dodgson to skate on thin ice. She came down to Oxford for the day on 21st July and helped Dodgson pose Frances Henderson 'in her favourite dress of nothing'. Leila Taylor, another don's daughter, was taken in bathing drawers and jersey and a few days later the Henderson girls appeared again in 'the same dress as before'. There was a quick dash up to London to see Offenbach's *Madame Favart* and then back to Oxford for more photographing: Annie Henderson naked on a blanket and all three Hatch sisters (Beatrice, Ethel and Evelyn) in the same condition, 'a kind of photo I have often done lately'. All this makes nonsense of his claim to Mrs Mayhew that he rarely had the opportunity to photograph the naked human form.

There was a kind of reckless abandon in what he was doing and courting danger always gave him a certain excitement. He simply could not see that he was putting himself at risk. It was elsewhere, he believed, that danger lay. When Gertrude Thomson hired a child model for him at her London studio, he was most concerned that she had had to travel there alone:

I don't quite like the idea of that small and pretty child going all that way alone on my account. If she had got lost or stolen I should feel an awful responsibility in having caused her to run the risk. I fear such beauty, among the very poor, is a very dangerous possession.[13]

1879 saw the renewal of his friendship with Ellen Terry. She had been a respectable married woman for nearly a year and although her husband Charles Wardell was an aggressive drunk, (according to her brother Fred, she had picked out his name from a hat full of suitors) she was now at least socially acceptable, even to Dodgson. Yet he still had misgivings about meeting her again. How was he to reconcile his own moral code with the fact that she had spent years in unwedded bliss with Godwin:

> I do not know, and have no means of knowing, <u>how</u> she regards that episode of her unhappy life: I think it quite possible she may even now believe that although she was breaking the law of the land she was not sinning in God's sight. But it is a matter which, unless she herself were to begin on it, I cannot think I have any right to question her about ... it is a question of fearful difficulty how far she was wrong.[14]

Dodgson decided to seek the advice of Canon King, the Regius Professor of Pastoral Theology, as to whether he could safely ignore her 'miserable past' and accept her for what she was now, 'a legally married wife'. King told him that it would be the right thing to do: he could renew the friendship without condoning what she had done. It was all rather like the difficulty of endowing Jowett's Greek Professorship without countenancing his theological opinions. He approached Florence Terry who told him that her sister would be only too pleased to meet him again. 'So I shall go and call. We last met on May 11th/67, I believe: nearly 12 years ago!'[15]

The meeting with Ellen Terry eventually took place in June. 'She was as charming as ever,' he noted in his diary, 'and I was much pleased with her husband (Mr C. Kelly on the stage). I also liked her two children, Edith and Eddie.' These were her children by Godwin. 'Poor little things!' he wrote to Tom Taylor. 'I hope they will never know their own sad history.'[16] Eddie, who was to grow up to be the actor and theatre designer Edward Gordon Craig, did not have a very high opinion of Dodgson:

> I can see him now, on one side of the heavy mahogany table – dressed in black with a face which made no impression on me at all.[17]

Dodgson tried to persuade the six-year-old Eddie to join in one of his puzzle games about getting five sheep across a river in a boat too small to hold them all, which he demonstrated with matches and a matchbox, but Eddie betrayed not the slightest interest. Despite this minor setback, Dodgson was pleased that he was now on good terms with Ellen again – 'she has not many <u>friends</u> now I fancy – <u>admirers</u> and <u>worshippers</u> she has by the thousand'.

Ellen Terry's performances at the Lyceum were a special treat for the Hull sisters, who were at Eastbourne again that summer. Agnes had become his particular favourite. One late afternoon he went down to the beach, 'after spending the day on the limits of π and found that she had cut her foot on a broken bottle'. 'I carried her up to the road, and took her home in a bath-chair, and then had the opportunity to do a bit of amateur doctoring with "calendula".' Rescuing children from the perils of the beach was all part of the excitement of Eastbourne. Dodgson was always on the alert for little girls who had fallen into the sea or had cut themselves, although when Norah Woodhouse fell off a breakwater and was soaked to the skin –

> Mr Dodgson ... looked me gravely up and down, and then tore a corner of blotting paper from his note-book and said, 'May I offer you this to blot yourself up?'[18]

As his friendship with Agnes Hull grew more intense, his letters became increasingly flirtatious. He began to address her as 'my darling' and to be very coy about kisses. When he heard that one of her friends had visited her while she was in bed with a cold, he wrote:

> I wished I had been with her. Only once have I had the chance of seeing that young person Agnes in that picturesque condition, and then I couldn't do it, because there was <u>another young person</u> (a great niece of Mrs Grundy) in the room, who objected to my coming in – so I was debarred from that pleasure.[19]

'He teased them unmercifully,' remembered Evelyn Hatch, 'pretending that they only tolerated his presence because of the treats he gave them.' But quite frequently it was Agnes who teased him, telling him that she only loved him because he had promised to take her to the Lyceum and, as time passed, the joke became less and less funny. Dodgson's dependence on the love of his child-friends made him intensely vulnerable to their caprices, and when this was combined with his strict sense of social propriety and his painful sensitivity, his life became a misery.

At the skating-rink in Eastbourne's Devonshire Park, 'two splendid beauties' caught his eye. He made a sketch of the elder girl who told him that her name was Irene Slade, and that she was eleven. Dodgson's code of etiquette forbade him to approach her again until he had obtained her parents' permission. He checked through the list of visitors to Eastbourne, found a 'Sir Alfred' Slade and sent him a brief note. 'I did not ask to be allowed to go on knowing the children, but provided at once for the worst by undertaking not to notice them again <u>unless</u> I receive permission to do so.'[20]

Dodgson received no reply and when he next saw the children with their father he pointedly ignored them. Three weeks later, to his considerable astonishment, Sir Alfred called when he was out, leaving his card with a message saying that he would be happy for Dodgson to get to know his children. But Dodgson considered that his *amour-propre* had been wounded and he wrote saying that if Sir Alfred had 'no good reason to give for neglecting to write before, I must decline the acquaintance'. The wretched Sir Alfred wrote to Dodgson 'with a sort of excuse for delaying to write' which was considered insufficient. Dodgson told him that he had made the situation 'extremely awkward'. Clearly the Slades had never been treated like this before and, on the following day, Lady Slade invited him to tea. Dodgson, who rarely accepted invitations, countered by arriving at twelve-thirty. Lady Slade proved to be extremely friendly and took him down to the beach to meet her daughters, but the younger, Constance, 'looked simply scared'. In the afternoon when he 'fell in with' the children walking with their governess, they regarded him 'with fear rather than friendliness'.

He decided that he must draw Lady Slade's attention to this state of affairs and told her that his attempt to make friends with her children had failed. At this stage no one could have blamed the Slades for withdrawing with a sigh of relief, but the children were sent round to try and make friends, and Sir Alfred himself called to look at Dodgson's photographs. Dodgson began to feel that the girls were 'growing decidedly more friendly' but by this time their holiday was over.

There were further troubles in store. The Hardings declined to allow him to continue to see their children at Reigate after their return from Eastbourne and a little girl with a 'singularly sweet expression' turned out to have parents who were decidedly middle-class. Dodgson was to be visited with tribulations like these every year but nothing could diminish his constant need to make new conquests.

'I am fond of children (except boys)' he told the twelve-year-old Kathleen Eschwege, whom he had met on a train that summer, 'and have more child-friends than I could possibly count on my fingers, even if I were a centipede (by the way, <u>have</u> they fingers? I'm afraid they're only feet, but, of course, they use them for the same purpose and that is why no other insects, <u>except centipedes</u>, ever succeed in doing Long Multiplication).'[21]

29
'Their innocent loveliness'

By the opening of the 1880s, Dodgson's life seemed in danger of losing direction. There had been no major work to claim his attention since *Euclid and his Modern Rivals*, and *Sylvie and Bruno* continued to be indefinitely becalmed. Ten years earlier, he had been so obsessed with the passing of time that he had drawn up a reading list 'which I hope will have the effect of redeeming from waste those stray half-hours I have so often lost from not having an occupation to turn to <u>at once</u>.' Now whole days drifted by with nothing very particular to mark them, and time seemed to be frittering itself away on a host of minor concerns.

Games seemed to occupy him more and more. There was 'Doublets', which he had devised for the Arnold girls. The game consisted of proposing two words of the same length and then devising a chain of words which would link them, changing one letter at a time. By this means, a 'Pig' could be driven into 'Sty':

> PIG
> wig
> wag
> way
> say
> STY

The game was published in *Vanity Fair* in 1879 and soon attracted an enthusiastic army of 'Doubleteers'. But Dodgson soon decided that 'Doublets' was really far too undemanding and 'invented a new way of working one word into another', which he christened 'Syzgies'. The game gave far more scope to his natural ingenuity and he busied himself over the difficulties posed by such propositions as 'Prove Prison to be Odious'.

> PRISON
> prismatic
> dramatic
> melodramatic
> melodious
> ODIOUS

Sketches
by Dodgson

Dodgson's
sketches
for the
White Rabbit

Bill the Lizard being comforted by two guinea pigs. Sketch by Dodgson

Alice in the Pool of Tears.
Sketch by Dodgson

Alice in the Pool of Tears.
By John Tenniel

'What I look like when I'm lecturing'
From a drawing in a letter
to Margaret Cunnynghame

One of Dodgson's highly original
and disturbing drawings for
Alice's Adventures Underground

She was a good deal
frightened by this very sudden
change, but as she did not
any further, and had
not dropped the top of the
mushroom, she did not give
up hope yet. There was hardly
room to open her mouth, with
her chin pressing against her
foot, but she did it at last,
and managed to bite off a
little bit of the top of the
mushroom.

     *   *   *   *   *

"Come! my head's free
at last!" said Alice in a
tone of delight, which changed
into alarm in another mo-
-ment, when she found that
her shoulders were nowhere
to be seen: she looked down
upon an immense length of
neck, which seemed to rise
like a stalk out of a sea of
green leaves that lay far
below her.

The Terry Family with Ellen in black in the centre and
Kate in white by her side.
Photograph by Dodgson in 1865

Gertrude Chataway,
drawing by Dodgson.
'Gert with a boyish garb
for boyish task'

Drawing by Dodgson
of girls on the beach
at Sandown, 1874

Sketch of a young girl
by Dodgson

at Regina House, Sandown.
June 26 1876

Dodgson's sitting room
at Christ Church

The Chestnuts, the Dodgson's
family home at Guildford

The four eldest children
of the Marquess of Salisbury,
photographed by Dodgson

Isa Bowman

Charles Dodgson

Gertrude Thompson,
'a young lady
who knew fairies'

Illustration by Gertrude Thompson for 'The Three Sunsets'

Evelyn Hatch, photographed by Dodgson, circa 1879

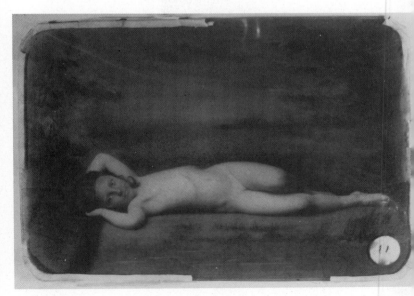

Not all his games were word games. There was 'Lanrick', played on a chess board, in which two players had to compete to move their men into a 'Rendezvous'. The name of the game derived from a line in Walter Scott's 'The Lady of The Lake': 'The muster place be Lanrick mead.' Like 'Doublets', the game had been devised as a diversion for the Arnold girls who were badly in need of entertainment.

In February 1880, Dodgson sent off a puzzle to Charlotte Yonge's *Monthly Packet*, a magazine with a high proportion of women readers. On the face of it, the problem appeared to be a straightforward mathematical one: 'If 6 cats kill 6 rats in 6 minutes, how many will be needed to kill 100 rats in 50 minutes?' The calculation seemed simple enough, but Mrs Yonge's 'fair readers' had reckoned without Dodgson entering into the spirit of the slaughter with quite so much dedication:

> Now there are at least <u>four</u> different ways in which the original feat of 6 cats killing 6 rats in 6 minutes can be achieved. For the sake of clearness, let us tabulate them:
> A. All six cats are needed to kill a rat; and this they do in one minute, the other rats standing meekly by waiting for their turn.
> B. 3 cats are needed to kill a rat; and they do it in 2 minutes.
> C. 2 cats are needed and they do it in 3 minutes.
> D. Each cat kills a rat by itself, and takes 6 minutes to do it.

Dodgson then goes to consider 'impossible' problems about rats and cats – 'If a cat can kill a rat in a minute, how many would be needed to kill it in the thousandth part of a second? The <u>mathematical</u> answer, of course, is 60,000 ... but I fancy that at least 50,000 of the cats would never even see the rat, or have any idea what was going on.' This is, in effect, the question about building a wall, which had so infuriated his pupils when he was a young lecturer, but Mrs Yonge's readers obviously loved it, for the following month Dodgson began a series of mathematical problems, tentatively entitled 'Romantic Problems' or 'Knots' – '"A knot!" said Alice ... "Oh, do let me help to undo it."' Each 'Knot' took the form of an anecdote in which was embodied, 'like the medicine so dextrously, but ineffectually concealed in the jam of our early childhood', a question in arithmetic, algebra or geometry.

Dodgson's 'Knots' included tales of medieval knights going out for a walk, boys trying to find 'eligible apartments' in 'Little Mendip', an elderly lady called 'Mad Mathesis' with her young charge, Clara, taking trains going opposite ways on a circular railway and a bizarre and grisly problem about injuries sustained by Chelsea Pensioners. The 'Knots' were eventually collected together and published in 1885 as *A Tangled Tale* with drawings by A.B. Frost.

Arthur Burdett Frost was a young American artist who had come to his notice through his pictures for works by Dickens and Mark Twain, at a time when Dodgson was considering bringing out an illustrated version of his humorous verse. Frost's first attempts, for *The Three Voices*, had delighted him, 'deliciously funny and extremely well drawn' though he had felt it necessary to give his transatlantic friend a few lessons in English etiquette:

> I notice that you have not guessed (and no wonder) that my address is 'Rev. C.L. Dodgson'. If you don't mind my mentioning it, the English form of address, where one is not 'Rev.', is 'So-and-so Esq,' not 'Mr So-and-so.' ... I should only write 'Mr J. Smith' if he were a tradesman. I am almost afraid of mentioning such trifles, for fear you should think I had taken offence at being directed to as 'Mr'. Nothing could be further from my thoughts.[1]

Frost was invited to stay at Christ Church – 'We don't <u>assume</u> evening dress for Hall dinner this term', and was entrusted with the task of illustrating the whole new *Phantasmagoria* volume, which included not only the title poem and 'Hiawatha's Photographing' but such problem pieces for the illustrator as 'Atalanta in Camden Town' and 'Fame's Penny Trumpet', which offered nothing in the way of pictorial subject matter. To all these challenges Frost rose superbly and Dodgson was encouraged to give him another commission, which may well have perplexed him, coming from such a highly respectable clergyman:

> a study from life (but not a Cupid) that I may keep it as a specimen of your power in drawing a beautiful figure. As it is <u>not</u> for publication, you need not put an atom of drapery on it, and I can quite trust you, even if you made it a full-front view, to have a simple classical figure. I had rather not have an adult figure (which always looks to me rather in need of drapery): a girl of about 12 is <u>my</u> ideal beauty of form.[2]

Dodgson's family were no longer quite so large a drain on his income (which was as well, as he had just lost over £1,000 on a shipping investment), but they were still a source of constant concern. Edwin had gone out to Zanzibar to be the principal of the Kiungani Missionary School, but the climate proved too much for him and he was struck down with 'ague'. He returned to England for a brief spell of recuperation and then went off to be Priest-in-Charge on Tristan da Cunha, a storm-swept, rat-infested, desolate volcanic cone in the south Atlantic, hundreds of miles from anywhere.

Skeffington was still no nearer finding a permanent parish. He had been through a variety of curacies but it was always, as Dodgson put it, 'the old story': he was not considered up to the work. By March 1880, Skeffington was curate to the Rev. Corbett, Rector of Blandford St Mary in Dorset. In the last week of term, Dodgson was alarmed to receive a telegram from Mrs Corbett asking him to come at once. Thinking that this could only mean that his brother was gravely ill, Dodgson packed his portmanteau and caught the next train to Bath. He passed a restless night in a small commercial hotel next to the railway station, and caught the first train to Blandford. Mrs Corbett was waiting for him at the station and poured out her strange story. She was on the verge of separating from her husband and it seemed that Skeffington was the main cause of it. He persisted in remaining in the house 'by Mr Corbett's wish, but totally against that of Mrs C to whom his presence has become intolerable'.³ The poor woman had been reduced to taking a room in the house of her sister.

Dodgson could only conclude that Mr Corbett was deranged, and he thought that his brother was 'going on as if he were deranged too...'. He did his best to persuade Skeffington that, 'as a matter of ordinary decency', he should leave the house, but could only secure a promise that he would 'think of it'. After this 'masterpiece of comfort' there seemed nothing more that Dodgson could do, and he left on the next train, promising to send a copy of *Through the Looking Glass* to Mrs Corbett's niece. This incident seems to have been as baffling to him as it still is to us.

There is no further reference to the affair in Dodgson's diary, but there is no doubt that it cast a considerable cloud over his relationship with his brother. His dearly-loved Aunt Lucy died later that year at The Chestnuts at the age of seventy-five and, when the brothers met at her funeral, Skeffington did not even mention that he was going to be married in six days time to Isabel Mary Cooper, a young lady from Bridlington. 'He had kept it a secret,' Dodgson noted when at last his sisters broke the news to him, 'and I am thankful to have no responsibility.'⁴ Dodgson's fits of pique never lasted for long and he was soon writing to Skeffington asking for news of his latest curacy and sending brotherly regards to his wife – 'it is hard to devise a message to one I have never set eyes on'.⁵ Isabel was to have a transforming effect upon Skeffington's life – two years after his marriage, Skeffington became Chaplain and Stipendiary Curate at Alfrick in Worcestershire where he was to remain for the next thirteen years.

Dodgson described his brother's religious opinions as 'very moderate High Church – not Ritualistic' and as he grew older Skeffington's views became increasingly evangelical. Dodgson himself, as he neared his fiftieth year, was becoming ever more tolerant of all faiths and was more concerned with what united men in their beliefs than what divided them:

> More and more, as I read of the Christian religion as Christ preached it, I stand amazed at the forms men have given to it, and the fictitious barriers they have built up between themselves and their brethren.[6]

He told Ellen Terry that he had been shocked by the cruelty of Shylock being forced to become a Christian at the end of the trial in *The Merchant of Venice*. Could not Irving be persuaded to cut the lines out?

In Oxford, storm clouds were steadily gathering. A girl named Atty Owen and her little brother came to wait in Dodgson's rooms for their father, Sydney Owen, Reader in Law and Modern History. When they left Dodgson gave the girl a kiss and was surprised to learn from her father that 'Atty' was seventeen and well beyond the permitted kissable age.

> I was astonished, but I don't think either of us was much displeased at the mistake having been made! Wrote a note of mock apology to Mrs Owen, assuring her that the incident has been 'as distressing to her daughter as it was to myself'! but adding that 'I would kiss her no more.'[7]

Mrs Owen was not amused. 'We shall make sure it does not occur,' she informed him. She had heard all about Dodgson and the scandalous goings-on in his rooms. Even Mrs Henderson was beginning to grow uneasy. She told him that she did not wish the children to be photographed naked because of the cold, but Dodgson brushed her objections aside. The temperature in his studio, he informed her, was 'nearer 80° than 70°' and he continued to indulge himself taking pictures of the girls with 'nothing to wear'.

> Their innocent loveliness is very beautiful, and gives one a feeling of reverence, as at the presence of something sacred ...[8]

For Dodgson, the naked beauty of a little girl was something approaching a divine revelation, a feeling, as he put it in *Sylvie and Bruno*, that he was standing on 'holy ground'. It was a highly Victorian response, a sublimation of a sexual impulse into religious awe.

At the same time, in a strange blend of the sacred and profane, Dodgson was taking pictures of his old headmaster at Rugby, Doctor Tait, who had been enthroned as Archbishop of Canterbury. The President of Trinity wrote to him telling him that Cardinal Newman would be happy to sit for a portrait but Dodgson grew oddly obstinate; he was not prepared to transport his apparatus over to Trinity and since Newman, very frail at seventy-nine, could not possibly have managed the stairs to his studio, the enterprise was abandoned.

Gertrude Thomson was still much in evidence and she described a visit to his studio when he had asked her to come and photograph 'human fairies', when Dodgson and the little girls and his toy animals all gathered together on the floor and his laugh rang out like a child's.

> And the delightful nonsense he talked! It was like pages out of the Alices, only more delightful, for there was his own voice and smile to give the true charm to it all. I used to try and record it. It was impossible – as impossible as to catch the gleam of colour on sunlit water, or grasp a drifting rainbow.[9]

But the happy days of photographing little fairies were numbered. Dodgson was rash enough to ask permission for Atty Owen to pose for him. Her father came round to see him 'and he looked like a thunder-cloud'. Mrs Owen had heard all about the kind of pictures that Dodgson had been taking and was condemning them 'in strong language'. But it was not just Mrs Owen who was up in arms, the scandal was spreading through the university.

Dodgson's old friend, Mrs Kitchin, was drawn into the growing fracas to intervene on his behalf with Mrs Owen, but already there were signs that he was beginning to find doors closed against him. On 15th July, 1880, Dodgson took his last recorded pictures. He photographed Gertrude and Gerida Gage, whom he had met through the Arnolds, but there was no suggestion at this stage that he was contemplating giving up photography, nude or otherwise. Although there is no evidence of more photographic sessions, there is no hint of repentance in a letter he wrote to Mrs Henderson in June the following year about the 'full-front' pictures he had taken of her daughters:

> I quite hope that picture on your drawing-room table will serve as a sort of 'decoy-duck' and reveal to you (and through you to me) other parents who possess well-made children who have a taste for being taken without the encumbrance of dress. But they <u>must</u> be <u>well-made</u>. ... Ill-made children should be taken in full dress.[10]

Nine days later he was writing to Mrs Henderson again, but in a very different frame of mind. She had warned him of some of the things that were being rumoured against him:

> If the remarks that have been made have caused <u>you</u> any annoyance [he told her], I am sorry to have (indirectly) caused them; otherwise, for <u>my</u> part, I am not only indifferent to being gossiped about, but even regard it as being possibly useful as an advertisement![11]

But in fact, despite his bravado, he was far from indifferent to what was being said. A 'terrible remark' had been made in Annie Henderson's hearing. He had no wish to know the name of the person who had made it, but he wanted to know what had been said – 'as a warning of the risk incurred by transgressing the conventional rules of society'.

After this there was no more talk of photographs. Four years later, Dodgson was writing nostalgically to Gertrude Thomson of his 'photographic days' with the Hendersons: 'It is 3 or 4 years since I have photographed – I have been too busy.' Are we to take him at his word or did he in fact renounce photography because of the scandalous stories that were being circulated among the wives and mothers of Oxford? He may well have been advised by Mrs Kitchin or one of his other close women friends that he was putting himself beyond 'the conventional rules of society'. There is evidence that he 'dropped' many of his Oxford acquaintances at this time and even the Kitchins disappear from his letters and diaries.

In 1893, nearly twelve years after he gave up photography for good, he wrote a letter to Gertrude Thomson which shows that nothing had diminished his interest in the camera, or in little girls:

> ... as a means of making <u>memoranda</u> of attitudes, etc. it is invaluable. Every figure artist ought to practise it. If I had a dry-plate camera, and time to work it, and could secure a child of really good figure, either a professional model, or (much better) a child of the upper classes, I would put her into every pretty attitude I could think of, and get in a single morning 50 or 100 such memoranda. Do try this with the next pretty child you get as model and let me have some of the photos.[12]

The development of the dry-plate process has been suggested as a reason for Dodgson's renunciation of his hobby, but from this letter it sounds as if he were not wholly opposed to it, and anyway he could have continued to use the wet plates if he so wished. A second, and more plausible, explanation is that Dodgson had abruptly come to the conclusion that photography was taking up far too much of his time. He had always been haunted by a horror of the way in which the days slipped by with nothing to show for them, and now, in his early fifties, the work still to be done nagged away at him. He grew more and more preoccupied with the thought that he might die before the tasks he had set himself were completed. As so often with Dodgson, his fear expressed itself in the form of a Biblical text: 'The night cometh, when no man can work.'

Even so, it is difficult to put aside the idea that his real reason for abandoning the 'black art' was to silence the wagging tongues of the wives of Oxford. For all his jests about 'defying Mrs Grundy' and his contempt for the opinion of others, Dodgson was highly sensitive to the demands of conventional morality. He had, after all, had to consult an Oxford divine about the propriety of renewing his friendship with Ellen Terry. To have abandoned only nude photography would have been as good as admitting his guilt. There was something splendidly reckless and disdainful in throwing over the whole art to which he had devoted himself for a twenty-five years. Fundamentally, he was totally unrepentant and he continued to draw naked little girls in Gertrude Thomson's studios. The thought that there might be a sexual element in capturing the nakedness of a little girl in a photograph or a sketch would have outraged him. His relationships ended with kissing and cuddling – nothing even remotely approaching the sexual act was required of him. Children for Dodgson were a defence against the impossible reality of sexuality. Sex would have destroyed his sacred vision of the innocence of children which was so central to him that it was virtually a religious belief. '... how much nearer to God than our travel-stained souls can ever come,' he told Edward Draper, 'is the soul of a little child.' Even so, although the little girls may have been entirely safe from him, the act of photography was beginning to come perilously close to a kind of substitute for the sexual act.

There was one other factor which may well have contributed both to Dodgson's obsession and his renunciation of photography. It may also have accounted for his inability to settle down to any steady programme of work. Throughout the last years of the 1870s Alice Liddell was being courted by Reginald Gervis Hargreaves. In July 1880 he proposed and was accepted, and on 15th September they were married.

Reginald Hargreaves was not the kind of suitor whom Dodgson would have regarded with favour (supposing that he could have accepted anyone in that role). His chief concern was to shine at cricket and athletics and it took him eight years to plod his way to an undistinguished BA at Christ Church. He was exactly the kind of 'abominably handsome', empty-headed young man Dodgson would depict in Captain Eric Lindon, the successful contender for the hand of Lady Muriel in *Sylvie and Bruno*. Hargreaves was aware that he was marrying not just the beautiful daughter of the Dean of Christ Church and Vice–Chancellor of the University, but the 'fabulous monster' created by Lewis Carroll, well on her way to becoming a national heroine. Alice too was acutely conscious of her double identity. After Reginald took her down to Hampshire to show her Cuffnell's, which was to be their home, she wrote:

> I hope it will be a real fairyland to us both as long as we are both permitted to enjoy it, dear; 'Wonderland' come true to 'Alice' at last![13]

They were married by Alice's father's old friend, Dean Stanley, with Stainer, composer of the celebrated *Crucifixion*, presiding at the organ. At Christ Church the bells rang out for over an hour, but Dodgson was in Eastbourne. There is no mention of Alice's wedding in his diary, but he did join with Vere Bayne in sending her a present, a framed watercolour of the Great Quadrangle.

It was an event for which Dodgson must have long prepared himself and anticipated with fear. It had been possible to live without Alice and to dismiss all thoughts of the marriage that never could have been, as long as Alice was not actually married to anyone else. Now the little girl whom he had immortalised by his writing and whom he had photographed with such love was lost to him. 'It is quite likely,' wrote his nephew Stuart Collingwood, 'that Alice's marriage to Hargreaves may have seemed to him the greatest tragedy of his life.'[14]

'The love of children is a fleeting thing'

As the sales of the two Alice books steadily advanced, Dodgson began to find his fame a considerable liability: 'people seem to assume that everybody likes notoriety'. It was one thing to see the faces of little children light up when he revealed that he was the author of their favourite books, but it was quite another to be pointed out in the streets of Oxford and to be pestered by total strangers for an autograph. 'I so much hate the idea of strangers being able to know me by sight,' he told his old *College Rhymes* friend Francis Atkinson, who had asked for a photograph, 'that I refuse to give my photo, even for the albums of relations.'[1] His response to autograph hunters became whimsical, to say the least. He persuaded his fellow dons to supply him with forgeries of the signature of 'Lewis Carroll' which were sent off to hopeful applicants.

At the end of November 1880, Dodgson heard from Falconer Madan that his name, 'coupled with the anonymous name Lewis Carroll', was to appear in a dictionary of anonymous and pseudonymous literature, edited by Caroline Laing. Within the hour, he hurtled off a letter begging her to remove his name from the publication.

> I use a name, not my own, for writing under, for the one sole object, of avoiding personal publicity: that I may be able to come and go, unnoticed, in all public places. And it would be a real unhappiness to me to feel myself liable to be noticed, or pointed out by strangers.[2]

If his work had ever given her any pleasure he entreated her not to repay it by the cruelty of breaking through his disguise. She complied at once, but told him that she had gained the information from a reference slip in the Bodleian, and all his efforts could not prevail to get his name removed from there.

As he grew older his understandable anxiety turned into something of an obsession. Letters addressed to 'Lewis Carroll' at Christ Church were returned to the sender or directed to the dead-letter office. His little friends were sternly rebuked if their mothers revealed his true identity. Tea parties at Oxford where there was the least risk of his cover being blown were automatically avoided:

I would much rather come to you some time when you have <u>not</u> a party – and not even the friends you mentioned, who are admirers of Alice. It may be morbid but I do heartily dislike meeting strangers who talk to me about my books, and much prefer being unknown in connection with them. You will do me a real kindness, if I should ever chance on any of your friends in calling, if you would leave them in ignorance of my 'anonym'.[3]

For all his morbid horror of being 'lionised', Dodgson had no reservations about promoting the books themselves and he was continually dreaming up schemes to reinvent them and find a wider audience. He was concerned that the sophistication of his writing was far beyond the understanding of some of the little children he took on his knee, and had the notion of rewriting the Alice books so that they could be appreciated by a younger reader. A Dutch abridgement of *Alice's Adventures* helped him to see his way towards *The Nursery Alice*, a picture book to be 'read, to be cooed over, to be dogs' eared, to be rumpled, to be kissed by little children'.[4] He approached Tenniel to find out whether he would be prepared to make enlarged and coloured versions of some of the pictures. Tenniel assented, but it was to be another eight years before *The Nursery Alice* eventually went on sale.

From *The Nursery Alice* Dodgson turned his attention to a nursery Shakespeare. He wanted to find out whether it would be possible to produce an edition containing a selection of the plays,

in which many of the beauties should be preserved, and yet the whole made so absolutely free from objectionable matter, whether in plot or in language, that any English mother might, without scruple, put it in the hands of her daughters from the age of 10 or 12 up to 16 or 18.[5]

There was no shortage of expurgated editions of Shakespeare in nineteenth-century England. Thomas Bowdler's notorious emasculation, published in 1818, had given a new word to the nation, but it did not go nearly far enough for Dodgson:

Looking through it, I am filled with a deep sense of wonder, considering what he has left in, that he should have cut <u>anything</u> out![6]

In a leaflet, published in Charlotte Yonge's *Monthly Packet* and in *Aunt Judy's Magazine*, he invited his lady readers to send in their own lists of selections founded on recollections of their own girlhood or on observation of their daughters' reading.

Dodgson continued to try and drum up support for his campaign until the end of the decade and enlisted the help of Miss Cooper, a mistress at Birmingham High School, for his 'School-room Shakespeare'. He even began work on his own version of *The Tempest*, though he never got very far with it. He did send off a circular letter to a great number of women asking for their help including, 'emboldened by memories of ancient friendship', the ailing Emily Tennyson. It is not known whether he ever received a reply.

Tennyson himself was enjoying an unprecedented theatrical success with Irving's production of his two act tragedy, *The Cup*. Dodgson took Agnes Hull to see it, and was distinctly unimpressed. 'Really as a play,' he told Helen Feilden, 'there is no action in it.' He was perplexed by why the heroine, Gamma, played by Ellen Terry, having despatched the 'poor worm' of a villain, Synorix, played by Irving, with a cup of poisoned wine, should go on to kill herself. 'The moral of the play is obvious:' he wrote to Ellen Terry, 'Had Synorix only been a total abstainer ...'[7] Agnes Hull, of course, adored it all. Dodgson had suggested to Ellen Terry that she 'would raise the child to the seventh heaven of delight', if she could send a copy of the play, autographed by herself, round to Agnes,[8] '... to have such a gift from you at such a moment would make it a memorable night for the rest of her life!' But Tennyson had been far too cautious about *The Cup* to let it appear in print, and Agnes had to be content with a bunch of violets and a copy of *The Corsican Brothers* which was running with *The Cup* as a double bill. Dodgson continued to pester Ellen Terry to let him see a copy of the play, so that he could show it to his cousin Dorothea Wilcox, and she sent him her own personal copy inscribed by Tennyson. In spite of his previous brushes with the testy bard over reading unauthorised copies of his work, Dodgson had clearly not learned anything.

Dodgson commemorated the occasion in a poem which he sent to Agnes later that year. It was a parody of Tennyson's 'The Miller's Daughter', in which Dodgson continued to tease her about the pecuniary nature of their relationship:

> *It is the lawyer's daughter*
> *And she is grown so dear, so dear,*
> *She costs me, in one evening,*
> *The income of a year!*
>
> *'You can't have children's love,' she cried,*
> *'Unless you choose to fee 'em!'*
> *'And what's your fee child?' I replied,*
> *She simply said ...*[9]

The missing word is 'Lyceum', but the paper was torn by Dodgson so that Agnes could work it out for herself. His teasing was wearing rather thin; he told her that her affection for him was cooling down:

But is that any reason why <u>mine</u> should cool down to match? I put it
to you as a reasonable young person ... haven't I got the right to be
affectionate if I like? Surely, just as much as <u>you</u> have to be as
unaffectionate as <u>you</u> like.[10]

Dodgson was perilously close to emotional blackmail, and it was a very
odd argument for an adult to put to a child. But it was the child in him that
was responding, not the adult. Agnes was nearly fourteen, past the age
'where the stream and river meet' and Dodgson told her that she would
soon be offering him only 'the extremity of her left ear' to kiss. He
scrutinised her letters for any variation in terms of affection, and when she
protested it did not matter how one began a letter, he responded 'Hateful
Spider'.

Agnes was not with him when, in January 1881, he attended a
performance given by children of Gilbert and Sullivan's *HMS Pinafore*,
when he was deeply shocked to hear the voices of little girls enunciating the
words: 'He said damme.' The horror of the experience haunted him for
years and he was still protesting about it seven years later:

> I cannot find words to convey to the reader the pain I felt in hearing
> those dear children taught to utter such words to amuse ears grown
> callous to their ghastly meaning. Put the two ideas side by side – Hell
> (no matter whether <u>you</u> believe in it or not: millions do), and those
> pure young lips thus sporting with its horrors – and then find what
> <u>fun</u> in it you can![11]

Dodgson had been a mathematical lecturer for over twenty-five years and
he could no longer summon up much enthusiasm for teaching. He had
persevered with it in recent years so as to have money to provide for the
family, but he now reckoned that the £300 a year it brought him would be
amply made up for by the additional time he would be able to devote to
writing. He decided to give himself the summer to decide.

Never had his affection for Christ Church or his loyalty to it been
stronger, a loyalty which now even extended to his former adversary,
Dean Liddell. On the night of 25th May, 1881, there was an outburst of
undergraduate rioting in the college – 'The row-loving men in College are
beginning to be troublesome again, and last night some 30 or 40 of them,
aided by out-college men, made a great disturbance and regularly defied
the censors.'[12] Liddell took prompt action and announced that a few men
would be sent down and some fifteen others would be summarily
punished. However, it soon emerged that most of those responsible for the
really serious rioting had been 'out-college men' and the punishments were
modified accordingly.

The *Observer* took the opportunity to mount a savage attack on Christ Church and its Dean, and Dodgson instantly leapt to the Dean's defence in a long letter to the paper:

> The truth is that Christ Church stands convicted of two unpardonable crimes – being great and having a name. Such a place must always expect to find itself a wide mark for scorns and jeers – a target where the little and the nameless may display their skill.[13]

He suggested that if the writer of the offending piece had found in any similar place of education such a gentlemanly, orderly or more pleasant set of men than Dodgson had found in Christ Church, 'I cannot but think him an exceptionally favoured mortal.'

The letter was signed 'Charles L. Dodgson', but 'Lewis Carroll' too had started to write to the newspapers. His chosen means of communication with his rapidly growing public was *The St James's Gazette*, a forbear of *The Evening Standard*. Over the next nine years Lewis Carroll discoursed on a wide variety of topics from lawn tennis tournaments to hydrophobia. The subject of the first letter was 'Purity of Election'. At that time, when voting at a general election was spread over a period of several days, individual constituencies were permitted to announce their results before voters elsewhere had gone to the polls. Dodgson, who was concerned with the mechanics of fair play, had observed that the announcement of one batch of results could frequently influence those about to vote: 'the passion for being on the winning side still flourishes with unabated vigour as regards constituencies'. Dodgson proposed that all ballot boxes should be sealed and not opened until the last election had taken place, and sent off copies of his letter to both Gladstone and Lord Salisbury:

> Most gladly would I have left it to some abler writer to ventilate the subject: but I have not seen it treated in print <u>at all</u>: and it appears to me to be a matter of really national importance: and I feel that, in urging a change, I am writing neither in Conservative or Liberal, but in British interests.[14]

Salisbury was sympathetically disposed towards Dodgson's proposal, but it was to be thirty-six years before it was put into effect.

As far as his creative writing was concerned, Charles L. Dodgson was faring considerably better than Lewis Carroll. His book on the elements of Euclid was moving steadily onwards and he was revising *Euclid and His Modern Rivals*. He was even making 'good progress' on a pamphlet on 'The Limits of Circle Squaring', a controversy into which he had been drawn by a certain 'Mr B' who had accused him of contradicting Euclid.

Sylvie and Bruno was getting nowhere at all, and the new edition of *Phantasmagoria* was indefinitely delayed.

He wrote a letter to one of his girl friends defending his failure to write to her:

> What with teaching, and looking over answers to questions, and writing lecture-business, and letters, sometimes I get that confused, I hardly know which is me and which is the inkstand. Pity me, my dear child! The confusion in one's mind doesn't so much matter – but when it comes to putting bread-and-butter, and orange marmalade into the inkstand: and then dipping pens into oneself, and filling oneself up with ink, you know, it's horrid![15]

His new pupils in the Michaelmas term of 1881 included, for the first time, a 'black from Sierra Leone', 'with a face as black as coal, and frizzy wool for hair. I have to keep a label on the coal scuttle, and a label on him, marked "THIS IS THE COAL SCUTTLE" and "THIS IS HIM" so as to know which is which.'[16] There is a terrible innocence about Dodgson's cheerful racism which is entirely consistent with an age of 'nigger minstrels' and 'gollywogs'. But despite this novel addition to his mathematical flock, Dodgson decided that it was time to resign and he told Liddell that he proposed to give up his fellowship at the end of the year.

> I shall now have my whole time at my disposal, and, if God gives me life and continued health and strength, may hope, before my powers fail, to do some worthy work in writing.[17]

Liddell told him that he would be reluctant to lose Dodgson's services but allowed that he had 'earned the right to retirement' and would do his best to carry out his wishes. 'So my lectureship seems to be near the end.'

Having made the break, Dodgson instantly regretted it. He wanted to hold on to at least some aspect of his job and wrote to the Dean, asking to be allowed to retain the Euclid lecture, which was worth, he prudently noted, £51 per annum. But it was too late; the Dean had already allocated the lecture to Dodgson's old friend Sampson, and since this had been accepted, he could hardly revoke it.

On 30th November Dodgson noted:

> I find in my journal that I gave my first Euclid lecture in the Lecture room on Monday Jan 28, 1856. It consisted of twelve men, of whom nine attended. This morning I have given what is probably my last: the lecture is now reduced to nine ... this morning being a Saint's Day, the attendance was voluntary, and only two appeared, E.H. Morris and G. Lavie. I was lecturer when the father of the latter took his degree, viz, in 1858. There is a sadness in coming to the end of

anything in life. Man's instinct clings to the Life that will never end.[18]

Dodgson seems to have been in no hurry to take advantage of his new-found freedom, and his life continued much as before: he drew up a list of books to be read, sent off a letter to the *Guardian* criticising a letter from its Oxford correspondent who had complained about the poor results in elementary mathematics in the Responsions examinations, and produced a poem for the Rev. C.E. Hutchinson who had dreamed of a procession of 'the heroes of past days' complete with accompanying words and music. The music had survived intact into his waking memory, but only two lines of poetry remained. He had applied to Dodgson, as an acknowledged expert on the world of dreams, to supply what was missing, and Dodgson obligingly drafted verses for his melody:

> *When midnight mists are creeping,*
> *And all the land is sleeping,*
> *Around me tread the mighty dead,*
> *And slowly pass away ...*

This scarcely qualified as 'worthy work in writing'. He was more engaged by a proposal of Dubourg's to found a School of Dramatic Art, a cause which he took up with considerable enthusiasm. He sent out a circular in which the stage was described as 'an engine of incalculable power for influencing society' and soliciting 'all the material help that the wealthy can give' for the school. Lord Salisbury was asked to lend his support for the project – 'your <u>name</u> would be a tower of strength to the <u>cause</u>' – but the great man declined.

Dodgson had taken to using the Hulls' house as one of his London bases, dining there, staying there when he took the girls to the theatre and frequently dropping in at lunch-time or even for breakfast. He was probably over-estimating his welcome. Agnes continued to be as fickle as ever, at times refusing to reward him with the little terms of endearment that were so precious to him, at times granting him a morsel of affection, for which he would be pathetically grateful:

> I haven't for a long time had a letter that has pleased me so much as yours just received, [he wrote to her.] It is pleasant to find one is not quite forgotten, when one is getting old and grey, and stupid: but to be so lovingly remembered is very charming. Thank you, very much, for the photograph: it is quite first-rate. But the letter I prize even more: the one is your <u>face</u> only – the other is <u>you</u>.
> Always your loving old friend (and mean to be so till you are 'fair, fat and forty'.)[19]

The holiday at Eastbourne that summer began pleasantly enough. He managed to write a couple of pages of *Sylvie and Bruno* but soon found that 'Work is hard to keep up, by the sea, when all is voluntary.' There were so many distractions – visits to Brighton to the Chain Pier and the Aquarium, little girls to be taken to see *Patience*, a performance of *Far from the Madding Crowd*, which he found painful but not vicious. He weighed himself on Eastbourne Pier: 10 stone $3\frac{1}{2}$ pounds.

He suddenly came to the conclusion that the Hull girls did not care for his company any longer. He had met Agnes and Evie in the road, 'but they gave themselves airs so much that I decided to go no further'. It was five years to the day that he had first met them; now he realised that their affection for him depended on his doing what 'exactly suits their inclination ... Such friends are hardly worth having.' For years he had joked about their mercenary attitude: now it was turning out to be all too true.

He tried to divert himself with other friends but the heartlessness of the Hulls had begun to obsess him. He thought of writing to Mrs Hull, but decided that his best plan was to 'hold aloof from calling at the house'. His resolution held good for six days and then he wrote to Mrs Hull. Agnes arrived the following day 'Dies creta notandus' to make friends again. 'It is a great relief to feel no longer estranged,' he wrote and went round to take tea with them all. But a few weeks later his fragile happiness was shattered again, not by the children, but by Mrs Hull herself.

Dodgson had been spending more and more time with Jessie, at eleven years the youngest of the girls, perhaps because he knew that the fifteen-year-old Agnes was growing steadily away from him. On 25th September he had spent six-and-a-half happy hours in Jessie's company and asked Mrs Hull if she would let her daughter stay for a few days with him at Lushington Road. Mrs Hull had refused on the grounds that Jessie 'would not quite like it', and when Dodgson suggested that Jessie should spend an evening with him, perhaps going to a concert in the park, permission was again refused. Dodgson was angry, hurt and bewildered. To avoid a painful confrontation with the Hulls he took himself off to Hastings on the day they left Eastbourne and tried to entertain himself by going to a concert. 'The day was lovely, and the music good, but I enjoyed nothing. The break-down of the "Hull" friendship is the fennel in my goblet of life, which gives a bitter taste.'[20]

Dodgson was incapable of keeping silent. He sent off an aggrieved letter to Mrs Hull, protesting not so much at her refusing him permission to take out Jessie, as at the one-sided nature of his friendship with the children:

> It will probably cause an estrangement for some time, if not

permanently. If, however, it all tends to the girls learning to try and treat friends in some sort of self-sacrificing spirit, I shall have done some good, and all the vexation I have suffered will not be quite wasted.[21]

It seems a curious way of putting it. Did he really want to be treated in a 'self-sacrificing spirit'? It is difficult not to suspect that he gained some kind of emotional satisfaction from all these quarrels and reconciliations.

When Mrs Hull's reply reached him at Guildford, it was some time before he could bring himself to open the letter. It was surprisingly conciliatory and was followed by a letter from Agnes and Jessie thanking him for the photographs he had sent to them. But they began 'Dear Mr Dodgson' not 'Dearest' and they were 'affectionate' and not 'loving' and Dodgson was once again hurt. 'The love of children is a fleeting thing,'[22] he wrote in his diary. He seemed totally incapable of learning from experience. Where his little girl friends were concerned, the same pattern of love, disappointment and loss would be endlessly repeated.[23]

'It will take me out of myself a little'

At the end of November 1882, Dodgson's oldest friend, Vere Bayne, resigned the Curatorship of the Common Room, amidst scenes of considerable acrimony. The post was certainly no sinecure since it was centred on the most important aspect of the dons' lives: their well-being. The Common Room was the centre of their communal life, an exclusive club where their privileges were closely guarded. There the Senior Students of Christ Church would sit and read the daily papers, the magazines and the reviews. They would gather there after Hall, sometimes with an honoured guest, to drink port and wine, to exchange gossip or highly academic anecdotes. Even Dodgson would sometimes relax his 'tantalising taciturnity' and present his colleagues with a 'knot' or conundrum, or on very rare occasions, to let fall 'a tiny drop of fantasy'. 'Heard this evening,' noted Edward Lee Hicks, a fellow of Corpus Christi, 'the last new joke by the author of "Alice in Wonderland". He knows a man whose feet are so large that he has to put his trousers on over his head.'

Although a happy haven, the Common Room was also a focus for continual bickering and discontent, where the fellows were constantly complaining about the quality of the wine or the uncomfortable armchairs or the absence of a favourite print from the walls or paper from the table or the draughts or the smells. Somehow Vere Bayne had managed to ride out the storms for twenty-one years, but, charged with 'obstinacy and extravagance' by the more belligerent members, he had finally given up. Dodgson had done his best to rebut the accusations levelled against his friend but, when it was proposed by Holland and Harcourt that he himself should be the new Curator, he rather surprisingly accepted, though 'with no light heart'.

> ... there will be much trouble and thought needed to work it satisfactorily: but it will take me out of myself a little, and so may be a real good. My life was tending to become too much that of a selfish recluse.[1]

His writing, his theatre-going and his constant entertaining of his little girl friends were taking up so much of his time; with the result that he had become alienated from many of his fellow dons.

For such a gentle, sensitive, quietly-reserved man, Dodgson made enemies with ease. Even Vere Bayne had had occasion to rebuke him for what he saw as disloyalty to his college and his colleagues. Friendship was all too frequently sacrificed to what Dodgson saw as principle, and with the best of intentions he could stir up a hornet's nest of hostility. Some years earlier, in 1876, he had brought upon himself the wrath of most of his fellow dons by his virulent opposition to a proposal to endow a project undertaken by Max Müller, the Professor of Comparative Philology. Müller was a fellow of Christ Church, an eminent German orientalist, mythologist and translator who had taken refuge in England after the revolutions of 1848, and was generally regarded as one of the most distinguished men in Oxford. Since 1863 he had been a friend of Dodgson, who had dined with him and photographed him and pronounced his daughters to be 'quite the loveliest children I have seen for a long while'.[2]

In February 1876, a proposal was put before Convocation allowing Müller, who was in the early stages of a massive enterprise for the University Press involving the editorship of translations of the sacred books of the East (some 50 volumes), to put aside his professorial cares and pursue his Eastern activities without interruption, and to appoint a deputy at half his salary. As Dodgson put it, 'the other half will be virtually a pension, and the Deputy will be virtually a new Professor'. In a series of papers, Dodgson questioned the propriety of the University's actions – was Oxford really so poor that it could not afford to 'pension a retiring Professor unless by mulcting his successor?' Dodgson defended his rushing into print on the subject on the grounds that he was 'no orator' (presumably a reference to his stammer) but, at the same time, he was actively canvassing for supporters and he did in fact speak in Convocation: 'the advocates of the Decree persisted so much in praising M. Müller, and ignoring the half-pay of the deputy, that I rose to ask them to keep more to the point'.[3] The decree was carried but Dodgson had managed to muster thirty-five opponents. Dodgson's intransigent integrity was the problem and his refusal to compromise earned him not only the enmity of his friend Müller but of the considerable body of his supporters.

When Dodgson took on the Curatorship, he was very conscious of the fact that, although he was generally respected, he was far from being well-loved and that he had lived for too long in isolation from his colleagues. The office was to prove an exacting test of his patience and was to show him to be far more capable of dealing with them than either they or he could have imagined.

The Curator's most important duty was the care and maintenance of the wine cellar, but his responsibilities also involved providing mineral waters, food, newspapers, writing paper and coal; keeping strict and detailed accounts and ensuring that the College servants carried out their tasks and were properly paid. It was rather like running a London club with a highly critical, eccentric and querulous membership.

Dodgson took his tasks very seriously and, from the beginning of 1883, Common Room matters were never far from his thoughts. It is curious that at a time when he had abandoned all his teaching work in order to give himself more time for his writing, he should have taken on something which would effectually absorb all the time he had gained. It is as if he took fright and shied away from writing, burying himself in activities which would prevent him thinking about it. Perhaps it was the realisation that nothing now stood between him and the daunting task of completing *Sylvie and Bruno*.

Dodgson made no pretension to being an expert on wine, though he was by no means an abstainer. He had a Wine Committee to whom he was responsible, but he was not going to take their views for granted and set about mastering everything he should know on the subject. On his return to Christ Church in January, he wrote to Juliette Dieudonnée of the Dieudonnée Hotel in St James's asking her to recommend a claret to be drunk in a year's time and to provide him with samples:

> To avoid confusion he wishes every bottle to be labelled with the dealer's name and with a letter (A, B, etc.) to distinguish one kind from another: and he would also wish to know the name and price of each kind.[4]

On the same day he asked his old friend Robert Bosanquet at St John's College for the best way to go about a wine-tasting:

> Is it a regular sit-down meal, with meat, etc., or <u>merely</u> for tasting, for which I suppose biscuits would be all required? ... How much of each kind of wine do you provide for each taster?[5]

Dodgson soon grew highly sceptical of his colleagues' professed knowledge of fine wines and of their ability to distinguish one wine from another. According to Claude Blagden, who knew Dodgson in his later years:

> He held the view that amateur wine-tasters deceived themselves when they professed to distinguish one vintage from another, and that they were really guided by the label supplied by the wine merchant. To

prove this he once secretly interchanged the labels on the bottles which the Wine Committee had met to taste, and maintained that his colleagues had reacted exactly as he had foretold.[6]

He was nevertheless prepared to go to endless lengths to ensure that the Wine Committee had no cause for complaint and that the wine was kept in the best possible condition. He began by drawing a detailed map of the wine cellar and its contents. To make sure that a proper temperature was maintained he sent off to Elliott Brothers for suitable thermometers, and he wrote off to Barrett and Clay of Old Burlington Street asking their opinion as to:

1. What amount of damp is desirable in a wine cellar?
2. Is ventilation desirable?
3. Should light be admitted?[7]

It hardly needs to be said that in all his dealings Dodgson was frostily incorruptible. Firms were told not to send their representatives to Christ Church, as they had done in Vere Bayne's day, and all gifts and inducements were angrily repudiated:

> Mr Dodgson has given directions to return to Messrs Snow the box of Portugal Fruit. He would have thought it hardly necessary to point out that the Curator whose duty it is to try to procure the best goods he can for Common Room, cannot possibly accept presents from any of the tradespeople concerned.[8]

In all his Common Room activities, Dodgson depended on the services and support of the butler, James Telling. Dodgson being Carroll could not resist the obvious possibilities for puns: 'I'll be telling the Common Room Man, and he'll be telling till further notice.'

The members of the Common Room were bombarded with a series of notices and circulars drawing their attention to wine tastings, to the price of tea, to a new five-light chandelier with 'incandescent burners' and, on one occasion, to pots of marmalade which Skeffington was offering for sale: '... it can also be guaranteed as absolutely genuine, and not, as is the case with much that is supplied in shops, largely composed of vegetable marrow'. Then there were rules to be enforced which Dodgson carried through with characteristic determination. Members were not allowed to sell Common Room brandy to the Henley Boat Club, nor were they to take publications away to their rooms or, worse still, remove the pictures.

Dodgson had a terrible tendency to get obsessed with trivial detail at the best of times, and was now frittering his time away with Common Room trivia:

To Messrs Snow and Co.

Mr C.L. Dodgson finds, on measuring, in ounces, half-bottles of the 3 liqueurs received from Messrs Snow and Co., that the half-bottle of Green Chartreuse contained 18 ounces, of Dry Curaçao $14\frac{3}{4}$, and of Maraschino 10. He will be obliged if Messrs Snow and Co. will send him the exact numbers of ounces contained in half bottles of the other liqueurs named in his letter of May 17 ... The 'Benedictine' is stated to be 'direct from the monastery'. He would be glad to know what Monastery is here alluded to.[9]

Drink took up a vast amount of Dodgson's time. It had to be selected and stored and nurtured, and the members of the Common Room could be fickle in their attachments. Vere Bayne had laid in considerable stocks of Madeira, but as Dodgson recorded in his pamphlet, *12 Months in a Curatorship by One Who Has Tried It*, which was published in 1884:

The consumption of Madeira (B) has been, during the past year, zero ... After careful calculation, I estimate that, if this rate of consumption be steadily maintained, our present stock will last us an infinite number of years. And though there may be something monotonous and dreary in the prospect of such vast cycles spent in drinking second-class Madeira, we may yet cheer ourselves with the thought of how economically it can be done.[10]

Despite all Dodgson's efforts, there were the inevitable complaints. Especially vocal was John Barclay Thompson, who, to judge from his photographs, had all the attributes of the classic school bully. It had been Thompson who had been chiefly responsible for unseating Vere Bayne and he was not pleased to discover that in Dodgson he had a far more skilful and less tractable opponent. He complained about everything – why were there no olives and preserves on Sundays, who was responsible for the installation of the 'hideous' fire-screen, why did the Curator no longer order green chartreuse or dry curaçao? Dodgson suggested that Thompson should order them from his own wine merchant.

Have been working 6 or 8 hours a day at Common Room ledgers, and have received a series of letters from J.B. Thompson reprimanding me for my conduct as Curator. It would be disheartening work if it were more than a single individual who did this.[11]

Dodgson did everything in his power to keep his temper and to hold on to his sense of humour. He wrote to Thompson begging him, 'that no difference of <u>views</u> may effect our <u>personal</u> friendship'. Dodgson emerges from this protracted conflict with a quite remarkable humility and humanity and a refusal to let himself be rattled by Thompson's pompous and humourless hostility.

Sadly, Dodgson did not always demonstrate such qualities when dealing with the College servants, who had very mixed feelings about him. Although he often came out strongly on their side over such matters as wages and working hours, and he would conduct their church services and visit them and sit by their bedside when they were sick, he could be impossibly exacting in his demands. In a series of letters to the Steward of Christ Church, Michael Sadler, he complained that too much milk had been sent up with his breakfast: was he to be charged for it? He had specifically 'negatived' cauliflower because it was always so badly cooked. Why had it been included in a meal sent up to his room, and was he to be charged for that? There was a dangerous 'effluvium' arising from under the Scout's room which made the new Common Room 'uninhabitable'. Could not someone take a broom to the pools of water which habitually formed at 'Tom' Gate whenever there was a shower of rain? He had sent away a window cleaner who had arrived at a time when Dodgson was in his bathroom. The man had not returned. Couldn't it be arranged for his ginger beer to be sent in bottles which had a glass ball in the neck, so that they could be stacked without going flat? There was also the little matter of the Messenger's Box which was supposed to be cleared precisely at the stroke of three. He had gone down with a note while the clock was striking the quarters and found that the box had already been cleared, would Sadler look into this matter? Sadler did so and only succeeded in making Dodgson more indignant than ever:

> How you <u>do</u> puzzle me! Are you engaged in composing riddles for a Xmas party? I complained that the Messenger, instead of coming just <u>after</u> 3, came just <u>before</u> it, and so missed some notes I took down while the clock was striking. <u>You</u> reply that the hour of collection is 'now 2.30' and, in corroboration thereof, refer me to a bluebook, in which I find the words, 'the Boxes are cleared during Vacation at 10 am, 12 noon, and at <u>3</u> and 8 pm'. I give it up! Never <u>was</u> much good at conundrums.[12]

The list of Dodgson's publications for his first year in office as Curator is characteristically eclectic. He printed a pamphlet on *Lawn Tennis Tournaments*, and one on *Rules for Reckoning Postage*, which does not seem to have survived and *The Times* republished his *Science of Betting* which had previously been seen in *The Pall Mall Gazette*.

His only major book that year was the eccentrically titled *Rhyme? and Reason?* which was, he told Henry Holiday, nearly all a '*réchauffé*' of previous work. It consisted of the humorous poems from *Phantasmagoria*, 'The Hunting of the Snark', 'Fame's Penny Trumpet', 'Atalanta in Camden Town', four riddles and two new poems, 'A Game of Fives', and

'Echoes'. The real novelty of *Rhyme? and Reason?* is the illustrations by Arthur Frost which have great satirical impact. The hideous screaming children on the beach in 'A Sea Dirge', the 'gentle popinjay' in 'The Lang Coortin' ' with a beak like a cornered pterodactyl, all give Dodgson's verses an unexpected force and a different dimension.

The publication of the book gave Dodgson a rare opportunity to write to Alice, enclosing a presentation copy:

> Dear Mrs Hargreaves,
> Perhaps the shortest day in the year is not <u>quite</u> the most appropriate time for recalling the long dream summer afternoons of ancient times: but anyhow if this book gives you half as much pleasure to receive as it does me to send, it will be a success indeed.[13]

This is the earliest surviving letter from Dodgson to his heroine. All the letters he had written to her as a child were destroyed by Mrs Liddell and so we can form no real idea (outside the Alice books) of how Dodgson actually spoke to her. In all the letters he wrote to her as Mrs Hargreaves his tone is cautious and respectful with nothing of the gaiety or fantasy which mark his letters to other former little girl friends. They read as if he had to pluck up his courage to speak to her at all, and he is always careful to be on his best behaviour. It is as if she were the adult, and he the child. He inscribed her copy of *Rhyme? and Reason?* to 'Mrs Hargreaves, with sincere regards and many pleasant memories of bygone hours in Wonderland from the Author'.

By December 1883, when Mrs Hargreaves received the book, she was the mother of two children, Alan and Leopold, the latter named after the Prince who had consented to be the boy's godfather. A third son was born in November 1887. He was named Caryl, but Alice firmly denied that this had anything to do with the creator of Wonderland. She said that she had come across the name in a novel.

'I hope you will not find it an impertinent suggestion'

While Dodgson was busily engaged in charting the tropics and zones of the Common Room wine cellar, his brother Edwin was fighting a losing battle with his bleak and inhospitable parish in Tristan da Cunha, where he served his hundred parishioners as 'post master, potato-patch digger, arbitrator, librarian, meteorologist and social entertainer'. The desperate plight of his miserable flock is best summed up in a letter which Dodgson later wrote to Lord Salisbury:

> The people were thriving enough, so long as whalers came that way, who were good customers for fresh meat and vegetables. But the whales have deserted those seas, and no ship comes near them, and, to crown all, the island is swarming with rats, who eat all the crops. The people are on the verge of starvation.[1]

Edwin had appealed to his brother for help and advice. Dodgson's projected solution to the islanders' miseries was highly imaginative, but distinctly drastic. He urged that the entire population, together with their sheep and cattle, should be transported either to the Cape or to Australia. On a more mundane level, he appealed, through *The St James's Gazette*, to any clergyman who was a reader of the *Guardian* to pass on his copies to Edwin:

> ... my brother lives almost in another Planet, so little does he hear of what goes on in the busy world he has left in order to devote himself to the spiritual needs of these poor islanders ... a batch of old Guardians would be very welcome to him, even if months old when they reach him ...[2]

The copies could be sent to the nearest point, St Helena, two hundred miles away, at which boats regularly called.

Dodgson set to work with a vigour and determination which could not have been exceeded if he himself had been the islanders' priest. He campaigned tirelessly on his brother's behalf for the next four years, but from the outset he was frustrated by the complexities, evasions and obduracy of the Civil Service whose machinations made those of Dickens' Circumlocution Office look positively obliging.

The Admiralty informed Dodgson that he had no authority to act on the islanders' behalf, and that, in any case, it was a matter for the Colonial Office. The Colonial Office said that nothing could be done until the Admiralty agreed to send a boat to transport the islanders to the Cape and, once they had arrived, the Colonial Office would do its best to interest the Cape authorities. Dodgson was then informed that no move could be initiated without the Cape government first sending for the islanders, but the next official to whom Dodgson applied told him that there was no point in approaching the Cape authorities since they had no jurisdiction over Tristan. The home government must begin the action.

The only person to show any sympathy at all for Dodgson's campaign was Sir George Smythe Baden Powell, an expert in colonial affairs, who had met Dodgson at Oxford in bizarre (though not untypical) circumstances at the house of Dodgson's old friend, the Reverend Hatch:

> Entering his house one day, and facing the dining room, I heard mysterious noises under the table and saw the cloth move as if some one were hiding. Children's legs revealed it as no burglar, and there was nothing for it but to crawl upon them, roaring like a lion. Bursting in upon them in their stronghold under the table, I was met by the staid but amused gaze of a reverend gentleman. Frequently afterwards did I see and hear 'Lewis Carroll' entertaining the youngsters in his inimitable way.[3]

Baden Powell was certainly impressed by Dodgson's efforts to help the people of Tristan da Cunha and spoke warmly of his sparing no pains to organise relief and assistance:

> At his instance I brought the matter before Government and the House of Commons and from that day to this frequent communication has been held with the islanders and material assistance rendered them – thanks to the warm heart of Lewis Carroll.[4]

But the truth was far from the happy ending suggested by Baden Powell. Although Dodgson believed that he had managed to secure an undertaking from the government agent for New South Wales to accept the islanders, when Dodgson and Edwin went to see Lord Salisbury in 1885, he told them that he was not confident of remaining in office long enough for anything to be achieved. The islanders were left to battle it out with the rats, and poor Edwin, exhausted with living so long 'as a second Robinson Crusoe', applied for missionary work in Africa.

Dodgson being Dodgson, there were other causes occupying his relentlessly busy mind. He was now concerned by the excessive profit of
booksellers. Out of every 1,000 copies of *Alice* sold, Macmillan's profit
was £20.16s 8d, his own £56.5s.od and that of the bookseller £70.16s.8d.
This seemed to him to be out of all proportion to the actual effort involved
by each of the participants.

> Account of share borne by the 3 parties in producing the book:
>
> 1. Bookseller – gives no time, thought, or trouble – merely sinks a
> little capital.
> 2. Publisher – gives time, thought, trouble, and results of experience.
> (Here I propose to say something of the amount of trouble I give you
> in bringing out a book!)
> 3. Author – gives brain-work chiefly, but of a kind not always
> procurable from any quarter, but scarce and so worth much.[5]

Dodgson's first move was to instruct Macmillan to fix the price for the
trade at a figure which would not yield such a high profit for the
bookseller, and a notice to this effect was inserted in his books:

> In selling Mr Lewis Carroll's books to the Trade, Messrs Macmillan
> and Co. will abate 2d in the shilling (no odd copies), and allow 5 per
> cent discount within 6 months, and 10 per cent for cash. In selling
> them to the Public (for cash only) they will allow 10 per cent discount.

The book trade responded with a letter from a 'Firm of London
Booksellers' which appeared in the *Bookseller*, suggesting that the trade
would do well not to take copies of Lewis Carroll's books:

> ... when an attempt is made to dictate terms to the whole of the
> booksellers of the United Kingdom by one individual, contrary to all
> the usages of the trade, and entailing nothing but unpleasantness
> between buyers and sellers, then the time has come for the trade to say
> it will not submit to dictation of this kind from any individual, be he
> whom he may ...[6]

If Mr Lewis Carroll wished to contest the system why did he not follow
Ruskin's example, and let the public order his books from the publisher?

Dodgson, who was never one to draw back from a good fight, began to
prepare a pamphlet on the subject of the disparity between profit and
labour contributed, entitled *The Profits of Authorship*. Dodgson paid
generous tribute to 'that most patient and painstaking firm' (Macmillan)
and set out, with disarming honesty, exactly what being publisher to Lewis
Carroll involved:

> The day they undertake a book for me is a 'dies nefastus' [unlucky

day] for them. From that day till the book is out – an interval of some two or three years on average – there is no pause in the pelting of the pitiless storm of directions and questions on every detail. To say that every question gets a courteous and thoughtful reply – that they are still outside a lunatic asylum – and that they still regard me with some degree of charity – is to speak volumes in praise of their good temper and of their health, bodily and mental. I think the publisher's claim on the profits is on the whole stronger than the bookseller's.[7]

The argument rumbled on for the next year, with the *Bookseller* surprisingly coming out strongly in Dodgson's favour, urging that his stand 'deserves support instead of condemnation'.

Dodgson could well have been accused of acting in his own interest, but, as ever, his chief concern was to see fair play, which was again at the heart of his next campaign – proportional, or as he would have called it, 'Proportionate' representation. In 1884 Gladstone was about to extend the franchise to all male householders, thereby increasing the electorate by some 2,000,000 people. There were predictable terror stories about the effect that this leap in the dark would have upon the country. Dodgson was convinced that the time was ripe to change the principles which governed parliamentary elections and to put forward a system by which the proportion of members sent to parliament would more accurately reflect the voting intentions of the electorate.

In a series of letters and pamphlets, Dodgson outlined a steadily evolving proposal for 'Proportionate' representation. Basically what he advocated was that districts should be formed which would return three, four, or more members, in proportion to their size:

When the poll is closed, divide the total number of votes by the number of Members to be returned plus one, and take the next greater integer as 'quota'. Let the returning officer publish the list of candidates, with the votes given for each, and declare as 'returned' each that has obtained the quota. If there are still Members to return, let him name a time when all the candidates shall appear before him; and each returned Member may then formally assign his surplus votes to whomsoever of the other candidates he will, while the other candidates may in like manner assign their votes to one another.[8]

A copy of Dodgson's scheme was presented to every member of Parliament. Lord Salisbury responded sympathetically but told Dodgson there was little hope of getting 'a patient hearing' for anything new – 'however Conservative its object'. When Gladstone's bill to extend the franchise reached Parliament in the spring of 1884, Salisbury did his best to hamper its passage through the House of Lords. Dodgson who by this time felt sufficiently at ease with Salisbury to give him the benefit of his advice told him, when the bill came up for its second reading in November:

> I hope you will not think it an impertinent suggestion if I express an <u>earnest</u> hope that the Lords will not a second time give Mr Gladstone a chance of going into the highways with the cry – untrue though it may be – 'the Lords have rejected the Franchise Bill!'[9]

Lord Salisbury was also the recipient of a frantic letter from Dodgson on the subject of W.T. Stead's campaign against child prostitution. It might have been expected that this would be an issue close to Dodgson's heart, but, although he admitted that child prostitution was a 'great evil', he was far more concerned about the excessive and highly lurid coverage of the issue and the unsavoury reports 'of the most loathsome details of prostitution' published 'in a daily paper sure to be seen by thousands of boys and young men'. After writing to Lord Salisbury he sent off an article to *The St James's Gazette* questioning whether all the publicity drummed up by Stead's campaign was not doing more harm than good:

> Not so many years ago, Vice was fashionable, and the literature of the day was <u>openly</u> profligate: no pretext of piety was offered to readers who would only have despised it. But in our day, to be popular, one must profess the very highest and purest motives. Straightway Satan is transformed into an Angel of light and with an air 'devout and pure, sober, steadfast and demure', offers us his old wares, furbished up in new colours.[10]

In September 1884, Dodgson went to stay with Edith Draper and her husband at Alfreton Vicarage in Derbyshire. He had known Edith since 1864 when she was the nine-year-old Edith Denman and they had met at a fête in Mitcham. Over the years he had kept in touch with her, sending presentation copies of his books and she had received an acrostic poem of her name accompanying his gift of 'The Hunting of the Snark':

> *Even while the blinding bandage lies,*
> *Daughter of a judge, upon thine eyes ...*

They met again in 1878 when she was twenty-three and Dodgson had marked the day with a white stone. He wrote to her about her 'very interesting drawings' and sent her a bunch of fritillaries, wrapped in wet cotton wool, for her to paint. She was married five years later to William Draper, 'a handsome young clergyman', despite considerable opposition from her family. It has been suggested that Dodgson was in love with her and that he accepted her invitation to stay at Alfreton because he knew she was now safely out of reach.

'Mr Draper met me at the station and walked up with me, about a mile. At night an ague-like "cold fit" attacked me.'[11] Dodgson stayed in the vicarage, working on an article on Proportional Representation, and Edith brought in some little girls from the village to cheer him up, but his ague grew steadily worse, and his three-day stay steadily extended itself into twelve. On the 25th September the house was invaded by Samuel Reynolds Hole, a Canon of Lincoln and an old friend of Tenniel and of the *Punch* staff in general. What followed is best described by Draper:

> ... there came to call a certain genial, and by no means shy, Dean, who without realising what he was doing, proceeded, in the presence of the other callers, to make some remark identifying Mr Dodgson as the author of his books. There followed an immense explosion immediately on the visitor's departure, with a pathetic and serious request that, if there were any risk of a repetition of the call, due warning might be given, and retreat secured.[12]

All of which makes it even stranger that Dodgson should have agreed to give a public lecture at the vicarage some days later, something that would have been highly unusual at the best of times. Dodgson's address, which Draper described as a 'sparkle from the pen of Lewis Carroll' was a highly characteristic little piece called 'Feeding the Mind':

> Breakfast, dinner, tea; in extreme cases, breakfast, luncheon, dinner, tea, supper, and a glass of something hot at bedtime? What care we take about feeding the lucky body! Which of us does as much for his mind? And what causes the difference? Is the body so much the more important of the two?

Draper remembered Dodgson's 'nervous, highly-strung manner as he stood before the little room full of simple people, few of whom had any idea of the world-wide reputation of the shy, slight figure before them'. One cannot help wondering what on earth they made of it all, as Dodgson's lecture slowly but surely deviated down paths of Carrollean fantasy, as he speculated on the idea of taking the mind to the doctor and having its pulse felt (a ritual which must have been very present in the midst of his ague).

> 'Why, what have you been doing with this mind lately? How have you fed it? It looks pale and the pulse is <u>very</u> slow.' 'Well, doctor, it has not had much regular food lately: I gave it a lot of sugar plums yesterday.' 'Sugar plums? What kind?' 'Well, they were a parcel of conundrums, Sir.' 'Ah, I thought so. Now, just mind this: if you go on playing tricks like that you'll spoil all its teeth.'[13]

Dodgson's lecture had a serious purpose, of course, as did, by this time of his life, nearly all his work. It was one's duty, he informed his audience, to 'Read, mark and inwardly digest' the good books that came their way. After the talk was finished, he handed the text over to Draper, telling him to 'Do what you like with it.'

That December Edith Draper gave birth to a son, but she was taken ill shortly afterwards and died on 30th December. Dodgson recorded simply in his diary: 'Heard of the death of my dear old friend Edith Draper.'

Dodgson was beginning to enter into a series of friendships with girls rather older than his customary little child-friends. Charlotte Rix, a young lady who had hopes of becoming an actress, sent her mother a long account of her first meeting with 'the Great Lewis' when he took her to an exhibition at the Grosvenor Gallery:

> He was absurd and liked the pictures so much himself (at least he criticised them enough) that I liked them too. It is quite absurd how fond he is of children – at least of <u>girls</u> ... and whenever he saw a picture of one he flew to it ... he <u>looks</u> eccentric and he is deaf with his right ear ... It <u>was</u> fun, and I felt as if I was dreaming all the time ...[14]

Charlotte was the younger sister of Edith Rix, whom Dodgson considered one of the most intelligent women he ever met. She became a close friend and one of his most regular correspondents. Edith first came to his notice through her answer to the 'Knot' of the ghastly injuries to the Chelsea Pensioners. She was a highly individual, determined young woman with a keen interest in mathematics and Dodgson immediately took her under his wing, constantly giving her advice about her studies: 'Never leave an unsolved mystery behind ... only go on working so long as the brain is <u>quite</u> clear.' It was to her that Dodgson dedicated *A Tangled Tale* when it appeared in October 1885, after the now customary series of tribulations and vituperations over the printing. The book was prefaced by an acrostic poem to Edith which, by using the second letters of each initial word to spell out her name, successfully skated round the problem posed by 'Rix':

> *Beloved pupil! Tamed by thee,*
> *Addish-, Subtra-, Multiplica-tion,*
> *Division, Fractions, Rule of Three,*
> *Attest thy deft manipulation!*
>
> *Then onward! Let the voice of Fame*
> *From Age to Age repeat thy story,*
> *Till thou hast won thyself a name*
> *Exceeding even Euclid's glory.*

Dodgson soon got to know the whole family and his friendship with

Edith's mother even survived her sending him a letter addressed to Lewis Carroll, Christ Church. He was greatly dismayed that she was proposing to send Edith to Cambridge, and if that was not bad enough, to Girton College:

> There is not a nice tone about 'Girton Girls'. They have an uncomfortable reputation for being fast and 'mannish'. I believe Newnham is much better. But why not Oxford? There is I believe no grounds for thinking that, because her turn is for Mathematics, she ought to go to Cambridge. Oxford teaching is, I am sure, all that she can possibly need, for a great many years to come.[15]

The status of women at Oxford in the mid-1880s was still unrecognised – the university had adopted the stance it took to any unwelcome innovation, and convinced itself that women did not exist. Ruskin refused to let the 'bonnets' into his lectures. Woman's intelligence, he announced, was for 'sweet ordering and arrangement' not for 'invention and creation'. Dodgson's reaction was more complex and considerably less dogmatic. He did not wish to see impediments placed in the way of the education of women, nor did he consider them inferior beings, but he was perturbed about where they were going to reside and what their effect would be on the young men of the university. For the time being he chose an easy way out, and when the question came up in Congregation in 1884, he said he was concerned that women were not physically capable of the demands on their stamina made by higher education, and quoted a report of a doctor who had observed that the majority of pupils in a large girls' school were suffering from curvature of the spine. Edith Rix, he was convinced, was pushing herself too hard. 'I hope you will interfere if she should seem much knocked-up and make her rest,' he told her mother. 'Several of my girl-friends have been seriously affected by this modern craze of excessive brain-stimulation.'[16]

That summer, Mrs Rix and Edith stayed as Dodgson's guest at Lushington Road. Much of the time was taken up with giving Edith lessons in mathematics and logic (which was fast becoming his major preoccupation), although they did find time for the traditional Eastbourne entertainments, concerts and swimming displays. When Mrs Rix returned home, Edith was allowed to stay on for a day unchaperoned. Initially the Rixes had ruled out such a notion 'because of Mrs Grundy' but they had relented. 'It will make an excellent precedent for having other visitors, of any age up to 19.'[17]

Mrs Rix had been worried that Dodgson might take offence at Edith's extreme High Church views, but he assured her that he had been brought

up in the same views by his father, although theological differences were
fast coming to mean less and less to him.

> More and more it seems to me … that what a person <u>is</u> is of more
> importance in God's sight than merely what propositions he affirms
> or denies. <u>You</u> at any rate, can do more good among those new
> friends of yours by showing them what a Christian <u>is</u> than by telling
> them what a Christian <u>believes</u>.[18]

On their day together, Dodgson and Edith went for a long walk and
attended a firework display and, since he had forsworn photography, he
arranged for Edith to have her picture taken. She sits, short-haired and
rather podgy, gazing curiously into the camera, a pen to her lips and a
book open on her lap.

33

'The extraordinary popularity the books have had'

> My dear Mrs Hargreaves,
> I fancy this will come to you almost like a voice from the dead, after so many years of silence – and yet those years have made no difference, that I can perceive, in my clearness of memory of the days when we did correspond. I am getting to feel what an old man's failing memory is, as to recent events and new friends ... but my mental picture is as vivid as ever, of one who was, through so many years, my ideal child-friend. I have had scores of child-friends since your time: but they have been quite a different thing ...[1]

Dodgson's memory was at fault on one point, at least. It was less than two years since he had last written to Alice, when sending her a copy of *Rhyme? and Reason?* He was now writing with a very specific purpose: to ask her consent to the publication in facsimile of the book she had once asked him to write for her more than thirty years earlier. If she had any objection, that would be the end of the matter. If she did not, would she lend it to him?

> I have not seen it for about twenty years: so I am not sure that the illustrations may not prove to be so awfully bad, that to reproduce them would be absurd.

Their position was now curiously reversed. Dodgson was no longer an obscure, eccentric, mathematical clergyman, but a famous author, already becoming something of a legend. Alice was no longer a 'fabulous monster', daughter of the most powerful man in Oxford, but a mother of three children living quietly in a large house outside Lyndhurst, with a husband whose chief interest was in playing cricket for Hampshire. And now the man who had transformed the child he had loved into a national heroine wanted to put before the public the manuscript which he had written for her as a token of his love.

> There can be no doubt that I should incur the charge of gross egoism in publishing it. But I don't care for that in the least: knowing that I have no such motive: only I think, considering the extraordinary popularity the books have had (we have sold more than 120,000 of the two) there must be many who would like to see the original form.

Undeniably there was a degree of egoism involved in his estimation of the degree of public interest in his work. Perhaps he was determined to squeeze every possibility that *Alice* afforded. *The Nursery Alice* was moving painfully slowly towards publication; the facsimile edition was another way of hashing up the same basic material. He may have wanted the public to see an *Alice* that was entirely his own, liberated from the clutches of Tenniel. Whatever his reasons, there is a slightly disturbing aspect to the whole enterprise, a feeling of disinternment of something essentially private. Alice was at first reluctant to part with the manuscript, but Dean Liddell told her that she could not refuse Dodgson even though he had sold 120,000 copies.[2] She agreed, with the reservation that she did not wish the photograph of herself which Dodgson had pasted on to the last page to be reproduced. With this agreed and her permission secured, Dodgson wrote off to Macmillan proposing a venture which would 'probably prove a considerable loss' as far as he himself was concerned, 'but it will at any rate put an honest penny into your pocket'. The problem was how to reproduce the facsimile; Dodgson was against lithography which he considered a rough and gritty process. He suggested that the books should be photographed page by page and cut on to woodblocks. The great difficulty, however, was how to protect the precious manuscript itself:

> I know exactly the state I should get the MS book back in, if I let it go (under whatever guarantees) into workmen's hands. It would not be much injured perhaps – just enough to spoil the look of it as a whole ...[3]

The only solution was for the book to be photographed in Dodgson's studio. Dodgson would himself pay for the photographer's rail fare and contribute towards his board and lodging at a modest hotel close to Christ Church. Macmillan selected Mr Noad from Eastham in Essex who duly presented himself at the College and took the pictures under Dodgson's close supervision.

> Whether the publication will be a source of gain or not, it is impossible to say [he wrote to Alice]. But if it is, I hardly like the idea of taking the whole profits, considering that the book is now your property, and I was thinking of proposing to send half of them to you. But a better idea has now occurred to me, which I now submit for your approval: it is to hand over the profits to Hospitals and Homes for Sick Children.[4]

By August 1885, all seemed to be going smoothly. Dodgson wrote to Alice again, telling her that Macmillan proposed to get the book out well in time for Christmas (he should have known better by now not to tempt

Providence), but that he needed to hold on to the manuscript for a little longer in case any corrections should be needed during the course of the zinc block process. Alice would of course receive one of the earliest copies of the facsimile.

> May I also have the pleasure of presenting one to your eldest daughter (even if she be <u>not</u> an Alice – which I think unlikely).[5]

New vistas of an entirely new *Alice* adventure must have seemed to be opening up for Dodgson, and he must have been greatly disappointed when he heard that her children were all boys. According to Alice's son, Caryl Hargreaves, she asked Dodgson whether he would care to stand as godfather to one of them, but he did not reply.

Dodgson had provided a preface to the book, a heartfelt and sincere attempt to put into words something of the mystery which he felt in the presence of children. The man who has loved 'one true child', he wrote, will have known:

> ... the awe that falls on one in the presence of a spirit fresh from GOD's hands, on whom no shadow of sin, and but the outermost fringe of the shadow of sorrow, has yet fallen: he will have felt the bitter contrast between the haunting selfishness that spoils his best deeds and the life that is but an overflowing love – for I think a child's <u>first</u> attitude to the world is a simple love for all living things ...[6]

It was a theme which he would develop at greater length in *Sylvie and Bruno*.

By November, the first 'electros' of the little book began to arrive from Noad, and Dodgson decided that the original could safely be returned to Alice. Suddenly, disaster struck. Dodgson heard that Mr Noad was in financial difficulties and was unable to pay Mr Swain, the man who was making the zinc blocks. Dodgson sent money off to Mr Noad, but heard nothing and on Boxing Day 1885, Mr Swain told Dodgson that he was preparing to bring a court case against Noad. Dodgson, who was genuinely sorry for his unfortunate photographer, paid Swain off, but this changed nothing:

> ... there is no getting anything, not even a letter from Mr Noad! He may have left the country for all I know.[7]

What made matters much worse, as far as Dodgson was concerned, was that he had entrusted to Noad the manuscript of *The Rectory Umbrella*, preserved intact from his childhood at Croft, which he had also planned to reproduce in facsimile.

In April 1886, Noad left four blocks at Macmillan, but again vanished into obscurity. With fourteen blocks still missing, Dodgson sought the advice of a solicitor who told him that he must 'frighten' Noad by a summons before a magistrate. Dodgson appeared before a court at Stratford-le-Bow, and although Noad did not put in appearance, the magistrate decided to proceed in his absence. Dodgson described what followed in a long letter to Alice:

> Then I had the new and exciting experience of being put into the witness box, and sworn, and cross examined by a rather savage Magistrate's Clerk, who seemed to think that, if he only bullied me enough, he would soon catch me out in a falsehood! I had to give the Magistrate a little lecture on photo-zincography, and the poor man declared the case was so complicated he must adjourn it for another week.[8]

He did, however, issue an order for Noad's apprehension, and the missing negatives and the precious manuscript of *The Rectory Umbrella* were rapidly returned. This left Dodgson with the expense of paying a second time for the fourteen blocks to be made, but he was heartily thankful that it was all over. By 21st November, 1886, he had a proof of the book in his hands, but, of course, he was not happy with it. 'The pages are not so placed that the tops of two opposite pages shall be at the same level ...' This was duly rectified and Dodgson had a bound copy by 17th December. The whole process had taken seventeen months, but at least the book was out before *a* Christmas.

On the day after *Alice's Adventures Underground* at last went on sale to the public, Alice appeared in yet another incarnation. The operetta *Alice in Wonderland* received its first performance at the Prince of Wales's Theatre, 'a tolerably eventful week for me!'[9]

Despite his failure to persuade Sullivan to set the Alice songs, Dodgson had by no means given up his dream of bringing *Alice's Adventures* to the stage. In 1883 he had approached Alexander Mackenzie, who had recently completed an opera entitled *Columba*, and who had been very enthusiastic. All that was needed was a suitable libretto, and Dodgson sat down to write one, but the task proved too much for him. It was not in his nature to regard anything as being beyond him, but the splendidly anarchic spirit of *La Guida di Braggia* had long since deserted him. He had grown prematurely old and cautious, his imagination blunted by sentiment and increasing religiosity, and perhaps dulled by too much exposure to second rate children's entertainments.

When in August 1886 he received a letter from Henry Savile Clarke asking for leave to make a two-act operetta out of *Alice's Adventures* and *Through the Looking Glass*, Dodgson's response was cautious rather than enthusiastic. His first condition was that his 'dream child' should not be exposed to the 'tastes of dirty-minded youths and men in the Gallery', and Dodgson wanted a written guarantee that 'neither in the libretto nor in any of the stage business, shall any coarseness, or anything suggestive of coarseness, be admitted'.[10] Nor was Dodgson very happy about a libretto that would combine both the Alice stories:

> In London Pantomime they constantly make the mistake of mixing <u>two</u> Nursery Tales together. I do not believe there is <u>one</u> child of their audience who would not be ready to say 'Give us the one or the other, but not <u>both</u> in one entertainment'.

On this point, however, Clarke stood firm. He was a professional writer, a drama critic and a newspaper editor. A three-act play of his, *A Fight for Life*, had met with moderate success, and he had written and produced a musical comedy, *The Duke's Doctor*. Above all what he had in mind was not some misty prospect for an unspecified future. He wanted to put *Alice* on the stage that Christmas. A compromise was agreed on by which each book was to be confined to a separate act.

Clarke wanted the piece to be performed entirely by children, but on this point Dodgson stood firm:

> By admitting grown-up performers you will certainly get a much higher sum total of skill, and probably much greater success – There is no reason why all the characters should be the same size as Alice – Many of them were much larger – at least, so far as my ideas went. Tenniel has rather reduced some more than I meant – the Kings and Queens ought surely to be grown up.[11]

The next difficulty was the choice of composer. Dodgson would almost certainly have favoured another approach to Sullivan, but Clarke had set his sights considerably lower. The composer he chose was Walter Slaughter, a young cellist and pianist who was to spend most of his short life as a conductor in the West End. His music for *Alice* was bland and unadventurous, but Dodgson, to whom music was largely a mystery, seems to have been perfectly happy with it.

Dodgson was in no doubt as to who should play Alice. He recommended 'a dear little friend on the stage – Phoebe Carlo, now playing in "The Governess"', but, whoever Clarke chose it must not be 'an Alice that drops her H's'. Since Phoebe Carlo's pronunciation was far from perfect, it seems an odd point for Dodgson to make. Nor was she in the least like Alice, neither Tenniel's nor Dodgson's, and certainly nothing like little Alice

Liddell. Phoebe Carlo was plump and dark, with distinctly Mediterranean features; nor was she, by any stretch of the imagination, a young lady. She was the daughter of a packer, born in 1874 in Peabody Square, and Dodgson had first noticed her in *Dick Whittington* at the Avenue, singing 'They call me such a pretty little thing'. He thought that she was charming and lost no time in calling on her family and carrying Phoebe off to see Holman Hunt's astonishing *Triumph of the Innocents*. Subsequently she was invited down to Oxford, where he escorted her round the colleges and where she received her first lawn tennis lesson: 'After which my tired little friend had a good nap on my knee ...'[12] Everything went so well that Phoebe went to stay with Dodgson at Lushington Road. She played on the sands, was taken to Devonshire Park and to church. Dodgson had hoped that she might stay a whole week, but her mother telegrammed to say that she was needed at the Princess's Theatre. She was photographed, dragged up Beachy Head and returned home. Phoebe was the first of his working-class girl friends, and he was obviously fascinated by her very positive personality. He also realised that working-class mothers, particularly those associated with the theatre, were far more likely to let him take their daughters off to Eastbourne without protesting, and would even consider it quite an advantage.

Savile Clarke was only too happy for his famous author to collaborate as fully as possible in the preparations for the production and Dodgson delighted in devising lively bits of 'business':

> Enter Cook, carrying a large soup-tureen, with a ladle: she pushes her way round the Court, and, wherever she goes, those around her are in fits of sneezing – the fits beginning suddenly as soon as she is within 2 yards of anyone, and ceasing as suddenly, when she has passed by. (I think that a great wave of sneezing might be rather funny).[13]

Given Clarke's distinctly vapid adaptation, it seems a pity that Dodgson did not feel himself capable of tackling the whole thing.

Believing that he was assured of Savile Clarke's sympathy, Dodgson suddenly came up with a thoroughly alarming suggestion. Why not interpose between the first act of *Alice's Adventures* and the second of *Through the Looking Glass*, a further act consisting of 'The Hunting of the Snark'? It would give the audience plenty for their money, and three hours would not be too long,

> But my main reason for wishing for this interlude, is to give a <u>real</u> rest for Phoebe, in the middle of her hard task. I am greatly afraid of her breaking down <u>physically</u> before the thing has run a fortnight.[14]

Savile Clarke would positively have no 'Snark'.

Dodgson did not attend the first performance. Given his obsessive concern for anonymity, this is not surprising. The operetta was well received and reviewed in terms that could only have pleased him. 'A pretty tale, delightfully told' said the *Illustrated London News*, 'a sweet and wholesome combination of drollery and fancy', said the *Daily News*, 'one of the most wholesome and innocent of the productions of the Christmas season', said the *Graphic*. Phoebe Carlo was generally praised.

Dodgson went to see the production on 30th December. He considered Phoebe to be 'a splendid Alice' – he pronouced her song and dance with the Cheshire Cat 'a little gem', and he was greatly charmed by the six-and-a-half-year-old Dorothy d'Alcourt as the Dormouse. But he found the second half flat and he was horrified by the performances of the Rosa Troupe who were playing the adult roles and who he thought 'largely spoilt' the production.

He made no mention of the operetta in any of his letters to Alice Hargreaves. He perhaps suspected that she might not be flattered to see herself and her adventures incarnated by Phoebe Carlo.

'All teetotallers like sugar'

On New Year's Day, 1887, Dodgson preached one of his rare sermons at St Mary's in Guildford, and Gertrude Corrie, who was sitting in the congregation, jotted down what she could recollect of it in her diary. 'We liked him immensely', she recorded, 'he has a fine face, especially profile.' Dodgson had taken the precaution of noting down the headings of his sermon, but when he stepped into the pulpit he kept them in his pocket. He spoke of people expecting to enjoy a sermon much as they would a musical play or an opera:

> There was a danger of his being new to us, and we to him. We were to look on him as a fellow wanderer in the garden – a fellow traveller groping for light like ourselves.

Dodgson then recalled the question put by Jesus to the blind man, 'What wilt thou that I should do to thee?' and of its application to everyone. He spoke of suffering, of the fear of death, of the loss of loved ones, 'But the real most overwhelming ill of all was sin – the blackness of sin in the world.' He then embarked on a very odd and very individual illustration:

> Most of us knew the terrible feeling of unforgiven sin – the load which even seemed to affect the lower creation. Children's dog flew at one when it stumbled over him; found his mistake, and did not bite; but the nurse left him behind the next time they went out, and the dog could not bear it, and went and lay in a ditch of water, and drowned himself.[1]

Even by the standards of the Victorian sermon it is a preposterous anecdote. Miss Corrie called in at The Chestnuts a few days later and was introduced to Dodgson – 'smaller and more shadowy than in church'.

Dodgson lost no time in getting back to London for urgent discussions with Savile Clarke about changes he wished to see made in the production of *Alice in Wonderland*. He attempted to relieve the flatness of the second half by writing in a new finale for the Walrus and the Carpenter scene in which the unfortunate oysters returned as ghosts.

The operetta had been due to finish its London run on 20th February, before setting out on a provincial tour, but there was such a clamour for seats that after a brief excursion to Brighton, *Alice* played at the Prince of Wales's until 18th March. By then, Dodgson was longing for it to end. All he wanted was to revise the piece and recast it, and he was determined that the next time the operetta was presented he would not let Clarke have quite so free a hand.

In the meantime he had written for *Theatre* an article called 'Alice on the Stage' which was published that April. It is a curious production, rather in the manner of some of his addresses to his readers in *The St James's Gazette*. He cautiously avoided saying anything in Savile Clarke's favour, but vaguely praised the production. What is so strange about the article is the view he presents of his heroine. He evokes the 'golden afternoon' when the tale was told as a kind of lyrical dream, and Alice herself is sentimentalised almost out of existence:

> What wert thou, dream-Alice, in thy foster father's eyes? How shall he picture thee? Loving, first, loving and gentle: loving as a dog (forgive the prosaic simile, but I know no earthly love so pure and perfect), and gentle as a fawn: then courteous to <u>all</u>, high and low, grand or grotesque, King or Caterpillar, even as though she were herself a King's daughter, and her clothing of wrought gold.[2]

The description may be an appropriate compliment to little Alice Liddell, but this saintly figure bears no resemblance to the Alice Dodgson had created. Where in all this is the girl who kicked Bill up the chimney or who shouted 'Nonsense!' to the Queen of Hearts?

In February 1887 *The Game of Logic* was published after a long and desperate struggle with the printers, during which the first edition, like that of *Alice's Adventures*, was scrapped and sent off ignominiously to America. As Dodgson grew older the study of logic began to assume a central position in his life and he put no limits on its possibilities. He lectured on the subject for the most part to young ladies, in schools and lecture halls, but he was perfectly happy, as in the case of Edith Rix, to impart his enthusiasm to a 'single individual girl'. Evelyn Hatch remembered him taking a logic class at St Hugh's, Oxford, before: 'a dozen students assembled solemnly in the library, armed with note-books and pencils, prepared to listen to a serious lecture on a difficult subject'.[3] But always behind Dodgson's lessons in logic was an anarchic Carrollean spirit at work and, however fundamentally serious in purpose the lectures might have been, the examples he chose teetered perilously on the verge of

the absurd and sound as if they might have been devised by the Mad
Hatter:

> Some new Cakes are nice
> No new Cakes are nice
> All new Cakes are nice.

or

> All teetotallers like sugar
> No nightingale drinks wine.

As the lessons in logic progressed, his 'propositions' became curiouser and
curiouser, with silent oysters and waddling puppies, fossils that were not
crossed in love and Emperors who were not dentists, and in his later years
they grew wilder and wilder still: all ducks waltz, no sugar-plums of mine
are cigars, no ostrich lives on mince-pies, no kitten with a tail will play with
a gorilla, and a rainbow cannot bear the weight of a wheel-barrow.

Dodgson's original idea had been to publish the lectures under the title
Logic for Ladies, but he changed his mind in favour of a small pamphlet,
with a board and counters – The Game of Logic. The board and counters
were the means by which the pupil would learn the processes of logic.

> Now please to look at the smaller Diagram on the Board, and suppose
> it to be a cupboard, intended for all the Cakes in the world (it would
> have to be a good large one, of course). And let us suppose all the new
> ones to be put into the upper half (marked 'x') and all the rest (that is
> the not new ones) into the lower half (marked 'x¹'). Thus the lower
> half would contain elderly Cakes, aged Cakes, ante-diluvian Cakes –
> if there are any: I haven't seen many myself – and so on.

Dodgson presupposes a very intelligent, very patient child, and one cannot
help wondering how many actually survived the course and finished the
book, let alone the game. Irene Barnes (the actress Irene Vanbrugh), who
was one of Dodgson's child-guests at Lushington Road, remembered:

> His great delight was to teach me his Game of Logic. Dare I say this
> made the evening rather long, when the band was playing outside on
> the Parade and the moon shining on the sea?[4]

The summer of 1887 at Eastbourne saw Dodgson doing his best to divide
his energies between logic and the highly illogical epic of Sylvie and Bruno,
then titled The Four Seasons. He had committed himself to making a
serious attempt to push forward with the book and was working six hours
a day and more. The reason for his new determination was that at long last
he had found an illustrator whom he intended to keep supplied with the

copy which Clay was printing up for him in slip. He had set himself the target of having the book ready for Christmas 1888.

The illustrator he had settled on was Harry Furniss, a leading *Punch* artist and as great a contrast to Dodgson as could be imagined. Furniss was tubby and bearded, an ebullient, hearty extrovert, a wit and raconteur and very much a man of the world. Tenniel had warned him that he would give him a week with Dodgson – '<u>you</u> will never put up with that fellow a day longer'. The Furniss–Dodgson collaboration was to survive almost intact, despite many alarms and vicissitudes, for the next ten years.

> Carroll [wrote Furniss in one of several highly-coloured accounts of their partnership] was as unlike any other man as his books were unlike any other author's books. It was a relief to meet the pure simple, innocent dreamer of children, after the selfish, commercial mind of most authors. Carroll was a wit, a gentleman, a bore and an egotist – and, like Hans Andersen, a spoilt child ... Carroll was not selfish, but a liberal-minded, liberal-handed philanthropist, but his egotism was all but second childhood.[5]

Dodgson told Furniss that he had 'a considerable mass of chaotic materials for a story', and Furniss was set to work on the poem of 'Peter and Paul' and from then on was supplied with odds and ends of episodes, poetry and stories without, at first, having any clear notion of the book as a whole. At that stage, neither, it seems, did Dodgson.

Alice in Wonderland was playing at Brighton again that summer and greatly to Dodgson's surprise, his sister Henrietta consented to be taken to see it. She had lived in Brighton since the beginning of 1885 when she had decided to set up on her own, independent of her sisters at The Chestnuts. Dodgson, Henrietta and Phoebe and her sisters went to see Louey Webb's aquatic entertainment on the pier, which so fascinated him that he went back to see it again and again.

> She performs in a tank, like those in the aquarium, with light behind ... and the water just deep enough for her to stand with her head out. She did some sewing, writing on a slate, etc., under water ... Miss Webb is 18, and as she is perfectly formed, the exhibition is worth seeing, if only as a picture.[6]

The St James's Gazette was carrying reports of a campaign to prevent children under ten from performing in the theatre, alleging that acting would impose 'physical strain' which might lead to 'fatal results'. Dodgson immediately sprang to the children's defence and wrote to the paper giving a lively account of the day he had spent in Brighton with the Carlo sisters:

I think that anyone who could have seen the vigour of <u>life</u> in those three children – the intensity with which they enjoyed everything, great or small, which came their way – who could have watched the younger two running races on the Pier, or could have heard the fervent exclamation of the eldest at the end of the afternoon, 'We <u>have</u> enjoyed ourselves!' – would agree with me that here at least was no excessive 'physical strain', nor any <u>imminent</u> danger of 'fatal results'.

These were, he went on, stage children who had been acting every night with a matinée on Thursdays, working until 10.30 at night and getting up every morning to bathe at seven.

On the fly leaf of his diary, Dodgson noted '27/9/87. First meeting with Isa.' It was a date of particular importance, for Isa Bowman was to become the closest and, after Alice, the most important of his girl friends. She wrote a memoir about their friendship, *The Story of Lewis Carroll*, which, for all its coyness and sentimentality, gives us a vivid picture of Dodgson. It has been said that she lays too much emphasis on the passionate hugs and kisses, but it is likely that in this she is probably more reliable than other, more reserved, witnesses. Kisses, by the hundred, even by the million, were an essential part of any girl's relationship with Dodgson. Problems only arose at the time 'when the kissing had to stop'.

Isa was thirteen and the eldest of three sisters and one brother, all of whom were to go into the theatre. She was wide-eyed, with pretty, delicate features and had a certain stylish elegance. On 27th September Dodgson had arranged for her mother to bring her to Fenchurch Street Station. They visited an exhibition in Bond Street where Dodgson admired a painting of the Magdalen and they got on so well that, when he took her back to her home at Stratford, he obtained her mother's agreement for Isa to go to Lushington Road with him.

At Eastbourne, there were daily Bible-readings and Isa was taught three propositions of Euclid. On the Sunday she was taken to church and in the afternoon they took the long walk up Beachy Head:

> I used to like it very much when I got there, but the walk was irksome. Lewis Carroll believed in a great amount of exercise, and said one should always go to bed physically wearied with the exercise of the day.[7]

He did his best to beguile her by making his handkerchief into a playful mouse and in telling her stories of scaly dragons and strange talking beasts:

> The consummation of a story was always heralded by the phrase, 'The children now came to a deep dark wood.' When I heard that

sentence which was always spoken very slowly and with a solemn
dropping of the voice, I always knew that the really exciting part was
coming. I used to nestle a little nearer to him, and he used to hold me
a little closer as he told of the final adventure.[8]

She was distressed by his almost total indifference to flowers, which she
loved. He would do his best to share her raptures but, 'he would always
rather invent some new game for us to play at'. Nothing much seems to
have changed since his childhood days at Daresbury and Croft – Dodgson
was always happiest in a world which he had himself created. Yet there
were occasions when she observed him drifting off into a melancholy
reverie. At sunset on Beachy Head, he would take off his hat and look out
to sea, letting the wind play in his long hair. Once she noticed tears in his
eyes, and when they turned to go he gripped her tightly by the hand.

Dodgson escorted Isa back to London at the end of the week, and
rounded off their holiday with a visit to Buffalo Bill's *Wild West Show*.
They may have discussed together the possibility of Isa playing Alice in a
new production of the operetta, and the thirteen-year-old girl could have
been gently but effectively manipulating the 'old professor' she was now
allowed to call her 'Uncle'. They had not been in London a week before
Dodgson was writing to Savile Clarke about the *Alice* revival – 'I was very
near calling the other day, and bringing Isa Bowman with me.'

The Alice books had been introduced to yet another audience. For a long
time Dodgson had been trying to persuade Macmillan to issue a popular
cheap edition, priced at 2s 6d. The publisher was not happy about the use
of the word 'cheap' on the cover and suggested 'People's Edition', in which
form *Alice's Adventures* appeared in December 1887 with a cover
showing the pack of cards flying at Alice, and *Through the Looking Glass*
the following month, with Alice reaching up to shake Humpty Dumpty's
hand. Yet a third edition, combining both books in one, appeared the same
month. Within three months the three books had sold over 10,000 copies.

Dodgson was also becoming quite a cult in America and a group of girls
from the Boston Latin School decided to launch a magazine called
Jabberwock. They wrote to ask his permission to use the name, obviously
hoping to get a letter from him, and Dodgson's reply fulfilled all their
wishes. Not only did he provide them with an elucidation of the name:

> He finds that the Anglo-Saxon word 'wocer' or 'wocor' signifies
> 'offspring' or 'fruit'. Taking 'jabber' in its ordinary acceptation of
> 'excited or voluble discussion', this would give 'the result of much
> excited discussion'.

He followed this up with a poem, 'A Lesson in Latin',

> Our Latin books, in motley row,
> Invite us to our task –
> Gay Horace, stately Cicero:
> Yet there's one verb, when once we know,
> No higher skill we ask:
> This ranks all other lore above–
> We've learned '"Amare" means "to love"!'.[9]

But 'amare' also means 'bitter' and so the lesson that they finally learn is that 'Love is bitter sweet'. Their relationship with Dodgson progressed merrily enough, until he read, in one of the issues which they sent to him, a limerick:

> There was an old deacon of Lynn
> Who confessed he was given to sin,
> When they said, 'Yes, you are,'
> Oh, how he did swear!
> That angry old deacon of Lynn.[10]

Dodgson was not amused. The confession of sin was not a subject for levity, he told them, and he forbade them to send any more copies of the magazine. The Boston girls were not alone in incurring his wrath that year. The future Bishop of Chichester, Winfrid Burrows, who launched into a jolly anecdote on the Ten Commandments in the Common Room, was sharply rebuked. 'There is a terrible amount, just now, of jesting on sacred things', Dodgson informed him, 'which *must*, I think tend to make these things less and less real: so that in fighting against profane talk, one is practically fighting the battle of faith as against unbelief.'[11]

Dodgson's health had begun to give him trouble. In 1886 he had suffered what his doctor described as an 'epileptoform' attack. Dodgson had suspected for some time that he might have epileptic tendencies, which may account for why he was so preoccupied with the condition and consulted various books as to how it should be treated. The attacks, none of them very serious, were to persist for the rest of his life. He was also suffering from pain in the knee, which was diagnosed as 'synovitis'.

While confined to his sofa, he tried to set down a few of his thoughts on blasphemy in an article, 'The Stage and the Spirit of Reverence', which he sent to *The Theatre*. He told his readers that he had heard blasphemies from the lips of clergymen far worse 'than would be even possible on the stage', attacked the casual taking of the Lord's name in vain so common in Shakespeare's plays, and complained about the way in which W.S. Gilbert portrayed ministers of religion as contemptible. The whole story of the children saying 'damme' in *HMS Pinafore* was trotted out again and he concluded his rather directionless article with an outline for a dramatisation of the Prodigal Son, translated into modern life.

While Dodgson saw evil in what others considered harmless anecdote, he firmly rejected any suggestion of evil in his own preoccupation with naked little girls. Although he had forsworn photography, this did not rule out drawing and, at the beginning of 1888, he visited the studio of Mrs Shute, the widow of a Christ Church colleague, to make nude studies of the fourteen-year-old Ada Frost: 'I think a spectator would have to be really in <u>search</u> of evil thought to have any feeling about her than simply a sense of beauty, as in looking at a statue.'[12]

'L.C. was the pink of propriety,' Mrs Shute remembered, and at their cosy drawing sessions, Dodgson would bring the cakes and entertain the models with his stories while she supplied the tea. Dodgson told her that he had no interest in grown-up models and that he found more beauty in the undeveloped female form. '12 would be my ideal age: children are so thin from 7 to 10.' In spite of his enthusiasm, Mrs Shute had to admit that Dodgson's drawing abilities were not very great.[13]

Dodgson's synovitis had rather restricted his visits to the theatre, but on 18th June he managed to get up to London to give his nephew Stuart Collingwood his first experience of a live stage performance. The play was Frances Hodgson Burnett's dramatisation of her sensationally successful *Little Lord Fauntleroy*, in which the nine-year-old Vera Beringer was playing the 'curly-headed little fellow'. 'One of the cleverest children I have ever seen on stage',[14] he wrote in his diary, and sent her a copy of *Alice's Adventures*. He began seriously to consider whether she might not make a better Alice than Isa Bowman. Isa herself was taken to see the play on 11th July. 'Isa would have liked to play the part,' Dodgson wrote in a diary which he concocted for her, 'but the Manager at the theatre did not allow her, as she did not know the words, which would have made it go off badly.' Dodgson still had lingering doubts as to whether she would be the best choice for Alice. He had not heard her speak on stage, he told Savile Clarke, yet he would 'far rather Isa should have it than any other child'.

The visit to *Little Lord Fauntleroy* was the start of a holiday together. On the first afternoon Isa was taken to see the Panorama of Niagara, and Dodgson created a whimsical fantasy about the model of a little dog staring at the Falls. It was not a model at all, he told Isa, and if they waited long enough they would see an attendant bring him a bone. The dog had an understudy, his 'rather restless' brother, who had once darted straight out of the panorama after a little girl's sandwich.

Suddenly he began to stammer and looking round in some alarm I saw that a dozen grown ups and children had gathered around and were listening with every appearance of amused interest. And it was not Mr Carroll, but a very confused Mr Dodgson who took me by the hand and led me quickly from the scene.[15]

That evening they took the train to Oxford, where Isa was to stay with Mrs Symonds in Beaumont Street. For the next four days she was taken on the round of the colleges and was introduced to various friends. Dodgson was evidently rather proud of his new girl friend and enjoyed showing off his elegant little companion. Dodgson wrote up their adventures in a diary, *Isa's Visit to Oxford*, in which he figured as the 'Aged Aged Man':

> They had breakfast at Ch. Ch. in the rooms of the A.A.M., and then Isa learned how to print with the 'Type-Writer', and printed several beautiful volumes of poetry, all of her own invention. By this time it was 1 o'clock, so Isa paid a visit to the Kitchen, to make sure her dinner was being properly roasted. The Kitchen is about the oldest part of the College, so was built about 1546.

It may have been on this visit – Isa was to stay at Oxford several times – that Isa, irritated and jealous by Dodgson's praise for her friend Florence Jackson's rendering of 'The Holy City', kicked up her heels and launched into a music-hall song. Dodgson was appalled and ordered her to stop at once. Apart from the vulgarity of the song, Isa had raised her skirts.

On the day they returned to London, Dodgson called on Savile Clarke and told him that he hoped that he could engage Isa to play Alice. Phoebe Carlo, whom Clarke still favoured, was too old and too tall and lacked 'childlike freshness', and Isa's English was far better than Phoebe's: 'In one special and important point, the use of "H", she is altogether better ... Isa looks more of a lady than Phoebe.'[16] Moreover, Phoebe had had a good innings and Isa had a claim on the part because of the long time she had spent understudying the role. Clarke gave way. Not only should Isa play Alice, her brother Charlie should play the White Rabbit, her sister Susie the Dormouse and something would be found for little Maggie. The Rosa Troupe would not be re-engaged.

Delighted, the following day Dodgson went down to Eastbourne, more determined than ever to make progress with *Sylvie and Bruno*, and to keep Harry Furniss supplied with copy.

35

'My darling Isa'

For the first few weeks at Eastbourne, Dodgson worked conscientiously away at the adventures of his little fairy creatures, venturing out to see a ventriloquist on the pier and searching all over town for a suitable pair of gloves. He was making splendid progress with *Sylvie and Bruno*, but his thoughts were continually drifting off to the forthcoming revival of *Alice in Wonderland* and he wrote to Savile Clarke with ideas on every aspect of the production, from the kind of masks needed for the animal characters to the need to enforce a ban on ladies' hats and bonnets in the stalls and dress-circle. He was still haunted by memories of the Rosa Troupe and suggested that when Clarke gave out the parts the words that needed emphasis should be underlined:

> Very likely it wouldn't have saved the Red and White Queens from making nonsense of every sentence by leaning on the wrong word, but they were exceptionally idiotic ...[1]

Dodgson made certain that every stress in Isa Bowman's copy was carefully marked.

Isa was due to come down to Lushington Road at the end of August, and Dodgson eyed the rainy skies, fearing that they promised a 'gloomy prospect'. He had arranged that Isa should stay with him for a week, but as he told Winifred Holiday:

> ... we got on so well together, that I kept writing to Mrs Bowman for leave to keep her longer, till the week had extended to <u>five</u>! When we got near the end of <u>four</u>, I thought 'at any rate I'll keep her for over the normal <u>honey-moon</u> period.' I felt rather curious to see whether there was any young person of the feminine gender, whose company tête à tête, I could endure for a <u>month</u>. I didn't believe it possible: and used to say, when twitted with being a bachelor, 'I never yet saw the young lady whose company I could endure for a <u>week</u> – far less for <u>life</u>!' But alas, I can plead that argument no longer![2]

What made the curious chemistry of their relationship so effective was that Dodgson had at last found someone who reflected something of Alice's charm and elegance but who returned his affection in a more mature way, and who could enjoy his company without wearying of it, or feeling, as the Hulls did, that there was something inherently ridiculous about it.

At Lushington Road they soon fell into a regular routine. Isa's bedroom was opposite that of her 'grave professor' and in the mornings he would thrust a newspaper under his door as a sign that she might go in. There were daily readings from the Bible and Isa had to repeat the stories in her own words. There were lessons and puzzles and games and visits to the theatres, and while Dodgson was struggling away at *Sylvie and Bruno*, Isa was having swimming lessons at Devonshire Park. There was, however, a condition attached to this:

> He would never allow me to go to the swimming bath – which I revelled in – until I had promised him faithfully that I would go afterwards to the dentists.[3]

Since Isa had a swimming lesson nearly every day, her visits to the dentist must have been quite frequent, but then, according to her, Dodgson went to the dentist as frequently as he went to his hairdresser.

Although the days passed happily enough, Isa's long stay was not without its problems. Bored with a concert at Devonshire Park, she took out her crocheting and was rebuked for showing indifference to artists who had 'probably spent a lifetime perfecting themselves at their art'. On one occasion, Isa drew a caricature of Dodgson on the back of an envelope. when he saw it he turned very red, tore it to pieces and threw it in the fire.

> … afterwards he came suddenly to me and saying nothing, caught me up in his arms and kissed me passionately.

At the end of the five weeks, Isa had stayed longer than all the previous guests put together. Dodgson took her back to London at the beginning of October and returned to Eastbourne on the same day. But it was no longer the same:

> Oct 4. Life feels rather lonely without Isa. Cold weather has suddenly set in and I begin fires in sitting room in evening. Walked to Beachy Head and on return got caught in a tremendous storm of wind and rain.[4]

Alice in Wonderland had run into difficulties. The new management at the Prince of Wales's Theatre had decided against it and Savile Clarke was trying to find another venue. Isa was very distressed and Dodgson tried not to raise her hopes too much. Clarke eventually managed to persuade the American actor Richard Mansfield, who had scored a great success as Dr Jekyll and Mr Hyde, to take on the direction of the operetta at the Globe Theatre in the Strand. A new musical director was appointed, the twenty-six-year-old Edward German, who remembered the cast at rehearsals as being like one big happy family. Isa, however, was far from happy. The Mr Hyde aspect of Richard Mansfield was in the ascendant and he was bullying the poor girl ferociously. Fortunately she had the good sense not to complain to Dodgson, who seems to have been blissfully unaware of it all, sitting around the theatre, entertaining the children with games and stories until asked to leave by the stage manager.

He had no intention of being present on the first night and even when he did attend a performance on 3rd January he was desperately anxious that no one should know who he was. The press had been generally enthusiastic, praising Isa as a 'pretty, engaging and highly intelligent exponent of the part of Alice', despite her weak singing voice. Dodgson, who must have had some anxiety about the girl whose cause he had so positively promoted, thought her 'delightful' and he told Winifred Holiday that Isa was a 'much more refined and intelligent Alice even than Phoebe'.

He was less happy about the production. Alice's dress looked too long, the sound of Humpty Dumpty's crash came before he had fallen off the wall, and there were two pieces of real indecency:

(1) The White King, this afternoon, fell flat on his back, with his feet towards the audience who (at any rate in the stalls) were thus presented with a view of him which – which I leave to your imagination.
(2) The Red King, in order to dance ... actually <u>drew up</u> the long series of rings which formed his skirt, nearly to his waist – I don't say he was not fully clad, in tights, beneath that skirt: and I don't say he <u>needed</u> the skirt: nor that there would have been any indecency in appearing <u>without</u> the skirt: but I <u>do</u> say that, having the skirt on, it was distinctly indecent to pull it up.[5]

Dodgson was full of ideas for improving the operetta, but by the end of January it was running into financial difficulties. Dodgson offered to give £100 for extra publicity, posters at railway stations, advertisements in the papers, bills and circulars, all of which would prominently display Isa's name. But the management found a face-saving excuse for terminating the run. The School Board of London had put through their new regulations against the employment of children under ten and was insisting on 'efficient elementary education' for children up to fourteen. This had not prevented Mansfield from staging the play, but it now gave him a sufficient reason for terminating it. The run came to an end on 9th February. The production was not to be revived again until the December after Dodgson's death.

The curtailment of the operetta found Dodgson thoroughly enmeshed in what he hoped might be the final stages of *The Nursery Alice*. Initially the delays were Tenniel's fault: as always, he took his time in making changes to the pictures. Alice's appearance was subtly altered to conform with changing fashion: her hair was now neatly tied in a blue ribbon and her skirt was pleated and narrower. The reduction in the width of her skirt meant that Tenniel had slightly to redraw his backgrounds, so that curious details like the Gryphon's tail and the flamingo's legs emerged. Dodgson himself was responsible for the next hold up, for it was not until the end of 1888 that he got down to the text. Gertrude Thomson had been asked to provide a cover picture, 'which I expect will add much to the attractiveness of the book', but she too took her time, and then became unwell, and the publication date of Easter 1888 had to be abandoned.

When they came to print, there were the now familiar problems and delays and the whole print run of 10,000 copies was rejected outright. By 7th March, 1890, Dodgson was at last satisfied and, despite acute synovitis, was able to stagger up to London to sign presentation copies. The book was dedicated to Marie Van der Gucht, who was sixteen, and one wonders what on earth she made of the strange book. Gertrude Thomson's cover shows a hightly sentimentalised Alice lying asleep under a tree, and a White Rabbit who seems to have mislaid his waistcoat. *The Nursery Alice* is a very odd and rather frustrating work which shows how far Dodgson had grown away from the genius of his astonishing creation. He had, admittedly, set himself an almost impossible problem, in presenting Alice as a story for the under fives. After various attempts he decided he would not really try to tell the story of Alice's adventures at all: he would simply provide a running commentary on the twenty Tenniel pictures which he had selected.

Years of sitting little children on his knee and of devising commentaries for magic lantern entertainments had given him an idea of what he believed would be suitable. He would begin the story like any conventional fairy tale:

> Once upon a time there was a little girl called Alice: and she had a very curious dream. Would you like to hear what it was that she dreamed about? Well, this was the *first* thing that happened. A White Rabbit came running by, in a great hurry; and, just as it passed Alice, it stopped and took its watch out of its pocket. Wasn't *that* a funny thing? Did you ever see a Rabbit that had a watch and a pocket to put it in?

He later embarks on a very odd anecdote about some children who had a little dog called Dash and who decided to give it oatmeal porridge as a brithday treat:

> And then, do you know, it did <u>hate</u> it so, it wouldn't eat a bit more of it! So we had to put it all down its throat with a spoon!

At times the narrator sounds like a nagging maiden aunt – or is it Dodgson lecturing his sisters?

> What do you think that was? <u>You don't know</u>? Well, you are an ignorant child! Now, be very attentive, and I'll soon cure you of your ignorance!

That June Dodgson accepted an invitation to stay again at Hatfield and this time he allowed himself to be coaxed into story-telling. At luncheon he was next to the Duchess of Albany, the widow of Alice's former admirer, Prince Leopold. Her daughter, another Alice, was there and, at first, Dodgson had hopes of adding her to his gallery of child-friends. 'Now that I have made friends with a real live little Princess, I don't intend ever to <u>speak</u> to any more children that haven't titles,' he told Isa, but then, fearing that she might take him seriously, he hastened to reassure her:

> If I made friends with a <u>dozen</u> Princesses, I would love you better than all of them together, even if I had them all rolled up into a sort of child-roly-poly.[6]

Princess Alice rapidly fell from grace. Dodgson was in the middle of telling a story to the assembled children when his stammer struck, and Princess Alice asked in a loud voice, 'Why does he waggle his mouth like that?' and was hastily removed by a lady-in-waiting.

Later in the month Isa's sister Maggie, acting in *Bootle's Baby*, arrived at Oxford and was taken on Dodgson's tour of the colleges. An encounter with the Bishop of Oxford provided Dodgson with what became one of his favourite anecdotes: The Bishop asked her what she thought of Oxford: 'I think', said the little actress with quite a professional aplomb, 'it's the best place in the provinces!'

Another of the Bowman sisters, Nellie, came down to stay with Isa and Dodgson for the summer at Lushington Road. The children bathed in the sea instead of the baths at Devonshire Park, 'that I might see them swim, which they seem to do capitally'.[7] Mansfield was planning to take Isa to America on his forthcoming tour of *Richard III* (accompanied by the rest of the family) and Dodgson thought that it would be an excellent idea to accustom the girls to the discomfort of their Atlantic crossing by taking them on a steamer excursion to Hastings. The sea was rough and the children rapidly began to feel ill, while Dodgson constantly reminded them: 'Crossing the Atlantic will be much worse than this!'

Dodgson had been giving some thought to the new regulations which had been seized on by the management of The Globe as a pretext for ending the run of *Alice in Wonderland* and wrote to J. Coleman, who was compiling a book on stage children, with an eminently sensible proposal for the employment of children in theatres. Every child under sixteen should hold an acting licence, annually renewable, on the condition that they attained a sufficient educational standard. There should be a limit to the number of weeks a year for which a child could be engaged and children should receive a specified number of hours of education while they were acting. Finally, girls under sixteen should be provided with a proper escort to and from the theatre.

> But I do not believe that the law can absolutely prohibit children under ten from acting in theatres without causing a cruel wrong to many a poor struggling family, to whom the child's stage salary is a Godsend, and making many poor children miserable by debarring them from a healthy and innocent occupation which they dearly love.[8]

In October the Bowman family left for Boston on the first stage of Mansfield's American tour. Dodgson makes no mention of it in his diary, perhaps because he was too affected by Isa's departure and the gloomy prospect of not seeing her again until the spring; perhaps because he was now absolutely committed to bringing out *Sylvie and Bruno* by the end of the year. He had dedicated it to Isa.

36

'The length of Sylvie and Bruno has far exceeded my intentions'

The publishing history of *Sylvie and Bruno* spread over nearly half of Dodgson's life. The first short story about the two fairy children had been brought out in 1867, when he was thirty-five; now, in 1889, at the age of fifty-seven, he was about to publish the first part of a work which had grown beyond his wildest imaginings.

The stories which had begun with 'Bruno's Revenge' in *Aunt Judy's Magazine*, and which had grown in number as Dodgson found himself obliged to sing for his supper at Hatfield House, had developed in a wholly random fashion with no apparent link between them and, by his own account, it was not until 1873 that Dodgson began to see how the tales 'might serve as the nucleus of a longer story'. It was then that he sat down and wrote what would become the last paragraph of *Sylvie and Bruno Concluded*:

> Sylvie's sweet lips shaped themselves to reply, but her voice sounded faint and very far away. The vision was fast slipping from my eager gaze: but it seemed to me, in that last bewildering moment, that not Sylvie but an angel was looking out through those trustful brown eyes, and that not Sylvie's but an angel's voice was whispering "IT IS LOVE".

The composition of *Sylvie and Bruno* was every bit as erratic and bizarre as that of 'The Hunting of the Snark'. In 1874 Henry Holiday made a drawing of the fairy pair, the following year Dodgson told the children at Hatfield the story of Prince Uggug and, when Harry Furniss was eventually set to work, he was given a poem which did not figure until the eleventh chapter. Little by little the fragments for the book slowly accumulated: stories, poems, fragments of sermons, random thoughts jotted down in the middle of the night, puzzles, jokes and games.

> And thus it came to pass that I found myself at last in possession of a huge unwieldy mass of litterature – if the reader will kindly excuse the spelling – which only needed stringing together, upon the thread of a consecutive story, to constitute the book I hoped to write.[1]

Dodgson had gone through a similar process when he had constructed

Through The Looking Glass out of stories told years before to the Liddell sisters, and there was no reason why the same process should not be applied to the Sylvie and Bruno stories. The difficulty lay in the fact that Dodgson had no intention of simply stringing the stories together. Moreover he was determined to strike out in a new direction, away from the idiom of the *Alice* books, believing '... it would be courting disaster to attempt that style again'.

As a result, Dodgson set about courting a different kind of disaster. Summer after summer, the material was taken down to Eastbourne, and over the years, despite the attractions of the pier and Devonshire Park and the distracting charms of dozens of little girls, *Sylvie and Bruno* began to take on its highly individual shape. The structure which he eventually devised for the stories and for the vast disarray of material which had crystallised around them was, if ultimately self-defeating, something which only Dodgson could have devised and which bears witness to the astounding, if eccentric, originality of his mind. 'Whether it is better or worse than the Alice books I have no idea', he told Mrs MacDonald 'but I take a far greater interest in it, as having tried to put more real thought into it.'[2]

The Sylvie and Bruno stories themselves are framed in a rambling, rather loosely-knit narrative in which their father, the noble and kindly Warden of Outland, is ousted by his brother, the treacherous Sub-Warden Sibimet and his evil wife, Tabikat. The Sub-Warden spreads false rumours of the Warden's death and Bruno's claims as his father's heir are swept aside in favour of Tabikat's loathsome son, Prince Uggug. The good Warden is, however, the King of Elfland, and he lurks about in disguise until the time comes for him to reclaim his kingdom.

Running parallel to this story, and at times closely interwoven, is a conventional Victorian romance, set in what purports to be the real world. Dr Arthur Forrester is in love with Lady Muriel Orme, the daughter of the Earl of Elvedon, but he hesitates to declare himself, partly because of his own impecunious circumstances, partly because he suspects she is in love with her cousin, the dashing Captain Eric Lindon. Lady Muriel has grave reservations about her cousin, on account of his lack of committed religious principles, but she agrees to marry him and Forrester decides to go out to India.

At this point, on page 359, the first part of *Sylvie and Bruno* comes to an end, and the story continues in *Sylvie and Bruno Concluded*, published in 1893. In this the Warden returns to his rightful domain, but the Sub-

Warden, in a fit of remorse, pleads for forgiveness and is allowed to continue as ruler. The unrepentant Uggug, however, is transformed into a porcupine. Meanwhile, in the Elvedon world, Eric Lindon agrees to release Lady Muriel from her engagement because of her misgivings about his religion, and she marries Arthur Forrester who has conveniently come into a fortune. However, their joy is short-lived, for Arthur rushes off to give help to the inhabitants of a nearby port where the plague is raging and is shortly afterwards reported dead. Eventually, Eric Lindon, who is at last finding his way towards religious faith, discovers that Arthur is in fact still alive and restores him safely to Lady Muriel.

The two worlds are linked by the narrator, an amiable, benevolent highly Dodgsonian personality, in late middle-age, who slips effortlessly between Outland, Elfland and Elvedon through falling into 'eerie' trances which convey him instantaneously from one world to the other. Many of the other characters enjoy a simultaneous existence both in Outland and Elvedon. Sylvie is intended to be the same being as Lady Muriel, the sparkling Bruno finds a rather unlikely counterpart in the sober Arthur Forrester, and Sibimet has a counterpart in Eric Lindon, as has the Warden/Elf King in the Earl.

Dodgson himself appears in the book in various guises: as Arthur Forrester, particularly in the forceful originality of some of his religious views:

> Can you have a stronger proof of the Original Goodness there must be in this nation, than the fact that Religion has been preached to us as a commercial speculation for a century, and that we still believe in God?

He also figures more obviously as the narrator, endlessly perceptive and understanding. Eric Lindon, for all his heroic qualities represents the kind of man Dodgson most disliked, the manly, empty-headed athletic type incarnated in Alice's husband, Reginald Hargreaves.

The Earl has borrowed some of Lord Salisbury's reserve and bumbling good nature, the Sub-Warden's wife, Tabikat, immediately calls to mind Mrs Liddell in her ferocious ambition. By bringing together the fairy-child Sylvie and the adult Lady Muriel as one and the same person (Alice Liddell and Alice Hargreaves) Dodgson is making yet another attempt to carry his child romances into the adult world, which is of course impossible. Dodgson and his narrator can be no more than spectators: 'I am one of those subordinate characters that turn up for the development of the story,' says the narrator, 'and whose final appearance is outside the church, waiting to greet the happy pair.'

*

The book posed the most unlikely problems for the illustrator. Harry Furniss had begun his task considerably in awe of both Dodgson and of Tenniel:

> When I, a little, very little boy in knickerbockers, first enjoyed the adventures of Alice and worshipped the pen and pencil which recorded them, I little thought I would some day work hand in hand with the author.

But he soon came to realise that *Sylvie and Bruno* was a very different proposition to *Alice*:

> I therefore did not fear comparisons, but what I did fear was that Carroll would not be Carroll, and Carroll wasn't – he was Dodgson. I wish I had illustrated him when he was Carroll.[3]

Dodgson subjected Furniss to a relentless bombardment of photographs indicating what he thought the characters should look like, particularly Sylvie/Lady Muriel:

> If you take No. 3 and cover the chin up to one third of the way from its point to the mouth you will see the face I admire most … But photo No. 4 looks to me quite the expression I should like Lady Muriel to have while discussing some serious subject. And No. 1 would do capitally for her face when enjoying a joke or talking nonsense …[4]

Furniss maintained an imperturbable composure, listening patiently to all Dodgson's suggestions, but going his own way:

> He invited me to visit friends of his, and strangers too, from John O'Groats to Land's End, so as to collect fragments of faces … He was jealous that I would not disclose to him who my model was for Sylvie … Repeatedly he wrote to me: 'How old is your model for Sylvie? And may I have her name and address?' 'My friend Miss E.G. Thomson, an artist great in "fairies", would be glad to know of her, I'm sure,' and so on. The fairy Sylvie was my own daughter! All the children in his books I illustrate were my own children; yet this fact never struck him![5]

Under the circumstances, Furniss must have been rather disconcerted by Dodgson's insistence that Sylvie, the incarnation of all the little girls he had ever loved, should wear as little as possible, and that her dress should be transparent:

> I <u>wish</u> I dared dispense with all costume; naked children are so perfectly pure and lovely, but Mrs Grundy would be furious – it would never do. Then the question is, how little dress will content her? Bare legs and feet we must have at any rate.[6]

In the event Sylvie was most decently and opaquely clad, but Dodgson was entirely satisfied with the result: 'Sylvie is just delicious, just the face and figure I want, and what a pretty pair of legs you've given her!' Bruno, on the other hand, had to be thoroughly covered up. Dodgson had a disconcerting and rather disturbing horror of naked little boys:

> Excuse my coarse language (I don't know how to put it more euphemistically) but a picture exhibiting the naked posteriors, even of a very young boy, cannot possibly go into the book.

In addition to the dozens of photographs with which he supplied Furniss, Dodgson's letters were often accompanied by sketches of his own, to give some idea of what he had in mind. They are very different from Furniss's sturdily realistic illustrations; delicate, grotesque, fantastic, giving a wholly different dimension to the work and bringing the worlds of Outland and Elvedon much closer together. Dodgson was excessively modest about them but that did not always prevent him from finding his own ideas preferable to those of Furniss:

> Of course the herrings must not have sharks' heads, and the Badgers must not be the dogs I have made of them. But as to the disproportion in size, I fear you have been too much to the zoo, and have got ideas too accurate for our present purpose. Surely it is better to get the pictures as funny as we can, than to be zoologically correct?[7]

Furniss was remarkably tolerant of Dodgson's relentless fault-finding, but on one occasion, in August 1889, they fell out. Dodgson took exception to the proportions of the drawing of Sylvie with the Stag Beetle, and noted that, in the picture of Sylvie with the Hare, her height, which he had carefully measured, was just under six diameters of her own head, whereas in the picture with the beetle it was just over eight. Furniss had always resented Dodgson's habit of minutely examining every sketch under a magnifying glass and he told his pernickety employer that 'John Tenniel, George du Maurier, or Harry Furniss must be accepted as they are.' Dodgson briefly cast around among other illustrators in the hope of finding someone else who might take on the task which Furniss had abandoned and then decided to temporise and suggested that they should 'fight the point out in print'. Dodgson had for many years contemplated an article on 'Authors' Difficulties with Illustrators' and he now felt that this dispute gave him the opportunity to write it.

> You shall have your say first: and my paper will come out, most appropriately as an answer to yours. I not only fully authorise you to print the '5 pages' of my letter, which you say would win you 'the sympathy of all the Artists', but I call upon you to do so.[8]

He must not be identified other than as Lewis Carroll, he would pay any expenses involved in the reproduction of the offending illustration, and it must be pointed out that 'our <u>artistic</u> differences have left our <u>human</u> relations untouched'.

Furniss was completely won over by this highly novel way of settling their differences and offered not only to redraw the picture of Sylvie but also one of Tottles to which Dodgson had objected. It was now Dodgson's turn to be conciliatory and he told Furniss he would let the pictures remain as they were, although it would seem that Furniss did, in the end, amend the picture of Sylvie.

> I was a problem solver also, and we worked without further friction to the end of the volume, and through a second volume which occupied some years more.[9]

By the end of 1888, Dodgson had decided that he had far too much material for one book and he decided that it should be published in two long volumes. Although he was later to insist that the books were not written for money, he was to display his usual business acumen about the proper price:

> The length of Sylvie and Bruno has far exceeded my calculations: I now find it will be close on 400 pages, if not over that number. That is, it will be almost exactly equal to Alice and the Looking Glass (for which we charge 12s) put together, though with only 47 pictures instead of 92. Under these circumstances, I must beg you to carefully reconsider the question of <u>price</u>, and see if you do not think we might fairly put on another shilling, or even 1s 6d.[10]

For once there were no difficulties over the printing, and Sylvie and Bruno was sent out in time for Christmas. Among the many who received a presentation copy was John Ruskin, exiled to Coniston suffering from brain fever and nursed by Joan Severn. Receiving no response to his gift, Dodgson wrote to Mrs Severn, asking her to remind Ruskin that he had once expressed a hope that Dodgson's next book 'would not be a mere unconnected dream, but would contain a plot, and to be told that I have tried to do this in Sylvie and Bruno.' It is not known whether Ruskin in fact ever read the book. It would scarcely have helped his brain fever. The difficulty of Sylvie and Bruno, as we have already seen, is that it contains far too much plot: in fact it contains far too much of everything. Dodgson made use of the book, rather as he had employed The St James's Gazette, as a means of communicating with his public on the many axes he had to grind, on almost any thought which came, unbidden, into his head. In the preface he is discoursing on his old hobby-horses, a Child's Bible and a

Shakespeare for Girls, and dwelling on such thoughts as the horror of dying suddenly in the theatre while watching an immoral play:

> Be sure the safest rule is that we should not dare to <u>live</u> in any scene in which we dare not <u>die</u>.

The reader is forewarned of exactly what is in store in the book itself and of the new departure the author has taken:

> by introducing, along with what will, I hope to be acceptable nonsenses for children, some of the graver themes of human life.

Dodgson even provided each of the Sylvie and Bruno books with an index (even his journal had an index) and these give some idea of the astonishing profusion of ideas which Dodgson introduced into his work:

> Barometer, sideways motion of;
> Bath, portable for tourists;
> Books or mind. Which contain most science?
> Boots for horizontal weather;
> Brain, inverted position of;
> Bread sauce. What appropriate for?

It is as if the book had been concocted by the White Knight and the Mad Hatter under the guidance of the Bellman. One would like to believe that Dodgson compiled his index with his tongue firmly in his cheek, but it seems unlikely.

Sylvie and Bruno presents us with a mirror of Dodgson's own consciousness, his restless and compulsive inventiveness, his religious faith, his bigotry, his tolerance, his passion for mathematics and logic, his delight in devising tricks, games and puzzles, his sentimentality, his boundless humanity, and above all his almost mystical conviction that in the beauty of little girls there is a kind of revelation in the divine world:

> … it was in a London exhibition where, making my way through a crowd, I suddenly met, face to face, a child of quite unearthly beauty. Then came a rush of burning tears to the eyes, as though one could weep one's soul away for pure delight. And lastly there fell upon me a sense of awe that was almost terror – some such feeling as Moses must have had when he heard the words, *Put off thy shoes from off thy feet, for the place whereon thou standest is holy ground.*

Dodgson's readers were so completely baffled by the subtlety of the transitions between the different worlds in *Sylvie and Bruno* that he was obliged to write to *The St James's Gazette*, giving an explanation of what he had intended:

... the book is written on the theory of the actual existence of fairies, and of their being able to assume human form. The 'I' of the story goes through 3 different stages of being, (1) real life, (2) the 'eerie' stage, in which he can see fairies, (3) trance, in which, while his body remains apparently asleep, his spirit is free to pass into fairyland and witness what is going on there at the moment.[11]

This explanation proved to be of little help to the readers desperately trying to disentangle the narrative thread and, in the preface to *Sylvie and Bruno Concluded*, Dodgson found it necessary to supply a table of events, giving page by page indication of what passages in the book were taking place in what stage of consciousness and whether the characters were in normal or fairy form.

Even this could not help to save a book which was widely regarded as unreadable. It was not the problem of who was in which world at what time that constituted the obstacle, but the fact that Lewis Carroll had been ousted by the Reverend Dodgson. The fatal flaw in the design was that the story was intended to serve two mutually contradictory purposes: 'to suit those hours of innocent merriment which are the very life of childhood' and to suggest thoughts 'not wholly out of harmony with the graver cadences of life'. In the *Alice* books, Dodgson had never talked down (except a little in *The Nursery Alice*), never preached, never drawn a moral. In *Sylvie and Bruno* he rarely leaves off doing so. The 'graver cadences of life' invade the book at every turn. Dodgson's sincerity is never in question and this makes the failure of the book even more disheartening. He believed the fairy duet for Sylvie and Bruno in praise of love to be the finest thing he had ever written:

> Say, what is the spell, when her fledglings are cheeping,
> That lures the bird home to her nest?
> Or wakes the tired mother, whose infant is weeping,
> To cuddle and croon it to rest?
> What's the magic that charms the glad babe in her arms,
> Till it cooes with the voice of the dove?
>
> 'Tis a secret, and so let us whisper it low –
> And the name of the secret is Love.

There were compensations. The book contained some excellent nonsense verses in which the Carrollean spirit seems still undimmed:

> Little birds are feeding
> Justices with jam,
> Rich in frizzled ham:
> Rich, I say, in oysters
> Haunting shady cloisters –
> That is what I am.

He even created a character in the book worthy of being introduced to Alice, the Mad Gardener, the anarchy of whose wild song mercifully lingers in the mind after all its dreary sermonising has been forgotten:

> *He thought he saw an Albatross*
> *That fluttered round the lamp;*
> *He looked again and found it was*
> *A Penny-Postage-Stamp.*
> *'You'd best be getting home,' he said:*
> *'The nights are very damp'.*

But the cloying sentimentality, the interminable religious chit-chat, Bruno's baby-talk and the sheer ineptitude of much of the action fracture the work beyond repair. However, it remains an endlessly fascinating work, a kind of wrecked treasure ship.

Isa Bowman's presentation copy of *Sylvie and Bruno* was not trusted to the uncertain waters of the Atlantic:

> ... the whales are so inconsiderate. They'd have been sure to want to borrow it to show to the little whales, quite forgetting that the salt water would be sure to spoil it.[12]

When she did eventually receive her copy she failed to notice that the dedicatory poem was a double acrostic on the letters of her name. 'She was so long without working it out,' he told his friend Florence Jackson, 'that I've had to give her a hint.' Perhaps she can be forgiven for this for it was a singularly bleak, pessimistic and curiously godless piece:

> *Is all our Life, then, but a dream*
> *Seen faintly on the golden gleam*
> *Athwart Time's dark resistless stream?*
>
> *Bowed to earth with bitter woe,*
> *Or laughing at some raree-show,*
> *We flutter idly to and fro.*
>
> *Man's little Day in haste we spend,*
> *And from its merry noontide send*
> *No glance to meet the silent end.*

'A kind and Christian deed'

In the week following the publication of *Sylvie and Bruno*, Dodgson went to Edgbaston School for Girls in Birmingham to see a version of *Alice* devised by Mrs Freiligrath–Kroeker. 'I only hope you'll find me some obscure corner from which I can look on without being myself a spectacle!' he told the headmistress, Alice Jane Cooper, who had been helping him over his Shakespeare for Girls project. He went on, recklessly: 'Possibly, I might wish just to be allowed to kiss the Alice of the play: but that, of course, would be an unheard of liberty, and not to be permitted on any account.'[1] Whether or not he kissed his Alice is not recounted, but he did have to undergo the 'awful ordeal' of reading *Bruno's Revenge* to an eager audience of 250 children and parents.

On 13th January 1890, Dodgson heard that his brother Edwin has been ordered home from Tristan da Cunha on account of his rapidly declining health and was expected any day at Guildford. Edwin remained in England only long enough to recover his health and in October he went out to the less abrasive climate of St Vincent in the Cape Verde islands.

> It is a great change for him, [Dodgson told Gertrude Chataway]. At Tristan he was 'master of all he surveyed'; and could carry on matters ecclesiastical exactly as he liked – which was delightful for such an extreme 'Ritualist' as he is.[2]

At St Vincent, a Portuguese colony, the established church was Roman Catholic and he would be regarded as virtually a 'Nonconformist Minister'.

Dodgson's vast extended family continued to claim his energy, his time and his sympathy. There was, for example, Loui Taylor, the daughter of Charles Collingwood's sister, 'helplessly ill', paralysed in a Cowley hospital, where Dodgson visited her whenever he could. He gave her a copy of *Through the Looking Glass*, and so that she could read it comfortably he had a special book holder designed for her and taught the sisters how to operate it, but after a time the hospital could no longer cope with Loui and the unfortunate girl was moved round various nursing homes and private hospitals where Dodgson continued to visit her. Her condition seems to have had remissions and he was convinced that she could do more to help herself:

> Yesterday I got a letter from poor Loui Taylor, to whom I had written that I thought if she exerted her will she could do more, and might some day walk again, interpreting my words as charging her with deceit and saying she does not want to see or hear from me again! My suggestion may, however, perhaps do good.[3]

She continued to grow worse and the situation grew so desperate that Dodgson consulted a colleague of his Uncle Skeffington as to whether Loui might be admitted 'to some place where they take lunatics'. He wrote to his sister Elizabeth:

> It is very sad about Loui Taylor: and I sincerely sympathise with C.S.C. and Mary in their trouble. I wish I could offer <u>money</u> help, as well: but I haven't got the money![4]

Although money continued to flow in from *Alice*, his finances were considerably stretched. There were his sisters to support, The Chestnuts to be paid for and dozens of other family calls on his income, such as paying for the education of the children of the widowed Mrs William Wilcox.

In June 1890 Wilfred Dodgson's eldest daughter Edith, now nineteen, came up to Oxford to take the entrance examination for Lady Margaret Hall. She took up her place in October, and Dodgson took her under his wing, escorting her to various functions, but her Oxford career was short-lived. She failed the first term examination and it was decided it would be best if she were to withdraw for a year. She never returned. Dodgson wrote her a long letter, attempting to console her:

> You professed, when I last saw you, to have a mind absolutely blank of all ideas on the subject – in fact, to regard the life, that lies before you, with the same amount of clear perception, of the probable drift of it, as is professed by a young frog – which seems to me one of the <u>most</u> uncertain of living things, as to its future, even the events of the next minute: it has such fearful muscular powers that a single leap takes it in a minute beyond its visible horizon, and <u>which</u> of the four elements it will land in, earth, water, air or fire, it hasn't the faintest idea.[5]

Even the remotest of his relatives seemed to hope that the famous Lewis Carroll might somehow be able to transform their lives. Minna Quinn, the daughter of his cousin Menella Wilcox, wrote from Ireland telling him that she hoped to earn her living as an actress, and asking for his help and advice. He went to see her in a tour of *Mother Goose* at Banbury, where they 'seemed to become intimate friends at once'. Dodgson did everything in his power to help her, writing to everyone he knew in the theatre who might conceivably be of use to her in her career. He asked Marion Terry if she could find the girl an opening with the actor manager George Alexander, he wrote to Clement Scott, and to Mrs Beerbohm Tree. Minna was taken to see Tree's *Hamlet* and Irving and Ellen Terry in *Henry VIII* at the Lyceum. For months he trundled her round the London agents trying to get someone to take her on, but no one could be persuaded to share his belief in his *protégée*, who had taken on the name of Norah O'Neill. Eventually Ellen Terry agreed to give the girl employment as a 'super' in *Faust*.

> You did a very kind and Christian deed on Friday [he wrote to her] in <u>inventing</u> a vacancy (as I feel sure you did) for my cousin, Minna Quinn. She was getting, I think, quite low spirited about her prospects, it was so difficult to get any engagement at all.[6]

Isa Bowman had returned from her American tour and was receiving lessons in elocution from Ellen Terry. 'You really are too nice and kind for anything!' Dodgson wrote to his 'dear old friend':

> The very utmost I hoped for was that, after seeing Isa and ascertaining that she had some 'teachableness' in her, you would tell me that, if I applied to the manager of such-and-such a theatre, he would give me the address of some good teachers of elocution. It never crossed my thoughts that you would give her any lessons <u>yourself</u>! ... And so have you found out that secret – one of the deep secrets of Life – that all, that is really <u>worth</u> the doing, is what we do for <u>others</u>?[7]

Isa continued to come down and stay with him at Lushington Road. 'She has been my guest here for 4 summers now,' he told Mrs Waddy, an old Eastbourne acquaintance, 'now that I am nearly sixty I venture to do very unconventional things.'[8]

His health was beginning to give him cause for concern. On 6th February, 1891, he suffered an epileptoform attack which considerably unnerved him. He fainted at the end of morning chapel and came to himself lying on the floor of the Cathedral. He had struck his nose in the fall and was bleeding profusely.

> I remembered distinctly the reader of morning prayers having come to within a few words of the end [he told Edith Blakemore] and I find I remained kneeling when the others left the building. The two tutors, who went last, noticed that I did not get up, but concluded I was only going on in private prayer a little longer than usual, and thought no

more of it: and the verger never noticed I had not gone out, but barred the doors, and left by another door.[9]

Dodgson suffered from a series of headaches and felt himself unfit for brainwork. The headaches persisted well into April and he was reluctant to face railway journeys. He was plagued with synovitis in his knees and had bouts of cystitis. 'I don't feel justified in counting on many more years of life,' he wrote in a letter to an unidentified 'invalid':

> in the last attack it might so very easily have happened that the heart (it is weak, I know) might have simply ceased to beat, and my waking up might have been in that strange region we all look forward to seeing and know so little about! ...[10]

To the same correspondent he wrote what was probably closest to his philosophy of existence:

> It seems to me that, for every one of us, life is really a sort of school, or training time, meant chiefly for the building up of a character, and of disciplining the spirit, so that by its own free choice of good rather than evil, and of God's will rather than self-will, it may rise to a higher and higher state of Christian growth, and get nearer and nearer to God, and more and more like Him, and so more fit for higher forms of existence.[11]

Dodgson had begun preaching more frequently – to the College servants and at St Mary's in Guildford, where he reproved his sister Mary for telling him that he had preached a 'beautiful' sermon. He was, however, growing increasingly impatient with the sermons of others, and gave vent to his feelings in a speech which he gave to Arthur Forrester in *Sylvie and Bruno*:

> I must say that our preachers enjoy an *enormous* privilege – which they ill deserve, and which they misuse terribly. We put our man into a pulpit, and we virtually tell him 'Now, you may stand there and talk to us for half an hour. We won't interrupt you by so much as a *word*! You shall have it all your own way'. And what does he give us in return? Shallow twaddle, that, if it were addressed to you over a dinner table, you would think, 'Does the man take me for a fool?'.

Increasingly he began to associate bad preaching with bad logic. In Eastbourne he heard a clergyman tell his congregation 'We believe that the Bible is true, because our holy Mother, the Church tells us it is.'

> I pity that unfortunate clergyman, if ever he is bold enough to enter any Young Men's Debating Club, where there is some clear-headed sceptic who has heard, or heard of, that sermon. I can fancy how the young man would rub his hands, in delight, and would say to himself, 'Just see me get him into a corner, and convict him of arguing in a circle!'

Meanwhile Dodgson was devoting every moment he could to pressing on with the second part of *Sylvie and Bruno*, though he also somehow found time to issue a pamphlet on circular billiards and a little book entitled *Eight or Nine Wise Words about Letter Writing* which was issued with the recently developed Wonderland Stamp Case, which held twelve stamps of various values, and had on the front a picture of Alice carrying the Baby, which turned into a pig when the case was opened up. In the book he gave advice on such matters as 'How to begin a letter', 'How to go on with a letter' and included eminently sensible suggestions like always carrying letters you intend to post in your hand:

> If you put them in your pocket you will take a long country-walk (I speak from experience), passing the post office <u>twice</u>, going and returning, and when you get home, you will find them <u>still</u> in your pocket.

He went on to urge correspondents to keep a register of all letters received and sent, with a brief indication of their contents. He appended a specimen register which, since this was a Lewis Carroll publication, concerned the despatch of a White Elephant which, after various alarms and adventures, turned out to be a dozen bottles of port.

While Dodgson was still recovering from his epileptoform attack, his life was considerably brightened by meeting the girl who was to call herself 'his very last child-friend'. Enid Stevens was the younger sister of Winifred, one of the young ladies who had been attending his classes on Logic at Oxford High School. After his first encounter with the 'sweet, loveable child', he wrote to her mother:

> I have lost a considerable fraction (say .25) of my heart to your little daughter: and I <u>hope</u> you will allow me further opportunities of trying whether we can become real <u>friends</u>. She would be about my only child-friend in Oxford. The former ones have all grown up: and I've taken no trouble to find others, it's such a lottery, the finding of any loveable ones. Please don't think it's only her <u>beauty</u> that has attracted me ...[12]

Enid had dark curls and large dreamy eyes. Dodgson would call for her two or three times a week and carry the child off for long walks in the park which he would enliven with his customary repertoire of songs and stories. In his rooms they would curl up together in his armchair playing number games and devising ciphers, or sit down to a game of backgammon or chess. 'Chess was the most fun,' she remembered. 'He was, of course, master of the game, but when he played with a child the knights and bishops became alive and held heated discussions over the rights of queens and the ownership of castles ...'[13]

Dodgson wanted to take Enid down to Eastbourne with him, but Mrs Stevens would not allow it – perhaps there were still too many rumours about him in Oxford. 'He must have had wonderful patience,' Enid wrote many years later, 'for he tried again and again, but I was never allowed to go and shall never cease to the end of my days to regret it.' Dodgson had to be content with borrowing her for expeditions to galleries and theatres, or playing hide-and-seek among the chimney pots on the roof above his rooms.

Mrs Stevens' prohibition did not extend to Enid's twenty-year-old sister Winifred, who was taken to stay with him at The Chestnuts. According to Enid he was 'obviously terrified' of her mother, and he wrote to explain exactly what the house rules were:

> When there, I always use my bedroom as a sitting room also, and spend my morning there ... And when any young friend of mine is on a visit there, I like her to come and keep me company instead of sitting alone in the drawing room (for my sisters are never there in the morning). My eldest sister allows this arrangement, <u>when she knows that the mother approves</u>: otherwise, if the young lady is to be regarded as under her chaperonage, she would consider it too unconventional to let her be alone with a single gentleman ...[14]

On one occasion he took Winifred to meet Mrs Henderson, whose daughters he had so frequently photographed without any clothes, and whose second daughter he still from time to time sketched in that condition. While they were there, Mrs Henderson took the opportunity to show Winifred some nude studies of her daughter, and Dodgson was understandably alarmed about word of this getting back to the formidable Mrs Stevens, especially as he had suggested to Enid that she should go to Mrs Henderson to have her photograph taken. 'Let me assure you,' he wrote, 'that neither she, nor I, would <u>dream</u> of suggesting that Enid should be done in anything short of <u>full dress</u>'.[15]

Despite the fact that he was nearing sixty, Dodgson's reckless pursuit of little girls who took his fancy tended to land him in scrapes more suited to a clumsy teenager. At Eastbourne he glimpsed a pretty little girl in the theatre. After the performance he followed her and saw her go into a boarding house at 42 Grand Parade. He consulted the Visitors List and discovered that a Mrs Lawrence was living at that address. He wrote to her asking her permission to make friends with her daughter. Mrs Lawrence came round to Lushington Road and told him that she was not the mother of the young lady in question, but would pass on his letter.

> I then found, quite accidentally, that the 'young lady' she thought I was attracted by, is 17! It seems the child was not staying at the house: they probably went in to see some friends – so I fear I have an infinitesimal chance of ever seeing her again.[16]

In October 1891 Dean Liddell wrote to Lord Salisbury announcing his intention of resigning before Christmas. He was suffering from sciatica and had great difficulty in going any distance. He told Salisbury that he wanted to walk out of the Deanery rather than be carried out. All hatchets had been long and deeply buried and Dodgson wrote to Mrs Liddell that Oxford would suffer a permanent loss, not just from the Dean's departure, but from hers also:

> It seems but yesterday when the Dean, and you, first arrived: yet I was hardly more than a boy, then: and many of the pleasantest memories of those early years – that foolish time that seemed as if it would last forever – are bound up in the names of yourself and your children …[17]

Dodgson had heard nothing of Alice since the publication of the facsimile edition. He had, however, met her husband Reginald Hargreaves, when William Baillie Skene, Lorina's husband, brought him into the Common Room as his guest. Dodgson had barely noticed Hargreaves when he was an undergraduate struggling to acquire the minimum mathematical qualification, but now he was confronted with the man who had married his dream child.

> It was not easy to link in one's mind the new face with the olden memory – the stranger with the once-so-intimately known and loved 'Alice', whom I shall always remember as an entirely fascinating little seven-year-old maiden.

Alice herself arrived at the Deanery early in December and Dodgson wrote timidly asking whether she might care to look in for tea: 'You would probably prefer to bring a companion; but I must leave the choice to you …'[18] But Alice was either too apprehensive or too busy to spare the time for tea. Instead, she briefly looked in with Rhoda. Dodgson did no more than bleakly record the fact.

In January of the following year, he wrote what was to be his last letter to his Alice. A friend who specialised in ivory carving had produced a number of umbrellas and parasols with handles carved with figures from *Alice's Adventures* and *Through the Looking Glass*. Most of them were unsuited for use, but he thought that one carved with Tweedledum and

Tweedledee might be used 'without wearing out the life of the owner with constant anxiety'.

> So I want to be allowed to present to the original Alice, a parasol with this as the handle – if she will graciously accept it, and will let me know what coloured silk she prefers, and whether she would like it to have a fringe. Wishing you and yours a very happy New Year, I am
> Most sincerely yours,
> C.L. Dodgson.[19]

'I generally wrote down the answer first of all'

For the first time in his life Dodgson felt so constrained by his 'housemaid's knee' and his other ailments that he spent Christmas of 1892 at Christ Church. It was a lonely, miserable and melancholy occasion. For his Christmas dinner the cook sent up dishes of fried sole and roast mutton. 'Never, never have I dined before on Christmas day, without plum pudding,' he lamented to Gertrude Chataway, 'wasn't it sad?'[1]

Mrs MacDonald had invited him to stay with her and the family at Bordighera, but Dodgson saw no prospect of ever going abroad again. Sitting on his sofa, drafting new rules for Syzygies and feeling very sorry for himself, he wrote:

> I hope I am <u>ready</u> to go, if God pleases to call me, but I should <u>like</u> a few more years of work first! Specially to finish Sylvie and Bruno Concluded ...[2]

The book, like its predecessor, continued to give him endless trouble. Most of it was now in proof, but it was 'in the most chaotic order'. To a Mr C.A. Goodhart, a Sheffield vicar, who had sent him a 'sympathetic and encouraging' letter, he said that he had tried to introduce into it some reference to 'subjects which are after all the <u>only</u> subjects of real interest in life' and felt that the book 'was more suitable to a clerical writer than one of mere fun'.[3]

In March he severed another of his links with college life and resigned the Curatorship. For nine years he had done his best to keep his patience with a cantankerous and acrimonious committee with as much humour as he could muster. He had cared for the claret, ensured a decent wage for Telling, chosen tiles for the fireplace (by De Morgan), and tried to find a painless and humane way of putting down the cat. He had even done his utmost to protect the members from draughts and offensive odours. When his colleagues had tried to resist his move to recompense the servants for working overtime he had effectively quashed their rebellion by threatening to resign, and they had voted him the authority he needed. By the end of his tenure he had them eating out of his hand. But enough was enough:

> it is ... an office which entails on its holder a very considerable
> expenditure of time, and of work, which, though not needing severe
> efforts of thought, is almost as tiring to the brain as if it did ...[4]

Thomas Banks Strong was prepared to relieve him of the office and he gave
it up with a thankful heart. His withdrawal from the Curatorship should
have given the time he needed in which to finally see off *Sylvie and Bruno
Concluded* and he went down to Eastbourne determined that this would
be the last summer he would devote to it. But Furniss had underestimated
the number of illustrations that were needed and this gave Dodgson a valid
excuse (always supposing that he needed one) to fill up the time with little
girls. His first guest was a new acquaintance, Polly Mallalieu, aged twelve,
the daughter of an acting family, but 'very ladylike'. He sent off a whole
series of letters to her mother in preparation for the visit, detailing what
she was to wear – 'My little friend Isa Bowman is rather apt to dress in
gaudy colours, which I don't like as it makes us too conspicuous: but I do
not think I need fear that in Polly's case ...'[5] He also wanted to know what
height the girl was without her shoes.

At first all went well. Polly was collected from her parents in London,
and Dodgson stopped off at Guildford, where they climbed to the top of
the old Norman castle behind The Chestnuts, 'my first ascent'. They
reached Eastbourne that evening and Dodgson wrote off to Mrs Mallalieu
saying that Polly was such a delightful companion that he wanted her to
stay for a week. There were lessons in arithmetic, geography and geometry
and a little Bible reading, there was the usual round of seaside entertainments. And then a terrible thing happened. Dodgson discovered that Polly
was 4ft 10½ inches and not, as she had told him, 4ft 10 inches. Polly,
somewhat bewildered, told him that her father might have said that she
was shorter than she actually was in order to secure her a theatrical
engagement. Dodgson was horrified: the child was being encouraged in
falsehood.

He sat down and wrote an astonishing letter to her father, telling him
how very sad it made him that this should happen to Polly at a time when
children learned good and evil so readily:

> Perhaps you think I am making a fuss about a mere trifle: but no sin is
> a trifle in the sight of God: and a lie is a sin. (I know 'lie' is an ugly
> name for it, and one very likely to give offence: but it is the true
> name.)

If the child had secured the engagement he would have been guilty of theft,
and if some other girl had lost the job as a result 'you would have been
guilty of robbing that child of invaluable property.'[6]

Perhaps all might have passed off relatively calmly had Mr Mallalieu opened the letter, but it was his wife who found it first and she was greatly distressed. She said that Dodgson had been unjust and uncharitable and that it would not have happened had she not been a member of the theatrical profession. Dodgson coolly brushed all this aside. Polly stayed on with him for the full week and no more was said. Mrs Mallalieu was sent a copy of *Sylvie and Bruno*, which perhaps served her right.

Maggie Bowman came down to stay for a week, followed by Violet Dodgson, the sixth daughter of Dodgson's brother Wilfred. She was fourteen, and rather apprehensive about the prospect of spending ten days alone with her celebrated uncle, but she enjoyed all the lessons and the Bible readings and the symbolic logic and was excited to be taking her first steps in Euclid. The constant round of entertainments, however, took its toll. They saw five plays in five days, including *Lost to the World*, 'a rather sensational drama of the East End type'. They played backgammon 'almost into the small hours', and by the time the ten days were over, she was 'a somewhat washed out little person'. She felt that she had been rather a disappointment to her uncle:

> I probably bored him: he liked children to talk and we were rather dumb. But he never let me see it and was the most courteous, and unwearying of hosts. Moreover, he made one feel that one was of interest to him as an individual – a novel experience to a child picked out of the middle of a large family ... His face lighted up with appreciation of my feeble little jokes or my admiration of something he was showing or explaining ...[7]

Much of the summer was spent in happily organising the despatch of 'Looking Glass' tins to various children. The previous year he had been approached by Miss Mary Manners, who had written asking if he would give permission for her brother to manufacture tin boxes, which she referred to as 'nursery boxes', illustrated with scenes from *Through the Looking Glass*. Dodgson was only too happy to give his consent but was donnishly perplexed as to what they were to be used for:

> One possible 'nursery' use for such a box occurs to me. It might hold flour, or starch, or whatever it is that is dredged over babies after they have been washed, and is no doubt the cause of their continual crying. I would wail, most of the day, if so treated. Is <u>that</u> the raison d'être of 'nursery tins'?[8]

When a specimen at last arrived he was so enthusiastic that he ordered no less than 364 of them (he was given them free) to be despatched to virtually his entire acquaintance, including Christina Rossetti and Princess Alice:

They say children use them to keep biscuits in or sweets or anything. But I think you will find a much better use for the one I'm sending you. Whenever Charlie is very naughty, you can just pop him in and shut the lid!⁹

What Dodgson had failed to realise was that, although all the ones sent out on his behalf were empty, the tins were intended to contain Jacob's biscuits. The first he knew of this was when he found advertisements for them placed inside the tins and, what was worse, they contained a greeting sending 'kind regards' from Lewis Carroll. He was, predictably, furious at the vulgarisation of the boxes 'by turning them into "advertising columns"'and complained that he had not been told what the conditions of sale would be. However, he very sensibly realised that he was now too deeply compromised to do anything about it, and ordered a hundred more tins.

On 6th October, 1892, Dodgson noted in his diary the death of Tennyson. As far as Dodgson was concerned, there was only one poet worthy to succeed Tennyson, and that was Christina Rossetti:

> If only the Queen would consult me as to whom to make
> Poet–Laureate! I would say 'for once, Madam, take a lady!'¹⁰

In February 1893, he took the eleven-year-old Enid Bell with him to pay the poetess a short call. Christina had undergone an operation for breast cancer the previous year, which had left her very weak. She would certainly have told Dodgson of her anger at discovering that the S.P.C.K., who were publishing a collection of her devotional verses, had published a book which appeared to condone vivisection. She would not have approved had she known that Enid Bell's younger sisters, Cynthia and Iris, were posing as naked little fairies for Gertrude Thomson, who was embarking on a series of drawings which Dodgson had commissioned from her. Dodgson was doing all he could to help Miss Thomson, not just by creating work for her, but by taking her to the theatre (when no one else was available) and even turning over to her his rooms in Lushington Road when he was unable to occupy them and paying her rail fare down to Eastbourne. Not that his friendship for her prevented him from being highly critical of her work: her fairy girls were too thick in the wrist and ankle, he told her, and her fairy boy had the breasts of a girl.

The Bell girls, whom he had drawn to her attention, were the daughters of Gertrude Chataway's sister Ethel, and Dodgson thought their figures, though not their faces, far more fitting for fairies than the 'plebeian and <u>heavy</u>' models whom Gertrude Thomson was accustomed to using. He gave her detailed instructions for the attitudes in which he thought they should be posed, but he insisted on one promise:

> Would you kindly do no sketches, for <u>me</u>, on a <u>Sunday</u>? It is in <u>my</u> view (<u>of course</u>, I don't condemn anyone who differs from me) inconsistent with keeping the day holy.[11]

The sketching sessions at the Bells' were not, however, to last for long. Dodgson was disconcerted by the way in which the girls' eight-year-old brother Clive kept on bursting into the room, and decided it was putting the boy at risk to be confronted with his sisters' nudity and dangerous for the girls' 'purity of mind'.

Dodgson gave a unique insight into the way his own purity of mind was troubled in the preface to *Pillow Problems*, which he published under his own name in the spring of 1893. *Pillow Problems Thought out During Sleepless Nights* consisted of seventy-two questions in arithmetic, algebra, geometry and what Dodgson described as 'Transcendental Probability'. Some of the problems were presented in anecdotal form with beggars playing for pennies or a group of friends forming themselves into a wine company, but most are presented in purely mathematical terms.

Dodgson said that he had solved the puzzles in his head while lying awake at night and had not drawn a diagram nor written a single word until he had worked out a solution. Most of the problems seem to have come at him like the Snark, backwards: 'I generally wrote down the <u>answer</u> first of all: and afterwards the question and the solution.' Almost as soon as Macmillan had published the first edition, Dodgson insisted on withdrawing it and recalling any copies that were being offered for sale. He was concerned that the words 'Sleepless Nights' on the title page suggested that he suffered from insomnia and various friends had written to 'express their sympathy in my broken-down state of health, believing that I am a sufferer from chronic insomnia, and that it is as a remedy for that exhausting malady that I have recommended mathematical calculations'.

He was at some pains to point out that he had never been a victim of insomnia. His 'over-wakeful' night hours were often 'simply the result of the over-sleepy hours I have spent during the preceding evening!' The book was not intended as a 'recipe for inducing sleep': mathematical calculations were more likely to keep the reader awake than to send him to sleep. The *Pillow Problems* were conceived as a remedy for the 'harassing thoughts that are apt to invade a wholly unoccupied mind'. As a result, 'Sleepless Nights' was amended to 'Wakeful Hours' in the second edition.

In the original preface Dodgson enlarges on exactly what he means by 'harassing thoughts':

> There are sceptical thoughts, which seem for the moment to uproot the firmest faith; there are blasphemous thoughts, which dart unbidden into the most reverent souls; there are unholy thoughts, which torture, by their hateful presence, the fancy that would fain be pure. Against all these some real mental <u>work</u> is a most helpful ally.[12]

'Unclean spirits' and 'unholy thoughts' had been tormenting his night hours since his early twenties and he often gave the impression of a man desperately exercising his brain to keep random thoughts at bay, particularly those which led to sexual temptation or religious doubt. There is nothing in all this, of course, which would not have been typical of any deeply religious bachelor committed to a monastic lifestyle, but for a person of Dodgson's extreme sensitivity and unceasing mental drive, the problem must have been greatly intensified and the 'dreamy delirious fight' in which he confronted his tempters must have been an inescapable part of his existence.

The difficulty was that many of the ideas and problems that came into his mind while he was keeping his adversaries away were often too important to be trusted to a memory which sleep might easily erase, and Dodgson went to considerable lengths to devise a system by which he could commit his thoughts to paper without getting out of bed to light a candle. At first he experimented with writing within oblongs cut out of cardboard, but all too often he found the writing illegible the following day. Then he worked out a more practical solution:

> Today I conceived the idea of having a series of squares, cut out in card, and devising an alphabet, of which each letter could be made of lines along the edge of the squares, and dots at the corners. I invented the alphabet, and made the grating of sixteen squares. It works well.[13]

One would have thought that lighting a candle and writing the ideas down would be easy by comparison, but it suited Dodgson's complex mind perfectly.

Mrs Stevens's restrictions on his meetings with her daughter Enid began to irritate him more than ever:

> She says 'you may come to my house, and you may sit there as long as you like, and you may kiss her once in every half hour (<u>mind you don't do it oftener than that</u>): but you mustn't take her out of the house'.[14]

How would it be, he wrote to Enid, if a friend offered to lend her an umbrella on that principle? Dodgson seems to have seen no harm in pointing out to a child her mother's short-comings, but then, he was so perfectly confident that he was in the right – or did he perhaps hope that Mrs Stevens might read it and see reason?

Nothing, however, could persuade her to let her daughter accompany him to Eastbourne where he went in July, more determined than ever that this would be the last summer devoted to concluding *Sylvie and Bruno*. His guests that year were considerably older, Gwendolen Riadore, who was in her mid-twenties, and Gertrude Chataway who was twenty-seven. 'Twenty or thirty years ago,' he told a friend, '"ten" was about my ideal age for such friends: now "twenty" or "twenty-five" is nearer the mark.' He had boasted to George MacDonald's wife that he was now entirely defying Mrs Grundy and that the great advantage of being an old man was that he could do pleasant things forbidden to a younger man, but, as it happened, he was causing more scandal by his friendships with older girls than he had by those with his child-friends. That summer he invited the twenty-three-year-old Marion Richards, whom he had first met at Eastbourne when she was eleven, to have dinner with him, but when her mother got to hear of it, she was expressly forbidden to dine with him again or even to walk with him.

For the first time in his life one of his sisters dared to voice her concern about what he was up to and what people were saying about him. He thanked her for her 'kind and sisterly' letter, but dismissed her fears:

> The only two tests I now apply to such a question as the having some particular girl friend as a guest are, first, my own <u>conscience</u>, to settle whether I feel it to be entirely innocent and right, in the sight of God; secondly, the <u>parents</u> of my friend, to settle whether I have <u>their</u> full approval for what I do. You need not be shocked at my being spoken against.[15]

He was in a confidently exuberant mood when he took the twenty-five-year-old May Miller on a steamer trip to Brighton. The sea was 'delightfully rough' and they were both soaked to the skin. His idea had been to call on his sister Henrietta, but they were far too wet to be presentable, and on their return to Eastbourne, they dined together at Lushington Road with May dressed up in the maid's clothes. Mrs Grundy was certainly being given something to think about.

There seemed a real possibility that *Sylvie and Bruno Concluded* might be through the press in time for Christmas. Dodgson composed a

dedicatory acrostic to Enid Stevens in which the third letter of each spelled
out her name:

> *Dreams, that elude the Maker's frenzied grasp –*
> *Hands, stark and still, on a dead Mother's breast,*
> *Which never more shall render clasp for clasp,*
> *Or deftly soothe a weeping child to rest;*

It seems a very morbid and sickly way in which to open a dedication,
almost as if he were subconsciously hoping for Mrs Stevens' death.

The book was still progressing merrily along when Dodgson chanced
upon a copy of the sixtieth thousand of *Through the Looking Glass* which
he was inscribing for a friend:

> I found the pictures so badly printed that the books are not worth
> anything. Of the fifty pictures, twenty six are over-printed, eight of
> them being very bad.[16]

'The book is worthless', he told Frederick Macmillan, 'and I cannot offer it
to my lady-friend.' The fault was traced to an impression of one thousand
copies of which only sixty had been sold. 'The 940 copies must be at once
destroyed, and the book must be "out of print" for the present.'

Far worse was to come. The incident had so undermined his confidence
in the printers, Messrs Clay, and in Macmillans that he insisted that they
should call a halt to the printing of *Sylvie and Bruno Concluded*.

> This will very likely prevent it coming out this Christmas [he noted in
> his diary] and will be a heavy loss to me: but anything is better than
> offering the Public inferior work. Rather than that I would (as I have
> told Mr Macmillan) find a new publisher and end a connection of
> nearly thirty years.[17]

A thoroughly abashed and contrite Frederick Macmillan wrote that
Dodgson's complaints were well-founded. Clay believed that the plates
were worn out and that new ones must be made. The cost of this would be
shared between printer and publisher. Dodgson had unnerved him by a
telegram in which he alleged 'breach of contract' and in a subsequent letter
said that he could not help feeling 'that the Firm has suffered much by
losing the personal supervision of Mr Alexander Macmillan'.[18]

Frederick Macmillan's immediate concern, apart from the horrifying
possibility of Dodgson deserting to a rival, was to keep *Sylvie and Bruno
Concluded* progressing in time for the Christmas market, but Dodgson
was not going to yield easily. He had been examining the eighty-fourth
thousand of *Alice's Adventures* and found it 'distinctly inferior' to earlier

copies. No more books were to be made from the existing electrotypes until they had been carefully examined.

> Someone must be to blame, for this miserable 'fiasco'; and the culprit must be traced out, if confidence is to be restored between us.[19]

But it was not merely a matter of finding out who had stolen the tarts. He required written undertakings from Clay and from Macmillan that the quality of printing would be maintained. Until these arrived, Dodgson refused to allow *Sylvie and Bruno Concluded* to resume production. In fact, *Sylvie and Bruno Concluded* missed the Christmas market, but Dodgson was at Macmillan's, inscribing presentation copies, to the Duchess of Albany and Christina Rossetti, among many others, on 27th December. Most copies of the book contained an inserted notice informing the public of the disaster which had fallen upon *Through the Looking Glass* and requesting readers to return their faulty copies to Macmillan.

'We need two prim misses'

'I am giving all my time to logic,' Dodgson wrote in his diary on 11th December, 1894, and in fact the whole year had passed without his directing his energies towards anything else: no pamphlets, no poems, not even an acrostic. With the exception of an announcement in *The Times* about the withdrawal of *Through the Looking Glass* (because of the poor quality), and a summary of the rules of 'Co-operative Backgammon', Dodgson's whole output was devoted to a series of papers, puzzles and problems about Symbolic Logic.

Dodgson's perception of logic had broadened and deepened, and his wits had been sharpened by a confrontation with the Professor of Logic, John Cook Wilson. Wilson was a traditionalist, an advocate of a system of logic dating back to Aristotle, but Dodgson, such a conformist where Euclid was concerned, derived his system from George Boole's *The Mathematical Analysis of Logic*, which had been published in 1847.

Dodgson had sent Wilson a paper seeking to prove 'the fallacy of a view of his about Hypotheticals' which the Professor had refused to read. Wilson then offered to read what Dodgson had written if he, in turn, would read a paper of his which pointed out the contradictory data in a problem of Dodgson's. Their disagreement was published in 1894 as *A Disputed Point in Logic* where the argument was presented, mostly in Wilson's own words, as a dialogue between 'Nemo' (the Professor) and 'Outis' (Dodgson). This was followed by *A Logical Paradox* in which Dodgson recast the problem in the form of a story centred on a Barber's Shop, run by three men, Allen, Brown and Carr. There are two logical premises (or 'prim misses' as Arthur called them in *Sylvie and Bruno*); the three barbers cannot be absent from the shop at the same time, since this would leave the place empty. Allen is unwell and whenever he leaves the shop, Brown has to accompany him. But what happens if Carr is absent? The problem is presented in a dialogue between Uncle Joe and Uncle Jim who are on their way to the Barbers':

> 'My dear, but most illogical brother!' said Uncle Joe. (Whenever
> Uncle Joe began to 'dear' you, you may be pretty sure he's got you in a

cleft stick!) 'Don't you see that you are wrong by dividing the *protasis* and the *apodosis* of that Hypothetical? Its *protasis* is simply 'Carr is out;' and its *apodosis* is a sort of sub-Hypothetical, 'If Allen is out, Brown is in'. And a most absurd *apodosis* it is, being hopelessly incompatible with that other Hypothetical, that we know is *always* true, 'If Allen is out, Brown is <u>out</u>.' And it's simply the assumption 'Carr is out' that has caused this absurdity. So there's only *one* possible conclusion – '*Carr is in*'!'[1]

Cook argued that, on Aristotelian principles, given the premises, Carr could not go out. Dodgson, on algebraic principles, argued that he could. The problem was published in *Mind* and occupied the minds of logicians, particularly Bertrand Russell, for many years.

Dodgson was conducting logic classes whenever he could, and making a courageous attempt to establish logic as a popular science which could be learned with no special knowledge. But, as far as he was concerned, it was not merely a mental discipline. Like chess, it offered a means of 'approaching many of the fundamental problems of life, above all in the area of religious belief':

> One great use of the study of logic (which I am doing my best to popularise) [he told his sister Elizabeth] would be to help people who have religious difficulties to deal with them, by making them see the absolute necessity of having clear <u>definitions</u>, so that, before entering on the discussion of any of these puzzling matters, they have a clear idea <u>what it is they are talking about</u>. Many people talk on <u>this</u> subject, just as if the phrase 'I believe in the doctrine of eternal punishment' had one meaning, and one <u>only</u>, and that everyone knew what that meaning was.[2]

The problem of eternal punishment had become one of the central problems of Victorian belief. Tennyson told the Bishop of Ripon that he did not believe in Hell, and the Bishop had whispered back that he didn't either. Applying logic to the problem, Dodgson came up with a series of propositions which recalled the problem of the two clocks with which he had tormented his sisters at Croft Refectory:

(1) My watch says 10
(2) My watch is right
(3) It is not 10.

It was possible to believe in two of these propositions, he told Elizabeth, but not all three. He then put to her three further incompatible propositions:

(1) The God, whom we worship, is perfectly good.
(2) It would be wrong to inflict eternal punishment on a being, except

in the case of that being <u>continuing to sin</u>.

(3) The God, whom we worship, is capable of doing this, even in the case of that person <u>having ceased to sin</u>.

No sane person can believe all three of these. But it is quite possible to believe any two.

Those who believe (1) and (2) and deny (3) (which is <u>my</u> case) are usually called Broad Church.

Those who believe (1) and (3) and deny (2) (which is the case with Edwin) are mostly High Church.

And those who believe (2) and (3) and deny (1) are mostly Atheists: for I imagine nobody <u>now</u> could go on worshipping a God whom he believed capable of doing wrong.

If God were capable of inflicting 'punishment for all eternity' on a soul who had renounced sin, Dodgson told his sister, he would renounce Christianity.[3]

Not that all of Dodgson's logical studies had quite so fundamental an application. One of the problems he never tired of exploring in different ways was the 'lying dilemma':

> <u>two</u> thieves, each saying to the person he has robbed, if you say truly whether my friend will keep his word I will restore: if not, not.

The problem received its most Carrollean treatment in the 'Crocodile and the Baby'. A crocodile has stolen a baby from its mother on the banks of the Nile. The crocodile tells the mother that if she can say truly what he will do with the baby, he will return it. If she cannot, he will eat it. The anguished mother cries out that he will devour her child and the crocodile informs her that he cannot now give her back the baby, for if he does, she will have spoken falsely. The mother, who clearly has her wits about her, tells the beast that if he does eat her baby, she will be proved to have spoken truly, and he had promised that if she did that, he would restore it.

Symbolic Logic now took the place of *Sylvie and Bruno* as the work to which he would turn whenever he had a moment, day or night. It accompanied him to Eastbourne where he worked on it for four hours a day. It was to be a book in three parts. The first, which he told Macmillan would cover much of the same area as *The Game of Logic* was to be 'easy enough for boys and girls of (say) 12 or 14'. Part two, *Advanced Logic*, was designed for decidedly more advanced students, and was not published in his lifetime. (It did not resurface in fully published form until 1977.) The third part, *Transcendental Logic*, remained but a dream.

Dodgson had high hopes of publishing the first part by Christmas 1895, but, as ever, this was not to be. He did, however, embark on a very carefully planned marketing campaign. A pamphlet advertising it as 'a fascinating mental excercise for the young' was sent out to teachers in schools all over the country, selected from *The Educational Year Book*, and a notice about the book was inserted in 4,000 copies of *Crockford's Clerical Directory*. He had cherished the notion that the book might be taken up by schools, but he was forced to the conclusion that 'in the present state of logical thinking' there was very little hope of it becoming a 'school-book'.

In the 'Introduction to Learners' he carefully explained to his young readers exactly how they should go about tackling the book:

> (1) Begin at the <u>beginning</u>, and do not allow yourself to gratify a mere idle curiosity by dipping into the book here and there ...
>
> Some people I know make a practice of looking into Vol. Three first just to see how the story ends: and perhaps it <u>is</u> just as well to know that it all ends <u>happily</u> – that the much persecuted lovers <u>do</u> marry after all, that he is proved to be quite innocent of the murder, and that the wicked cousin is completely foiled in his plot and gets the punishment he deserves, and that the rich uncle in <u>India</u> (Qu. Why in India? Ans. Because somehow uncles never <u>can</u> get rich anywhere else) dies at exactly the right moment – before taking the trouble to read Vol 1.[4]

But what might be permissible in looking at a novel is 'sheer insanity' with a scientific book. Readers should not begin a fresh chapter until they have thoroughly understood the whole book up to that point and if they do not understand a passage they should read it again until their brains get tired, in which case they should put the book away until the next day.

Dodgson's logic classes almost invariably consisted of groups of young ladies in their late-teens. If a girl missed a lesson, Dodgson would happily call round at her house and help her to catch up. The classes would often lead to *tête à tête* dinners in his rooms with his pupils, and, since he insisted on seeing them alone – 'if you don't come on your own, you shan't come at all' – he was involved in a series of running battles with the heads of women's colleges. Edith Olivier recalled that he was the only person in Oxford for whom the rigid rule of chaperonage would be waived. Some of his letters to Oxford mothers were enough to strike alarm in the boldest heart:

> Would you kindly tell me if I may reckon your girls as invitable (not inevitable!) to tea, or dinner, singly? I know of cases were they are available in <u>sets</u> only (like the circulating library novels), and such friendships I don't think worth going on with ... Also are they kissable? I hope you won't be shocked at the question, but nearly all my girl friends (of all ages, even married ones!) are now on those

terms with me ..."[5]

Mrs Moore, the recipient of this letter and the widow of a former Canon of Christ Church, declined to let Dodgson dine and kiss her daughters. She said that she thought him a bit odd, which seems putting it quite mildly.

The only member of Dodgson's family who was seriously engaged in the study of logic was his sister Louisa. He had set her 'Jack Sprat could eat no fat' as a 'Sorites-Problem' and he teased her for her slow progress, in the way that he would when they were children at Croft. But the tone of the letter changes completely when Dodgson talks about the death of their cousin, Clara Wilcox:

> Such news comes less and less of a shock: and more and more one realises that it is an experience each one of us has to face before long. That fact is getting less and less dreamlike to me now: and I sometimes think what a grand thing it will be to say to oneself 'Death is over now: there is not that experience to be faced, again!'[6]

He went on to speak of utilising 'the splendid health I have had, unbroken, for the last year and a half, and the working powers, that are fully as great as, if not greater than, what I have ever had'. This was certainly true. All the ailments which had so plagued him had fallen away, and he was now taking vigorous walks of eighteen or twenty miles a day, striding purposefully through the villages around Oxford, his coat tightly buttoned, his top hat firmly on his head.

Logic was far from being the only topic on which Dodgson was lecturing. His experience addressing the girls at Edgbaston High School some years earlier seems to have given him quite an appetite for getting groups of young ladies together and talking to them. To the girls of Guildford High School he revealed the benefits of his 'Memoria Technica' while the younger children were introduced to the tales of *Sylvie and Bruno*, or to Dodgson's favourite party-piece, 'Mr C. and Mr T.', in which, while telling the story of these two friends, he would illustrate their adventures with a blackboard diagram which steadily assumed the shape of a cat.[7] He also lectured at a girls' boarding school in Eastbourne, run by a Mrs Barber. Her daughter, May, wrote to him asking, 'What did you mean the Snark was?' Dodgson would not be drawn and told her simply that the Snark was a Boojum. He continued:

> To the best of my recollection, I had no other meaning in my mind when I wrote it; but people have since tried to find the meanings in it. The one I like the best (which I think is partly my own) is that it may be taken as Allegory for the Pursuit of Happiness. The characteristic 'ambition' works well into this theory – and also its fondness for

bathing-machines, as indicating that the pursuer of happiness, when he has exhausted all other devices, betakes himself, as a last and desperate resource, to some such wretched watering-place as Eastbourne, and hopes to find, in the tedious and depressing society of the daughters of mistresses of boarding schools, the happiness he had failed to find elsewhere.[8]

Never one to confine himself to one issue at a time, Dodgson had been turning his attention again to the old problem of the admittance of women into the University. At the beginning of 1896, Congregation had thrown out a motion proposing to give the B.A. Degree to women. The misogynist old guard were triumphant, but Dodgson was beginning to have second thoughts. He could no longer plead, as he had done in the past, that women were not physically capable of the intellectual demands that would be made on them. He had, after all, gone to considerable lengths to help female friends and relatives find places in the new colleges for women and had got to know the women who ran them. He had given lectures in all the colleges on logic and had found that female audiences were more perceptive and teachable than male ones. He could no longer oppose the university education of women – what troubled him was whether Oxford was the suitable place for it.

In a paper which he published on *Resident Women-students* he recalled that his old friend Dr Liddon had said that women themselves would be the real victims if they were to reside in the University and Dodgson shared Liddon's fears about the influx of a large body of women into the University:

> Considering that we have over 3000 young Men-Students, and that the number of young Women, who are devoting themselves to study, is increasing 'by leaps and bounds', it may be confidently predicted that any such scheme will bring to Oxford at least 3000 more young Women-students. Such an immigration will of course produce a rapid increase in the size of Oxford, and will necessitate a large increase in our teaching-staff and in the number of our lecture-rooms.[9]

The solution which he proposed was undoubtedly well-meaning, and characteristically far-sighted, but it was a wholesale evasion of the issue: Oxford, Cambridge and Dublin should petition the Crown to grant a charter for a Women's University. At first the University might have to borrow its teachers from the older universities, but he was confident that 'Women-Lecturers and Women-Professors would arise, fully as good as any that the older Universities have ever produced.' He brushed aside the fact that this was not what the women themselves desired, nor did he take into account the fact that young women might not be prepared to wait ten or twenty years for a university to be built for them: 'Even <u>men</u> very often fail to "desire" what is, after all, the best thing for them to <u>have</u>.'

Dodgson might be able to hold back for a little longer the threatened flood-tide of women-students, but there was nothing he could do to prevent the little girls he had loved growing up and departing into adult life. When Edith Lucy, one of his former logic pupils at Oxford High School, announced her engagement, he wrote to her hoping she was not mistaking a:

> 'passing fancy' or 'the very natural wish to get settled in life, and to secure a protector and a home, for the genuine <u>love</u> – the absolute surrender of one's whole being to the love of just <u>one</u> human being, a love <u>far</u> beyond that felt for any <u>other</u> human being, and only second to the love which one must feel for God himself – without which marriage is only a desecration of holy things and a sin against God.[10]

With such a lofty concept of love and marriage, it is not surprising that he often felt that his girl friends' husbands fell far short of it.

There can be little doubt that the loss which hurt him most was that of Isa Bowman. She called on him at the end of May 1895 when she was touring as the leading lady in a musical comedy called *All Abroad*. She was twenty-one, and although she and Dodgson had grown apart over the years, he was unprepared for the news that she was engaged to be married. He snatched a little bouquet of roses from her belt and flung it out of the window, crying: 'You know I can't stand flowers!'[11] By the following day when Isa called to present her fiancé, Mr Weatherly, he was in control of himself again, but he was careful not to see them alone. He invited his friend Patrick Henderson, a Fellow of Wadham, and his daughter Annie to join them for an early dinner and he also asked Beatrice and Evelyn Hatch to meet them. For good measure he brought in the sixty-eight-year-old Holman Hunt whom he happened to meet in the Quad 'that Isa might have the memory of having met him'.[12]

Isa's engagement proved to be short-lived. 'It's a long time since I heard from Isa,' Dodgson wrote in November 1896, 'and I don't know whether the report is true, that I heard some months ago, that she is married.'[13] Isa did not, in fact, get married until the year following Dodgson's death, and her husband was a journalist, George Bacchus. Dodgson had once told her that if she and her husband ever quarrelled, they could retire to the twin turrets of his rooms in Christ Church until they made it up, but when Isa and her husband did quarrel, the rooms had long since belonged to someone else. Isa left Bacchus to live for the rest of her life with a man called Frank Barclay. One can only hope that Dodgson would have understood.

'Is your story going to be about a clergyman?'

The sales of *Sylvie and Bruno* had been so bad that Dodgson found himself forced to cut back on his Christmas presents for the family. At first he tried to convince himself that inadequate publicity might have been responsible but, by the end of 1896, he realised that no amount of advertising could possibly change the situation. Dodgson put the whole matter out of his mind and tried to concentrate all his efforts on *Symbolic Logic Part Two*. *Through the Looking Glass* had been re-issued with fresh electrotypes taken from the old wood blocks, and with a new preface, which was something of a rag-bag of Carrolleana. The other book he had on hand, *Three Sunsets* – a collection of serious verse with pictures by Gertrude Thomson – continued to give him endless trouble. As early as 1893 she had been working on a series of drawings of little naked fairies which he had commissioned for a collection of his games and puzzles, but she was a painfully slow worker and Dodgson was a remorselessly exacting critic:

> When this business began, I told you I could have no <u>clothed</u> fairies at all. My feeling is this. First I object to all <u>partly</u> clothed figures altogether, as being unpleasantly suggestive of impropriety. So I will have none but <u>wholly</u> clothed or <u>wholly</u> nude (which, to my mind, is not improper at all).[1]

In 1895 Thomson asked for Dodgson's permission to let the drawings she was working on for him appear in a public exhibition. His reply was uncharacteristically sharp and even vindictive, suggesting that his patience with her had been wearing thin for some time:

> It will very likely have occurred to you by this time, that a good deal of the value of the copyright of illustrations consists in their <u>novelty</u>: the right of publishing pictures, with which the public is already acquainted, is of very small commercial value.[2]

Thomson had complained that the size of the drawings as they would appear was lamentably small, and Dodgson agreed with her. He had warned her that the pictures were far too large to be reduced without 'losing much of their beauty', but she had ignored his advice:

... the pictures got larger and larger, reaching their maximum in the Nautilus-picture, which is actually $6\frac{1}{2}$ inches wide, and which will scarcely bear <u>any</u> reduction without sacrificing much of its beauty.[3]

The only solution that he could see, he told her, was for him to publish the book without any pictures and for her to repay him the £50 he had advanced for the copyright. He knew very well that she could not possibly afford to buy the pictures back, nor did she wish to forfeit her association with him. This was merely a softening-up operation before he prepared to surprise her with one of his fairy-godmother gestures. He wrote to her a few days later telling her that he proposed to use her drawings 'unreduced' as illustrations to a collection of serious poems, *Three Sunsets*. Her pictures of naked nymphets might perhaps show 'no <u>very</u> distinct connection with the text: ... the book will not pay its expenses: but I don't mind <u>that</u>. The public <u>must</u> have the pictures in their full beauty.'[4] The result was undoubtedly a beautiful book, but the naked fairy creatures sailing in cockle shells or riding a Nautilus, or coyly embracing in a cave, look curiously incongruous when placed against *The Path of Roses*, or *The Valley of the Shadow of Death*.

Gertrude Thomson was also designing the cover for a book by Dodgson's cousin, Georgina Wilcox (Mrs Egerton Allen), which was being printed at his own cost and which he had persuaded Macmillan to publish. He was so enthusiastic about the optical illusion by which 'the gold ornamentation seems to lift itself a good half-inch off the cover' that he drew attention to it in the introduction which he provided for the book. According to Georgina's nephew, the original of 'Fred Dale' in *The Lost Plum Cake*, Dodgson also wrote the last chapter. If he did write it, he matched his style very carefully to that of his cousin, for there is nothing outstandingly Carrollean about it.

> A man in the Show had some buns to sell.
> 'Oh let's buy one!' said Joey to Ben. 'And let's give it to the *Lion* and see him eat it!'
> 'No, you won't see *that*!' said wise Ben. 'No *Lion* will ever eat a *bun*, I'm very sure. But you can give it to the *Bear* if you like. *He'll* eat it – and ten more, if you like to give him so many!'[5]

The whole production of the book was rather a family and friends affair, since, apart from Gertrude Thomson's cover, the illustrations were provided by Mrs Shute in whose studio Dodgson had often sketched naked young girls. His own introduction, written at the suggestion of Macmillan, and the last piece of his writing to be published during his lifetime, was utterly typical of the man. He recommended *The Lost Plum*

Cake as the kind of book which mothers could take into church for their children to look at during the sermon:

> It goes to one's heart to see, as I so often do, little darlings of five or six years old, forced to sit through a weary half hour, with nothing to do, and not one word of sermon that they can understand. Most heartily I can sympathise with the little charity-girl, who is said to have written to some friend, 'I thinks, when I grows up, I'll never go to church no more. I thinks I'se getting sermons enough to last me all my life!'[6]

Dodgson's own sermons had become a matter of some concern to him. One of the college duties which had always given him a certain sense of fulfilment was preaching at the services for the Christ Church servants, but for two-and-a-half years he had not been invited to do so. When he asked the Dean why this was, he was told that only those who had parochial experience were now being invited to preach. He was, however, immediately asked to take the next sermon, but Dodgson, uncertain and offended, replied that it was better for things to continue as they were. In any case, in December 1896, he was approached by an old friend, H.L. Thompson, who had been installed as vicar of St Mary's, the University Church, and asked to preach a sermon to the undergraduates. To preach in the church where the students had flocked to hear the charismatic Liddon and the saintly Newman, was no small undertaking. Dodgson appeared in the pulpit of St Mary's on 6th December and his sermon became something of an Oxford legend.

> It was a privilege to be thankful for [he noted], 'but a formidable task: I had fancied there would be only a small audience, and the church was <u>full</u>, as well as the West Gallery, and the North was partly filled as well. I took as my text Mark IX, 24 – 'Lord, I believe: help Thou mine unbelief'.[7]

News had got round that the 'fabulous monster', the Snark Hunter was coming, but if his audience had expected a sermon by Lewis Carroll they would have been disappointed. 'What they did hear,' recalled Claude Blagden, later to become Bishop of Peterborough, 'was a plain, evangelical sermon of the old-fashioned kind, preached by one who held the faith of his childhood, undisturbed by the learning or the criticism of any later age.'[8] Others remembered him as weeping when he came to the serious parts of the sermon and H.L. Thompson wrote of:

> the erect, grey-haired figure, with the rapt look of earnest thought; the slow almost hesitating speech, the clear and faultless language; the intense solemnity and earnestness which compelled his audience to

listen for nearly an hour, as he spoke to them on the duty of reverence, and warned them of the sin of talking carelessly of holy things.[9]

In his last years, Dodgson's concern that sacred things should not be exposed to mockery became almost obsessive. A don dining next to him at High Table launched into an anecdote only to be immediately stopped short by Dodgson: 'Excuse me, but is your story going to be about a clergyman?' The storyteller lamely admitted that it was. 'Then,' said Dodgson, 'I would rather not hear it.' To a correspondent who has not been identified, Dodgson wrote, 'The favour I would ask is, that you will not tell me any more stories, such as you did on Friday, of remarks children are said to have made on very sacred subjects.' The story had quite spoiled the pleasure of his 'tiny dinner party' and he did not believe that these remarks were really ever made by children at all: 'I feel sure that most of them are concocted by people who <u>wish</u> to bring sacred subjects into ridicule – sometimes by people who wish to undermine the belief that others have in religious truths.'[10] Dodgson preached again in St Mary's in March 1897, on the theme of reverence. 'It has been the most formidable sermon I ever had to preach: and it is a <u>great</u> relief to have it over.'[11] Even the young ladies invited to his rooms for a *tête à tête* dinner were likely to find themselves engaged on the perils of looking at sacred things 'in a spirit of mockery'.

While Dodgson's horror of blasphemy grew stronger with increasing years, he was becoming more and more convinced that the divisions between faiths and churches were of no importance (the Salvation Army always excepted). His old friend Edith Rix had been received into the Church of Rome – and he escorted her to a service at St Aloysius, the yellow brick church where Gerard Manley Hopkins had been a parish priest twenty years before:

> There was much beauty in the service, part of which consisted in a procession, with banner, all round the church, carrying the Host, preceded by a number of girls in white, with veils (who had all had their First Communion that morning) strewing flowers. Many of them were quite little things of about 7.[12]

It rained steadily for much of Dodgson's last summer holiday at Eastbourne. Mrs Dyer had been forced to give up the house in Lushington Road, and had moved to Bedford Well Road, which was further from the sea and where Dodgson could not have his drawing room on the first floor. Nevertheless, he decided that he would not find anyone else who would fall in so readily with his long-established routine: 'It would take a good many drawbacks to drive me to look for another lodging.'

His guest that summer was Molly Rivington, the fourteen-year-old daughter of the vicar of Bladon near Blenheim. Whenever it was not raining, which was not often, Dodgson would escort her down to the bathing-machines. They saw *East Lynne* at the Seaside Theatre, twice went with Henrietta to the Flower Show and made an expedition to Winchelsea to see Ellen Terry at Tower Cottage. What distinguished that summer from all the other holidays at Eastbourne was that Dodgson was persuaded to talk to a large group of children at the Sunday Children's Service at Christ Church, Seaside. He took along Ellen Terry's daughter, Edith Craig, to give him moral support. He was happy enough telling his audience the story of 'Victor and Arnion', an allegorical fable about children and temptation, but he took great exception to the churchwardens and female teachers constantly walking about the church to make sure that their charges were behaving properly and paying attention. Dodgson returned to repeat the performance a week later, when, on his insistence, the children were left to themselves – 'all but one female teacher, who wouldn't let her little victim alone!'[13] Rather in the way in which he had previously lectured anyone within range on the subject of logic, Dodgson now went the round all the schools in or near Eastbourne, telling the Bruno stories or 'Mr C and Mr T' to the little ones, and explaining his 'Memoria Technica' to the older pupils and introducing a few of his favourite mathematical problems.

Dodgson's thoughts were not entirely given over to matters spiritual and educational. He had received a tempting account from Gertrude Thomson of the seaside resort she was staying in, where children played naked on the beach. He wanted to know if her landlady would take him in. But he could not possibly get there before the end of the month, 'And by that time the summer-heat will have gone, and your live fairies will have ceased to dress in "nothing".' Even if he did manage to get there, how was he to go about making friends with any of the 'little nudities'?

> ... what an embarrassing thing it would be to begin an acquaintance with a naked little girl! What could one say to start the conversation? Perhaps a poetical quotation would be best. 'And ye shall walk in silk attire.' How would that do? I'm afraid she would reply 'Do I look like it?'.[14]

If she had her camera with her, could she perhaps make friends with some of the little 'girl-fairies' and photograph them against a rocky background? And if she happened to make friends 'with any exceptionally nice little nudity (no matter whether she is beautiful or not: only nice ones will do)' who could be 'victimised' for his benefit, he would send a book for her.

In the autumn, Dodgson's old friend Thomas Gibson Bowles came to stay as his guest at Christ Church and they went with Miss Thomson to a performance of J.M. Barrie's *The Little Minister* at the Haymarket. Dodgson thought it a 'beautiful play, beautifully acted ... a play I should like to see again and again'. It was his last visit to the theatre. After the performance he sent a note to the actress playing the young boy asking whether he and Gertrude Thomson could come round and meet her. A note was sent back to 'Mrs Dodgson'. 'Well, we are certainly labelled now' remarked Dodgson.[15]

Throughout 1897, Dodgson was exchanging letters with an unnamed 'agnostic'. This rather fragmentary correspondence suggests that he had not completely abandoned the book on religious difficulties, and that he was putting to the test his logical approach to spiritual problems. Christianity, he told his correspondent, could not be proved like a proposition in Euclid:

> Some of the beliefs are what would be called in Science 'Axioms' and are quite incapable of being proved, simply because proof must rest on something already granted ...[16]

Logic, in fact, was ultimately of little use to Dodgson in his argument. Belief in Christianity, he told his agnostic, rests largely on a balance of probabilities as being a theory which fully accounts for certain facts:

> The facts as such are these:
> The nation of the Jews have existed, distinct from all other races, for 3000 years. They preserved prophecies, all pointing to a coming Saviour, and to the actual time when Jesus came. His life fulfilled these prophecies. He professed to have come as the Saviour of the world, and to do miracles as evidence of his divine power. He was executed, and his followers dispersed. But they at once took a new line, asserted his Resurrection, and on the strength of that alone, without learning, or money, or military force, changed the whole course of human history. And the church, which they founded, exists, and has been, for nearly 2000 years, one of the greatest facts in the world.
> If Christianity is true, it accounts for all these facts.[17]

It is far from being a satisfying or convincing argument, and one cannot help wondering what Humpty Dumpty would have made of it.

Dodgson ended the term in the best of health and spirits. He had continued his long walks, and his rooms were so warm, he noted, that there was no need to light a fire. His sister Margaret came up to stay in Oxford and they were joined by Wilfred's daughters, Nella and Violet, for a family dinner in his rooms. On the night of 19th December he sat up until four o'clock in the morning working on 'a tempting problem sent me from New York' to find three equal rational-sided right-angled triangles. He found two, but not three.

He set off for a quiet Christmas at Guildford, and on 5th January he received a telegram announcing the sad news of the death of his brother-in-law, C.S. Collingwood. Collingwood had been suffering from heart disease for some time and, two years previously, Dodgson had made the long journey north to be with him, but now he found himself confined by a 'feverish cold, of the bronchitic type' which his physician, Doctor Gabb, feared might turn to 'ague' and warned him not to travel. Dodgson wrote to his sister Mary:

> You know, better than I can say it, all that my heart feels for you in your irreparable loss. And you know, better than I can tell you, where to go for strength and guidance, and, in God's good time, comfort and peace.[18]

He sent her off a cheque for £50, reckoning that she must be in need of 'ready money'. To her son, Stuart Collingwood, he wrote on the same day, advising him to tell the undertaker that his charges must not exceed a 'stipulated sum': 'You and your mother will have to live with the strictest economy: you have no money to throw away.'[19]

These were the last words he wrote. His cold developed into pneumonia. He had difficulty in breathing, and had to be propped up with pillows where he lay feverishly dreaming mathematical rules and 'Memoria Technica'. What followed is best described by Stuart Collingwood, in an account based on the Dodgson sisters telling of their brother's last days:

> A few days before his death he asked one of his sisters to read him that well-known hymn, every verse of which ends with 'Thy Will be done'. To another he said that his illness was a great trial of his patience. How great a trial it must have been it is hard for us to understand. With the work he had set himself still uncompleted, with a sense of youth and joyousness, which sixty years of the battle of life had in no way dimmed, Lewis Carroll had to face death. He seemed to know that the struggle was over. 'Take away those pillows,' he said on the 13th, 'I shall need them no more.' The end came at about half past two on the afternoon of the 14th. One of his sisters was in the room at the time, and she only noticed that the hard breathing had suddenly ceased.[20]

He was thirteen days short of his sixty-sixth birthday.

*

Dodgson had left very specific details for his funeral, as precise as those he was accustomed to giving to his printer, illustrator, or publisher. He had never forgotten the excessive cost of his father's burial, as his letter to Stuart Collingwood testified, and he had been greatly moved by the simple effectiveness of his Aunt Lucy's funeral seventeen years earlier. No pall was to be employed, no hat-bands or scarfs were to be worn. The coffin was to be plain and simple with no inner coffin. Unless it should prove inconvenient, it was to be a 'walking funeral', no horses, no hearse, no plumes.

> And generally I request that all the details be simple and inexpensive, avoiding all the things which are merely done for show, and retaining only what is, in the judgement of those who arrange my Funeral, requisite for its decent and reverent performance.[21]

Dodgson's plain oak coffin, covered in flowers, was trundled on a hand-cart down from The Chestnuts, through the old Castle archway and along Quarry Street to St Mary's, where it was met by Dean Paget and Canon Grant. The hymns included 'The Saints of God, their conflict past' and 'My God, my Father, while I stray'. Because his death had come so suddenly and unexpectedly there was only a handful of mourners. From the family came all his sisters, Wilfred and Skeffington, and his nephew, John Hassard Dodgson. From Christ Church came the Reverend T.J. Prout, whom Dodgson had known since his earliest years as a student, A.V. Harcourt, who, with Vere Bayne, had witnessed his will, and Arthur Hassall who had taken over the thankless task of Curator two years earlier. From Macmillan came G.L. Craik, the only man Dodgson had trusted there over the last few years. And there was Gertrude Thomson, who wrote an account of it all for *The Gentlewoman*:

> A grey January day, calm and without sound, full of the peace of God which passeth all understanding.

The coffin proceeded from St Mary's down into the High Street, over the river Wey, past the railway station and up the steep hill to the Old Mount Cemetery.

Not far away, appropriately for the writer of 'Jabberwocky', was the old Anglo-Saxon burial ground and nearby were the Downs where the chilling line about the Baker's demise had come suddenly into Dodgson's mind. Dean Paget read the service by the graveside. Among the many wreaths there was one from the last of his girl friends, Enid Stevens, another from the 'chiefest', Isa Bowman, and one from his 'ideal child-friend', Alice.

'We shall miss him for a long time to come,' wrote Beatrice Hatch, whom he had known for more than twenty-five years, in an obituary for the *Guardian* – 'not for his books, for his story-telling days were past, but for himself. The well-known smile whenever we met; the long calls when one felt oneself a child again for old sake's sake and life one vast holiday: the familiar and characteristic handwriting in the frequent and amusing notes; above all, the true affection that grows scarcer in these latter days – these are now things of the past and we mourn.'

41
'Lewis Carroll told it like it is'

Hilaire Belloc, who was wrong about a great many things, wrote in *The Cruise of the Nona*:

> I am perfectly certain that <u>Alice's Adventures</u> will not survive the easy and unquestioned security of the England of Alice's day …

In fact, the metamorphosis from the author of two best-selling children's books into a figure whose universal fame is not far behind that of Shakespeare is one of the more curious stories in literary history. Far from being confined to the 'happy time of pinafores, treacle and innocence', the Alice books have been read by explorers, prisoners of conscience, distraught politicians and harassed surgeons, providing them with a still centre of reasoned unreason, a core of sanity in a world where nothing else makes sense.

At the time of his death, Dodgson's fame was at a comparatively low ebb. The Alice books were as popular as ever, but the disaster of *Sylvie and Bruno* had cast a shadow over his reputation. 'Lewis Carroll,' wrote a friend, 'had been really lost to us for some time: the magic wand was broken, and it is certain that he would never again reach the level of his best work.' The obituaries were appreciative and for the most part respectful with only 'One Who Knew Him' striking a sour note. In an article chiefly notable for some wild inaccuracies, he spoke of Dodgson as 'a humorist oppressed with a sense of gravity … the stiff but courteous don, all chastened eyes and repellent silence'.[1]

Everyone was united in praise of the Alice books as works of singular genius that would endure 'as long as the language of Shakespeare continues to be spoken', but only *The Times* had a premonition of the way in which they would become a universal metaphor:

> It is curious to note how frequently <u>Alice in Wonderland</u> is quoted in reference to public affairs, as well as to the ordinary matters of public life. Hardly a day passes without the employment of its whimsicalities to point a moral or adorn a tale.

At Christ Church Vere Bayne recorded the dismay with which Wilfred

Dodgson viewed the vast quantity of books, files, papers, photographs, toys and Carrollean curiosities which somehow had to be cleared out. Much that should have been preserved was destroyed, casually dispersed, or lost. The furniture, books and personal effects, including Dodgson's telescope, the nyctograph, his photographic apparatus, the children's dressing-up clothes and a human skull, were put up for auction.

Working with astonishing speed and devotion, Stuart Collingwood produced his remarkable biography of his uncle by the end of the year and, perceptively and sensibly, gave over seventy pages to Dodgson's little girl friends:

> ... the fact that they exhibit a very important and distinct side of his nature seems to justify me in assigning them a special and individual position.[2]

There was a general feeling that some kind of national memorial was needed. At that time no one seems to have considered that he might qualify for Westminster Abbey, and it was not until December 1982 that a memorial stone was placed in Poets' Corner, close to Lord Byron's and those of D.H. Lawrence and Dylan Thomas, inscribed with the first line of the dedicatory poem to *Sylvie and Bruno* which he had written for Isa Bowman:

> *Is all our life, then, but a dream?*

It was Audrey Fuller, daughter of Minnie Drury, (one of the 'Three Little Maidens weary of the rail'), whom Dodgson had entertained with his puzzles nearly thirty years earlier, who suggested that a cot should be endowed in a children's hospital in his memory. The idea was taken up by *The St James's Gazette* and a fund-raising appeal was launched for an 'Alice in Wonderland Cot' in Great Ormond Street Hospital. The list was headed by the Prince of Wales, who had done his best to avoid Dodgson in his lifetime, by the Duke and Duchess of York, and by Princess Alice, whom he had instructed in the art of making paper pistols. Sir John Tenniel, Mrs Humphrey Ward, George Meredith, Holman Hunt, Lawrence Alma-Tadema and Henry Irving all subscribed. The President of Corpus Christi, who had been with Dodgson in the Whitby reading party of 1854, contributed two guineas, Anne Thackeray Ritchie gave a pound and 'Little Nick' donated five shillings.

In the year of Dodgson's death Savile Clarke's operetta *Alice in Wonderland* was revived at the Opera Comique and was presented at the Vaudeville Theatre two years later with the twenty-nine-year-old Ellaline Terriss as Alice. Max Beerbohm thought her appearance 'a defiance rather than a compromise', but asserted – presumably he had not seen Phoebe Carlo or Isa Bowman – that 'no actress can play Alice till she is twenty, and then she doesn't look the part'. Dodgson would have been horrified at the idea of a mature woman playing Alice, but the operetta became a regular feature of London theatrical life, playing fifteen times during the next twenty years. Since then there have been more than four hundred dramatisations of Alice, but Dodgson's dream child was no longer confined to Wonderland or to Looking Glass House, finding her way into a host of bizarre and largely pointless new perspectives – *Through the Magnifying Glass, Alice in Movieland, Alice in Ireland, Alice in Blunderland meets the Tax Inspectors, Alice Down Under* and, two manifestations which would have infuriated Dodgson, *Alice in Bibleland* and *Alice in Sunday-school land*. There was even one highly original Italian dramatisation which somehow managed to combine scenes from *Alice's Adventures* with an episode from Rabelais's *Gargantua and Pantagruel*.

In 1907 Alice emerged from the rabbit hole of copyright into the public domain and no fewer than eight new editions appeared before the end of the year. Millicent Sowerby devised a magnificent Gryphon but an anaemic Alice; Charles Robinson produced a bewildered stick insect of a Gryphon and an Alice with a fringe like Alice Liddell's, who at times looks as though she has spent too much of her time reading *The Yellow Book*. Arthur Rackham drew Alice into his own tenebrous and rather sinister fairy world in which there was precious little opportunity for irony or humour.

While Alice was trying on her new faces, Lewis Carroll and the rest of his work remained in obscurity. Reminiscences trickled out – from former girl friends, his 'ugly duckling' Edith Litton, and Isa Bowman – and from would-be acquaintances like Lionel Tollemache, who spoke of him as an 'Oxonian Sphinx'. Henry Holiday told the story of the illustrations to 'The Hunting of the Snark' and Harry Furniss, who had meanwhile produced his own Alice illustrations, presented a hilarious version of the 'simple, innocent dreamer of children'.

In 1904 Edwin Dodgson made a determined attempt to salvage something from the wreckage of *Sylvie and Bruno* by producing a version – *The Story of Sylvie and Bruno* – from which everything not directly concerned with the fairy pair was excluded:

A few words only have in some places been added, when <u>absolutely necessary</u> to dovetail the different paragraphs together, so as to make the 'Story' one consecutive whole.[3]

It was a vain undertaking. There are frequent and confusing half-references to people and events that have been cut out, and occasionally characters from the original, like Eric Lindon, briefly surface, gasping for air, only to sink again. The unavoidable truth was that, for all its faults, the fascination of the book lay in its complexity and in its reflection of Dodgson's tortured personality. Sylvie and Bruno themselves were not really capable of standing on their own feet.

Alice, on the other hand, had taken on a wholly independent life of her own and scarcely a year passed without a new edition of her adventures in which she changed her dress, her hair style, her face and her shape according to the prevailing fashion. Mabel Lucie Atwell tried her hand, as did Harry Rountree and Thomas Heath Robinson and, in the course of time, Willy Pogany and Marie Laurencin. But it was the original Alice who unexpectedly launched her adventures and her creator into the full glare of international publicity.

By 1928 Alice Hargreaves was a lonely old lady of seventy-six living with her only surviving son, Caryl, at Cuffnells, the large and, by then, rather decaying Hampshire house which had been her home since her marriage. Two of her sons had been killed in the First World War and Reginald had died in 1926. If Cuffnells was to be saved, a considerable injection of cash was needed and she reluctantly decided to put on the market her only really valuable possession, the manuscript of *Alice's Adventures Underground*, which Dodgson had begun sixty-six years earlier. The book was placed in the hands of Sotheby's.

Overnight *Alice* became a national heirloom to be preserved at all costs; the difficulty was that no one was prepared to pay the price. Mrs Hargreaves was offered £5,000 by a firm of London dealers on behalf of a 'gentleman' who proposed to give the book to Christ Church. Sotheby's advised her to wait for a better offer. Two days before the sale there was a bid of £10,000, but this too was refused. There was much public agonising and a leader in *The Times*, but when the little book finally came up for auction on 3rd April, along with Samuel Johnson's last letter and a pair of Byron's duelling pistols, the British Museum's limit of £12,500 was rapidly overtaken and the manuscript was knocked down to A.S.W. Rosenbach, an American book dealer, for £15,400, the highest price that had ever been paid for a book in Britain. The press was predictably outraged, and *Alice* sailed off to begin a new series of adventures in the United States of America.

Four years later she was followed by her original. In 1932 the University of Columbia decided to mark the centenary of the birth of Lewis Carroll by mounting an exhibition in which the manuscript of *Alice's Adventures Underground* was to be the star item, and Alice herself was invited to receive an honorary degree. The opening ceremony was deferred from January until May so that she would not have to cross the Atlantic in the middle of winter and on 29th April Alice arrived in New York on board the *Berengaria* to be met by a film crew from Paramount News. The eighty-year-old lady showed all the calmness and presence of mind which had distinguished her seven-year-old fictional self:

> It is a great honour and a great pleasure to have come over here, and I think now my adventures overseas will be almost as interesting as my adventures underground were. I think that I have every prospect of having a most wonderful time, as I did down the rabbit hole.[4]

At the ceremony at Columbia she was hailed, somewhat to her surprise, as the 'descendant of John of Gaunt, time-honoured Lancaster' and admitted to the degree of Doctor of Letters. 'I love to think,' she said, 'however unworthy I am, that Mr Dodgson–Lewis Carroll knows and rejoices with me.' He would not, one suspects, have greatly rejoiced at the sight of Mrs Hargreaves being photographed with the massive Eldridge Johnson, the new owner of the manuscript he had written for his 'dream child'. 'I am very proud, as you will imagine, of being made a D. Litt,' Alice wrote to Dodgson's niece, Violet, 'all just through being Alice – for it is no merit of my own.'[5]

The centenary celebrations in London were considerably more modest. There was an exhibition in Bumpus's book shop, opened by Alice herself, accompanied by J.C. Squire, who had composed an excruciatingly embarrassing poem in honour of the occasion:

> *We've here today the girl who made*
> *A don in Academic shade*
> *Frisk and disport himself as one*
> *Who's lived a lifetime in the sun*
> *Oblivious of his position*
> *As a most eminent logician ...*[6]

Alice was not the only fabulous monster present. Beside her stood Peter Llewelyn Davies, who had the not unmixed blessing of being 'the real Peter Pan'. J.B. Priestley was there, as was Dodgson's girl friend, Irene Vanbrugh, and Leonard and Virginia Woolf, who had demonstrated their Carrollean credentials two years previously by appearing at a New Year party dressed as the Mad Hatter and the March Hare. Dodgson would have hated all the festivities, though he would have appreciated the endowment of a children's ward in his memory at St Mary's Hospital in

Paddington, sponsored by, among many others, Walter de la Mare, J.M. Barrie, A.A. Milne, and Alice.

Mrs Hargreaves was now beginning to weary of being Alice in Wonderland. She declined to unveil the White Rabbit memorial in Llandudno commemorating her wholly imaginary storytelling sessions with Dodgson there, but she could not avoid being involved by Paramount in their new film of *Alice*, in which she was asked to approve their choice of the nineteen-year-old Charlotte Henry. At a private showing at her home in 1933 she watched Gary Cooper as the White Knight, W.C. Fields as Humpty Dumpty and Bing Crosby as the Mock Turtle. She died the following year.

The centenary celebrations marked the point at which the Alice books began to take on a mythical status: Lewis Carroll had joined the immortals. The books had been translated into virtually every language in the world and had acquired the classic position of *The Pilgrim's Progress* or *Robinson Crusoe*. This was only the starting point of their astonishing universality. No one has manufactured a Pilgrim's Progress egg cosy, or a Robinson Crusoe tea-pot, but images of Alice and the Wonderland and Looking Glass characters began to spread like some unstoppable infection to any surface capable of carrying them. What had begun modestly enough in Dodgson's own time with stamp cases and biscuit tins and parasol holders now threatened to leave its mark on every object within its path – pencil cases and T-shirts, ashtrays and bedside lamps and babies' bibs, purses and thimbles and brooches, clocks and watches and tea-spoons, key rings and belt buckles, pencils and rubbers, calendars and tray cloths, mirrors and cots and braces and slippers. Alice and her companions in crime were dragged into giving their names to advertising all kinds of the most unlikely products – not merely predictable items like jams and sweets and biscuits and teas, but Shell petrol and Guinness, Pilkington's glass, Kraft freezer foods, Sanforised shrunk fabric. There was Alice in Ediswan Town, Alice in Thermland and even Alice in Debitland. It became virtually impossible to walk down any shopping street without being confronted by Alice, or the White Rabbit or the Mad Hatter.

By bringing out his work in so many different formats and editions, by scrapping print runs wholesale , by producing works that originated as pamphlets or papers or circulars as well as a vast range of bound editions, and by writing many thousands of letters, Dodgson's oeuvre and Dodgsonia became eminently and endlessly collectable and enthusiasts began to assemble whole private museums, so that the ever-growing field of Lewis Carroll scholarship threatened to become inextricably confused with the tracking down of rare items. By the time of the centenary, the Alice books had acquired the status of academic classics and were beginning to be used as books in schools and to be analysed and dissected in universities in Britain and in America:

> I am sorry to say it [wrote G.K. Chesterton in an article for the *New York Times*] but the soap-bubble which poor old Dodgson blew from the pipe of his poetry, in a lucid interval of lunacy and sent floating into the sky, has been robbed by educationalists of much of the lightness of the bubble, and retained only the horrible healthiness of the soap.

Dodgson had envisaged the possibility of the Alice books being used in the schoolroom, but only as a means of teaching French or German. What he had certainly not foreseen was that they would be set as literary texts, and that curiously searching questions would be asked:

> How does the question 'Who am I?' relate to the wish to eat and the fear of being eaten in Alice?

Even in his wildest nightmares he would not have foreseen that structuralist students would pick over every sentence, phrase and word and advance their findings as conclusive proof that he desired to deflower, or had actually deflowered, the little darlings who climbed upon his knee or posed before his camera.

A shy, stammering, clerical don who devoted all his time to the pursuit of little girls and whose most popular work opened with Alice dreaming that she had fallen down a rabbit hole was bound to provide the Freudians with a field-day, and in the thirties and forties the books were eagerly pounced on by analysts of every persuasion. According to A.M.E. Goldschmidt, falling down 'what seemed to be a very deep well' was 'the best known symbol of coitus'. The long, low hall in which Alice found herself with its locked doors and the tiny golden key and the little door opening on 'the loveliest garden you ever saw' were also symbols of coitus, the locked doors representing the adult women from whom Dodgson had debarred himself and the little door a female child.

> The whole course of the story is perhaps to be explained by the desire for complete virility, conflicting with the desire for abnormal satisfaction.[7]

Paul Schilder, a research professor of psychology in New York, questioned whether children should be exposed to the 'cruelty, destruction and annihilation'[8] of Wonderland and drew attention to the 'preponderant oral sadistic trends of cannibalistic character'. Martin Grotjahn speculated on Alice as a symbolic expression of the penis, while other adventurous spirits considered anal/oral reversibility as revealed in the Mad Hatter's Tea Party, saw the arrival of the Red Queen as marking Alice's first period (at seven?), interpreted the Pig and Pepper episode as a lesson in toilet training and saw Alice holding her flamingo as a symbol of masturbation. From out of this nightmare wood in which everything had the wrong name, Dodgson and his heroine have emerged unscathed and untroubled.

Just as Alice's appearance evolved with each new illustrator, so Dodgson's own persona was differently perceived in the light of new cultural fashions. The sentimental storyteller became Edmund Wilson's 'poet-logician'; the patron saint of childhood became the apostle of pedophilia; the nursery entertainer became a mysterious magus. During the heady sixties he was proclaimed as the prophet of drug culture and *Alice's Adventures* hailed as a testament of psychedelic experience. Thomas Fensch, author of an 'adult' film entitled *Alice in Acidland*, wrote:

> When you take something that tastes like cherry tarts, custard, pineapple, roast turkey and toast at the same time, and it makes you grow and shrink – baby, that's tripping out. Lewis Carroll told it like it is – and he told it in 1865.[9]

Lewis Carroll was recruited by the Beatles into the ranks of Sergeant Pepper's Lonely Hearts Club Band, and Alice found herself cast in a new role as 'Lucy in the Sky with Diamonds'.

Dodgson himself began to take on a parallel existence in plays and novels in which he figured as a character – in Dennis Potter's *Dream Child*, in Christopher Hampton's *Alice's Adventures Underground*, in Didier Decoin's *Lewis et Alice* in which he relates the story of his love for Alice in a series of unrequited letters to Charles Dickens (Dickens dies three quarters of the way through the correspondence which continues until Dodgson's deathbed), and, most bizarrely of all, in Graham Masterton's horror novel *Mirror*. The world on the other side of the Looking Glass is, quite literally, the domain of Satan, 'the ante-room of Hell', and Dodgson had a vision of it when close to death. He intended Jabberwock as a mirror image of the Antichrist and 'Vorpal' is an acronym for Victory Over Ruin, Pestilence and Lust.

Even in Dodgson's lifetime the imitations of Alice had grown so numerous that he had begun to make a collection of them. After his death the Wonderland formula produced hundreds of children's books, from Baum's *The Wizard of Oz* to Whoopi Goldberg's recent *Alice*. Dodgson's impact upon children's literature was a predictable and comparatively minor affair. What no one could possibly have predicted was that he would be unveiled as one of the precursors of the Surrealist movement and would be classed as one of its 'sponsors' by André Breton, along with Swift, De Sade, Poe, Baudelaire, Rimbaud and Jarry, a company in which he would have felt distinctly uneasy. The poet Louis Aragon, who described Dodgson as a professor with a fair pointed beard, and who produced a not very accomplished translation of 'The Hunting of the Snark', declared Alice the greatest poetic success of modern times. André Breton more plausibly saluted him as the first teacher of how to play truant. Salvador Dali illustrated Alice, and Max Ernst 'The Hunting of the Snark', as well as producing Logique Sans Peine, which derived from some of the weirder propositions in Symbolic Logic. Jean Cocteau, in a perceptive Hommage, spoke of Lewis Carroll as the 'Impuni don Juan des naïves amours' and dwelt on his love for barefoot girls in night-dresses with dishevelled hair.

'Lewd's carol' and the ambiguous nature of his relationships with little girls naturally intrigued James Joyce, and he summed this up in a sentence which managed to combine psychoanalytic intrusions with dirty doings in the darkroom:

> and so wider but we grisly old Sykos who have done our unsmiling bit on 'alices, when they were yung and easily freudened, in the penumbra of the procuring room and what oracular comepression we have had to apply to them![10]

Not only the language but the whole dreaming technique of Finnegans Wake, in which people, places, objects, time and theme are in a constant state of fluid motion, derive much from the Alice books, from 'The Snark' and from Sylvie and Bruno, with Wonderland and Looking Glass images and 'All old Dodgerson's dodges' woven so tightly into the fabric as to become part of it.

In 1946, following the death of Eldridge Johnson, Luther Evans, Librarian of Congress, launched a campaign for the return of the manuscript of Alice's Adventures Underground to England. Fifty thousand dollars was raised to buy the book back and in 1948 it was accepted for the British Museum by the Archbishop of Canterbury, who described the generous gesture as 'an unsullied and innocent act in a distracted and sinful world'.

Three years later, as if to restore the status quo, Walt Disney unleashed his film of Alice. 'It's a rollicking, astounding spectacle of mad-cap entertainment,' shrieked his publicity department, with commendable accuracy. The first film of *Alice* had been made three years after Dodgson's death by Cecil Hepworth at Walton-on-Thames, and *Alices* of every conceivable (and a few positively inconceivable) character followed, including *Alice in Wonderland or What's a Nice Kid Like You Doing in a Place Like This*, in which Alice followed her dog into a television screen; a soft-porn film called *Through the Looking Glass* and *Curious Alice*, made for the National Institute of Health in the USA, in which the Mad Hatter was hooked on LSD and the Dormouse was a barbiturate addict.

One could be forgiven for believing that by now everything that could happen to Alice and her creator has happened, but I suspect that we still have a long way to go. Every day, in some part of the globe, in Bournemouth or Kathmandu or Little Rock, someone is putting on an Alice musical or getting together a Lewis Carroll pageant or an Alice lookalike competition. Every day beleaguered parents make their way through the Wonderland Maze at Disneylands across the world and their children wait entranced for the Dormouse to pop out of its teapot, or clamber into outsize Mad Hatter tea cups to be whirled round and round. Every day a newspaper headline will liken whatever war happens to be raging at the moment to Wonderland or Through the Looking Glass. Every day politicians and town planners and bishops and police superintendents are compared to Tweedledum and Tweedledee, or the Mad Hatter or the Mock Turtle or the Queen of Hearts. A paper on Aggregation and Awarding Methods for the National Curriculum opened and closed with 'The Hunting of the Snark'. *The Health Visitor* used a picture of the Jabberwock to spearhead its campaign on Immunisation. Our speech, our thought processes, our way of looking at the world have been hopelessly conditioned by Lewis Carroll. Even the word processor's spell check recognises 'Jabberwocky'.

There are no indications that the next century will see the bandwagon slowing down. There are highly active societies devoted to Lewis Carroll in England, North America and Australia, and Alice seems to have made a wholesale conquest of Japan. Since its foundation in 1968 the Lewis Carroll Society has organised a constant stream of meetings, discussions, outings and conferences devoted to Dodgson and his work. Its newsletter, *The Bandersnatch*, has set itself the daunting task of reporting anything happening anywhere in connection with Lewis Carroll, and its journal, *Jabberwocky*, is devoted to the continual exploration of every aspect of Dodgson's life and writing, and the zeal and jealousy of error with which every line, every comma and semicolon in the many editions of his works have been studied and analysed, would have satisfied Dodgson himself. But there are Dodgsonians as well as Carrolleans, eagerly examining everything he ever penned, from the algebra questions he set for schoolchildren to the notices he pinned on the door of the Common Room. Dodgson and Lewis Carroll are in better shape than ever and Alice, the 'prime heroine of our nation', as Robert Graves called her, has achieved the status of a national myth.

Source Notes

References to the works of Lewis Carroll (outside the 'Alice' books and 'The Hunting of the Snark') are to the edition of the *Complete Works* published by The Nonesuch Press in 1939, reprinted by Penguin Books in 1982 and to the *Works of Lewis Carroll* edited by Roger Lancelyn Green, published by Spring Books, Paul Hamlyn Ltd in 1965.

The diary entries refer either to the edited and selected text made by Roger Lancelyn Green and published by Cassell in 1953 ('Diaries'), or to the complete surviving manuscript diary in the British Museum, for which I used a photoststat copy in the Guildford Muniment Room. ('MS. Diary'). The complete diary is currently being published by the Lewis Carroll Society and edited by Edward Wakeling.

Books and papers in the Dodgson Family Collection in the Guildford Muniment Room are listed as 'DFC', with the appropriate reference number.

Chapter 1

1 'Wilhelm von Schmitz', *The Complete Works of Lewis Carrol*. Nonesuch Press, 1939. Republished Penguin Books, 1982.
2 Roger Lancelyn Green, *The Diaries of Lewis Carroll*. Cassell. 1953.
3 Florence Becker Lennon, *Lewis Carroll*. Cassell, 1947.
4 Diaries, 29th November, 1890.
5 Robert Kee, *The Laurel and the Ivy*. Hamish Hamilton, 1993.
6 DFC, A/2/2.
7 Collingwood, *The Life and Letters of Lewis Carroll*. Fisher Unwin, 1898.
8 *The Cheshire Village Book*, CFWI and Countryside Books, 1990.
9 Christ Church Treasury Papers.
10 Christ Church Treasury Papers.
11 Collingwood, page 11.
12 Edna de Prez, 'Where the sun came peeping in at Morn'. *Cheshire Life*, April 1974.
13 'Terrors'. *The Rectory Magazine*. Edited Jerome Bump. Austin, University of Texas Press, 1975.
14 Derek Hudson, *Lewis Carroll*, page 27. Constable, 1954.
15 Collingwood, page 15.
16 DFC, A/1/1.
17 DFC, A/1/2 1–18.

18 Derek Hudson, *Lewis Carroll*, pages 23–24, Constable, 1954.
19 Collingwood, page 12.
20 A Sermon Preached in Ripon Minster by the Rev. Charles Dodgson M.A., 1838.

Chapter 2

 1 'Lays of Sorrow' No 2. Nonesuch, page 712.
 2 Diaries, pages 7–8.
 3 Ibid.
 4 Derek Hudson, pages 36/7.
 5 Diaries, page 6.
 6 Diaries, pages 7–8.
 7 Sue Chaytor, *Guide to St Peter's Church Croft on Tees*.
 8 Collingwood, page 3.
 9 Diaries pages 9–10.
10 'A Tangled Tale'. Knot III. Nonesuch, page 889.
11 'The Village School'. *The Rectory Magazine*. University of Texas.
12 Collingwood, pages 21–22.
13 Ibid.
14 Ibid.
15 Ibid.
16 Collingwood, page 24.
17 Collingwood, pages 24–25.
17a I have been informed by Donald Walker that the theatre in Richmond was in fact closed during the time that Dodgson was at school there.
18 *Useful and Instructive Poetry*, page 25. Edited Derek Hudson. Geoffrey Bles, 1954.
19 DFC, E/2/5.
20 Ibid.
21 Ibid.
22 Ibid.
23 Ibid.
24 Ibid.
25 Ibid.
26 'Lays of Sorrow' No 2.
27 'Brother and Sister'. Nonesuch, page 702.
28 'The Two Clocks'. Nonesuch, page 1108.
29 *The Letters of Lewis Carroll*, page 6. Edited Morton N. Cohen and Lancelyn Green. Oxford University Press. New York, 1979.
30 'My Fairy'. Nonesuch, page 700.
31 'Rules and Regulations'. Nonesuch, page 704.
32 Florence Becker Lennon, *Lewis Carroll*. Cassell, 1947.

Chapter 3

 1 *Letters to Skeffington Dodgson from his Father*, edited by Anne Clark Amor. The Lewis Carroll Society, 1990.
 2 Bentley and Davidson, *Life of Archibald Campbell Tait*.
 3 Collingwood, page 30.

4 Ibid.
5 'Lewis Carroll: An Interview with his Biographer'. *Westminster Budget*, 9th December, 1898.
6 Diaries, page 18.
7 Collingwood, page 30.
8 DFC, A/2/3.
9 Letters, pages 11–12.

Chapter 4

1 Collingwood, page 31.
2 *Mischmasch* (Preface). Cassell, 1932.
3 *The Rectory Magazine I*, University of Texas.
4 Ibid., page 56.
5 Ibid., page 94.
6 Ibid., page 30.
7 Ibid., page 71.
8 Ibid., page 61.
9 Ibid., page 29.
10 *The Lewis Carroll Picture Book*, edited Collingwood. Fisher Unwin, 1899.
11 Ibid.
12 Ibid.
13 *Life and Correspondence of Dr Arnold*, A.P. Stanley. London, 1882.
14 Ibid.
15 DFC, F/53/5.

Chapter 5

1 Bede, *The Adventures of Mr Verdant Green*, Chapter V. London 1853.
2 Collingwood, pages 45–46.
3 'The Walking Stick of Destiny'. *The Works of Lewis Carroll*. Edited Green, Hamlyn, 1965, pages 271 ff.
4 'Maggie's Visit to Oxford'. Nonesuch, page 844.
5 'The Deserted Parks'. Nonesuch, page 823.
6 Quoted in Hibbert, *The Encyclopaedia of Oxford*. Macmillam, 1988.
7 T.E. Kebbel, *The National Review* 1887.
8 Falconer Madan, *Oxford Outside the Guide Books*. Blackwell, 1923.
9 Collingwood, page 49.
10 Thomas Hughes, *Tom Brown at Oxford*. Routledge.
11 Letters, page 13.
12 Letters, page 1132–3.
13 'The Ligniad'. *Lewis Carroll Observed*, Lewis Carroll Society of North America. Clarkson Potter, Inc., 1976.
14 Ibid.
15 Ibid.
16 Ibid.
17 Diaries, page 28–29.
18 DFC, C/1/1.
19 Letters, page 146.

20 Nonesuch, page 860.
21 *Works*, Edited Green, page 226.
22 Menella Smedley, 'Weave me a Summer Crown'.
23 'The Sailor's Wife'. Nonesuch, page 870.
24 Green, Diaries, page 28–9.

Chapter 6

1 Letters, page 15.
2 Roger Fulford, *The Prince Consort*. Macmillan, 1966.
3 Collingwood, pages 51–52.
4 Ibid.
5 Ibid.
6 Isa Bowman, *The Story of Lewis Carroll*. Dent, 1899.
7 Diaries, page 35.
8 Letters, page 22.
9 Collingwood, pages 53–4.
10 DFC C/1/7–8.
11 'Mr Dodgson: Lewis Carroll at Oxford'. T.B. Strong. *The Times*, 27th January 1932.
12 Letters, pages 26ff.
13 *St James's Gazette*, 11th March, 1898.
14 Nonesuch, page 721.
15 Nonesuch, page 986.
16 Collingwood, page 58.

Chapter 7

1 Diaries, pages 38–9.
2 Nonesuch, page 797.
3 Letters, pages 31–32.
4 Diaries, page 43.
5 Diaries, page 41.
6 MS. Diary.
7 Diaries, page 45.
8 Diaries, page 46.
9 MS. Diary.
10 Diaries, page 50.
11 Violet Hunt, *The Wife of Rossetti*. John Lane, 1932, page 144.
12 Henry Thompson, *Christ Church*. F.E. Robinson and Co., 1900.
13 Diaries, page 51.
14 Loc cit.
15 Diaries, page 52.
16 Diaries, page 53.
17 Diaries, pages 53–54.

Chapter 8

1 MS. Diary, 10th July.
2 Diaries, page 62.
3 Diaries, page 65.

   4 Collingwood, pages 64–5.
   5 'Lays of Mystery, Imagination and Humour', No. 1. Nonesuch, page
     725. The question of the influence of Blake on the poetry of Lewis
     Carroll is examined by Morton Cohen in Chapter 4 of his biography.
   6 Thompson, *Henry George Liddell*. page 54. John Murray, 1899.
   7 Ibid, page 149.
   8 'Alice's Recollections of Carrollean Days, as told to her son'. *Cornhill
     Magazine*, 73, July 1932.
   9 Diaries, page 72.
  10 Diaries, page 75.
  11 Diaries, page 78.
  12 MS. Diary, 24th January.
  13 H.F. Howard, *The Times*, 23rd December, 1931.
  14 *The Listener*, 13th January, 1932.
  15 Diaries, page 67.
  16 T.B. Strong, 'Mr Dodgson: Lewis Carroll at Oxford'. *The Times*, 27th
     January, 1932.
  17 Diaries, page 96.

Chapter 9

   1 Diaries, page 81.
   2 DFC, Address by the Rev. C.L. Dodgson...at St Mary Magdalen
     Church, St Leonard's on Sea.
   3 'Hiawatha's Photographing'. *The Train*, December, 1857.
   4 Diaries, page 79.
   5 Colin Gordon. *Beyond the Looking Glass*, Hodder and Stoughton,
     1982.
   6 'Faces in the Fire'. Nonesuch, page 874.
   7 Christ Church College Library.
   8 Diaries, page 86.
   9 Collingwood.
  10 *Letters to Skeffington Dodgson From His Father*, edited Anne Clark
     Amor.
  11 Ibid.
  12 Diaries, page 88.
  13 MS. Diary.
  14 Nonesuch, page 979.

Chapter 10

   1 Diaries, page 93.
   2 'Alice's Recollections of Carrollean Days'.
   3 Diaries, page 95.
   4 Diaries, page 111.
   5 Diaries, page 113.
   6 Diaries, page 114.
   7 'Alice's Recollections of Carrollean Days'.
   8 MS. Diary, 30th July, 1857.
   9 Collingwood, page 355.

Chapter 11

1 Nonesuch, page 776.
2 Diaries, page 125.
3 Ibid.
4 Ruskin, *Life Letters and Works*. Cook and Wedderburn.
5 Diaries, page 340.
6 Diaries, page 130.
7 Letters to Skeffington Dodgson from his father.
8 Letters, page 35.
9 Quoted in Green. Diaries, page 157.
10 Diaries, page 164.
11 Holman Hunt, *Pre-Raphaelitism and the Pre-Raphaelite Brotherhood*.
New York. AMS, 1967.

Chapter 12

1 DFC,I/4, A Sermon preached in Ripon Minster at the Ordination.
2 Letters, pages 602–3.
3 Diaries, page102.
4 Letters, page 617.
5 J.O. Johnstone, *Life of Henry Parry Liddon*. London, 1904.
6 Letters, pages 602/3.
7 For an analysis of Dodgson's faith and the influence of Coleridge and
Morris, see Cohen, Chapter 11.

Chapter 13

1 Nonesuch, page 875.
2 'Alice's Recollections of Carrollean Days'.
3 Nonesuch, page 766.
4 Quoted in Green, *Diaries*.
5 Letters, page 51.
6 Letters, page 49.
7 Letters, page 53.
8 An Index to *In Memoriam*, British Museum.
9 Diaries, page 165.
10 Endowment of the Greek Professorship. *Works*. Edited Green, page
950.
11 MS.Diary.
12 MS.Diary.
13 Diaries, page 175.
14 Nonesuch, page 863.

Chapter 14

1 'Alice's Recollections of Carrollean Days'.
2 'Alice on the Stage'. *The Lewis Carroll Picture Book*.
3 'Alice's Recollections of Carrollean Days'.
4 *Alice's Adventures Underground*. Macmillan, 1886.
5 'Alice on the Stage'.

6 Duckworth, 'I figure as the "duck" '. *Lewis Carroll Picture Book.*
7 'Alice's Recollections of Carrollean Days'.
8 Collingwood, page 379–80.
9 Duckworth, 'I figure as the "duck"'.
10 'Alice on the Stage'.
11 Duckworth.
12 'Alice on the Stage'.
13 Diaries, page 188.
14 Anne Clark, *Lewis Carroll*. Dent, 1979.
15 'Alice on the Stage'.
16 Ibid.
17 'Alice's Recollections of Carrollean Days'.

Chapter 15

1 MS. Diary.
2 'The Majesty of Justice'. Nonesuch, page 812.
3 Diaries, pages 193–4.
4 'Alice's Recollections of Carrollean Days'.
5 'Alice on the Stage'.
6 MS. Diary, 17th April, 1863.
7 MS. Diary, 21st April, 1863.
8 MS. Diary, 12th June, 1863.
9 Letters, pages 45–6.
10 Diaries page 198.
11 MS. Diary.
12 Diaries, page 208.
13 Gernsheim. *Lewis Caroll, Photographer*. Dover Publications, Inc., 1969.
14 Hargreaves Papers. Christ Church College Library.
15 Ibid.

Chapter 16

1 MS. Diary.
2 Ibid.
3 Mackenzie Bell, *Christina Rossetti*. London, 1898.
4 Diaries, page 204.
5 British Columbia MSS.
6 Duckworth.
7 Greville MacDonald, *George MacDonald and his Wife*. London, 1924.
8 Letters, page 65.
9 MS. Diary, 6th April, 1866.
10 *Ellen Terry's Memoirs*. Gollancz, 1933.
11 Diaries, page 225.
12 Collingwood.
13 Langford Reed, *The Life of Lewis Carroll*. W. and G. Foyle Ltd, 1932.
14 *Ellen Terry's Memoirs*.

Chapter 18

1 Letters, page 74.
2 Diaries, page 226.
3 G. Thomson, 'Lewis Carroll', *The Gentlewoman* 16.
4 Diaries, page 235.
5 Letters, page 77.
6 Diaires, page 241.
7 Diaries, 11th May, 1865.
8 Letters, page 595.
9 MS. Diary.
10 Langford Reed, *The Life of Lewis Carroll.*
11 DFC. C/2/1/2.
12 Letters, page 81.
13 Ibid.
14 Letters, page 85.
15 *Lewis Carroll and the House of Macmillan.* Edited by Morton Cohen and Anita Gandalfo. Cambridge University Press, 1987, page 41.
16 *Lewis Carroll and the House of Macmillan*, page 43.
17 Diaries, page 239.
18 Ibid.
19 Letters, pages 86–7.
20 Diaries, pages 240–41.

Chapter 19

1 Diaries, page 209.
2 Nonesuch, page 826.
3 Nonesuch, page 1011
4 Nonesuch, page 1016
5 Bill and Mason, *Christ Church and Reform.* Oxford, 1970.
6 Ibid.
7 Diaries, page 249.
8 MS. Diary.
9 MS. Diary.
10 Diaries, page 249.

Chapter 20

1 Diaries, page 261.
2 'The Russian Journal II. A Record kept by Henry Parr Liddon of a Tour Taken with C.L. Dodgson in the Summer of 1867'. Edited by Morton N. Cohen, 1979. Reprinted in *Lewis Carroll, Interviews and Recollections*, Macmillan, 1989.
3 Journal of a Tour in Russia, Green, *Works.* 1965, page 968.
4 Journal, page 968.
5 Journal, page 969.
6 Russian Journal II.
7 Journal, page 970.
8 Russian Journal II.

9 Journal, page 973.
10 Journal, page 974.
11 Journal, page 976.
12 Journal, page 977.
13 Journal, page 979.
14 Journal, page 983.
15 Journal, page 985.
16 Journal, page 1002.
17 Letters, page 886.

Chapter 21

1 *Lewis Carroll and the House of Macmillan*, page 50.
2 *Lewis Carroll and the House of Macmillan*, page 70.
3 Collingwood, page 109.
4 Letters, page 109.
5 Letters, pages 119–20.
6 Diaries, page 270.
7 Alice Wilson Fox, *The Times*, 15th January, 1932.
8 Diaries, pages 251–2.
9 Letters, pages 99–100.
10 Diaries, page 264.
11 Collingwood, page 131.
12 Edward Wakeling, *Skeffington Hume Dodgson*. 1992.
13 Collingwood, page 132.
14 Letters, page 123.

Chapter 22

1 Diaries, page 271.
2 Diaries, page 273.
3 Diaries, page 274.
4 Letters, page 123.
5 'Lewis Carroll Interrupts a Story'. *Children's Newspaper*, 7th February, 1931.
6 Nonesuch, page 828.
7 Edith Haydon. DFC. H/1/1/36.
8 MS. Diary.
9 Ethel Arnold, *Reminiscences of Lewis Carroll*. Atlantic Monthly, June 1929.
10 Beatrice Hatch, 'In Memorian Charles Lutwidge Dodgson'. *Guardian*, 19th January, 1898.
11 *The Story of Lewis Carroll*, 1899.
12 Ibid.
13 Ibid.
14 'Nix'. *Oxford Mail*, 25th January, 1932.
15 Letters, page 135.
16 Walter De La Mare, *Lewis Carroll*. Faber, 1932.
17 *Lewis Carroll and the House of Macmillan*.
18 'To All Child Readers of Alice in Wonderland', 25th December, 1871.

Chapter 23

1 Diaries, page 288.
2 Letters, page 151.
3 Letters, page 152.
4 Ibid.
5 Ibid.
6 *Lewis Carroll and the House of Macmillan*, page 87.
7 Letters, page 147.
8 Diaries, page 289.
9 *Lewis Carroll and the House of Macmillan*.
10 Diaries, page 295.
11 Collingwood, pages 147–8.
12 Collingwood, page 148.
13 *The Wasp in the Wig*, with a Preface, Introduction & Notes by Martin Gardner. Macmillan, 1977.
14 Letters, page 163.
15 R. Engen, *Sir John Tenniel*. Scolar Press, 1991.
16 *Lewis Carroll and the House of Macmillan*.
17 Collingwood, page 146.

Chapter 24

1 *Reminiscences of Lewis Carroll*.
2 Ian Ker, *John Henry Newman*. Oxford University Press, 1990.
3 Letters, page 209.
4 *Reminiscences*.
5 *Pall Mall Gazette*.
6 Letters, page 165.
7 Mona Wallace Kidston, *The Times*, 27th March, 1928.
8 Diaries, page 305.
9 Nonesuch, page 1026.
10 Nonesuch, page 1036.
11 Letters, page 180.
12 *Lewis Carroll and the House of Macmillan*, page 99.
13 *The Lewis Carroll Picture Book*.

Chapter 25

1 Letters, page 207.
2 Letters, page 202.
3 'More Recollections of Lewis Carroll'. *Listener*, 5th February, 1958.
4 Nonesuch, page 1054.
5 The full text of 'Cakeless' has been reprinted in Anne Clark, *The Real Alice*. Dent, 1979.
6 *Ellen Terry's Memoirs*.
7 Letters, pages 1014–1016.
8 Ibid.
9 *Ellen Terry's Memoirs*.

10 Diaries, page 329.
11 'Alice on the Stage'.
12 Diaries, page 332.

Chapter 26

1 Diaries, page 334.
2 H. Holiday, *Reminiscences of my Life*. Heinemann, 1914.
3 H. Holiday 'The Snark's Significance.' *Academy*, 29th January, 1898.
4 Gertrude Atkinson, 'Memories of Lewis Carroll'. *Hampshire Chronicle*, 13th March, 1948.
5 Letters, page 232.
6 *Lewis Carroll and the House of Macmillan.*
7 *Lewis Carroll and the House of Macmillan.*
8 Dairies, page 351.
9 Letters, page 246.
10 Nonesuch, page 836.
11 Collingwood, page 166.
12 Nonesuch, page 1071.
13 Letters, page 224.
14 Diairies, page 348.
15 Quoted in *Letters*. Edited Morton N. Cohen.
16 Letters, page 240.
17 Ibid.
18 Letters, page 253.
19 Letters, page 254.
20 Ibid.
21 MS. Diary.
22 Letters, page 262.

Chapter 27

1 Diaries, page 359.
2 Diaries, page 360.
3 Letters, page 273.
4 Letters, page 274.
5 L. V. Fildes, *Luke Fildes R. A.* Michael Joseph, 1968.
6 Ibid.
7 Walter Crane, *Of the Decorative Illustration of Books Old and New*. Bell, 1896.
8 Walter Crane, *An Artist's Reminiscences*. London, 1907.
9 Collingwood, page 187.
10 Collingwood.
11 Collingwood, page 268.
12 Letters, page 279.
13 Diaries, page 365.
14 Letters, page 282.
15 *Euclid and His Modern Rivals*, Macmillan, 1879.

Chapter 28

1 Letters, page 321.
2 *The Life and Letters of Frederic Shields*, Longman, 1912.
3 Letters, pages 325–7.
4 *Lewis Carroll and the House of Macmillan*.
5 Letters, page 331.
6 Letters, page 337.
7 Letters, page 340.
8 Letters, page 341.
9 'Lewis Carroll: A Sketch by an Artist-Friend'. *Gentlewoman*. January/
   February, 1898.
10 Ibid.
11 MS. Diary. 18th July, 1878.
12 Letters, page 348.
13 Letters, page 1147.
14 Letters, page 377.
15 Diaries, page 380.
16 Letters, page 372.
17 Edward Gordon Craig, *Index to the Story of My Days*. 1957.
18 Reed, *The Life of Lewis Carroll*.
19 Letters, page 356.
20 MS. Diary.
21 Letters, page 351.

Chapter 29

1 Letters, page 305.
2 Letters, page 308.
3 MS. Diary.
4 MS. Diary.
5 Edward Wakeling, *Skeffington Hume Dodgson*.
6 Collingwood, page 340.
7 Letters, page 402.
8 Letters, page 381.
9 'Lewis Carroll. A Sketch by an Artist Friend'.
10 Letters, page 434.
11 Letters, page 435.
12 Gernsheim, *Lewis Carroll Photographer*. page 80.
13 *Beyond the Looking Glass*, Colin Gordon.
14 Letter from Stuart Collingwood to Menella Dodgson. 3rd February,
   1932. Quoted in Derek Hudson's *Lewis Carroll*. Constable 1954.

Chapter 30

1 Letters, page 446.
2 Letters, page 395.
3 Letters, page 463.
4 *The Nursery Alice*. (Preface.)
5 'A letter about Shakespeare for young people', *Aunt Judy's Magazine*.

April, 1882.
6 *Sylvie and Bruno*. (Preface.)
7 Letters, page 403.
8 Letters, page 405.
9 Nonesuch, page 839.
10 Letters, page 421.
11 *The Lewis Carroll Picture Book,* The Stage and the Spirit of Reverence.
12 Diaries, page 396.
13 Collingwood, page 214.
14 Letters, page 429.
15 Letters, page 440.
16 Diaries, page 401.
17 Diaries, page 400.
18 Diaries, page 402.
19 Letters, page 460.
20 MS.Diary.
21 MS.Diary.
22 MS.Diary.
23 Morton Cohen, in Chapter 7 of his biography, says that Agnes Hull broke off from Dodgson when she felt that one of his kisses was 'too sexual'.

Chapter 31

1 Diaries, page 411.
2 Diaries, page 260.
3 Diaries, page 350.
4 Letters, page 473.
5 Letters, pages 473–4.
6 Claude Blagden, *Well Remembered.* 1953.
7 Letters, page 476.
8 Letters, page 771.
9 Letters, page 515.
10 Nonesuch, page 1060.
11 MS.Diary, 15th November, 1883.
12 Letters, page 771.
13 Letters, page 520

Chapter 32

1 Letters page 609.
2 *St James Gazette.*
3 George Baden-Powell, *Life and Letters.*
4 Ibid.
5 *Lewis Carroll and the House of Macmillam*, page 175.
6 *Lewis Carroll and the House of Macmillam*, page 365.
7 Collingwood, page 226.
8 Collingwood, page 235.
9 Letters, page 554.
10 *St James Gazette*, 22nd July, 1885.

11 Diaries, page 428.
12 Diaries, page 429.
13 Green. *Works*, page 1071.
14 Letters, page 578.
15 Letters, page 565.
16 Letters, page 572.
17 Diaries, page 438.
18 Letters, page 618.

Chapter 33

1 Letters, page 560.
2 Hargreaves Papers, Christ Church Library.
3 *Lewis Carroll and the House of Macmillan*, page 190.
4 Letters, page 588.
5 Letters, page 597.
6 *Alice's Adventures Underground*. (Preface.)
7 *Lewis Carroll and the House of Macmillan*. page 198.
8 Letters, page 648.
9 Diaries, page 445.
10 Letters, page 636.
11 Charles Lovett, *Alice on Stage*. Meckler, 1990, page 38.
12 MS. Diary 26th June, 1885.
13 Letters, page 644.
14 Ibid.

Chapter 34

1 Quoted in Green, Diaries.
2 'Alice on the Stage'.
3 *A Selection from the Letters of Lewis Carroll to his Child Friends*, edited by Evelyn Hatch. Macmillan, 1933. (Introduction.)
4 Irene Vanburgh, *To Tell My Story*. Hutchinson, 1948.
5 Furniss, *Confessions of a Caricaturist*. Bradbury, Agnew & Co., 1901.
6 Diaries, page 452.
7 Isa Bowman. *The Story of Lewis Carroll*.
8 Ibid.
9 Letters, page 695.
10 Letters, page 706.
11 Letters, page 693.
12 Diaries, page 457.
13 'Lewis Carroll as Artist'. *Cornhill Magazine*, November, 1932.
14 Diaries, page 460.
15 *The Story of Lewis Carroll*.
16 Lovett, page 80.

Chapter 35

1 Letters, page 713.
2 Letters, page 730.
3 *The Story of Lewis Carroll*.

4 MS. Diary.
5 Lovett, page 87.
6 Letters, page 742.
7 Diaries, page 474.
8 Quoted in Diaries, page 473.

Chapter 36

1 *Sylvie and Bruno*. (Preface.)
2 Letters, page 886.
3 *Confessions of a Caricaturist.*
4 Beatrice and Guy Mackenzie, 'Lewis Carroll Shown in a New Light.' *New York Times Magazine*, 24th August, 1930.
5 *Confessions of a Caricaturist.*
6 Ibid.
7 Letters, page 651.
8 Letters, page 753.
9 *Confessions of a Caricaturist.*
10 *Lewis Carroll and the House of Macmillan*, page 269
11 *St James's Gazette*, 10th January, 1890.
12 Letters, page 789

Chapter 37

1 Letters, page 768.
2 Letters, page 814.
3 MS. Diary, 19th May, 1892.
4 Letters, page 1045.
5 Letters, page 827.
6 Letters, page 1013.
7 Letters, page 812.
8 Letters, page 862.
9 Letters, page 836.
10 Letters, page 853.
11 Letters, page 782.
12 Letters, page 825.
13 Quoted in Green. Introduction to Diaries.
14 Letters, page 906.
15 Letters, page 833.
16 MS. Diary.
17 Letters, page 870.
18 Hargreaves Collection, Christ Church Library.
19 Letters, page 883.

Chapter 38

1 Letters, pages 880–1.
2 Letters, page 880.
3 Letters, page 885.
4 Common Room Circular: Resignation. March 1892. Christ Church Library. Quoted in Edward Wakeling, *The Pamphlets of Lewis Carroll.*

(Vol One.) University Press of Virginia, 1993.
5 Letters, pages 912–3.
6 Letters, pages 918–9.
7 Quoted in Green, Introduction to Diaries.
8 Manners Collection, Guildford.
9 Letters, page 924.
10 Letters, page 986.
11 Letters, page 982.
12 *Pillow Problems*, (Preface). Macmillan, 1893.
13 Diaries, page 486.
14 Letters, page 939.
15 To Mary Collingwood. Letters, pages 977–8.
16 Diaries, page 503.
17 Ibid.
18 *Lewis Carroll and the House of Macmillan*, page 293.
19 *Lewis Carroll and the House of Macmillan*, page 296.

Chapter 39

1 Quoted in Bartley, *Lewis Carroll's Symbolic Logic*. Harvester Press, 1977, page 456.
2 Letters, page 1041.
3 Ibid.
4 Quoted in Bartley, page 51.
5 Letters, page 1095.
6 Letters, pages 1099–1100.
7 Quoted in Diaries, Appendix G.
8 Letters, page 1113.
9 Nonesuch, page 1068.
10 Letters, page 1040.
11 Green, Diaries, page 518.
12 Ibid.
13 To Mary Jackson. Letters, page 1104.

Chapter 40

1 Letters, page 1027.
2 Letters, pages 1053–3.
3 Ibid.
4 Letters, pages 1054–5.
5 *The Lost Plum Cake*. Macmillan, 1897, page 95.
6 *The Lost Plum Cake*. (Preface.)
7 Diaries, page 531.
8 Blagden, *Well Remembered*.
9 'The Late Rev.C.L. Dodgson', *Oxford Magazine*, 26th January, 1898.
10 Collingwood, page 337–8.
11 Diaries, page 533.
12 Diaries, page 536.
13 MS. Diary.
14 Letters, page 1134.

15 Gertrude Thomson, *A Sketch by an Artist Friend.*
16 DFC A/29/4/1–3.
17 Ibid.
18 Letters, page 1155.
19 Ibid.
20 Collingwood, page 347.
21 Harvard College Library.

Chapter 41

1 *Daily Chronicle*. 15th January, 1898.
2 Collingwood, page 359.
3 *The Story of Sylvie and Bruno*, 1904. (Preface.)
4 From *Paramount News*, 30th April, 1932. Quoted in *Jabberwocky*, Winter 1973.
5 Hargreaves Papers, Christ Church College Library.
6 Speech at the Lewis Carroll Centenary Exhibition. *Bumpus*, 1932.
7 'Alice in Wonderland Psychoanalysed.' *New York Outlook*, May, 1933.
8 'Psychoanalytic Remarks on Alice in Wonderland and Lewis Carroll'. *The Journal of Nervous and Mental Diseases*. (Vol 87), 1938.
9 A.S. Barnes, New York, 1970.
10 *Finnegans Wake*. Faber & Faber, 1939 page 115.

Published Sources and Bibliography

Amor, Anne Clark (editor), *Letters to Skeffington Dodgson from his Father*. Lewis Carroll Society. 1990.

Aspin, Roy, *Lewis Carroll and His Camera*. Brent Publications. 1989.

Auerbach, Nina, *Ellen Terry*. Phoenix House. 1987.

Bamford, T.W., *Thomas Arnold*. Crescent Press. 1960.

Bartley, W.W., *Lewis Carroll's Symbolic Logic*. Harvester Press. 1977.

Batey, Mavis, *The Adventures of Alice*. Macmillan. 1991.

Batey, Mavis, *Alice's Adventures in Oxford*. Pitkin. 1980.

Beerbohm, Max, *Around Theatres*. Hart Davies. 1953.

Bentley and Davidson, *The Life of Archibald Campbell Tait*. London. 1891.

Bill and Mason, *Christ Church and Reform Oxford*. 1970.

Bowman, Isa, *The Story of Lewis Carroll*. Dent. 1899.

Carpenter, Humphrey, *Secret Gardens*. Allen and Unwin. 1985.

Chaytor, Sue, *St Peter's Church, Croft on Tees*. Croft PCC. 1989.

Clark, Anne, *Lewis Carroll*. Dent. 1979.

Clark, Anne, *The Real Alice*. Michael Joseph. 1881.

Cohen, Morton N., *Lewis Carroll: Interviews and Recollections*. Macmillan. 1989.

Cohen, Morton N., *'Lewis Carroll and Victorian Morality'* (Sexuality and Victorian Literature). *Tennessee Studies in Literature Vol. 27*. University of Tennessee Press. 1984.

Cohen, Morton N., *The Russian Journal II. Henry Parr Liddor*. The Lewis Carroll Society of North America. New York. 1979.

Cohen, Morton N., 'Alice in Analysis'. *Sunday Telegraph Magazine*. 19th March, 1978.

Collingwood, Stuart, *The Life and Letters of Lewis Carroll*. Fisher Unwin. 1898.

Collingwood, Stuart, *The Lewis Carroll Picture Book*. Fisher Unwin. 1899.

Coveney, Peter, *The Image of Childhood*. Peregrine Books. 1967.

Davenport-Hines, Richard, *The Macmillans*. Heinemann. 1992.

De La Mare, Walter, *Lewis Carroll*. Faber and Faber. 1932.

Engen, Rodney, *Sir John Tenniel: Alice's White Knight*. Scolar Press. 1991.

Evers, C.R., *Rugby*. Blackie. 1939.

Faber, Geoffrey, *Oxford Apostles*. Faber and Faber. 1933.

Faber, Geoffrey, *Jowett*. Faber and Faber. 1957.

Fisher, John, *The Magic of Lewis Carroll*. Nelson. 1973.

Furniss, Harry, *Confessions of a Caricaturist.*. Bradbury, Agnew and Co. 1902.

Gardner, Martin, *The Annotated Alice*. Clarkson Potter 1960; Penguin Books.

1965.

Gardner, Martin, *The Annotated Snark*. Bramhall House, 1962; Penguin Books, 1967.

Gardner, Martin, *The Wasp in a Wig*. Macmillan. 1979.

Gattégno, Jean, *Lewis Carroll*. Allen and Unwin. 1977.

Gernsheim, Helmut, *Lewis Carroll Photographer*. Dover. New York. 1969.

Goodacre, Selwyn H., *Feeding the Mind. A Centenary Celebration of Lewis Carroll's Visit to Alfreton*. Princeton. 1984.

Gordon, Colin, *Beyond the Looking-Glass*. Hodder and Stoughton. 1982.

Guilliano, Edward, *Lewis Carroll. An Annotated International Bibliography*. Harvester Press. 1981.

Guilliano, Edward (editor), *Lewis Carroll Observed*. Clarkson Potter. New York. 1976.

Gulliano, Edward (editor), *Lewis Carroll: a Celebration*. Clarkson Potter. New York. 1982.

Hibbert, Christopher, *The Encyclopaedia of Oxford*. Macmillan. 1988.

Holiday, Henry, *Reminiscences of My Life*. Heinemann. 1914.

Hudson, Derek, *Lewis Carroll*. Constable. 1954.

Johnston, J.O., *The Life of Henry Liddon*. London. 1904.

Kincaid, James R. *Child-Loving*. Routledge. 1992.

Lennon, Florence Becker, *Lewis Carroll*. Cassell and Co Ltd. 1947.

The Diaries of Lewis Carroll, Edited by Roger Lancelyn Green. Cassell and Co Ltd. 1953.

Lewis Carroll's Diaries. Volumes 1 and 2, Edited by Edward Wakeling. The Lewis Carroll Society. 1993, 1994.

The Letters of Lewis Carroll, edited by Morton N. Cohen, with the asssistance of Roger Lancelyn Green. Oxford University Press, New York. 1978.

Lewis Carroll and the House of Macmillan, edited by Morton N. Cohen and Anita Gandalfo. Cambridge University Press. 1987.

A Selection from the Letters of Lewis Carroll to his Child Friends, edited by Evelyn Hatch. Macmillan. 1933.

The Lewis Carroll Society, *Mr Dodgson: Five Lewis Carroll Studies*. 1979.

The Lewis Carroll Society, *Jabberwocky*. 1973 onwards.

Levi, Peter, *Tennyson*. Macmillan. 1993.

Lovett, Charles C. *Alice on Stage*. Meckler, Westport.

Madan, Falconer, *Oxford Outside the Guide Books*. Oxford. 1923.

Manvell, Roger, *Ellen Terry*. Heinemann. 1968.

Morgan, Charles, *The House of Macmillan*. Macmillan. 1944.

Morris, Jan, *The Oxford Book of Oxford*. Oxford. 1978.

Muller, Max, *My Autobiography*. London. 1901.

Pearsall, Roland, *The Worm in the Bud*. Weidenfeld and Nicholson. 1967.

Philips, Robert (editor), *Aspects of Alice*. Gollancz. 1972.

Pudney, John, *Lewis Carroll and His World*. Thames and Hudson. 1976.

Raeper, William, *George MacDonald*. Lion Publishing. 1987.

Reed, Langton, *The Life of Lewis Carroll*. W. and G. Foyle Ltd. 1932.

Rose, Kenneth, *Some Later Cecils*. Weidenfeld and Nicholson. 1975.

Stanley, A.P., *Life and Correspondence of Dr Arnold*. London. 1844.

Steen, Marguerite, *A Pride of Terrys*. Longman. 1962.

Taylor, Alexander, *The White Knight*. Oliver and Boyd. 1952.

Tennyson, Charles, *Tennyson*. Macmillan. 1968.

Terry, Ellen, *Ellen Terry's Memoirs*. Gollancz. 1933.

Thompson, Henry, *Henry George Liddell*. John Murray. 1899.

Thomson, Henry, *Christ Church*. Robinson. 1900.

Wakeling, Edward, *Skeffington Hume Dodgson, Brother of Lewis Carroll*. 1992.

Wakeling, Edward, *The Pamphlets of Lewis Carroll. Vol. I*. University Press of Virginia. 1993.

Ward, W.R., *Victorian Oxford*. Frank Cass and Co. 1965.

Wenham, Leslie, *The History of Richmond School*. Arbroath Herald Press. 1958.

Weaver, Warren, *Alice in Many Tongues*. University of Wisconsin. 1944.

Williams and Madan (revised by Dennis Crutch), *The Lewis Carroll Handbook*. Dawson Archon Books. 1979. (Originally published Oxford. 1931.)

Woolf, Virginia, 'Lewis Carroll' in *The Moment*. Hogarth Press. 1947.

Index

References to publications, whether by Dodgson or 'Carroll' are to be found under the heading Dodgson, Charles Lutwidge: writings

A Selected List of Biographies and Autobiographies available from Mandarin

While every effort is made to keep prices low, it is sometimes necessary to increase prices at short notice. Mandarin Paperbacks reserves the right to show new retail prices on covers which may differ from those previously advertised in the text or elsewhere.

The prices shown below were correct at the time of going to press.

☐	7493 1685 3	**Dickens**	Peter Ackroyd	£7.99
☐	7493 2332 9	**The Perfect English Spy**	Tom Bower	£7.99
☐	7493 0238 0	**Maxwell the Outsider**	Tom Bower	£7.99
☐	7493 1546 6	**Autobiography**	Tony Curtis	£5.99
☐	7493 1438 9	**Churchill, a Life (Pocket Ed.)**	Martin Gilbert	£7.99
☐	7493 2200 4	**A Woman Named Jackie**	C. David Heymann	£7.99
☐	7493 22381	**Liz: An Intimate Biography of Elizabeth Taylor**	C. David Heymann	£6.99
☐	7493 2367 1	**Noël Coward**	Philip Hoare	£8.99
☐	7493 2288 8	**Brian Johnston: The Authorised Biography**	Tim Heald	£5.99
☐	7493 0544 4	**Jimi Hendrix: Electric Gypsy**	Shapiro & Glebbeek	£14.99
☐	7493 1614 4	**In No Uncertain Terms**	Helen Suzman	£5.99

All these books are available at your bookshop or newsagent, or can be ordered direct from the address below. Just tick the titles you want and fill in the form below.

Cash Sales Department, PO Box 5, Rushden, Northants NN10 6YX.
Fax: 01933 414047 : Phone: 01933 414000.

Please send cheque, payable to 'Reed Book Services Ltd.', or postal order for purchase price quoted and allow the following for postage and packing:

£1.00 for the first book, 50p for the second; **FREE POSTAGE AND PACKING FOR THREE BOOKS OR MORE PER ORDER.**

NAME (Block letters)..

ADDRESS...

....

☐ I enclose my remittance for ....

☐ I wish to pay by Access/Visa Card Number

Expiry Date

Signature ....

Please quote our reference: MAND